Not Since

CARRIE

By Ken Mandelbaum

o o o o o o o o o o o o o o o o o o o o o o o o o o o o o o o o

A Chorus Line and the Musicals of Michael Bennett

St. Martin's Press / New York

Not Since CARRIE

○ ○ ○ ○ ○ ○ ○ ○ ○ ○ ○ ○ ○ ○ ○ ○ ○ ○ ○ ○

FORTY YEARS OF BROADWAY MUSICAL FLOPS

KEN MANDELBAUM

Not Since *Carrie*: art and photo acknowledgments:

The reproduction of the covers of *PLAYBILL* Magazine by permission of *PLAY-BILL* Incorporated. *PLAYBILL*℠ is a registered Trademark of *PLAYBILL* Incorporated, New York, N.Y.

Photos courtesy of Peter Cunningham. (Pages 3, 6, 7, 350, 353)

Photos courtesy of N.Y. Public Library (Pages 11, 14, 33, 48, 51, 54, 60, 65, 71, 77, 83, 95, 106, 109, 115, 119, 122, 124, 130, 151, 155, 167, 174, 183, 188, 193, 203, 215, 229, 251, 258, 263, 268, 272, 293, 300, 311, 329, 343)

All other photos and materials courtesy of the private collection of the author.

Design by Chris Welch

Library of Congress Cataloging-in-Publication Data

Mandelbaum, Ken.
Not since Carrie : forty years of Broadway musical flops / Ken Mandelbaum.
p.   cm.
ISBN 0-312-06428-4 (hc.)
ISBN 0-312-08273-8 (pbk.)
1. Musicals—New York (N. Y.)—History and criticism.   I. Title.
ML1711.8.N3M13   1991
782.1′4′097471—dc20   91-21818
                                                                 CIP
                                                                 MN

First Paperback Edition: September 1992

10   9   8   7   6

To my father, who purchased a ticket to Merrily We Roll Along
*even after the reviews came out, and to all those who were
involved in the shows herein, this book is lovingly dedicated.*

CONTENTS

○ ○

AUTHOR'S NOTE AND ACKNOWLEDGMENTS

○ ○ ○ ○ ○ ○ ○ ○ ○ ○ ○ ○ ○ ○ ○ ○ ○ ○ ○ ○

It has become quite common in recent decades for Broadway musicals to run for a year or more and not return their initial investment. So it is not especially helpful to define a flop musical as one that failed financially. Indeed, a book devoted to postwar flop musicals which defined flops as shows that lost money would have to cover the vast majority of musicals produced. For the purposes of this book, I have defined a flop as a musical that had a short run; I have made 250 performances the maximum, although most here are well under that figure and many had single-digit runs. I have also defined a flop musical as one that had no national tour after its Broadway engagement, and has not been performed with any regularity since its initial production. Only Broadway musicals qualify; a few that premiered off-Broadway are included because they went on to Broadway engagements. I have also excluded British musicals, revues, revue-like musicals, and bookless song cycles. I have, however, included musicals that closed prior to Broadway openings or during Broadway previews.

This study covers musicals that opened on Broadway between 1950 and 1990, but I have not included all Broadway musicals that ran under 250 performances during that period, only the ones that I consider worthiest of discussion.

○ ○ ○ ○ ○

In order to reevaluate these musicals (I saw more than two-thirds of them), I read their scripts, in many cases more than one version. I read novels, short stories, and plays, and watched movies on which these shows were based; listened to commercially released recordings, "live" tapes and demos; and watched videotapes where available.

It is important to keep in mind that with a few exceptions, the principal reason these shows flopped was that whatever their merits, they received bad reviews from the critics. But the musical is a complex art form, and it can be difficult to absorb all the elements of a musical in a single viewing. So critics, through no fault of their own, may fail to fully appreciate a show after a single viewing. Quite a few of these shows contain strong elements, and a number of them are worthy of revival. This study may, I hope, stimulate those who put on musicals to consider some of these shows for production, whether it be in a concert version, a reading, or a full-scale mounting.

The parentheses that appear next to the first occurrence of a show's title contain the name of the theatre where the show first played (or, if the show closed before its New York opening, the city in which it first played), the opening date of the original production, and the number of performances the original production played.

The resources of the Billy Rose Theatre Collection of the New York Public Library at Lincoln Center were invaluable to this study. I would like to thank Jeffrey Dunn, Charles Willard, Donald Oliver, Steve Cole, Mike Kuchwara, Ray Evans, and especially Richard Norton for the loan of scripts and other materials. I wish that my wonderful friend Dennis Soens, who died just as I was beginning this book, was here to read it. Broadway musicals, hits or flops, meant so much to him, and it is for people like Dennis that this book was written.

I would like to thank my editor, Michael Denneny, for believing in the project and seeing it through; Benjamin Dreyer, for his scrupulous and thorough copy editing; and Eric Meyer and Keith Kahla for their supervision of the final manuscript. I cannot begin to express my gratitude to Ethan Mordden for his enormous generosity, unerring advice, incisive observation, and constant help.

PROLOGUE

CARRIE: FIRST
NEW YORK PREVIEW,
APRIL 28, 1988

○ ○

Word is out among New York's flop connoisseurs: Don't miss the first preview of *Carrie*. During its tryout in Stratford, England, Broadway diva Barbara Cook jumped ship, and some who made the trip to Stratford reported back that *Carrie* was a lulu. *Carrie* postponed its New York previews more than once, and for a while it looked as if *Carrie* might never begin performances here at all. Finally *Carrie* sets a date to begin: April 28, 1988. To those who care about collecting flops, attending the performance is de rigueur; some present are saying that this could be the only performance of *Carrie* in New York, and such gossip gains credence when the opening of the house is delayed for half an hour.

Another ominous note sounds in the Virginia Theatre on West Fifty-second Street: the entire auditorium has been painted black. Why? We are plunged into darkness, and the lights come up on a white enameled box with side panels capable, we discover, of rotating into mirrors. In togalike white exercise outfits, a dozen ladies—most looking too old and hard for the high-school girls they are meant to be—are engaging in strenuous aerobics under the guidance of gym teacher Miss Gardner (Darlene Love), who is clad in a Greek-style lounge outfit. The scene, in which the girls sing the intense "In," a song about the pressures of adolescence, does not begin to resemble any high school on earth. Clearly, something is wrong.

A row of translucent, revolving panels representing showers is hydraulically borne aloft, the girls rising into the air as they sing out their romantic fantasies in "Dream On." The stage is filled with smoke, although there is no water, and these girls take showers in bras and panties. Carrie White (Linzi Hateley), her plump body covered by a towel, discovers that she is bleeding, and the girls taunt her for her ignorance of menstruation. A light bulb mysteriously explodes overhead. Why? Left alone, Carrie performs the title number, one of the most overwrought and lengthy solos ever in a Broadway musical, in which she expresses her isolation and longing for acceptance. Some theatregoers gape at the stage—others give Hateley an ovation.

The scene shifts to the White home, which for some reason appears to consist solely of a wooden floor, a trapdoor, and a chair. Carrie's mother, Margaret (Betty Buckley), is discovered prostrate on the floor. Margaret is a religious fanatic, yet her fashionable, all-black ensemble includes stylish boots. She sings an eerily beautiful hymn, "Open Your Heart," in which she is soon joined by her daughter. When Mrs. White learns what transpired in the shower room, she interprets the incident as

○ ○ ○ ○ ○

evidence of Carrie's sin and begins stalking Carrie all over the stage as the two perform a grandly operatic duet, "And Eve Was Weak." Suddenly, something wonderful happens in the show: there's searing writing and a tremendous performance by Buckley and Hateley. Margaret forces Carrie down through the trapdoor, sparks fly up, and Buckley finishes sola to a wall of bravos.

Now an assemblage of automobile fronts and headlights moves on. Coupling high-school kids sing "Don't Waste the Moon." Good girl Sue expresses her regrets about mocking Carrie, while bad girl Chris sings of her hatred for Carrie. The scene is jarringly cute, totally out of style with what we've already seen. Doubts about director Terry Hands' control of the evening's tone become exacerbated.

On a bare stage, Margaret and Carrie perform "Evening Prayers," mother and daughter expressing their love and torment in pop-religioso music of passionate beauty. Moving back to the gymnasium set, the show's only moment of warmth arrives as Miss Gardner (in gym attire but with white high-heeled pumps) helps Carrie to believe that love will one day find her, in the song "Unsuspecting Hearts." What is *Carrie*? So far, half of it is thuggish camp, half of it is gorgeous music-theatre.

The evening goes off the track completely in the next scene, set on a bare stage referred to in the program as "Night Spot," supposedly a typical gathering place for middle-American high-school students. But the kids, in studded leather, are moving in a kind of early-middle neurotic disco. Apparently they date not at the local soda shoppe but in a back-room bar. Chris, bad girl in red body stocking, plots revenge on Carrie with help from hip and mean boyfriend Billy. Good girl Sue, in pink body stocking, persuades sweet and nice boyfriend Tommy to take Carrie to the prom. By now, anyone unfamiliar with the Stephen King novel on which the musical was based, or the subsequent film version, wouldn't have the slightest idea what's going on, or who the characters are, or even where the show is taking place. Could Hands' staging be a perverse put-on?

Another vivid mother–daughter scene closes Act One. Carrie informs her mother that she's been invited to the prom, triggering Mrs. White's lurid recollections of the "sin" that produced Carrie. The song, "I Remember How Those Boys Could Dance," is ravishing. But when mother forbids daughter to go, the show becomes unhinged again. The stage floor opens, and Carrie, hands aflame—yes, her hands really appear to be aflame—stands in front of a large strip of simulated fire behind which

○ ○ ○ ○ ○

Four glimpses of the typical, middle-American teenagers of *Carrie*: Above, the opening frenzy, to the tune of "In." Below, the shower scene, with the young ladies taunting ignorant Carrie, who has just experienced her first period.

Above, "Don't Waste the Moon": Is this Carrie or Bye Bye Birdie? Below, "Do Me a Favor": Is this a malt shop or a leather bar?

her mother is pinned. Stephen King buffs know, of course, that Carrie has the power of telekinesis. But as these powers have barely been hinted at until now, the rest of the audience is bewildered—why are Carrie's hands aflame, and what just happened to the stage?

The buzz among habitual first-previewgoers is contradictory. Some have already written the show off, some find it alternately thrilling and ridiculous, some can't believe what they're seeing. Those willing to suspend judgment up to now find that they no longer can as Act Two opens, according to the program on "The Pig Farm." It is with this scene that *Carrie* stakes its claim to a special niche in musical-theatre history. Billy slaughters pigs for Chris (we hear "oinks" through the sound system) to obtain the blood they will use to humiliate Carrie. In the number, called "Out for Blood," boys in leather perform dangerous choreography around and over the fire strip, which doubles here as a pig trough, chanting the refrain "Kill the pig, pig, pig." Chris sings, "It's a simple little gig/You help me kill a pig," and Billy, topless and with his hair in braids, smears his chest repeatedly with the blood of the squealing pigs. When the number ends, a few applaud dutifully, but most look at the stage or at each other with mouths open, just like the audience at *Springtime for Hitler*, the show-within-the-movie in *The Producers*.

A nightmare from which no show could possibly recover, the number is followed by the show's most dispensable sequence: Sue sings "It Hurts to Be Strong," about how hard it is to stand up to one's peers, and it's a good opportunity to sneak out for a cigarette. This is followed by Carrie alone, flanked by two ultraviolet tubes. As she prepares for the prom, Carrie sends her hairbrush, hand mirror, powder puff, shoes, and gown dancing around her in a display of "black lighting" magic. The number is cutesy rather than ominous, the tone way off; Carrie's powers are supposed to be expressions of her emotional upheaval, not a second-rate magic act. Carrie leaves, and Mrs. White sings a lovely, melancholy solo, "When There's No One," in an improbably low-cut negligee.

Now we're at the prom, and a mirrored, rotating ball is, for some reason, secured to the floor. Another overchoreographed sequence culminates in a Verdi-like assemble in which all the principal characters voice their sentiments. Chris's big moment of revenge is so poorly staged it gets laughs: Billy runs on and plunks a small bucket of raspberry topping over Carrie's head, instead of the elaborately rigged device of the *Carrie* novel and film.

○ ○ ○ ○ ○

Next, in "The Destruction," Carrie, hydraulically lifted on a white platform, extends her arm, and laser beams shoot out over the audience. What looks like a plastic shower curtain traps the revelers, and they feign death throes. A roof descends (with a hole cut so that Hateley, still aloft, is not decapitated), and when the lights come up, the roof has become an enormous white staircase covering the entire stage and disappearing up into the flies. Where are we? In heaven? On the high-school steps? At Jacob's Ladder? Jacob's Pillow? Mrs. White, in a cocktail dress, descends the steps, singing the title song as a lullaby. Still singing, she takes out a knife and stabs Carrie. Carrie touches her mother lightly and her mother falls dead. Carrie descends the stairs; crawling backward, she smears blood all over the white steps, drawing barely suppressed laughter from the audience. Carrie joins Sue downstage. Sue comforts the dying Carrie, Mrs. White lies dead on the platform, and as the lights dim to black, boos ring out from the upper balcony while below, others begin an ovation.

As the audience files out, some appear thrilled, others appalled; the word most frequently bandied about is "unbelievable." For show freaks, this has been a night unlike any other, the kind for which they have waited a lifetime. They cannot wait to get home to call their friends, and phone lines, particularly those on the West Side, will continue to steam for hours to come. These fans are aware that what they have just witnessed has set a new standard, one to which all future musical flops will be compared and found waiting. The ad copy, which read "There's Never Been a Musical Like Her," has proved prophetic. These fans will tell their friends to get to the Virginia Theatre immediately, and many of them will return to *Carrie* two or three times during the two weeks of previews that remain. *Carrie* has become an instant legend.

One

CATASTROPHES & CAMP

"Nor will I say that *Portofino* is the worst musical ever produced, because I've only been seeing musicals since 1919."—Walter Kerr, *Herald Tribune*

"*Kelly* is a bad idea gone wrong."—Walter Kerr, *Herald Tribune*

"Like such famous Broadway fiascos as *Kelly*, *Rachael Lily Rosenbloom* and *Rockabye Hamlet*, this one has the courage to meet vulgarity far more than halfway."—Frank Rich, *The New York Times*, on *Marlowe*

Sylvia Syms, Romo Vincent, and Susan Johnson in Whoop—Up *(above)*

There are flop musicals that cause those who remember them to evince regret over how far short their creators fell of their admirable goals. Other flops cause fans to speak fondly of a wonderful score, an unforgettable star performance, some great sets. Certain flops can provoke tirades from those horrified at such utter incompetence. Sometimes the mere mention of a flop musical evokes chuckles at the silliness and stupidity conjured up by its title. But no matter what the degree of awfulness, there's no use denying that flops exert a perverse fascination. There is a decided cachet attached to having seen the musicals to be discussed herein, and musical-theatre lovers are often more eager to discuss a show that played for three performances than one that played three thousand.

Flops are just as much a part of musical-theatre history—indeed, a bigger part—as hits and often involve the same creators. Almost no one in the theatre is immune to flops, and the finest writers, directors, stars, producers, and designers have all had big ones. These theatrical artisans devoted just as much time and energy to their bombs as to their triumphs. And those who have never stopped playing the original cast recordings made from these flops never tire of debating what went wrong or attempting to relate to the uninitiated what it was like to be there.

Carrie was every category of flop rolled into one, capable of provoking all of the reactions mentioned above and then some. But if *Carrie's* unprecedented highs and lows provided it with the immediate aura of legend, it was only the latest in a long series of classic catastrophes. Musical flops are a seasonal Broadway staple, but for a variety of reasons, some are not soon forgotten: their titles are summoned up by aficionados as exemplars of disgrace, humiliation, and utter chaos.

Say "flop" in a word association test, and the title that might come up most frequently, at least prior to *Carrie*, is **Kelly** (Broadhurst; Feb. 6, '65; 1). The most notorious flop of postwar musicals, it is curiously not one of the all-time worst shows—or at least it wasn't when it opened in Philadelphia in December 1964. *Kelly's* notoriety is more the result of its aftermath than of its intrinsic quality.

Based on the true-life story of Steve Brodie, who may or may not have jumped off the Brooklyn Bridge in the 1880s, *Kelly* was the work of Eddie Lawrence (book and lyrics) and Moose Charlap (music). Charlap's career had already encompassed two flops, *Whoop-Up* and *The Conquering Hero*, and his music for Mary Martin's *Peter Pan* had been augmented by the

○ ○ ○ ○ ○

work of other writers. Lawrence, a performer, had never written a musical before—and never would again. *Kelly* went through numerous possible producers, directors (Lindsay Anderson, Peter Coe), and stars (Richard Harris, Gene Kelly, Tommy Sands, Frank Gorshin) before it finally was taken up by David Susskind, Joseph E. Levine, and Daniel Melnick, none of whom had ever produced a Broadway musical. They hired Herbert Ross, a talented choreographer whose only direction thus far had been his takeover of two flops, *House of Flowers* and *The Gay Life,* from other directors. Canadian actor Don Francks was hired for the title role, and Ella Logan, who had not appeared on Broadway since creating the lead in *Finian's Rainbow* in 1947, signed on as Ma Kelly. Anita Gillette got the ingenue lead: she had recently opened *The Gay Life* by jumping off a bridge (the scene and her part were cut on the road); bridges, clearly, were not to be lucky for Gillette, whose career would be beset by flop musicals.

As the curtain rises on *Kelly,* young busboy Hop Kelly has already chickened out of three previous attempts to jump off the Brooklyn Bridge and in so doing has placed himself in considerable jeopardy with Bowery gamblers. Kelly ultimately foils the gamblers' plans to substitute a dummy in his place, accepting the challenge and triumphing at the end.

By the time *Kelly* reached Boston, the producers had brought in three new writers (one of whom was Mel Brooks) to fashion a largely new book. Lawrence and Charlap promptly took the producers to court to prevent them from opening the show on Broadway unless their material was restored. A Supreme Court judge ruled that arbitration was in order but that the opening could not be stopped. Susskind, who was heard in Boston to say, "We haven't got a Chinaman's chance—the truth is this is a bad show," now told the *Daily News,* "I predict it'll be the biggest hit since *Hello, Dolly!*" Susskind invited a group of clairvoyants onto his weekly television show the week before the New York opening; each of the five declared that *Kelly* would be a smash.

Logan, who withdrew from the show when her part was whittled away, attended the opening, as did Charlap, who sat upstairs with his lawyer and a tape recorder. Howard Taubman of the *New York Times* began his notice by saying, "Ella Logan was written out of *Kelly* before it reached the Broadhurst Theatre Saturday night. Congratulations, Miss Logan." The reviews were uniformly terrible, far worse than they had been for the show's two tryout engagements, and *Kelly's* opening night performance was its last.

○ ○ ○ ○ ○

Three major catastrophes. Above, Ella Logan (before
she was written out) with Don Francks in Kelly.
Right and below, the Playbills for those twin disgraces
of 1972, Dude and Via Galactica.

Many worse shows had opened before, but *Kelly*'s failure turned into a media event. The show became the subject of a lengthy, fly-on-the-wall piece in the *Saturday Evening Post*; in it, featured lead Eileen Rodgers was said to have broken into tears in Philadelphia and exclaimed, "I wish I was back in *Tenderloin*. It was a flop, but at least people were friendly." Newspapers trumpeted the fact that *Kelly* was the most expensive ($650,000) failure in Broadway history. Perhaps for the first time, it was brought home to the public the stakes involved, and the decline of a system that could produce an evening so obviously headed for doom. *Kelly* was scary—it made people ask, "How do these things happen?"

From the time they went to court to stop the Broadway opening to this day, the writers of *Kelly* maintain that theirs was a promising show destroyed on the road by lack of producing know-how. In its original form, *Kelly* aspired to a *Threepenny Opera*-like grit mixed with the colorful lowlifes and lovable hoods of *Guys and Dolls*. There are interesting lyrics and some decent attempts at local color and salty dialogue. But it's a strange and perilously thin story, and one is never made to care about Hop and his plight. Moreover, *Kelly* was unwise to hinge its entire plot around an event—the bridge jump—that could not possibly be shown on stage. If *Kelly* in Philly was better than *Kelly* on Broadway, it was never strong to begin with.

Kelly's score contains one notable song, "Never Go There Anymore," an ambitious ballad that extends into a dramatic scene in which the hero recalls his slum upbringing. Otherwise, the score is not much more interesting than the story. The only recording of *Kelly* is a "demo" recorded by the authors and commercially released fifteen years later, an indication of how desperate someone was to put out an album of the most famous flop of them all. With its tinny sound and wailing voices, it is arguably the most unlistenable show record ever released.

Kelly is mostly famous for being famous; it was unpromising from its inception. **Breakfast at Tiffany's** (Majestic; Dec. 12, '66; closed in previews), though, would seem to have had everything going for it. It was produced by David Merrick, its book and direction were by Abe Burrows, and its score was by Bob Merrill, who had already written *Take Me Along*, *Carnival*, and two songs interpolated into Merrick's *Hello, Dolly!* during its tryout. It starred two glamorous television names, Mary Tyler Moore and Richard Chamberlain, and was based on Truman Capote's heartbreaking novella, which had already been made into a hugely successful 1961 film.

○ ○ ○ ○ ○

Indeed, *Breakfast at Tiffany's* was the most anticipated musical of the 1966–67 season, with an advance sale far exceeding that of *Cabaret, I Do! I Do!*, or *The Apple Tree*, other autumn '66 musical attractions.

Capote set his book in the forties and made it a flashback narrated by an unnamed writer, obviously Capote himself, who is fascinated by his eccentric neighbor Holly Golightly but who has no romantic relationship with her. In the movie version, reset to the present, writer Paul falls in love with Holly, the attraction complicated by a newly invented affair between Paul and a rich, married older woman. The film also was given a happy ending in which flighty Holly finally commits to someone and stays with Paul; in the novel, Holly leaves the country forever. The film, if far less moving than the novel, represented a capable job of turning a plotless mood piece into a conventional sixties romantic comedy.

Originally, Merrick had asked Capote to adapt his own novella for the musical stage, but Capote, who had already adapted one of his own short stories into the book for the musical flop *House of Flowers*, declined. Joshua Logan was asked to direct, and Nunnally Johnson wrote a book for the show, which was rejected. When Burrows agreed to write a new book and to direct, the project became a reality. It's worth noting, however, that Merrill had already written most of his score—to Johnson's book—before Burrows was hired.

Under the title *Holly Golightly*, the musical played two tryout engagements, in Philadelphia and Boston, to mostly negative reviews. The critics were particularly harsh on the show's leading lady. Mary Tyler Moore told the *New York Post*, "I've got to clear my name. We were a month in Boston. It seemed like fourteen. You can imagine how I felt having to go on every night when I read that Tammy Grimes or Diahann Carroll would replace me. Tammy was never in Boston waiting to take over as reported. And Miss Carroll was the original choice for the part. In Philadelphia, they made Holly very tough. The critics rapped us for that, so in Boston we made her sweet and they rapped us for that. David Merrick has been wonderful to me. With those reviews, I'm sure other producers would have replaced me."

Capote saw the show in Boston and told *Women's Wear Daily*, "I don't like the score or the leading lady." It was clear that drastic measures were called for: Burrows, known as the ace play doctor of his time, seemed unable to fix his own show, so Merrick took the surprising step of asking Edward Albee—whose only experience with musicals was as coauthor of the libretto for a forgotten 1961 off-Broadway musical adaptation of

Melville's "Bartleby the Scrivener"—to write a new book. Merrick and Albee wanted Burrows to stay on as director, but Burrows walked out when he read Albee's words to Kevin Kelly in the *Boston Globe* near the end of the tryout: "All those awful jokes will be thrown out, and I hope to substitute some genuine wit. The characters, from Holly down, will be redefined, and she won't have any of those borscht-circuit lovers she's saddled with now."

Joseph Anthony took over the direction; Larry Kert and others joined the cast, while other performers were dropped; the score was substantially revised to fit Albee's script; and the show, now called *Breakfast at Tiffany's*, limped into New York. In spite of disastrous reports from the road, nothing could stop people from buying tickets for what they still believed to be a sure thing, and the advance sale continued to build.

After watching the first Broadway preview on December 12, 1966, during which members of the audience walked out or talked back to the actors, Merrick decided to cancel the scheduled December 26 opening. He allowed the show to play three more previews—performances to which the Broadway cognoscenti flocked—then called a press conference to make an unprecedented statement: "Rather than subject the drama critics and the theatregoing public—who invested one million dollars in advance sales—to an excruciatingly boring evening, I have decided to close. Since the idea of adapting *Breakfast at Tiffany's* for the musical stage was mine in the first place, the closing is entirely my fault and should not be attributed to the three top writers who had a go at it." With tongue in cheek, Merrick added that he was shutting the show down "because Tiffany's the jeweler promised to pay off the loss. Their competitor, Cartier's, wanted me to keep it open to damage Tiffany's."

The announcement made Merrick a hero. Never before had a producer admitted at this stage that his show was a disaster and stated that he did not wish to cheat his customers. No show had ever been stopped prior to its Broadway opening with an advance sale as large as that secured by *Tiffany's*. The show cost $500,000, but thanks to sell-out business in both road engagements, it wound up losing $425,000, thus making it a bomb that actually returned a portion of its investment.

Just as remarkable is the fact that the *New York Times* actually ran a semireview, written by second-stringer Dan Sullivan, the day after the final preview. Sullivan wrote, "The preview audience left the Majestic immeasurably depressed . . . Both [Moore and Chamberlain] are troupers, but neither was ready for a Broadway musical."

○ ○ ○ ○ ○

HOLLY GOLiGHTLY

Mary Tyler Moore and Richard Chamberlain, the stars of Holly Golightly,
later Breakfast at Tiffany's. They're smiling, but that's because this photo was
taken for the Philadelphia Playbill before all the trouble started.

Many mediocre-to-poor musicals, by dint of hefty advance sales, opened in the sixties and managed to play out a season. How did a show so promising become such a disgrace that it had to be withdrawn? Burrows' version went astray because it attempted to make Capote's ethereal character study into a boisterous, conventional, sixties-style Broadway show. The character of Holly, more annoying than charming, got lost in a series of mostly extraneous production numbers. Humor was in very short supply, and Merrill failed to musicalize the most dramatic or emotional moments of the story. The road version was simply not very entertaining.

Albee took an unconventional and fascinating approach that managed to destroy every scene, every moment. In Albee's virtually plotless book, Holly becomes a character being created by Jeff Claypool (as the writer was called in both Burrows' and Albee's versions). Jeff invents Holly as he goes along, instructing, rebuking, interrupting, and correcting her throughout. In their scenes together, Holly and Jeff are no longer people, but a writer and the character he's improvising. The central conceit is particularly confusing when Jeff, supposedly inventing the action, becomes upset with what's happening to Holly: if he's making up the story, why does he allow these things to happen? In addition, Albee's hard-bitten Holly was even less suited to Moore's personality than Burrows' had been. Deadly to any possible dramatic interest, Albee's script did include one amusing in-joke: after a television news report about Holly's arrest for her unwitting involvement in a drug ring, the newscaster introduces a review of a new David Merrick musical, based on Chekhov's *The Cherry Orchard* and called *Cherry!*

Both versions contained some good songs, but Merrill's work was too conventional for the material, and people missed the film's hit song, "Moon River." Capote's touching heroine never got the imaginative musicalization she might have had and didn't even receive the successful, if revisionist, treatment she got in the movie. Hiring Albee to fix what was already a deeply troubled show was the wrong decision, and by the time it reached Broadway, *Breakfast at Tiffany's* had gone wildly astray. Advance ticket buyers lined up for refunds, not quite believing that it could have been that bad.

Capote's colorful Holly and the success of the *Tiffany's* movie meant that a Broadway musical would inevitably follow, and in fact, there was never anything wrong with the idea of *Tiffany's* as a musical. But Peter Allen playing Prohibition-era gangster Legs Diamond was an idea doomed

○ ○ ○ ○ ○

to failure from the start. Allen and his close friend Charles Suppon began to write the book for **Legs Diamond** (Mark Hellinger; Dec. 26, '88; 64), dimly based on the 1960 Warner Brothers film *The Rise and Fall of Legs Diamond*, in 1983. The show that got to Broadway five years later, just months after *Carrie*, was one of the greatest personal humiliations Broadway has ever witnessed.

Singer—songwriter Allen is a star with a passionate following who has on occasion been known to fill Radio City Music Hall but who otherwise lacks hit records and is not really all that famous. In 1971, Allen had appeared in a Broadway flop called *Soon*, a rock opera which closed after three performances and which also featured Richard Gere, Barry Bostwick and Nell Carter; but by the time of *Legs Diamond* he was much better known, and *Legs Diamond* was meant to be the vehicle that would allow him to make the transition from concert performer to Broadway star.

After a 1987 workshop of the Allen—Suppon book, Harvey Fierstein, who had already won Tony Awards for his play *Torch Song Trilogy* and the book for *La Cage aux Folles*, was hired to write a new script. (Suppon retained coauthorship credit, thus qualifying as the only librettist in Broadway history to also win the Coty Award for women's wear design.) The first book had been dark and serious; it was Fierstein's idea—an idea that ultimately made little sense—to make his hero a hoofer in Prohibition-era New York who only becomes a gangster to further his desire to break into show business.

Initially, *Legs Diamond* was scheduled for out-of-town tryouts in various cities, but David Mitchell's needlessly intricate set designs made a tour impossible; the cancellation of the pre-Broadway tour would prove to be the most crucial of many producing errors. Also abandoned early on were elaborate "black art" designs, whereby bullets and the front pages of newspapers would have hurtled across the footlights in 3-D fashion.

As the only new book musical on the horizon when the 1988–89 season began, *Legs Diamond* built up a huge advance sale throughout the summer. The first public sign of trouble came in August when the show's choreographer, Michael Shawn, was dismissed and replaced by Alan Johnson. Shawn later took the show's producers to court, claiming that he was fired because he had tested positive for the AIDS virus and the producers feared he would be unable to continue working. Long after *Legs Diamond* closed, the case was settled out of court, and Shawn was awarded $175,000. He died in April 1990.

After several postponements, eight weeks of previews began in late

○ ○ ○ ○ ○

October. Poisonous word of mouth spread almost instantly; even those who had little interest in Broadway musicals became aware that *Legs Diamond* was a dog. More unusual was the series of articles that appeared in major newspapers which let those who had not already heard know how bad the show was supposed to be.

Not since *Merrily We Roll Along* in 1981 did a show experience such a troubled preview period and undergo such radical change. Within a week a leading role, that of Legs' wife, Alice (Christine Andreas), had been eliminated. Then Legs' brother, Eddie (Bob Stillman), a character central to the 1960 film, was also dropped. Allen's lack of acting ability was addressed late in previews by giving him monologues that enabled him to talk directly to the audience as he would in his club act. Audiences were paying fifty dollars a head to see a chaotic show in constant flux.

Director Robert Allan Ackerman, who had directed the workshop but had no experience with big-time musicals, retained his job throughout previews, probably because no better director was willing to take over. After several canceled opening dates, *Legs Diamond* premiered the night after Christmas. Standing on his own coffin at the beginning of Act Two, Legs said, "I'm in show biz. Only a critic can kill me!" A critic? The reviews were *unanimously* horrendous. The advance sale, which had filled most of the theatre during previews, fell away, and the show closed after eight weeks, losing over $5 million. At the final performance, Allen thanked everyone, saying, "I guess I'm not going to be able to do this at the Tonys."

Warning bells should ring when a show's creators announce that they only want to give the audience a good, old-fashioned, escapist time. The creators of *Legs* thought they were providing the public with a respite from pretentious, overblown British pop-opera spectacles, but even the weakest of those imports was more entertaining than *Legs*. From previews to opening, the show had progressed from an unprofessional, often incomprehensible embarrassment to a more polished, clearer embarrassment. Dull and above all humorless, it was a star vehicle without a star. Allen looked ridiculous throughout and was particularly unconvincing romancing the many ladies supposedly a part of his life. His music wasn't all bad, but his lyrics were often awkward and didn't always rhyme. Cabaret goddess Julie Wilson, forced to speak entirely in B-movie clichés, continued her record of creating roles only in Broadway bombs (*Jimmy, Park*) but provided *Legs* with its only touch of class.

Legs Diamond's lousiness is less important, however, than its stark dem-

∘ ∘ ∘ ∘ ∘

onstration of the lack of producing know-how on Broadway in the late eighties. The idea of Allen as a twenties gangster—Lothario was a bad one to begin with. The workshop, with most of the Broadway production's songs and cast already in place, should have demonstrated to all the inadvisability of continuing. *Legs* could and should have been aborted in 1987; the Nederlander Organization's insistence on going ahead with it made it clear that landlords, rather than artists, were running the show. Immediately after the closing, the Times Square Church took possession of the Mark Hellinger Theatre, the Nederlanders having rented it out to them for five years as an admission of the hopelessness they felt after *Legs Diamond*. Without realizing it, Peter Allen was standing atop the coffin of Broadway professionalism itself.

Lack of professionalism, however, is by no means a recent development on Broadway. Professionalism was seriously threatened in the late sixties and early seventies as a result of the rock musical *Hair's* taking Broadway by storm. It was a time when zanies and no-talents of a sort far less equipped for Broadway than Peter Allen suddenly turned up on the posters of big-budget Broadway musicals, largely because Clive Barnes, then critic for the *New York Times*, decided after seeing *Hair* that the sounds of contemporary music were what Broadway needed. What Barnes didn't realize was that those interested in writing in that style generally had no idea how to write a musical. **Dude** (Broadway; Oct. 9, '72; 16) and **Via Galactica** (Uris; Nov. 28, '72; 8), which opened about a month apart and which both featured music by *Hair's* composer Galt MacDermot, were the two most salient horrors that resulted.

For *Dude*, the enormous Broadway Theatre was converted into an environmental arena. The forestlike, in-the-round setting included a band placed around the house in various locations, ramps, a central stage on top of what used to be the orchestra seats, and seats where the stage used to be. Actors roamed throughout the theatre and even flew overhead. The seat locations were given cute names: the best seats (seven dollars) were the "Foot Hills," and one could also purchase "Trees," "Mountains," and "Valleys."

Dude, subtitled *The Highway Life*, with book and lyrics by *Hair's* coauthor Gerome Ragni, seemed to be about Dude, who represented Everyman, and his temptation by Zero, who represented Satan. God, here called #33, ultimately won out and gave Dude back his innocence. Perhaps the most incomprehensible show ever presented on a Broadway stage, it was mostly sung, but its songs were barely related and could have been performed in any order or by any "character" with the same result. MacDermot, a talented composer, wrote his least interesting score for *Dude*, and the lyrics were gibberish, seldom rhyming and deficient in craft or meaning.

Previews were halted after three days so that the show's original director, Rocco Bufano, could be replaced by *Hair's* director, Tom O'Horgan (though the show seemed like pure O'Horgan from the beginning). Late in previews, the producers, Adela and Peter Holzer, told Ragni they would close the show if he didn't make the book intelligible. But Ragni never did, and after a critical drubbing (with rock-musical champion Clive Barnes joining in), the show closed in two weeks, losing a million dollars. In 1989, Mrs. Holzer again joined forces with O'Horgan for a rock opera called *Senator Joe*, which closed after three previews at the Neil Simon Theatre; Holzer's financing ploys for that production landed her in jail.

It's amazing to think that anyone involved with *Dude* ever thought they'd get away with it. *Via Galactica* was a somewhat more imaginative project, but also incoherent: a synopsis had to be inserted into programs just prior to the opening. The lyrics for this all-sung show were by Christopher Gore, who in 1977 would write the book and lyrics for *Nefertiti*, which closed on the road. But the man most responsible for *Via Galactica* was Peter Hall, then director of the Royal Shakespeare Company and about to take over the National Theatre of Great Britain. Hall conceived and directed *Via*, his first musical; he later staged the disastrous, but far more interesting, *Jean Seberg* at the National.

A precursor of later pop opera spectacles like *Starlight Express* and *Time*, *Via Galactica* told its story of a band of nonconformists on an asteroid one thousand years in the future with such appurtenances as six large trampolines (to help the actors simulate the weightlessness of space), laser beams, and a flying spacecraft. The complexities of the production, not helped by the fact that *Via Galactica* was the first show booked into the new Uris Theatre, were so enormous that the show's textual problems took a back seat. (The show's original title, *Up!*, had to be abandoned when the producers realized that the marquee would contain an unwanted pun if it read "*Up! Uris.*")

Nothing in *Via Galactica* could possibly have entertained a drug-free audience. With a pretentious, confusing libretto and a dull score heavy

○ ○ ○ ○ ○

on country and gospel rhythms, it was an enormous, million-dollar mess. In his *Diaries*, Hall wrote: "If you can't have a monumental success, I suppose you may as well have a monumental failure."

Dude and *Via Galactica* were two expensive embarrassments that actually had a salutary effect on musical theatre. With their back-to-back awfulness, they put a quick end to the idea that rock would "save" the Broadway musical. People were not willing to stand for overproduced nonsense just because it had a rock beat. Soon, even the most hackneyed old-school Broadway writers were warmly welcomed back. *Dude* had one other positive effect: its gutting of the Broadway Theatre paved the way for the environmental production of *Candide* that moved in there the following season.

As all-out catastrophes go, *Dude* and *Via Galactica* retain a certain fascination for collectors—like a train wreck from which it is hard to tear oneself away. But another all-out catastrophe, **The Little Prince and the Aviator** (Alvin; Jan. 1, '82; closed in previews), is remembered as one of Broadway's most difficult-to-sit-through musicals ever. The fact that Alan Jay Lerner, Frederick Loewe, and Stanley Donen had had little success adapting Count Antoine de Saint-Exupery's 1943 classic, *The Little Prince*, into a movie musical should have said something to A. Joseph Tandet, a coproducer of the 1974 film who held the rights to the property and produced a variety of stage and film versions of it during the last twenty years. In the early eighties, Tandet got Hugh Wheeler (*Sweeney Todd, A Little Night Music*), John Barry (*Billy, Lolita, My Love*), and Don Black (*Song and Dance, Aspects of Love*) to write a musical stage version of the story, and after the original director and choreographer were fired, *The Little Prince and the Aviator* began Broadway previews without benefit of tryout. In the stage version, which starred Michael York in his only musical appearance, the focus was equally on the prince and on the pilot who is grounded in the Sahara and meets the little refugee from an asteroid. York's character was explicitly de Saint-Exupery, and the musical alternated flashbacks to the Count's life with scenes involving the prince. While the concept was not necessarily a bad one, *The Little Prince and the Aviator* proved to be grisly, a boring evening of disconnected scenes and unmotivated song cues. No one involved knew until the day before the scheduled January 20 opening that the show had already been aborted.

What was most interesting about this particular debacle was what happened after. Tandet sued the Nederlander Organization, claiming that

○ ○ ○ ○ ○

they had coerced him into closing the show by demanding more money than they had originally asked for to keep the show open through the final week of previews. In 1986, Tandet was awarded $1 million, the jury having decided that the Nederlanders *had* forced the show to close by making unreasonable demands. The $1 million reward represented two thirds of the show's cost, and *The Little Prince and the Aviator* became one disaster that almost returned its investment.

All the above shows were essentially sorry spectacles, in retrospect sadder still. But there is another genus of catastrophe, the camp flop. While generally no better than the disasters already discussed, these have an amusing side. Their very titles conjure up ineffable mental pictures in the minds of show freaks. Their cast recordings—if they ran long enough for recordings to be made—are played with glee in the privacy of collectors' homes, sometimes more often than the albums of *My Fair Lady* or *Carousel*. These shows were horrible, but wonderfully, deliciously horrible. These shows were a hoot.

The 1950s produced what are arguably the four worst musicals ever seen on Broadway. They were, for the most part, written and directed by nobodies, and in the way that *Carrie* has become a standard for shows that followed it, these four titles were invoked throughout the sixties and seventies whenever a new bomb arrived..

Chronologically, the first two fall into the category of "floperetta," a term coined by the writer Ethan Mordden. After the Rodgers and Hammerstein musical-theatre revolution in the forties, shows that in any way smacked of Victor Herbert and Sigmund Romberg operetta were deemed particularly unacceptable. But old ways die hard, and there continued to be Broadway musicals that, while taking token notice of the changes of the forties, were hopelessly antiquated in plot, composition, and performance. These tended to be the work of amateurs, but there are four professional figures who define the floperetta genre. They are Edwin Lester, producer of the Los Angeles Civic Light Opera seasons, who continued to present works from the twenties while creating new musicals in the forties, fifties, and sixties that were homages to the past; Robert Wright and George Forrest, who adapted the works of classical composers and came up with two hits, *Song of Norway* and *Kismet,* then wrote numerous old-style shows that failed to find favor; and Irra Petina, a one-time Metropolitan Opera mezzo who appeared in several of the most notorious floperettas.

○ ○ ○ ○ ○

Buttrio Square (New Century; Oct. 14, '52; 7), the first of our "four worst," was about a village in 1946 Italy seeking to qualify as a town. One more citizen is needed for township, and Marisa, daughter of the baron who owns the village, becomes pregnant. The pregnancy must be kept secret, however, because the father of the child is American Captain Steve, who has married Marisa in spite of the fact that fraternization between the Italians and the occupying GIs is forbidden. Childless Papa Mario, the village's baker and would-be mayor, is led to believe that his own wife is pregnant and that it is his child that is on the way. For comic relief, there is Terry Patterson, who wants to become a WAC but who, because of her male name, has been accidentally designated as a GI and been unable to correct her status.

Billy Gilbert, who played Mario, was a popular comic star of films and the stage who had recently appeared on Broadway in two floperettas, *Gypsy Lady* and a revival of *The Chocolate Soldier*. Gilbert cowrote the book, and one Gen Genovese was colibrettist, lyricist, producer, and author of the story on which the show was based.

Buttrio Square had a terribly troubled history. During rehearsals, a post-dated check written to cover the Equity bond bounced, and Equity stepped in and halted rehearsals. Both Boston and Philadelphia tryouts were scratched when a major backer withdrew funding. Eugene Loring, the choreographer, took over the direction as well, replacing Dale Wasserman. At the last minute, Loring was forced to form a syndicate of fifty enthusiastic cast members, each of whom invested two hundred dollars so that the show could open. But critics were horrified, with good words only for talented newcomer Susan Johnson as the would-be WAC.

Two years after *Buttrio Square*, another all-time worst, **Hit The Trail** (Mark Hellinger; Dec. 1, '54; 4), arrived and defined the camp flop. For two years, one Elizabeth Miele had attempted to get a vehicle for Irra Petina on the boards. With music by Portuguese composer Frederico Valerio, Miele's production, then called *On with the Show*, finally opened in New Haven and Boston. Petina sustained an ankle injury in Connecticut, but worse was to come in Bean Town; understudy Vera Brynner (Yul's sister) had to sub for the ailing Petina, and when Miele went backstage to chastise Brynner for her lack of familiarity with the part, producer and understudy had to be separated. (Brynner, who was playing a featured role, left when her one big number was given to Petina.) The choreographer was fired, and cast members threatened to walk, claiming the show needed far more work than it was receiving.

○ ○ ○ ○ ○

Billy Gilbert starred in—and coauthored the book for—Buttrio
Square. Floperetta queen Irra Petina was given her very own
vehicle, but was soon asked to Hit the Trail.

Opening on Broadway as *Hit The Trail*, the show, set during the Nevada gold rush, tells of a stranded operetta troupe. Company diva Lucy Vernay (Petina) is forced to choose between her former lover, the company's corrupt manager (Paul Valentine), and an honest local banker (Robert Wright), who gives her money to open a beauty emporium in town. Completely irrelevant to the Broadway of 1954, *Hit The Trail* reached new depths in stilted dialogue, tuneless quasi-operetta love duets, and transparent hopelessness. The title change was appropriate: *Hit The Trail* did so two days after opening.

Perhaps because no one could believe it, *Hit the Trail* was quickly forgotten. But to this day, **Portofino** (Adelphi; Feb. 21, '58; 3) is still often pointed to as the worst Broadway musical ever. It was produced and written by Richard Ney, an actor whose main claim to fame was that he had once been married to Greer Garson. The music was by jazz composer Louis Bellson (husband of Pearl Bailey), and Sheldon Harnick, whose first Broadway show, *The Body Beautiful*, had just opened, was called in for help with the lyrics.

Portofino was about a cynical auto-racing Italian duke (Georges Guetary) who falls for a rival driver from Texas (Helen Gallagher). A single actor (Robert Strauss) played both the local padre and his look-alike, an emissary from the Devil in danger of losing his position. The plot was further complicated by the duke's granddaughter, a young witch. After its poor Philadelphia reception, Ney posted a closing notice but left it up to the cast to decide whether or not to bring the show to New York. They voted to go in, thus demonstrating the perils of democracy. In the *Daily Mirror*, Robert Coleman greeted the show with, "After being bored by *Buttrio Square* and plagued by *Portofino*, we think it's about time for the Italian Tourist Bureau to mount a musical of its own. In self-defense."

It was another career setback for Helen Gallagher, whose first leading role on Broadway had been in the flop *Hazel Flagg* a few years earlier. Gallagher described the three performances of *Portofino*'s run as "the longest performances of my life," and critics sympathized with Gallagher's having to utter such lines as, "When I think of him kissing me, I don't know whether to fall down, sit down, or Miltown."

Portofino's Adelphi Theatre was renamed the 54th Street, and when the last of our four all-timers, **Happy Town** (54th Street; Oct. 7, '59; 5), opened there, Thomas R. Dash wrote in *Women's Wear Daily*, "The nadir of Broadway musicals of the recent past has been attained by *Portofino* and *Buttrio Square*. They can now move over and leave room for *Happy Town*."

○ ○ ○ ○ ○

Again, the Playbill credits said it all: "B & M Productions present," "book adapted by Max Hampton" (but who wrote it?), lyrics by Harry M. Haldane, music by Gordon Duffy, directed by Allan A. Buckhantz. Who were these people? Paul Nassau, who later wrote two flop musicals better than *Happy Town*, contributed additional music and lyrics. The less-than-stellar cast was headed by Biff McGuire (who was asked to deliver most of his lines and songs standing on a barrel), Lee Venora, and Cindy Robbins.

Happy Town, backed by Texas millionaires, was set in Back-A-Heap, the only town in Texas without a millionaire. Four Houston trillionaires send their innocent brother to Back-A-Heap, ostensibly to help the populace by buying property, but actually to obtain the land to exploit the big cave below the town as an oil storage basin. The hero ultimately joins forces with the townspeople to foil his brothers. *Happy Town* had closed after a week's tryout in Boston for a complete rewrite, but it unwisely came in to town as the first musical of the 1959–60 season. There have been camp flops since, but perhaps none as completely without merit or reason for being.

Buttrio Square, Hit The Trail, Portofino, and *Happy Town* never intended to be laughed off the stage. But there is one show, **Rachael Lily Rosenbloom** (Broadhurst; Nov. 26, '73; closed in previews), that stands as the only intentionally camp musical in Broadway history. It opens like this: an actress made up to resemble Barbra Streisand strides onstage to present the Academy Award for Best Actress. She reads the nominees: "Angela Lansbury for *The Rosalind Russell Story*, Goldie Hawn for *Via Galactica*, Diana Ross for *The Angela Davis Story*, Angela Davis for *The Diana Ross Story*, and Rachael Lily Rosenbloom for *Cobra Goddess on Pink Flamingo Road.*"

That opening sets the tone for all of *Rachael Lily Rosenbloom*. The show traces the rise and fall of its eponymous heroine (the extra "a" in Rachael was the "a" that her idol, Streisand, dropped from her first name) from Brooklyn's Fulton Fish Market to fame in Hollywood as a gossip columnist, then star. At the end, strung out from nervous exhaustion, Rachael attempts, unsuccessfully, to return to her roots.

With its wholly gay sensibility, *Rachael Lily Rosenbloom* was a show that might have been produced by *After Dark* magazine. It was instead produced by hotshots Robert Stigwood and Ahmet Ertegun, and it was the work of Paul Jabara, a performer in *Hair* on Broadway and in Stigwood's London

Three flops: The two above were unintentional camp, the one below actually aimed for camp.

production of *Jesus Christ Superstar.* Jabara was a sort of court jester to the Stigwood empire, and Stigwood and Ertegun put up $500,000 to indulge his whims, which included playing one of the leads. *Rachael* was written for Bette Midler, who wisely passed, and the lead went to cabaret performer Ellen Greene, who, with *Rachael* and *The Little Prince and the Aviator* on her resumé, has the singular distinction of having created the female leads in two musicals that closed during New York previews.

Tom Eyen, a writer known for camp epics, was brought in to help with the book and replace original director Ron Link. Grover Dale came in to "supervise" Tony Stevens' choreography. The result was a mess, closer to the shows Eyen and drag queen Jackie Curtis were then doing off-off-Broadway than to a Broadway musical. There were flashes of potent dirty humor, but by the end of eight previews, it was obvious to all that the show was woefully out of place on Broadway. Sylvia Miles and other key figures of New York's then "in set" raced to the final performance.

Four musicals of the eighties and one of the seventies stand out for their unintentional hilarity and overall ridiculousness. In 1974, fifty-five-year-old Yul Brynner decided it was time to find another musical vehicle, his last Broadway appearance having been in *The King and I.* Brynner tossed in his lot with three of the more flop-prone figures in the modern musical: director Albert Marre, actress Joan Diener, and composer Mitch Leigh. Marre had had two major hits with *Kismet* and *Man of La Mancha* and a mild success with *Milk and Honey;* otherwise, his credits featured bomb after bomb (*Chu Chem, At the Grand, Cry for Us All, La Belle, Shangri-La, The Conquering Hero, Halloween, Winnie*). Diener, Marre's wife, had been in the two big Marre hits but also in many Marre flops. And the talented Leigh had made his debut with *Man of La Mancha,* but after that triumph, he, too, had had an unbroken string of flop musicals.

Leigh wrote the score, Marre directed, and Diener costarred with Brynner in a show originally called *Odyssey,* loosely based on Homeric legend. Brynner was Odysseus, and Diener, surrounded by beefy suitors, was the long-suffering Penelope back in Ithaca. The show touched briefly on the end of Odysseus' journey but concentrated on his return home. With book and lyrics by Erich Segal (*Love Story*) and a relatively small cast of eighteen, *Odyssey* began a year-long tour in December 1974. Brynner's hotel and dressing room accommodation list became an industry joke: every dressing room had to be painted a particular shade of brown

○ ○ ○ ○ ○

and every hotel-suite kitchen had to be stocked in advance with "one dozen brown eggs—under no circumstances white ones!"

The tour was beset with litigation and unhappiness. In April 1975, Brynner, Diener, and Marre filed a $7.5 million suit against Trader Vic's restaurant in New York, where the three and Brynner's wife, Jacqueline, had dined just prior to commencing the tour. They alleged that the spareribs they consumed that evening were "poisonous," causing them to fall "ill, weak, and infirm" and forcing Brynner and Diener to miss shows. Marre claimed he had "been unable to perform his theatrical work with his accustomed energy and vigor," and Jacqueline averred that she sustained an "impaired and depreciated" marital association with her husband as a result of the tainted ribs.

When Diener's name was, contrary to contractual stipulation, left off the marquee of the Colonial Theatre in Boston, she insisted that the marquee be shrouded in black, causing some theatregoers to believe that Brynner had died. During the Los Angeles run, Segal asked that his name be removed from the credits, and it was, although much of his work remained. (The book was ultimately credited to Marre and Roland Kibbee, the lyrics to Charles Burr and Forman Brown.) Marre also removed choreographer Billy Wilson and took over the musical staging himself.

In August, Brynner brought suit to terminate his contract but was threatened with a $1 million damage claim if he should leave the show. In November, when producer Roger L. Stevens decided to close the show in California, Brynner did an about-face and threatened to walk out of the current engagement if the show was not brought to New York. In the fall, Segal sued again, demanding that the show be closed, and it was—for a while.

Renamed **Home Sweet Homer** (Palace; Jan. 4, '76; 1) and billed as "A Musical Romantic Comedy," the show opened and closed on a single Sunday matinee. Terminally silly, *Homer*'s score included a lovely duet for Odysseus and son Telemachus called "How Could I Dare to Dream," and Diener's reckless combination of high notes and chest tones made a couple of other numbers amusing. But *Homer* should never have risked Broadway. On the road, it had received consistently poor reviews but had done strong business. Because of the constantly shifting personnel, however, the show, a disaster that played over a year, recovered none of its cost. Brynner took up the role of the King of Siam immediately after *Homer* folded and continued to play it for the rest of his life. His final tour in the part was produced and directed by Mitch Leigh.

○ ○ ○ ○ ○

The flop-prone team of Mitch Leigh, Albert Marre, and Joan Diener came up with the ridiculous Yul Brynner vehicle first called Odyssey, then Home Sweet Homer. Pictured is the unique Diener as Penelope, surrounded by suitors who, one suspects, may not really be all that interested in Penelope.

An exemplar of unintentional humor, **Into the Light** (Neil Simon; Oct. 22, '86; 6) is likely to stand as the only Broadway musical about the Holy Shroud of Turin. In 1978, a team of American scientists performed tests on the Shroud, believed by many to be the burial cloth of Jesus, to determine its origin. The program stated, *"Into the Light,* while a work of fiction, has remained faithful to the findings of that expedition."

It was once again the work of a composer, lyricist, librettist, director, choreographer, and producers with few or no Broadway credits. But it starred Dean Jones, who had opened and promptly withdrawn from the brilliant *Company* at the same theatre sixteen years earlier. The deeply religious Jones told the press why he believed in *Into the Light:* "Theatre should inspire," he said, "and lift the human spirit."

Was *Into the Light* the worst idea ever for a Broadway musical? If not, the show was at least a camp classic to be treasured. The stage was filled with smoke and laser beams (press releases said it would "take Broadway into the twenty-first century"), while the story alternated scenes involving Jones and his crew of scientists performing tests with scenes of his neglected wife and son at home. (The son had an imaginary friend, performed by a mime, who followed him everywhere.) The evening's most memorable moment may have been the number "Let There Be Light," in which an archbishop, nuns, and priests all kicked up their heels to express their approval of the project. The show's not-quite-hidden agenda was the validation of the Shroud's authenticity; those wondering how *Into the Light* ever got to Broadway were not surprised to find out that the entire cost of the show, over $3 million, was raised from an audience of the devout and monied in a single backers' audition in California.

Even more amusing than *Into the Light,* and only a marginally better idea, was **Marilyn—An American Fable** (Minskoff; Nov. 20, '83; 16), the third of our five funniest camp flops. The Playbill credits for the show listed nine songwriters and sixteen producers, one of whom had secured official blessing from Monroe's acting coach, Anna Strasberg, making this show the "authorized" Marilyn Monroe musical. During rehearsals, the original Marilyn, Gerolyn Petchel, was dismissed and replaced by Alyson Reed, a more experienced performer already featured in such flops as *Oh, Brother!* and *Dance A Little Closer.* During previews, director–choreographer Kenny Ortega was replaced by *Chorus Line* alumni Thommie Walsh and Baayork Lee, neither of whom took credit. More than ten numbers and forty-five minutes were dropped before opening night; there were so many changes that even the opening night Playbill did not reflect the exact final version.

Marilyn—An American Fable was—with the exceptions of Reed's gallant and touching performance and a song by Wally Harper and David Zippel called "Cold Hard Cash" interpolated in previews—completely without merit. But it is now treasured by Broadway camp collectors because it contained some of the most inane dialogue and lyrics ever heard on Broadway. In the middle of the second act, Marilyn looked hard at her current spouse and exclaimed, "But you're Arthur Miller! How can you be so boring?" The show seemed to be the work of eight-year-olds assigned to write a musical about Monroe; so dumb it was almost inspired, *Marilyn—An American Fable* had a giddy innocence that was very rare.

And it was indeed a fable: set entirely on an enormous and ugly sound-stage, the largely fictional script made no mention of Marilyn's childhood insecurities; her only problem seemed to be producers who refused to take her seriously as an actress. At the end, the musical's Monroe was happily reunited with Joe DiMaggio and, more incredibly, did not die but instead walked off into the sunset with Norma Jean, the child she once was. Throughout, Marilyn was trailed by an awkward trio identified in the program as "Destiny," which commented on her travails and urged her on to glory.

While it was unwise to use Monroe and her life as the basis for a musical—there is no way to make DiMaggio, Arthur Miller, and Lee Strasberg sing without looking ridiculous—*Marilyn–An American Fable* was far worse than it had to be. Just how much worse can be seen by comparing it to *Marilyn!*, another musical on the same subject, written by Americans and presented in London earlier the same year. A pop opera closely modeled on *Evita*, it featured an interesting score, a vibrant first act, and a stunning performance by leading lady Stephanie Lawrence. If it didn't avoid being silly, it at least took Monroe's life seriously, filtering it through the comments of a figure called "Camera," Monroe's "one true lover."

Unwanted laughter was audible throughout **Marlowe** (Rialto; Oct. 12, '81; 48) and **Prince of Central Park** (Belasco; Nov. 9, '89; 4), our two remaining comic camps. *Marlowe* was yet another amateur night, but unlike some others not worthy of mention, it was a riot from start to finish. A program note stated, "The story of this drama is essentially true and

○ ○ ○ ○ ○

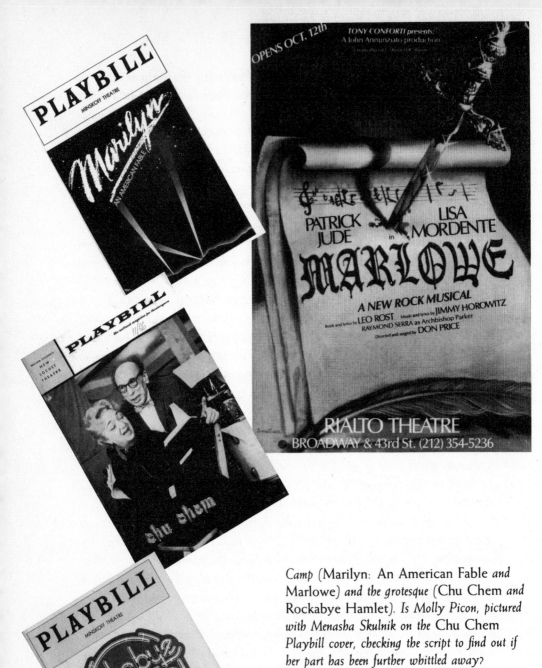

Camp (Marilyn: An American Fable and Marlowe) and the grotesque (Chu Chem and Rockabye Hamlet). Is Molly Picon, pictured with Menasha Skulnik on the Chu Chem Playbill cover, checking the script to find out if her part has been further whittled away?

accurate, except for minor adjustments in time for dramatic purpose." The characters included Christopher Marlowe (here described in a lyric as "a fifteenth-century man with a twentieth-century mind"—which was supposed to rhyme with "born before his time"), Shakespeare, Queen Elizabeth I, and Richard Burbage. But if *Marlowe* was "essentially true and accurate," why did the queen and Archbishop Parker frug to a number called "Rocking the Boat"? Why did the characters speak with Bronx accents? Why did Sir Walter Raleigh offer Marlowe, Shakespeare, and Burbage pot he had obtained from Pocahontas? Why was the flimsy set made out of tinfoil? In the finale, Marlowe (in a wildly self-indulgent performance by Patrick Jude, who had already had a lead in a 1979 Broadway bomb called *Got Tu Go Disco*) returned from the dead and, clad in a silver-lamé jump suit, exhorted the audience in song to "Eat, drink, and sing the Madrigal Blues/Christopher Marlowe has paid his dues." *Marlowe* somehow stayed opened for six weeks, and Lisa Mordente, daughter of Chita Rivera, was somehow nominated for the Best Musical Actress Tony Award for her portrayal of Emilia Bossano, in love with Marlowe and Shakespeare and forced to live life as a boy in order to act in sixteenth-century England.

On the subject of *Prince of Central Park*, Mimi Kramer wrote in the *New Yorker*, "All those who relish the chance to see a really bad musical (or are still kicking themselves for having missed *Carrie*) should hurry along to the Belasco while it lasts." Originally a novel by Evan H. Rhodes, then a television movie starring Ruth Gordon, the musical, with a book by Rhodes, kicked around for years—Albert Marre was signed to direct it at one time, with Martha Raye to play the lead. Finally, Jan McArt, often dubbed First Lady of South Florida Theatre because of her chain of dinner playhouses, presented the show in Key West with Nanette Fabray in the star part. It was then picked up by real estate magnate Al Hirschfeld, who presented it at his theatre in Miami Beach. McArt and Hirschfeld decided to take the show to New York; the Broadway Playbill informed readers that "[McArt's] record 'Pray For Peace' is in the permanent collection of Voice of America" and that Hirschfeld was "the innovator of the magnetic refrigerator door" and "the originator of the open-air parking system."

Fabray, whose career had been plagued by a series of interesting musicals that didn't make it, wisely chose not to make *Prince of Central Park* the vehicle for her return to Broadway. Gloria De Haven was hired, then dismissed, and Jo Anne Worley ultimately took the part of middle-aged Margie Miller, who befriends Jay-Jay, a twelve-year-old who escapes an abusive foster mother by taking refuge in a tree house in Central Park.

Like *Marlowe, Prince* was often camp heaven, mostly because of its wildly-out-of-touch-with-reality portrayal of New York City. The musical's Central Park featured a friendly park ranger, a gang of not-very-threatening, misunderstood teens, a quaint bag lady, and a couple of well-dressed men seen emerging from the park bushes. Specific camp highlights were a number set in Bloomingdale's called "Red" (when Margie arrives in the dress department, a sweet old saleslady comes right up to her and says, "May I help you?"), which culminated in a Dance of the Mannequins, and all the numbers for the gang, which defy description. *Prince of Central Park* was also notable for its constant textual plugs for Tavern on the Green; one scene took place there, and the restaurant hosted the show's opening night celebration.

From the uproarious, we move to the bizarre, even goofy. Perhaps no show ever had a weirder initial idea and story than **Chu Chem**, which opened and closed in Philadelphia in November 1966. The self-described "Zen Buddhist–Hebrew musical comedy" had a book by Ted Allan, who was inspired to write it when he visited Kaifeng Fu, China, and learned of the Jews who had migrated there in the tenth century. Otherwise, it was another perverse inspiration of the Albert Marre–Mitch Leigh axis. It followed their smash *Man of La Mancha* by exactly a year and was coproduced by Leigh with Cheryl Crawford, whose musical productions ranged from major hits (*Brigadoon, One Touch of Venus*) to bizarre, if usually interesting, failures (*Regina, Flahooley, Reuben Reuben, Celebration*). Jack Cole, a tyrant of enormous talent who choreographed *La Mancha* and *Kismet* for Marre, was hired to stage the dances and also to appear as Mongol Lord Hoo Hah. The stars were beloved Yiddish theatre and Broadway performers Menasha Skulnik and Molly Picon.

Chu Chem's intricate plot focused on the title character, a scholar–wanderer (Skulnik) who, with his wife, Rose (Picon), and daughter, Lotte (Marcia Rodd), journeyed to Kaifeng Fu eight hundred years ago to search for traces of the Jews who had ventured there three hundred years earlier and to find a husband for Lotte. Prince Eagle (James Shigeta) becomes enamored of Lotte but wants to make her one of his concubines, unthinkable for the very liberated young woman. After many convolutions,

○ ○ ○ ○ ○

there are two denouements: the prince abdicates, thus avoiding the requisite harem, and Chu Chem discovers that the Jews he was studying assimilated into Chinese when, for a change, they were not persecuted in their new homeland.

This story may appear to be the reasonably sound basis for a musical, but it was not presented straightforwardly. It was done as a play-within-a-play, in which Skulnik, Picon, and Rodd played Occidental actors joining a troup of Chinese performers to enact a story. The production featured all the trappings of Chinese theatre, and when the Prince halted the action for intermission, two huge sumo wrestlers (one of whom was Man Mountain Dean, Jr.) took over to maul each other for fifteen minutes.

Dissastisfied with cuts in her part, Picon walked out twice during rehearsals and previews, the second time for good. The Philadelphia critics were utterly nonplussed: Ernest Schier wrote, "like blintzes and soy sauce . . . a better title might be *The King and Oy*." Such was the chaotic state of the production that on opening night, Picon's successor, Henrietta Jacobson (another Yiddish stage veteran), turned to the audience at one juncture and said, "There was a song here, but you'll be better off without it." *Chu Chem* promptly cancelled its scheduled Broadway opening at the George Abbott Theatre.

Chu Chem was indeed an original, but it was wildly overplotted and far too silly to support its elaborate conceptual framework. What is most unusual about *Chu Chem*, however, is that it came back. In 1988, Allan and Leigh decided to take another look at the show, and they were able to get Marre back to direct the show at the tiny Jewish Repertory Theatre on East Fourteenth Street. The new version eliminated most of the actors-playing-roles concept, and the Picon–Jacobson role was no more. Greater emphasis was placed on the romance between the prince and the daughter, and the score was augmented or cut here and there—but the plot remained essentially the same. Stripped of the original's elaborate scenic production and impressive Cole choreography, *Chu Chem* was now just small and silly. A good review from a third-string *New York Times* critic provoked Leigh into attempting to rewrite history by bringing the show to Broadway (Ritz; March 17, '89; 44). Hoping to garner Tony Award nominations at the end of the worst season for Broadway musicals since World War II (the *Carrie–Legs Diamond* season), Leigh kept the show running at a heavy loss for almost two months, with the public mostly disliking it or ignoring it completely. When it received no Tony nominations—even with many vacant slots in the categories—Leigh finally closed what was essentially a vanity production. *Chu Chem* is one of the few examples of the "double flop" genre.

Our second entry in the grotesquerie sweepstakes, **Rockabye Hamlet** (Minskoff; Feb. 17, '76; 7), demonstrated that *Dude* and *Via Galactica* had not completely killed off the rock horrors of the early seventies. Originally entitled *Kronberg: 1582* and performed in Canada on radio and on stage, *Rockabye Hamlet* was entirely the work of the Canadian Cliff Jones. What has given this almost-all-sung rock version of Shakespeare a controversial reputation is the fact that it was directed for Broadway by one of the musical theatre's top professionals, Gower Champion, then in the midst of a slump period that included *Prettybelle*, *Mack and Mabel*, and *A Broadway Musical*.

Champion went all out with an enormous production staged like a rock concert. There were hundreds of lights, movable ramps, bridges, an onstage band, and heavy sound equipment. The cast, which featured black actors as Hamlet, Gertrude, and Claudius, held hand mikes as they sang, and Ophelia took her life by strangling herself with her mike cord.

The song titles speak volumes about the show's quality: "He Got It in the Ear" (about the murder of Hamlet's father) and, yes, "Something's Rotten in Denmark" were among them. Very few of Shakespeare's words remained, and the lyrics were howlers: in his first solo, Hamlet sang, "Loving does strange things/Messes up your mind," and Polonius told Laertes, "Good son—you return to France/Keep your divinity inside your pants."

Author Jones did not take the show's dismissal by New York critics at all well. To avenge it, he first recorded his own album of the show's songs, with liner notes describing how the show played three weeks of New York previews "to packed houses of cheering, madly applauding audiences" and how "five critics killed it." He then wrote and recorded a bitter single called "Broadway Wipeout," which began with the sound of an audience cheering and averred that uptight New York critics could not forgive the show for "messing around with the Bard." The song's refrain went, "Thank you, *New York Times*."

What was most disturbing about *Rockabye Hamlet* was that it never addressed the question, "Why do *Hamlet* as a rock opera?" At least Andrew Lloyd Webber and Tim Rice, in their *Jesus Christ Superstar* a few years earlier, were attempting a comment by portraying Jesus as a contemporary

○ ○ ○ ○ ○

superstar. No such idea was discernible in *Rockabye Hamlet*, and Champion's involvement seemed to be his desperate attempt to jump on a bandwagon that had already moved on (but which returned with the Lloyd Webber–Rice *Evita* two years later).

As crazy as *Chu Chem* and *Rockabye Hamlet* but rather more endearing in its stupidity was **I'm Solomon** (Mark Hellinger; April 23, '68; 7), based on a hit 1964 Israeli musical called *King Solomon and the Cobbler*. For Broadway, only the story of the Israeli show remained, and a new book and score were written. The book was originally by Erich Segal and Anne Crosswell, and as he did with *Odyssey/Home Sweet Homer*, Segal removed his name before the show got to Broadway; the show's original title, *In Someone Else's Sandals*, was also dropped. Directing his first musical was Michael Benthall, who would follow it with *Her First Roman* and *Coco* and be more or less removed from both. The music was by Ernest Gold, composer of film scores, who may have been hired because he had written the score for the movie *Exodus*—*I'm Solomon* was clearly aimed at the Jewish theatre-party trade.

Dick Shawn played both King Solomon and a humble cobbler in the show, set in Jerusalem in 100 B.C. The king experiences an identity crisis, wondering if he is respected and loved for himself or for his title, and thus decides to change places with a look-alike cobbler to explore the question. *I'm Solomon* featured two of the most flop-prone performers of recent musical-theatre history, Carmen Mathews (*Courtin' Time, Zenda, The Yearling, Dear World, Ambassador, Copperfield*) and Karen Morrow (*I Had a Ball, A Joyful Noise, The Selling of the President, The Grass Harp*). When the show closed in a week, coproducer Zvi Kolitz told the press that *I'm Solomon* had been the "victim of the arbitrariness, haughtiness, shallowness, and heartlessness of the television critics." It lost over $700,000, making it and the then recent *Darling of the Day* the most expensive musical flops to date.

I'm Solomon, which featured a memorably tacky song about the frequency with which Solomon's many wives got to sleep with their husband ("Once in 2.7 Years"), had a couple of nice songs and an extremely silly book. But what places it firmly in the category of the bizarre was the absurdly overblown production it received. "With a Cast of 60" boasted the program, and there were enormous sets, large choral numbers, harlots, concubines, and belly dancers, all swamping the slender plot, which might have been the basis for a cute off-Broadway musical.

○ ○ ○ ○ ○

The final four productions in this section represent a better class of camp: while equally silly, they were somewhat more respectable, had longer runs, or involved bigger names. On the morning of April 19, 1955, Walter Kerr was provoked to begin his review of the earliest of these four, **Ankles Aweigh** (Mark Hellinger; Apr. 18, '55; 176), by stating, "Some of us have been campaigning lately for a return to the old-fashioned, gags-and-girls musical comedy. Some of us should be shot." *Ankles* had a book by Guy Bolton (*Anything Goes, Oh, Kay!*) and Eddie Davis, with lyrics by Dan Shapiro and music by Sammy Fain. Bolton, Davis, and Shapiro had collaborated on *Follow the Girls*, a musical of dubious quality which had managed to chalk up 882 performances on wartime Broadway.

Ankles Aweigh was indeed an overt, unabashed throwback to musicals of the twenties and thirties, with stale burlesque jokes, stock characters, pretty chorines, and a book that allowed its stars—hardworking, rowdy nightclub performers and sisters Betty and Jane Kean—to drop everything and perform impersonations of Mary Martin's recent Peter Pan, the Gabors, and Marlene Dietrich. By 1955, Broadway audiences had become accustomed to the seamless integration of elements in such musical plays as *Kiss Me, Kate, Guys and Dolls*, and the Rodgers and Hammerstein shows. Even for the tired businessman, *Ankles* was an incredibly dated effort.

The plot, indistinguishable from that of many an earlier musical, told of Wynne, a starlet making a film in Italy, who marries her lieutenant boyfriend, thus violating a clause in her contract. With the aid of her sister, Elsey, and two of her husband's navy pals, Wynne is smuggled aboard her husband's aircraft, which then sails for Morocco, where the lieutenant is implicated in a spy ring.

Coproducer Reginald Hammerstein's brother, Oscar, and Oscar's partner, Richard Rodgers, invested in *Ankles Aweigh*. During rehearsals, leading male clown Myron McCormick was replaced by Lew Parker. In New Haven, leading man Sonny Tufts was replaced by Mark Dawson. Jerome Robbins, who had recently helped out *Wonderful Town, Wish You Were Here*, and *Silk Stockings* on the road, worked on the show for two weeks in Boston. But the New York critics didn't buy it, and the Kean sisters were at best B-level stars for a Broadway musical. The closing notice was posted almost immediately, but the owner of the Mark Hellinger Theater, Anthony Brady Farrell (nephew of Diamond Jim Brady), decided to take over and keep *Ankles* kicking. Broadway columnists like Walter Winchell

o o o o o

and Ed Sullivan took it upon themselves to defend the show, decrying the fact that highbrow critics were unable to enjoy an old-fashioned extravaganza. But the publicity didn't help sufficiently. When Equity permitted Farrell to institute salary cuts, Jane Kean, along with Mark Dawson and featured chanteuse, Thelma Carpenter, left, leaving Betty Kean to play sister to an understudy. Thanks to the losses during its six-month run, *Ankles* managed to close at a deficit of $340,000 on an investment of $275,000.

Ankles Aweigh did have one thing going for it: its composer, Sammy Fain. Fain, who wrote five consecutive Broadway musical flops (*Toplitzky of Notre Dame, Flahooley, Ankles Aweigh, Christine, Something More!*), never failed to come up with a few catchy tunes, and the cast recording of *Ankles Aweigh* is the kind that collectors rarely admit to playing as often as they do. It includes an opening number, "Italy," that sounds like every tacky opening number rolled into one, and "Headin' for the Bottom Blues," a choice cut for drag performers to mouth the words to in their acts. And such other *Ankles* songs as "Walk Like a Sailor," "Nothing Can Replace a Man," and "Skip the Build Up" define fifties Broadway fun-trash. As heard on the cast album, their cheesiness can be cut with a knife.

Ankles, like *Chu Chem*, is one of the few disasters that was tried again. The Goodspeed Opera House in East Haddam, Connecticut, which usually presents reputable titles from the twenties and thirties, chose to revive it, mainly on the strength of its score, in the summer of 1989. Goodspeed, aware that the show would never play satisfactorily without rethinking, had the inspired notion of asking Charles Busch, founder of Theater-in-Limbo and author and star of such off-Broadway camp efforts as *Vampire Lesbians of Sodom* and *Psycho Beach Party*, to write a new book. Retaining plot essentials, Busch made *Ankles Aweigh* into a tribute to *Gentlemen Prefer Blondes*-style fifties movie musicals; transmuted through Busch's camp sensibility, *Ankles Aweigh* became an affectionate salute to a period and a satiric comment on it as well. Audiences enjoyed the new version, but critics, who had done their homework by looking up the original notices, hated it. It's unlikely that Goodspeed will be presenting *Hit The Trail* or *Portofino* in the near future.

Our second example of the more respectable camp flop, **13 Daughters** (54th Street; Mar. 1, '61; 28), might get another chance, but if that happens, it is more likely to be in Hawaii, where it originated, than anywhere else. The curtain rises on *13 Daughters* with a prologue in which

o o o o o

Above, Betty and Jane Kean at sea in the immortal Ankles Aweigh. *Below, the stupid* In Someone Else's Sandals, *which became* I'm Solomon *for Broadway.*

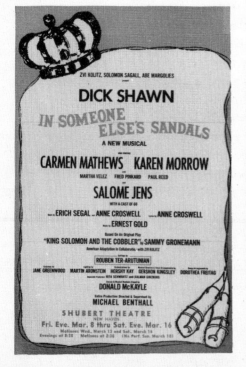

the Hawaiian Emmy defies her gods and marries Chun, a foreigner. It is thus prophesied that they will have thirteen daughters who will not marry until thirteen trees blossom. The show then flashes forward thirty years; Chun (played by Don Ameche) is attempting to arrange a marriage between his eldest daughter, Isabel, who must marry before the other daughters, and a local prince. But Isabel, a missionary, is secretly in love with her colleague, Doctor Willoughby. Still, she agrees to marry the prince (who is actually in love with Chun's daughter Malia) when she is dismissed from the mission over a dispute involving her use of the hula to teach the alphabet to her students. Emmy, meanwhile, blames herself and her mixed marriage for all the trouble that has ensued and attempts to sacrifice herself in a storm. Eventually, Chun saves the precarious finances of Hawaii and is made a "true Hawaiian"; the curse is lifted; and the daughters marry.

Hawaii was the newest state in the Union at the time of 13 Daughters, so it was perhaps inevitable that a musical would reach Broadway that exploited its culture and music. The show was entirely the work of Eaton ("Bob") Magoon, Jr., a wealthy Hawaiian real-estate broker–songwriter. The show was first done in Honolulu in 1956, and the financing for the Broadway version came mostly from Hawaiians, the balance provided by ABC-Paramount in exchange for recording rights. John Fearnley, casting director for Rodgers and Hammerstein, was the original director but was replaced on the road by choreographer Rod Alexander; the Broadway Playbill ultimately listed no director at all but one Billy Matthews as "book stager."

With Don Ameche as the show's sole draw, and John Battles, not seen on Broadway since he took leads in On the Town and Allegro in the forties, playing Ameche's secretary and understudying the role of Chun, 13 Daughters, in spite of its absurd plot and weak score, somehow received several favorable reviews. But by then Broadway had seen much better musicals set in exotic locales, and audiences stayed away. One theatre-party lady, when asked by a friend how the show was, shrugged and said, "With Don Ameche as a Chinaman, how good could it be?" ABC-Paramount did not record the show, but there was an album (with execrable singing) made of a post-Broadway Hawaiian revival; Dean Pitchford, later the author of Carrie, played a child in that revival. Magoon, Jr., returned to Broadway in 1972 as the author of the musical Heathen!; it lasted one performance at the Billy Rose Theatre.

○ ○ ○ ○ ○

Expert magician Doug Henning had made his Broadway debut in *The Magic Show*, which ran over four years. Henning got by in that one by playing himself, but he was not up to the real role he attempted a few years later in **Merlin** (Mark Hellinger; Feb. 13, '83; 199), our third example of classier camp. Elmer Bernstein, who had one previous flop (*How Now, Dow Jones*) to his credit, wrote the music, with lyrics by Don Black, who had begun the year with *The Little Prince and the Aviator*.

The entire cast, crew, musicians, and even the ushers were required to sign "secrecy contracts" promising not to reveal how any of Henning's magic was done. Early in previews, director Frank Dunlop was replaced by the show's coproducer, Ivan Reitman. Christopher Chadman, who had replaced Ron Field as choreographer during rehearsal, was joined by Billy Wilson. All of Henning's singing was eliminated in previews.

Merlin tells of a queen so evil she has no name and her attempt to put her son, Prince Fergus, on the throne of England. Aware that Arthur is the rightful heir and that the novice magician Merlin will be the key to putting Arthur on the throne, the queen attempts to destroy Merlin. The intricate plot was a transparent excuse for Henning to ready his succession of magic tricks, and several of these were dazzling: a horse and rider disappeared into thin air stage right, only to reappear stage left; a black panther was turned into a woman; pieces of a suit of armor were transformed into an enormous black knight.

The one trick Henning couldn't perform, however, was making the critics disappear. When previews dragged on for eight weeks and three opening dates were cancelled, Frank Rich of the *New York Times* and Douglas Watt of the *Daily News* chose to review the show two weeks prior to its latest opening date. This prompted intense debate, with Clive Barnes in the *New York Post* condemning his colleagues' actions and coproducer Marvin Krauss asking the press, "Why didn't [the critics] cover *A Doll's Life* when it began previewing here after ten weeks in Los Angeles?"

The critics were especially harsh on Henning's nonperformance. While using Henning as Merlin and integrating his magic into a story about a legendary magician was not necessarily a bad idea, Henning's lack of rudimentary acting and singing skills did the project in. The show was fortunate to have Chita Rivera as the queen, who brought her customary class and skill to bear on a role that had her saying lines like, "I have devoted my life to the black arts—now I shall be repaid." The nicest things about *Merlin* were ballerina Rebecca Wright as a unicorn and the

o o o o o

Camelot-like ending, with Merlin meeting young Arthur and then magically turning into the old Merlin. Henning's name kept one of the silliest evenings in years going for seven months.

It is doubly fitting to end this survey of camp flops with **Whoop-Up** (Shubert; Dec. 22, '58; 56), for among fans no other title is so closely associated with the sheer pleasure of unreconstructed trash, and because *Whoop-Up* had music by Moose Charlap, who later wrote *Kelly*. Based on Dan Cushman's novel *Stay Away, Joe, Whoop-Up* told of the unfunny romantic complications of a half-Indian rodeo star and his on-again, off-again girlfriend (Susan Johnson, singled out for praise in *Buttrio Square* and the best thing in *Whoop-Up*), whose saloon is half on and half off an Indian reservation in Montana. The plot was immensely complex, its hero, Joe, was singularly unappealing and dull, and virtually every scene revolved around a car that one or another of the characters was either trying to buy, sell, or hide. Curiously, in the middle of this tired-businessman show, there was an attempt to comment on white conde-scension toward Indians. Typical of the period, however, *Whoop-Up* had only one real Indian in the cast.

By 1958, producers Cy Feuer and Ernest Martin had had an unbroken string of hit musicals: *Where's Charley? Guys and Dolls, Can-Can, The Boy Friend,* and *Silk Stockings.* They had their first flop with *Whoop-Up*, which they also cowrote and which Feuer directed. It was to have had a score by Richard Adler and Jerry Ross, but Charlap and lyricist Norman Gimbel, protégés of Frank Loesser's (as were Adler and Ross), got the show. Bob Fosse, Ernie Kovacs, and Edie Adams were announced for roles, but none of them wound up in the production, whose biggest name was Paul Ford, of television's "Sergeant Bilko," in a nonsinging role.

Whoop-Up faced competition from *My Fair Lady, West Side Story, The Music Man, Bells Are Ringing, Flower Drum Song,* and *Jamaica* when it arrived on Broadway, and the critics, with two exceptions, were negative, all emphasizing the noise of the show while praising Onna White's chore-ography, Johnson, and a young lady called simply Asia, whose figure and walk attracted the lion's share of attention. The cast album of *Whoop-Up* has always been treasured for its mixture of incredible clinkers like "No-body Throw Those Bull" and irresistible if trashy numbers like "When the Tall Man Talks" and "Flattery." Johnson, possessor of one of the finest vocal brass sections in Broadway history, made everything with which she came into contact sound better, and Sylvia Syms, who created only

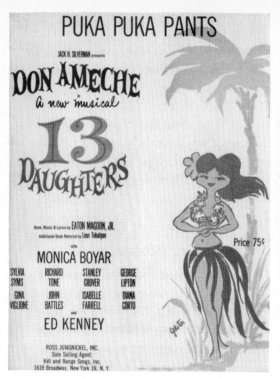

Hawaiians and Native Americans were respectively celebrated in 13 Daughters and Whoop-Up. That's Sylvia Syms about to serve Romo Vincent, not singing "Nobody Throw Those Bull," in the Whoop-Up photo below.

two musical roles, in *Whoop-Up* and *13 Daughters*, movingly performed a ballad called "Sorry for Myself." As is the case with so many flops, *Whoop-Up*'s failure could not be traced to its songwriters. But they could not avoid or disguise the fact that *Whoop-Up*'s two and a half hours were really about nothing but a car.

How could any intelligent person wish to collect catastrophes like *Legs Diamond* and *Kelly* or camp disasters like *Home Sweet Homer* and *Whoop-Up*? There has always been something in show followers that enjoys seeing people fail, and the shows we've just encountered represent failure in its most extreme and unadulterated form. Total calamities have a morbid fascination; fans relive them and ask, "How come these people didn't know better?" The funny bombs are loved for their absurdity, their lack of sense, their undiluted ineptitude. And those who care about these shows treasure the fact that catastrophic flops are rarely if ever mentioned in books on musical theatre, which most often trace only the significant points in the development of the art form. Fans of flops know about these shows, can sing songs from them, and love the kinship they feel with others who know them. Casual followers of the musical have some idea about why *Oklahoma!*, *West Side Story* and *A Chorus Line* are important; but the world of *Breakfast at Tiffany's* and *Into the Light* is a private world, and those who are part of it can't wait for each new Broadway season to make, as it inevitably does, its contribution.

∘ ∘ ∘ ∘ ∘

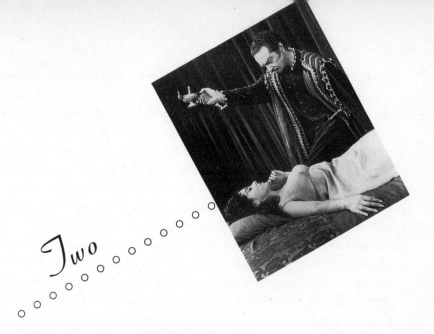

Two

STAR FLOPS

"Members of the Nancy Walker Association will now have to adopt a new set of officers. *Copper and Brass* proves that the present policy is not working at all."—Brooks Atkinson, *The New York Times*

"Everyone wanted to love Lucille Ball, but her show didn't make it easy."—Howard Taubman, *The New York Times*, on *Wildcat*

"In *A Joyful Noise*, every time a song is over the lights go out immediately. This, I believe, is to prevent dialogue . . . [There is] a double difficulty. One is to know in what century the musical takes place. The other is to know in what century it was written."—Walter Kerr, *The New York Times*

Alfred Drake and Lee Venora in Kean (*above*)

Musical librettos of the twenties and thirties were often little more than transparent excuses for beloved performers to do their specialties. The rest was filler, only there so the star could change costumes or take a breather. As American musicals matured after World War II, writers sought to create serious, integrated pieces that could not easily be interrupted for star turns. Even if forties and fifties musicals like *Lady in the Dark, South Pacific, The King and I,* and *Gypsy* were, to some extent, star vehicles, they were also mature musical plays that were not totally dependent on their leading performers' presence for their success.

Musicals came to be seen as ensemble efforts which often had no need of stars; if *Call Me Madam* and *Happy Hunting* might not have been produced without Ethel Merman's participation, and if *Bells Are Ringing* was written specifically for Judy Holliday, *The Pajama Game, West Side Story, Fiorello!, Cabaret, Company, A Chorus Line,* and *Les Misérables* were not dependent on "name" performers for their acclaim. The last thirty years have also seen a sharp decline in the number of musicals produced; fewer musicals obviously means fewer chances for stars to find vehicles.

But star vehicles have never entirely disappeared, and with the exceptions of Merman and Gwen Verdon, every major musical star of the last forty years has appeared in at least one flop musical. In most cases, the show's failure had little to do with the star's performance. On the contrary, that performance was often the only thing that made the show worth attending. Some stars were able to rise above their failures; if unable to sell a weak show to the public, they were at least able to put it behind them and go on to the next, hopefully better, one. In some cases, however, stars' careers were seriously damaged by shows in which they appeared. There were also stars who made one-shot appearances as musical-theatre headliners, then returned to the show business genre in which they had gained fame. Whatever their effect on a performer's career, the musicals in this chapter are remembered mainly for their stars: without them, many of these shows would never have been produced.

It is appropriate to begin our survey of star flops with Mary Martin, for only Merman rivaled her as a musical-theatre star in the last half-century. Martin, the entrancing, ageless gamine of Broadway, had a career filled with such smashes as *South Pacific, Annie Get Your Gun* (on tour and on television), *The Sound of Music, Hello, Dolly!* (in London, Tokyo, and Vietnam), and *I Do! I Do!* But Martin did come to Broadway with one genuine flop, and she turned down *Funny Girl,* then called *My Man,* to do it.

○ ○ ○ ○ ○

Jennie (Majestic; Oct. 17, '63; 82) had an extremely convoluted history. It was always meant to be about the early life of the legendary actress Laurette Taylor to some degree, but that degree kept changing. First it was to be based on *Laurette,* a book by Marguerite Courtney, Taylor's daughter. When the musical stalled, and *Laurette* was made into a nonmusical for Judy Holliday which closed after a week in New Haven in 1960, Martin's vehicle was to be based on a book about Laurette and her first husband, the melodrama king Charles A. Taylor, by their son, Dwight. The show, to be called *Blood and Thunder,* was to have had a book by S. N. Behrman, and Martin was to have played seven women (one of them the actress) in Charles's life. Ultimately, it was decided to revert to the Courtney book but to fictionalize its real-life characters, and Arnold Schulman (*A Hole in the Head*) did the adaptation.

Jennie, as the show was finally called, was coproduced by Cheryl Crawford—in one of her less ambitious ventures—and Martin and her husband, Richard Halliday, the couple clearly retaining the production's clout. The score was by the distinguished team of Howard Dietz and Arthur Schwartz: only the fourth book show of their thirty-four-year partnership, it was also to be their last show together. Vincent J. Donehue, Martin's director of choice, who had already guided her through *Annie Get Your Gun, The Skin of Our Teeth, The Sound of Music,* and the televised *Peter Pan,* continued his association with the Hallidays, who supplied half of the show's $550,000 price tag.

Jennie was beset by troubles. In Boston, Constance Carpenter, who played a friend of Jennie's, was written out, and Carol Haney replaced Matt Mattox as choreographer, without taking credit. Schwartz sued *Boston Globe* critic Kevin Kelly when the latter wrote that the score "poaches on the melodies of other composers, from Rodgers and Hammerstein to Meredith Willson, Frank Loesser, and Bob Merrill." In Detroit, George Wallace replaced leading man Dennis O'Keefe. By this time, considerable enmity had developed between Schwartz and Dietz and the Hallidays. Martin refused to sing the lyric, "Before I go to meet my maker/I want to use the salt left in the shaker," deeming it dirty. Schwartz threatened to take the matter up with the Dramatists Guild, and he and Dietz were barred from the theatre for a while. Near the end of the Detroit run, Martin and Halliday decided not to bring *Jennie* into New York. But the advance sale had reached $1.35 million, and the composers declared that they would sue the Hallidays for that figure if the show did not go on

o o o o o

Above, the entrancing Mary Martin, performing "Waitin' For The Evening Train" with Dennis O'Keefe, before he was fired, in Jennie. Below, the Boston and New York Playbills. Note that the first cover shows Mary beginning to look her age, while the second features the ageless Mary audiences loved.

to Broadway. The Hallidays chose not to attend *Jennie's* opening night party at Sardi's.

Jennie concerned a romantic triangle involving Jennie Malone, her husband James O'Connor, with whom she has barnstormed across the country in spectacular melodramas, and Englishman Christopher Lawrence Cromwell, a drawing-room playwright who gives Jennie a job when she leaves James. It was a remarkably unexciting book, one of the weakest ever to be accepted by a major star in the fifties and sixties. Neither of the men in Jennie's life was very interesting, and the show had just three things going for it: Martin, as always irresistible to her audiences; an attractive score; and the physical production. *Jennie* offered elaborate and satiric recreations of early twentieth-century melodramas. The show's high point was its opening, with Martin hanging from the limb of a tree over a working waterfall, struggling to rescue her baby while pursued by a bear and a coolie. There was also the "Sultan's 50th Bride" sequence, in which Martin, who in other shows had washed her hair and flown onstage, sang upside down, lashed to a torture wheel and rotated while chanting "Lonely Nights." That was followed by a simulated fire in which O'Connor's new theatre was destroyed. But these sequences served mainly to rouse the audience from its torpor; *Jennie* was simply a dull show. It was amazing that so soon after one of Martin's greatest triumphs, *The Sound of Music,* the Hallidays could ever have believed that *Jennie* would be a worthy new vehicle for one of Broadway's first ladies. So embarrassed was Richard Halliday that when *Jennie* closed after three months, he told the press that the show had returned its investment and actually shown a small profit. But the end-of-season tallies proved otherwise.

Even so established and beloved a musical comedy dancer–comedian as Ray Bolger could not carry a weak vehicle. Bolger's career as a Broadway star extended back to the twenties, but his biggest personal success was in *Where's Charley?* in 1948. After an absence of more than a decade, he returned to Broadway for two final appearances in the sixties. If Martin was able to recover after *Jennie* with one more hit musical, *I Do! I Do!,* Bolger's last two shows were both flops, providing an unfortunate conclusion to a distinguished stage career. The first of these was originally to be a vehicle for Ron Moody or Charles Boyer, but Bolger, rather miscast, wound up playing Professor Fodorski, an immigrant from behind the Iron Curtain, who comes to teach engineering at the Southern Baptist

Institute of Technology, in **All American** (Winter Garden; March 19, '62; 80).

The book, based on Robert Lewis Taylor's novel *Professor Fodorski*, was by Mel Brooks, who, it is said, never got around to writing the second act, which was pieced together by the rest of the creative staff. The score was the work of Charles Strouse and Lee Adams, their second show after the triumphant *Bye Bye Birdie*, and *Birdie's* producers also presented *All American*. Joshua Logan, whose directorial triumphs included *Annie Get Your Gun*, *South Pacific*, and *Fanny*, began a chain of flops with *All American* that he was never able to break: *Mr. President*, *Hot September*, *Look to the Lilies*, and *Miss Moffat* were Logan's next, and final, musicals. *All American* had a lot to do with football, thus allowing for several locker-room scenes in which Logan, as he had done in *South Pacific*, *Mister Roberts*, *Wish You Were Here*, and *Fanny*, filled the stage with well-built men bare to the waist. In the number "Physical Fitness," fifteen gypsies formed a four-tiered human pyramid while extolling the joys of getting in shape; the cast album liner notes explain, "The stripped-down athletes may be wretched football players but they have glorious muscles, and prove it acrobatically."

A throwback to weakly plotted star vehicles of the thirties and forties, *All American's* story was silly: would football strategy really help the teaching of college-level engineering, and would the principles of engineering really make for a winning football team? In Act Two, Fodorski's new fame was exploited by Madison Avenue, by 1962 too well worn a satirical target. The score, while not as good as *Birdie's*, was far better than the book and included one semistandard, "Once upon a Time." In desperation, Bolger attempted to repeat a ploy that had worked well in *Where's Charley?* by asking *All American* audiences to join him in singing a reprise of the song "What a Country!" during the curtain call. But audiences had loved the song "Once in Love with Amy" and had enjoyed singing along with it at *Where's Charley?* They didn't take to "What a Country!," and the response was tepid at best. *All American's* brief run indicated that during his absence from Broadway, Bolger's public had shrunk.

Even less admired was Bolger's last show, **Come Summer** (Lunt-Fontanne; Mar. 18, '69; 7), in which he played a peddler in Connecticut at a time—1840—when pastoral New England was giving way to the Industrial Revolution. Just as Bolger was making one last stab at Broadway, his character in the show, Phineas, was making the most of his final summer on the road before factories supplanted his function entirely.

Based on *Rainbow on the Road*, a novel by Esther Forbes, *Come Summer*

○ ○ ○ ○ ○

Flops starring two of Broadway's best leading men. Above, Ray Bolger's two final Broadway musicals, All American and Come Summer. Below, John Raitt in the not-good-enough Three Wishes For Jamie and the awful A Joyful Noise.

was also the final Broadway show for Agnes de Mille, who had given new meaning to Broadway choreography in the forties. The New England setting offered natural opportunities for the de Mille style, and the show featured a series of notable dance sequences. De Mille also chose *Come Summer* as her third directorial effort: she had been more or less removed as director from both *Allegro* and *Out of This World*, and this time she was supplanted by Burt Shevelove, who was brought in, in Boston, for help with both book and staging.

In addition to the dancing, *Come Summer* had other things going for it. The quality score, with music by David Baker and lyrics by Will Holt (the latter involved in such subsequent flops as *Music Is* and *Platinum*), contained several fine items, especially a duet for romantic leads David Cryer and Cathryn Damon called "Wild Birds Calling," an amusing dead-pan number for Barbara Sharma called "Fine, Thank You, Fine," and Cryer's closing song, "So Much World." The company was strong, too: Bolger was reunited with Margaret Hamilton of *The Wizard of Oz*, and Cryer made such a strong impression that he appeared likely to become a major Broadway leading man. He followed *Come Summer* with *Ari*, however, and that may have been one flop too many. Damon, who had heretofore scored while scantily clad in frivolous comic-relief parts, demonstrated a range of which few had been aware.

On the debit side, *Come Summer*'s book, if charming, had an unwieldy plot, with Act Two drifting into incoherent fantasy. Oddly enough, though, the show's biggest problem may have been Bolger himself. Cryer's character, Jude Scribner, was the novel's hero, and in the musical Jude was still quite obviously the most interesting and important character. Because Bolger had to have a number of scenes, songs, and dances commensurate with his reputation and billing, he was frequently dragged into the action even when his character was peripheral to it. At the final call, Bolger ended his Broadway career by silencing the applause and delivering a bitter speech denouncing the New York critics, all of whom had panned *Come Summer*. When he told the audience that the show was closing that night, they responded with a cry of "Oh, no!" "Oh, yes," answered Bolger.

Martin and Bolger each enjoyed five or six big musical successes in their careers. Carol Channing, on the other hand, reached a high level of Broadway musical stardom with only two parts. After winning fame with her devastating portrayal of not-so-dumb Lorelei Lee in *Gentlemen Prefer Blondes* in 1949, Channing was able to find only one other successful

○ ○ ○ ○ ○

vehicle, *Hello, Dolly!*, fifteen years later. She would continue to play Dolly and Lorelei for years thereafter, her talents too unusual for most conventional musical comedy parts. Her only other book musical, falling in between *Blondes* and *Dolly!*, was the big and disastrous **The Vamp** (Winter Garden; Nov. 10, '55; 60).

It was not a bad idea to star Channing as Flora Weems, a simple farm girl who allows herself to be transformed into a Theda Bara–Nita Naldi-style silent screen siren in order to win the affection of Dick Hicks, cowboy movie star. But *The Vamp*'s book was laborious and overplotted, with occasional broad satirical swipes at moviemaking scoundrels of the era. It was coauthored by John Latouche, who, one year earlier, had written the libretto for one of the decade's best musicals, *The Golden Apple*. Latouche also wrote *The Vamp*'s superb lyrics to James Mundy's only Broadway score.

The Vamp's authors relied heavily on their star, who was given number after number. Channing, of course, delivered, and the show's highlights were her entrance pantomime, in which she performed countless farm chores nonstop, and her eleven o'clock showstopper, "I'm Nobody's Baby." Otherwise, *The Vamp*, coproduced by Alexander Carson, Channing's husband at the time, was a plot-heavy, one-joke affair; critics and audiences were not amused, and Channing took to touring her nightclub act for most of the next decade until *Dolly!* happened.

No musical leading man was more talented and dynamic than Robert Preston, but like Channing, Preston was able to find only two hit musicals. After his astonishing musical-theatre debut in *The Music Man* in 1957, there was just one more success: *I Do! I Do!*, opposite Mary Martin, in 1966. There were, however, four musical flops, in which Preston appeared respectively as Pancho Villa, Ben Franklin, Mack Sennett, and (pseudonymously) Yiddish-theatre star Boris Thomashefsky. Of his four flops, two folded on the road, and only one, *Mack and Mabel*, was worthy of him.

Preston's second musical appearance saw him play Mexican revolutionary Pancho Villa in **We Take the Town** (New Haven; Feb. 19, '62, closed on the road), based on Ben Hecht's screenplay for the 1934 Wallace Beery movie *Viva Villa!* The score was by the somewhat obscure team of Harold Karr and Matt Dubey, whose only other musical was *Happy Hunting*, Merman's least successful vehicle. But some major names turn up here along with Preston's. Because Columbia Records provided the financing,

Carol Channing created the roles of Lorelei Lee, Dolly Levi—and Flora Weems in
The Vamp. Above, Channing, Robert Rippy, and Patricia Hammerlee: Could
anything that looked as strange as this ever be a hit? Below, Flora is transformed
into vamp Delilah Modo and presented to the public at Grand Central Station.

their new singing star Barbra Streisand recorded one of the show's songs, "How Does the Wine Taste?" Stuart Ostrow made his producing debut with the show, and Pia Zadora was one of four children in the company. Most major of all was Jerome Robbins, who toyed with the idea of replacing director Alex Segal out of town but decided against it. Potentially an interesting subject for a star-vehicle musical, *We Take the Town* was done in by a melodramatic book, and it canceled its scheduled April 5, 1962, opening at the Broadway Theatre. Years later, Preston would tell people that Villa was his favorite role.

Preston's next musical, **Ben Franklin in Paris** (Lunt-Fontanne; Oct. 27, '64; 215), managed to run seven months on Broadway thanks to advance ticket buyers who liked the idea of Preston as Franklin. The musical, which had book and lyrics by Sidney Michaels and music by Mark Sandrich, Jr., stuck fairly close to historical fact in its delineation of Franklin's 1776 journey to Paris to gain French recognition of the American Revolution, and the script borrowed liberally from Franklin's famous aphorisms. Two major adjustments in fact were made for the purposes of the musical: Franklin, actually past seventy at the time of his Paris visit, became the fiftyish Preston (who shaved his head for the part), and the four women Franklin romanced during his trip became one, Diane. To play the role, Simone Signoret, Arlene Dahl, and Danielle Darrieux were sought; ultimately, the part went to Ulla Sallert, first lady of Sweden's musical stage and a baroness in real life, but not one of the great articulators of the English language. Noel Willman and Herbert Ross were to have directed and choreographed; they were replaced by Michael Kidd prior to rehearsals.

While in Philadelphia, Jerry Herman came in to write two songs, "To Be Alone with You" and "Too Charming." Jacqueline Mayro, the original Baby June in *Gypsy*, was replaced by Susan Watson just before previews began in New York. The show that greeted largely theatre-party audiences in New York was decently constructed, not insulting to the intelligence, but formulaic and lacking any spark of surprise. Moreover, the time of shows set in royal court rooms had passed: *Ben Franklin* had the unmistakable whiff of an Edwin Lester-style floperetta. "Look for Small Pleasures" and "To Be Alone with You" were fine songs, but a show this stodgy needed a wonderful score to get by. Preston, of course, helped enormously, but Ben Franklin wasn't to have a Broadway hit until *1776* five years later.

Preston's last musical, **The Prince of Grand Street** (Philadelphia; Mar.

○ ○ ○ ○ ○

STUART OSTROW presents

ROBERT PRESTON
as PANCHO VILLA

WE TAKE THE TOWN
A Musical Adventure

Lyrics by MATT DUBEY
Music by HAROLD KARR
Book by FELICE BAUER & MATT DUBEY
Choreography by DONALD SADDLER

with MIKE KELLIN JOHN CULLUM CARMEN ALVAREZ KATHLEEN WIDDOES ROMNEY BRENT LESTER RAWLINS

Settings by PETER LARKIN
Costumes by MOTLEY
Musical & Vocal Direction by COLIN ROMOFF
Orchestrations by ROBERT RUSSELL BENNETT & HERSHY KAY
ORIGINAL CAST ALBUM BY COLUMBIA RECORDS

Production Directed by ALEX SEGAL

SHUBERT THEATRE
NEW HAVEN
Saturday, Feb. 17 thru Saturday, Feb. 24
Evenings at 8:30 -:- Matinees Wed., Feb. 21 and Sat., Feb. 24 at 2:30

BEN FRANKLIN IN PARIS

PLAYBILL
FORREST THEATRE

PLAYBILL
Shubert Theatre

The Prince of
Grand Street

Three of Robert Preston's four flop musicals. He was Pancho Villa in We Take The Town, *the eponymous Ben Franklin in* Paris, *and, in his last show,* The Prince of Grand Street, *Boris Thomashefsky.*

7, '78; closed on the road), died in Boston. It was also Bob Merrill's last Broadway-bound musical to date. Merrill wrote not only the music and lyrics but also the book; his only previous book had been for *Prettybelle*, which also closed in Boston. Most of Merrill's hits were based on plays or movies, but *Prince of Grand Street*, while it retained real-life actor Boris Thomashefsky's propensity for playing adolescent parts in his sixties and adding a Jewish slant and happy endings to Gentile tragedies, was an original, and there lay the problem. Thomashefsky (here renamed Nathan Rashumsky) seemed a likely hero for a musical, but Merrill, after supplying a colorful central character and setting, failed to come up with a plot. There was only the ups and downs of Nathan's relationship with his young wife, and that relationship lacked conflict or development. Preston also found his least congenial role here; not ideally cast as a veteran Yiddish star, he read his lines as if he were still playing Mack Sennett. Even Sam Levene, as the wife's grandfather, and Werner Klemperer, as Preston's severest critic, were awkwardly cast in roles that didn't have a single song between them.

There were compensations in the highly amusing scenes from Nathan's productions at the Grand Street Tivoli Theatre. Nathan, well over sixty, was seen playing both fifteen-year-old Huck Finn and *Young Avrum Lincoln* (promising that if elected, he would turn the state of Illinois into a homeland for the Jews). Merrill's score, heavy on Jewish harmonies, was pleasant, but not strong enough to carry the thin story. The show's producers, who should have demanded a more dramatic book from Merrill, were probably correct to cancel *Prince's* scheduled Broadway opening at the Palace Theatre on May 11, 1978, but doing so deprived Broadway audiences of the chance to see one of their princes in his last show.

One of their princesses, Judy Holliday, in her first musical, the 1956 *Bells Are Ringing*, gave one of the finest star performances Broadway has ever seen. But Holliday was to do only one more musical, **Hot Spot** (Majestic; April 19, '63; 43). In *Bells*, Holliday played a big-hearted girl who kept getting into trouble by becoming involved in the lives of others. In *Hot Spot*, she played the same basic character, this time a hygiene teacher in the Peace Corps who, as the curtain rises, has already gotten into hot water in three different countries. For her fourth and last chance, she is sent to D'hum, the most remote country possible, where she inadvertently stirs up a phony Communist threat, thus assuring D'hum of United States aid.

○ ○ ○ ○ ○

Hot Spot's book was by Jack Weinstock and Willie Gilbert, who had been credited along with Abe Burrows for the libretto of *How to Succeed in Business without Really Trying*. But it was common knowledge that Burrows had been responsible for that show's triumph by taking Weinstock and Gilbert's nonmusical adaptation of Shepherd Mead's novel and transforming it for the musical stage; Weinstock and Gilbert had not shared in the Pulitzer Prize that went to *How to Succeed*. The music for *Hot Spot* was by Mary Rodgers (Richard's daughter), who had already written a remarkable score for *Once upon a Mattress*. Martin Charnin, who had recently turned from performing to writing, did the lyrics. Charnin ranks high on the list of flop masters, and *Hot Spot* was the first of his long string of Broadway failures, which came to include the old-fashioned *Zenda*, the accident-prone *Mata Hari*, the grim *La Strada*, the out-of-control *I Remember Mama*, the unfulfilled *The First*, and the unnecesary *Annie 2*.

Charnin and Rodgers both wanted newcomer Barbra Streisand to play their heroine, but the show's producers and director felt she was too plain to carry off the romantic aspect of the story. Holliday, who was supposed to star in a musical version of Anita Loos' *Happy Birthday*, singing her own lyrics to music by her boyfriend Gerry Mulligan, had recently undergone a mastectomy and took *Hot Spot* mainly to extricate herself from I.R.S. debts.

By the time *Hot Spot*'s tryout was over, Holliday had given up all hope. Original director Morton Da Costa had become ill and withdrawn from the show, and Holliday's choice for a replacement, Richard Quine (who had directed her in two pictures), came in, then quickly fled. Herbert Ross eventually took over the direction and choreography (from Onna White) without credit. Herb Gardner and Larry Gelbart doctored the book, and during previews in New York a new opening number for Holliday, called "Don't Laugh," was added. Quite the best thing in the show, it was mostly the work of Stephen Sondheim, a close friend of Mary Rodgers'. Even Holliday's character's name was changed, from Dulcie to Sally Hopwinder. *Hot Spot* had one of the longest Broadway preview periods ever, canceling its opening four times in an attempt to avoid critics and take advantage of the advance sale.

It finally opened, and on a Friday, a sure admission of trouble: no one, it was thought, read the papers on Saturday. No director or choreographer was listed in the opening night Playbill for the Majestic Theatre, which had become available when Mary Rodgers' father's new show, *I Picked a Daisy*, was postponed. Setting Holliday loose in the Peace Corps was a

○ ○ ○ ○ ○

Even Judy Holliday couldn't save Hot Spot. In the photo, four citizens of D'hum find Holliday, as Sally Hopwinder, fascinating in the song "Smiles."

perfectly good notion for a musical, but the political satire in *Hot Spot* was heavy-handed: the level of humor is indicated by the name D'hum (alternately pronounced "doom" or "dumb"), the leader was the Nadir of D'hum, and local currency was the *dreg*. Structurally, the show made the mistake of introducing its main plot event, the fake Communist threat, at the end of Act One, with little having happened up to that point. To make matters worse, the score was no match for that of *Bells Are Ringing* and couldn't begin to carry the book. Holliday had two nice ballads, "Hey Love" and "Gabie," and an eleven o'clock tour de force called "A Far, Far Better Thing." But it was a sad finale to a potentially great musical-theatre career: Holliday was diagnosed with cancer of the throat immediately after *Hot Spot* closed and died two years later.

Alfred Drake was equally able to command the stage as a cowboy, a poet, or a ham actor, and his panache and voice made him the male equivalent of Merman and Martin on Broadway in the forties and fifties. The original Curley in *Oklahoma!*, Fred Graham in *Kiss Me, Kate,* and Hajj in *Kismet,* Drake found three flops and no hits after *Kismet.* **Kean** (Broadway; Nov. 2, '61; 92) was the first.

In Jean-Paul Sartre's 1953 comedy, *Kean,* based on a play by Alexandre Dumas, Edmund Kean, the foremost actor of Regency London, is profoundly troubled by the gap between illusion and reality. An admired star on stage, he remains an outcast of society when off, and a bastard, drinker, and womanizer to boot. Kean becomes increasingly unable to differentiate between playing his roles and living his life. The idea of Alfred Drake, Broadway's grandest, wittiest musical actor, as Kean was an inspired one, and Drake had himself bought the rights to Sartre's play with an eye to starring in its New York premiere. There were no takers, so Drake and his personal manager, Robert Lantz, decided to turn it into a musical. Peter Stone wrote his first musical book for *Kean,* and the show featured the first original Wright and Forrest score to reach Broadway. *Kean* reunited Drake, Wright and Forrest, and Jack Cole from *Kismet;* it was also Cole's second try at choreography *and* direction. Columbia Records provided most of the over $400,000 capitalization.

Interestingly, *Kean's* reviews were wonderful in Boston (where Drake missed half the run), less good in Philadelphia, and still worse in New York. Howard Taubman in the *New York Times* gave it a strong notice, but *Kean* demonstrated that a good *Times* review doesn't always guarantee success. During the fifth week of the run, twenty minutes, including one

○ ○ ○ ○ ○

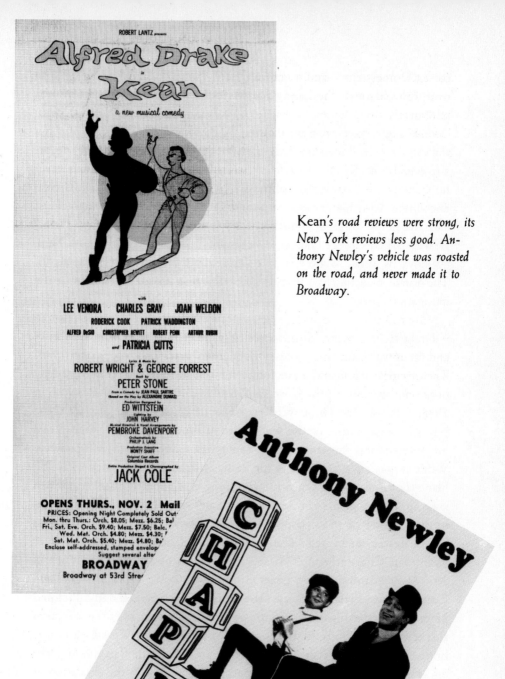

Kean's road reviews were strong, its New York reviews less good. Anthony Newley's vehicle was roasted on the road, and never made it to Broadway.

ROBERT LANTZ presents

Alfred Drake
in
Kean

a new musical comedy

with

LEE VENORA   CHARLES GRAY   JOAN WELDON

RODERICK COOK   PATRICK WADDINGTON

ALFRED DeSIO   CHRISTOPHER HEWITT   ROBERT PENN   ARTHUR RUBIN

and **PATRICIA CUTTS**

Lyrics & Music by
ROBERT WRIGHT & GEORGE FORREST

Book by
PETER STONE
From a Comedy by JEAN-PAUL SARTRE
(Based on the Play by ALEXANDRE DUMAS)

Production Designed by
ED WITTSTEIN

Lighting by
JOHN HARVEY

Musical Direction & Vocal Arrangements by
PEMBROKE DAVENPORT

Orchestrations by
PHILIP J. LANG

Production Executive
MONTY SHAFF

Original Cast Album
Columbia Records

Entire Production Staged & Choreographed by
JACK COLE

OPENS THURS., NOV. 2 Mail
PRICES: Opening Night Completely Sold Out
Mon. thru Thurs.: Orch. $8.05; Mezz. $6.25; Bal
Fri., Sat. Eve. Orch. $9.40; Mezz. $7.50; Balc.
Wed. Mat. Orch. $4.80; Mezz. $4.30;
Sat. Mat. Orch. $5.40; Mezz. $4.80; B
Enclose self-addressed, stamped envelop
Suggest several alte
BROADWAY
Broadway at 53rd Stre

Anthony Newley

CHAPLIN

song ("Domesticity") and a bathtub scene, were dropped, but even with over 550 balcony seats going for $1 each, the Broadway Theatre was seldom full.

Kean might have been an incisive study of acting versus real life, but the show received the standard, semi-floperetta treatment in score, decor, and even book. Kean's identity crisis was frequently announced but never fully dramatized, while most of the action was given over to Kean's farcical encounters with his mistresses, would-be or real. Drake was marvelous, and the score offered compensations in the opening, "Penny Plain," Drake's ballad "Sweet Danger," the production number "Chime In," and "Willow, Willow, Willow," for a Desdemona opposite Kean's Othello. The Sartre play has had several successful revivals in England since the musical's failure.

Drake's chief rival as Broadway's best male singer—actor in the forties and fifties was John Raitt, whose first musical lead was in *Carousel* in 1945. But after that landmark, Raitt found himself in four flops interrupted by only one hit: *The Pajama Game*, in 1954. The first flop was *Magdalena*, in 1948, followed by **Three Wishes for Jamie** (Mark Hellinger; Mar. 21, '52; 94). *Jamie* is one of the few shows in Broadway history that closed out of town for repairs and actually came back to life to open on Broadway. While it was always a vehicle for Raitt, with music and lyrics by Ralph Blane (*Best Foot Forward*), nearly everything else about it changed. When it was produced at the Los Angeles and San Francisco Civic Light Operas in the summer of 1951, coproducer Albert Lewis was the director, and Edwin Lester supervised. The book was by Charles O'Neal (father of Ryan) and Charles Lederer, based on O'Neal's novel *The Three Wishes of Jamie McRuin*, and the show (then in three acts) costarred Marion Bell and Cecil Kellaway. For Broadway, Abe Burrows, who had recently doctored *Make a Wish* after his triumph with *Guys and Dolls*, took over the direction and rewrote the book. Burrows replaced most of the West Coast cast, bringing in Anne Jeffreys, Bert Wheeler, and Charlotte Rae, among others. The New York critics were generally positive, with the exception of Brooks Atkinson in the *Times*, to whom any whiff of operetta was invariably an anathema.

The show told of young Jamie McRuin (Raitt), who leaves Ireland for America to fulfill the three wishes that the fairy queen Una has granted him: travel, a beautiful wife, and a son who speaks Gaelic. Jamie has no trouble with the first two, but at his wedding to Maeve (Jeffreys) at the

○ ○ ○ ○ ○

end of the first act, he learns that she has been cursed with barrenness. Jamie and Maeve adopt a mute son, who in the show's touching conclusion miraculously utters his first words, and in the Gaelic that Jamie's friend Tavish (Wheeler) taught him.

While not an unpleasant evening, *Three Wishes* had the look and sound of several major successes of the late forties and early fifties (e. g. *Brigadoon*, and *Paint Your Wagon*) without delivering in equal measure. Its story and score were never as strong as one would have liked, and the show had marked similarities to well-known hits. As in *Finian's Rainbow*, the leading characters arrive in America from Ireland at the beginning of the evening. As in *Brigadoon*, Act One ends with a rejected suitor threatening the happiness of the lovers by activating a curse. There was a secondary comic couple featuring a raucous girl right out of *Brigadoon*, and *Jamie's* original female lead, Bell, had made her name in *Brigadoon*. The similarities served to point up the gap in quality between *Jamie* and the hits of which it was reminiscent.

Raitt's last book show to date was **A Joyful Noise** (Mark Hellinger; Dec. 15, '66; 12), easily his least interesting musical and notable only for the fact that it featured the first Broadway choreography by Michael Bennett. It was another of those shows that underwent wholesale changes in personnel from its tryout (in summer tents) to Broadway. Throughout, the score was by Oscar Brand and Paul Nassau, who, two years later, wrote a much nicer flop called *The Education of H*Y*M*A*N K*A*P*L*A*N*. But the book, originally by the show's producer Edward Padula, was rewritten by Dore Schary, who also took over the direction from Ben Shaktman. When Schary quit, Padula and Bennett were left with the directing chores. Donna McKechnie, later Bennett's star dancer, had the nondancing ingenue lead; for Broadway, she was replaced by Susan Watson. Likewise, Mitzi Welch and James Rado (coauthor of *Hair* the following season) of the tour were replaced by Karen Morrow and Clifford David.

A Joyful Noise, which told of the effect of a wandering minstrel on a small town in the Tennessee hills, had laughably stilted dialogue and an unconvincing plot. Even the names of the characters rang false: Raitt played Shade Motley, apparently so his backup band could be called the Motley Crew. Well before *A Joyful Noise* reached Broadway, Raitt—too old for his part—was aware of the show's shortcomings and of the difficulty of finding good roles in a musical theatre that had become the provenance of star ladies like Carol Channing, Angela Lansbury, and Barbara Harris. While on tour, Raitt gave singularly frank, even bitter

○ ○ ○ ○ ○

interviews; he told a Boston reporter, "We could never get by the New York critics with this show. What's wrong with it? The story, the basic story, that's all. The dialogue is so bad I was embarrassed to be saying it on stage." A far cry indeed from *Carousel*, which Raitt had recreated at Lincoln Center the previous summer.

Barbara Cook was not quite a star in the way Alfred Drake, John Raitt, Mary Martin, or Judy Holliday were. She was an incomparable singer and an actress of conviction, but people didn't necessarily buy tickets because of her presence in a musical; her greatest personal triumphs came after her Broadway career, in concerts and cabaret. She had one musical smash, opposite Robert Preston, in *The Music Man*, two mild successes with *Plain and Fancy* and *She Loves Me*, and five flops. Of the flops, one— **Something More!** (Eugene O'Neill; Nov. 10, '64; 15)—had virtually nothing going for it except Cook.

Something More!, with a book by Nate Monaster, was to have had the same title as the Gerald Green novel on which it was based—*Portofino P.T.A.*—until someone remembered that one of Broadway's worst turkeys had had almost the same title. *Something More!* was Sammy Fain's last Broadway flop and Cook's second Fain flop (*Flahooley* was the first). It was the only Broadway musical directed by Jule Styne, who, it is said, also had a hand in the music. The lyrics were by Marilyn and Alan Bergman, whose only other Broadway musical to date has been Michael Bennett's 1978 flop, *Ballroom*.

Florence Henderson was first announced for the female lead, but it went to Cook: it was one of the few times in her career when she got to play a contemporary woman, even sporting a bikini in one scene. Cook was cast as the wife of a best-selling novelist who becomes discontented with suburbia and takes his family off to Italy in search of "something more." Husband and wife are tempted by jet setters but ultimately return to Long Island.

In Philadelphia, Joe Layton replaced Styne as director, taking no credit, and Viveca Lindfors, as the sculptress who attempts to seduce the husband, was replaced by Joan Copeland. But the show's biggest problem, a book lacking in wit or originality, was never properly addressed, and $350,000 was promptly lost. Fain's score varied from lovely to junk; Cook, in her only unrecorded Broadway performance, made all of her songs sound better than they actually were. Aside from Cook, Bob Herget's musical staging—including a passel of Santini Brothers moving the family

○ ○ ○ ○ ○

Above, bikini-clad Barbara Cook consults with Peg Murray in Something More!
The Philadelphia Playbill cover, above right, features Arthur Hill, Viveca Lindfors
(before she was fired), Cook, and Ronny Graham. Below, Nanette Fabray and
Georges Guetary's celebrated bundling scene in Arms and the Girl was used to
promote Sumter Springmaid sheets.

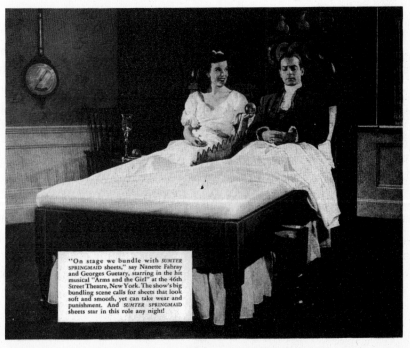

"On stage we bundle with *SUMTER SPRINGMAID* sheets," say Nanette Fabray and Georges Guetary, starring in the hit musical "Arms and the Girl" at the 46th Street Theatre, New York. The show's big bundling scene calls for sheets that look soft and smooth, yet can take wear and punishment. And *SUMTER SPRINGMAID* sheets star in this role any night!

Bundling without Bungling

from Mineola to Portofino and a scorching beach dance for Jo Jo Smith and Paula Kelly—was the show's only asset. *Something More!* demonstrated yet again that musicals set in Italy (*Buttrio Square, Portofino, Ankles Aweigh, Bravo, Giovanni, Do I Hear a Waltz?, La Strada, Carmelina*) rarely succeed.

Musicals about movies (*The Vamp, Goldilocks,* and *Mack and Mabel* on Broadway, *The Biograph Girl* and *Blockheads* in London) rarely succeed either. And by the eighties, the bio-musical was just about dead, too. But Anthony Newley attempted both in **Chaplin** (Los Angeles; Aug. 12, '83; closed on the road).

In his two hit collaborations with Leslie Bricusse, *Stop the World—I Want to Get Off* and *The Roar of the Greasepaint—The Smell of the Crowd,* Newley had played the same "little man" character, and that character was often dubbed Chaplinesque. Indeed, Newley identified with Charles Chaplin: they were both cockneys from the East End of London, and both were raised without a father. For *Chaplin,* Newley collaborated on the book and score with television writer Stanley Ralph Ross, and Michael Smuin was hired to direct and choreograph. Playing three of Chaplin's wives was Andrea Marcovicci, who had already appeared in the flop *Ambassador* on Broadway and in *Nefertiti,* which, like *Chaplin,* closed on the road. Coproducer James M. Nederlander allowed David Susskind to invest $250,000 in *La Cage aux Folles,* which opened on Broadway when *Chaplin* was beginning its tryout, with the stipulation that Susskind would also put up $500,000 of *Chaplin's* $4 million cost.

Chaplin opened an eight-week engagement in Los Angeles, where the critics had praise only for Douglas W. Schmidt's lavish sets. Doctors were called in: Leslie Bricusse (naturally), Larry Grossman, Ellen Fitzhugh, George Schaefer, and even Susskind lent a hand. But an additional million dollars was needed to bring the show to New York, and a deal whereby Susskind would put up most of it and take top producing billing fell through. The show's failure to make it to Broadway was the subject of a front page story in the *New York Times:* it ran on November 10, 1983, the day *Chaplin* was supposed to have opened at the Mark Hellinger Theatre.

The main problem with *Chaplin* was obvious: the show featured three narrators (Newley as "himself," Newley as Chaplin, and an actor playing Stan Laurel), and almost everything that happened in the show was announced rather than dramatized. The show's point of view was also confused, with three actors playing Chaplin as boy, teenager, and man,

○ ○ ○ ○ ○

sometimes all onstage at once. The score, with tunes strongly reminiscent of other Newley shows, was mediocre, and many of the numbers were "onstage" songs, unrelated to what little story there was. The show almost never dealt with Chaplin's artistry, only with the events of his personal life. Newley's performance was not good, but then he never had a chance, as he spent the evening announcing things happening offstage rather than acting them out. Newley revived the show in the summer of 1985 at Houston's Theater under the Stars, this time serving as star, coauthor and director. But *Chaplin* was not a good idea from the beginning, and after this second try Newley promptly took to the road in a revival of his biggest hit, *Stop the World*.

Although she made two appearances in Broadway musicals early in her career, the second in the Gershwins' *Girl Crazy* in 1930, Ginger Rogers is thought of primarily as a film star. Almost thirty years after *Girl Crazy*, she returned to the musical stage in the unwisely chosen vehicle **The Pink Jungle** (San Francisco; Oct. 14, '59; closed on the road). In this would-be satire of the beauty industry, Agnes Moorehead played the head of a cosmetics empire who, Liliom-like, dies but is barred from Heaven until she returns to earth and performs her first good deed. She sees to it that Rogers, playing one of four company vice presidents, takes over for her. But this being the late fifties, Moorehead's ultimate good deed is telling Rogers that love is more important than a successful career. *The Pink Jungle* concludes with Rogers marrying Moorehead's eldest son and Moorehead entering Heaven.

The Pink Jungle was originally announced as a light comedy by Leslie Stevens (*The Marriage-Go-Round*), to have a few incidental songs by Vernon Duke. While on the road, the show ballooned from an intimate play with four songs and a cast of fifteen to an elaborate musical with a cast of thirty, ten songs (with more to come), and a sizable orchestra. The original concept had gone out the window when Donald Oenslager's enormous sets and Rogers' $130,000 Jean Louis wardrobe (with fourteen costume changes) arrived.

The idea of a play with a few songs was probably unworkable from the start; the script needed to be fully musicalized or left as a straight comedy. When it became a full-scale musical, what satirical edge *The Pink Jungle* had disappeared, and the show became a labored musical sitcom. Original director Joseph Anthony was replaced by Stevens, and Rogers,

○ ○ ○ ○ ○

playing a vice president when the show began its tryout, was playing a humble beautician by the time the show folded in Boston, canceling its January 14, 1960, opening at the flop-prone 54th Street Theatre.

Moorehead got the best reviews and had the only real fun, cracking wise about those who could not see her, taking on the guise of a lady cop, a waitress, and a stenographer, and even flying. (Moorehead would soon be doing pretty much the same thing on the TV series "Bewitched.") Rogers, who reportedly feuded with Moorehead on the road, was given two big dance numbers, including one good one with Matt Mattox set in Central Park, but her puny singing voice was a liability. When it was announced that the show would return after a face-lift, Rogers told the press, "It needs more than a face-lift. They better bury it. It had no substance; it was a big nothing. We would have been foolish to face the seven New York critics. They would have shot us out of the water." Rogers never again created a role in a musical, choosing instead to play Wildcat, Molly Brown, Dolly, Mame, and Coco in stock or abroad after other actresses had created the parts.

All of the stars mentioned above had already enjoyed a degree of success sufficient to assure that their reputations would not be permanently damaged by the flops in which they appeared. But there were performers who might have made it to the Martin–Bolger–Drake level were it not for the failures that plagued them. Nanette Fabray had sufficient versatility and star quality to rival Martin, but after her first big personal success in *High Button Shoes* in 1947, she remained a talent in search of a *South Pacific* or an *Annie Get Your Gun* who instead got several almost-but-not-quite shows. First came *Love Life* in 1948 (Fabray received a Tony Award for her performance), followed by two fifties flops that sent Fabray straight to television, where she had considerable success with Sid Caesar.

The Theatre Guild had already presented two big hit musicals based on plays and directed by Rouben Mamoulian, *Oklahoma!* and *Carousel*. The Guild went back to a play they had presented in 1933 called *The Pursuit of Happiness*, written by Lawrence Langner and his wife, Armina Marshall, two-thirds of the Guild. Under the title **Arms and the Girl** (46th Street; Feb. 2, '50; 134), the play, set in Connecticut during the Revolutionary War, was refashioned for the musical stage by Herbert and Dorothy Fields, with a score begun by Burton Lane. But Lane withdrew just a few months before the show went on the road and was replaced by Morton Gould (*Billion Dollar Baby*), who composed his score to an already written

○ ○ ○ ○ ○

book. Mamoulian directed, and the Guild coproduced with Anthony Brady Farrell (of *Ankles Aweigh* fame).

Fabray had a plum role here, that of Jo Kirkland, who, zealously committed to playing her part in the fight for independence, winds up creating chaos rather than helping the cause. Jo becomes involved with Connecticut (Pearl Bailey), a runaway slave who takes the name of whatever state she's in, and Franz, a Hessian deserter, played by Continental star Georges Guetary. At the end, General Washington himself arrives; Jo expects to be decorated for her war efforts but is instead ordered by Washington to "stay the hell out of the Revolution."

Much fuss was made over a plot element taken from the original play, that of "bundling," in which young ladies and gentlemen of the period had dates while snuggled in bed (for warmth and to conserve fuel) with a wooden board raised between them. There were only two bundling scenes in *Arms and the Girl*, but it was a good angle for publicity photos. The show received mixed reviews in Philadelphia but very good ones in Boston, and it looked like a hit by the time it came in. But the New York reviews were divided, with Atkinson again invoking the "o" word. The production was plagued by cast illnesses, and all three leads withdrew within three months.

Arms and the Girl reads pleasantly, and the show had charm and several fine songs. Bailey's two solos, although barely integrated into the plot, were the show's peaks. She won raves, was elevated to above-title billing three weeks after the opening, and walked away with what was meant to be Fabray's show. Unfortunately, the kind of sweetly amusing, old-fashioned entertainment that *Arms and the Girl* provided was no longer acceptable to a public now used to the likes of *South Pacific, Finian's Rainbow,* and *Kiss Me, Kate.*

One play by Ferenc Molnár, *Liliom,* had been made into a hit musical, *Carousel,* but lightning was not to strike again when Molnár's *The Good Fairy,* which had served as a vehicle for Helen Hayes on Broadway and Margaret Sullavan on film, was made into the musical **Make a Wish** (Winter Garden; Apr. 18, '51; 102). Fabray got her name alone above the title for the first time, and had the show been a smash she might have entered the top echelon of Broadway stardom. It was also the first book show choreographed by Gower Champion, the show that began Abe Burrows' career as a sought-after doctor, and the first book musical produced (along with Jule Styne and Harry Rigby) by Alexander H. Cohen. Cohen would go on to produce an uninterrupted series of flop

○ ○ ○ ○ ○

book musicals, including *Courtin' Time, A Time for Singing, Dear World, Prettybelle,* and *I Remember Mama.*

With music and lyrics by Hugh Martin, *Make a Wish* was about a young war orphan, Janette, who, while touring the Louvre, escapes her fellow orphans and plunges into the glittering world of Left Bank Paris. She is tempted by meat packer Marius Frigo (Melville Cooper, in a nonsinging lead), one of the richest men in town, but succumbs to indigent law student Paul Dumont (Stephen Douglass). The book was written by Preston Sturges, who had done the screenplay for the Sullavan movie, but Sturges quit in Philadelphia and returned to Hollywood. Burrows wrote an almost entirely new book and even took over the direction when John C. Wilson became ill late in the tryout.

Make a Wish was another pleasant show with a decent if uneventful score, and its highlight was Champion's brilliant "Sale" ballet, set in the Galerie Napoléon Department Store and comparable in quality to Jerome Robbins' Mack Sennett ballet in *High Button Shoes.* But *Make a Wish* suffered greatly when compared to *Guys and Dolls, South Pacific, Kiss Me, Kate, The King and I,* and *Call Me Madam,* all on Broadway at the time of its arrival.

Helen Gallagher and Harold Lang played a dance team from Texas working at the Folies Labiche in *Make a Wish.* Jule Styne took Gallagher from a featured dance spot in his *High Button Shoes* and put her first into *Make a Wish,* then into his smash revival of *Pal Joey,* for which she won her first Tony Award. Determined to make Gallagher a star, Styne may have done her less than a favor by producing and writing the music for a star vehicle for her: **Hazel Flagg** (Mark Hellinger; Feb. 11, '53; 190).

The book was by Ben Hecht (based on the 1937 Carole Lombard movie, *Nothing Sacred,* which Hecht had written with Charles MacArthur) and told the story of Hazel Flagg of Stoneyhead, Vermont, who mistakenly believes she is dying of radium poisoning as a result of her job painting dials in a watch factory. When she finds out that she has a lot more than three weeks to live, she decides to go to New York and have a fling anyway, courtesy of *Everywhere* magazine, whose editor Laura Carew believes she is fulfilling Hazel's last wishes.

Sticking close to a caustic, amusing film, *Hazel Flagg* was fun, but the satire was softened in the musical. Moreover, Gallagher was never the kind of performer audiences fell in love with: she was too tough to make Hazel—who was, after all, duping the public—a sympathetic character. Judy Holliday, who would have been able to touch the audience the way

○ ○ ○ ○ ○

Three stars whose careers were not helped by a string of nonhits. Above, Helen Gallagher as Hazel Flagg, who believes she is dying of radium poisoning, bids farewell to Stonyhead, Vermont. Below left, Nanette Fabray achieved solo, above-the-title billing for the first time in Make A Wish. Below right, Nancy Walker as lady cop Katey O'Shea in Copper and Brass.

Lombard did in the film, might have made the show a hit; as a star showcase for Gallagher, who had a marathon-sized part, *Hazel Flagg* hurt Gallagher's career more than it helped it.

The show received mixed reviews, with praise for Gallagher, Robert Alton's dances, Thomas Mitchell in a nonsinging lead, and veteran Jack Whiting's comeback as the mayor of New York, singing the show's hit, "Every Street's a Boulevard." But business was slow, and after five months the show suspended its run, having recouped half of its $240,000 investment. After eight weeks, *Hazel* reopened, with Tony Bavaar replacing the original leading man, John Howard, and getting two new songs. Donald Saddler choreographed a new ballet for the second act, but *Hazel Flagg* closed for good two weeks after reopening. Not a disaster, it was a marginal show overshadowed by its source. A film version of sorts, called *Living It Up*, was released in 1954, with Jerry Lewis—as "Homer" Flagg—and Dean Martin. The film retained four of the show's songs.

As for Gallagher, she went on to replace Carol Haney in *The Pajama Game*, do revivals at City Center, star in the notorious *Portofino*, take supporting roles in *Sweet Charity* and the flop *Cry for Us All*, then finally make a comeback, winning a Tony Award for the 1971 Broadway revival of *No, No, Nanette*.

When Helen Gallagher left the *Pal Joey* revival for *Hazel Flagg*, she was replaced by Nancy Walker, a sign that the theatre's most gifted clown had not managed to parlay her early successes in *Best Foot Forward* and *On the Town* into the top star career she deserved. Walker had the lead in two subsequent musicals of the forties, *Barefoot Boy with Cheek* and *Look, Ma, I'm Dancin'!*, neither of which proved a great success, and she closed on the road in a musical called *A Month of Sundays* in 1952. In 1957, Walker's husband, David Craig, wrote the lyrics and cowrote the book for **Copper and Brass** (Martin Beck; Oct. 17, '57; 36), in which Walker played Katey O'Shea, a lady cop who falls for a jazz musician she meets when investigating a noise disturbance. The music was by David Baker, who wrote one more Broadway score later, for Ray Bolger's *Come Summer*.

During the show's Philadelphia tryout, Joan Blondell, playing Walker's mother, was replaced by Benay Venuta; director Mark Daniels was replaced by Burt Shevelove (who had written and directed *A Month of Sundays*), with Daniels retaining credit; and most of Anna Sokolow's choreography was redone by Bob Fosse, who took program credit for only one dance.

○ ○ ○ ○ ○

Walker was pretty much on her own, and she had some choice comic highlights: becoming entangled in her nightstick and fur stole, battling a modern "womb chair," and creating havoc in the Holland Tunnel. But Walker's unique comic abilities were unwisely placed in the service of a drearily conventional romance plot. Hoping to do for Walker what *Bells Are Ringing* had done for Judy Holliday, or what *Wonderful Town* had done for Rosalind Russell, *Copper and Brass* actually did Walker a disservice. It was probably her last chance at top Broadway stardom, and it was followed by only one more book show, *Do Re Mi*, in which she had the female lead (with below-the-title billing) opposite Phil Silvers.

After kicking around as a replacement for other stars in several shows in the early sixties, Joel Grey staked his claim to Broadway legend with his portrayal of the Master of Ceremonies in *Cabaret* in 1966. But Grey's Emcee, if it dominated the evening, did not have to carry it; the part had virtually no dialogue, consisting of a series of musical numbers which commented on the action. Still, Grey's success and Tony Award meant that producers would now have to come up with vehicles for him. The first was the moderately successful *George M!*, a revuelike show in which Joe Layton's nonstop staging camouflaged Grey's lack of warmth as George M. Cohan. But his second starring vehicle, the first of his two flops at the Palace Theatre, indicated that finding vehicles for Grey was not going to be so easy. Grey quickly became another on our list of stars whose Broadway musical career was damaged by flops.

Goodtime Charley (Palace; Mar. 3, '75; 104) had a book by Sidney Michaels (*Ben Franklin in Paris*) and a score by Larry Grossman and Hal Hackady, their second for Broadway after the flop *Minnie's Boys*. Grossman, a talented composer, wrote four interesting scores for four Broadway flops, *Minnie's Boys*, *Goodtime Charley*, *A Doll's Life*, and *Grind*. *Charley* had Grey playing the meek dauphin of France, under the thumb of a corrupt general and archbishop, to Ann Reinking's Joan of Arc. Their relationship is a rocky one, but Joan's belief in Charley eventually inspires him to take command and become a man.

The kind of old-style vehicle once fashioned for Ray Bolger or Eddie Cantor, *Charley* was by no means terrible and was well-tailored to Grey's talents. But the Joan of Arc story had been recounted onstage several times already, and even though the telling was from the point of view of the Dauphin this time, few were interested. Moreover, no matter the point of view, this *is* Joan's story, and she really has to be the central

○ ○ ○ ○ ○

character. Grossman and Hackady wrote a few nice numbers, especially a duet for peripheral characters, "Merci, Bon Dieu," and Rouben Ter-Arutunian's sets and Willa Kim's costumes, in the style of Maxfield Parrish illustrations, were attractive. The recipient of six Tony nominations, *Goodtime Charley* lost $1.1 million, well over its original investment, thanks to consistent operating losses.

A comic demon possessed of a wonderful way with a song, Dorothy Loudon had an entire Broadway career that seemed to be made up of bombs, until she finally got a hit, *Annie*, in 1977. She made her Broadway debut in **Nowhere to Go but Up** (Winter Garden; Nov. 10, '62; 9), in which she was fourth-billed. The only Broadway musical directed by Sidney Lumet, it was the first show choreographed by Ron Field, who was assisted by Michael Bennett. *Nowhere to Go but Up* was about celebrated Prohibition agents Izzy Einstein and Moe Smith, known for their integrity and clever disguises, and had strong similarities to a later Prohibition-era disaster, *Legs Diamond*. Tom Bosley had his second Broadway lead; all together, he would star in three musicals, but only the first, *Fiorello!*, was successful. Miss America of 1959, Mary Ann Mobley, was the ingenue.

Nowhere was an uninspired formula show with a weak score. The idea of a musical about Izzy and Moe was a good one, but the show required a pair of star clowns like Victor Moore and William Gaxton, rather than actors like Bosley and Martin Balsam. The choreography and Loudon— playing Wilma Risque ("It's French—I ain't, it is"), a part similar to Adelaide in *Guys and Dolls*—were singled out for praise. When Kermit Bloomgarden and his coproducers announced the closing after a week, a group of investors hired a lawyer to file an injunction preventing the producers from shutting down the show. The investors picketed the theatre, but when Bloomgarden made it clear that *Nowhere* was doing no business whatsoever, they dropped the complaint.

The turning point in Loudon's career came with another instant flop, **The Fig Leaves Are Falling** (Broadhurst; Jan. 2, '69; 4), one of the numerous musical failures (*Flora, the Red Menace, Anya, The Education of H*Y*M*A*N K*A*P*L*A*N, Music Is*) directed by George Abbott late in his career. *Fig Leaves* had book and lyrics by Allan Sherman, then famous for his song parody album *My Son, the Folk Singer*. The music was by Albert Hague; the show was the second of three flops with which Hague would end a Broadway career that started with *Plain and Fancy* and *Redhead*.

Fig Leaves tells of Harry Stone (Barry Nelson), who leaves his wife, children, and comfortable home in Larchmont for a fling with young Pookie Chapman, founder of the Sexual Freedom League. It was the kind of show that while pretending to deal with contemporary society and its changes was actually stroking the prejudices of theatre-party audiences. It attempted to satirize the generation gap, the new morality, and the sexual revolution, but did so with a consistent leer, winding up distasteful and unfunny. Pookie, meant to be an appealing free spirit, came off as a pushy home wrecker. And there were no surprises, as there was never the slightest doubt that Harry would return to wife Lillian. In the show's most desperate moment, Harry and Pookie, celebrating their newfound happiness, raffled off a chicken to an audience member.

During New York previews, Abbott took the song "All of My Laughter" away from Jenny O'Hara, playing Pookie, and gave it to Loudon, playing Lillian. With that song, "We," and "Lillian, Lillian, Lillian," Loudon had sufficient opportunity to show what she could do. Everyone who saw *Fig Leaves* came out wondering when Loudon would find a good show, and Loudon received her first Tony Award nomination.

Rumple (Alvin; Nov. 6, '57; 45) was a musical about the creator of one of America's most popular comic strips who, after a plane accident, stops drawing. His two leading strip characters, Rumple and Anna, come to life; they must get their creator drawing again or they will be consigned to Oblivia, where obsolete comic strip characters wind up. A completely forgotten show today, *Rumple* was first done as a straight play called *Caricature*, and it still reads like a nonmusical farce into which songs have been uneasily plopped. Written by nobodies, it was a throwback to pre-Rodgers and Hammerstein shows, but it seems unlikely that it would have thrived even in the thirties or forties.

The only thing interesting about *Rumple* is its demonstration of the perils of maintaining a star career in postwar Broadway. Eddie Foy, Jr., made a big hit in *The Pajama Game* in 1954, but the remainder of his Broadway career went poorly. There were four flops: *Rumple* (in which he played the title role), *Royal Flush* (1964), from which he withdrew in rehearsal (it folded in Philadelphia), *Donnybrook!*, and *Drat! The Cat!*, from which he withdrew during the tryout.

For Gretchen Wyler, a highly enjoyable performer in the Gwen Verdon–Chita Rivera mold, *Rumple* meant even more. She gained recognition on Broadway in *Silk Stockings*, a show she joined during its tryout as a replacement for Yvonne Adair. She then replaced Gwen Verdon in *Damn*

○ ○ ○ ○ ○

Yankees. Rumple was the first musical she was in from the start, and as the cartoon strip's writer, she was billed above the title. Had *Rumple* been a hit, there might have been other new roles. Instead, Wyler spent most of her career playing parts that Verdon, Rivera, or some other star originated.

Thus far, we have looked at some star flops that stained but did not do permanent injury to careers and others that did. We now move to our third category of star flop, comprising shows headed by performers who are not thought of primarily as musical-theatre stars. While they may have later chosen to forget that it ever happened, such stars as Katharine Hepburn, Lucille Ball, Bette Davis, Julie Harris, and Buddy Hackett all performed in musicals. Through sheer willpower and a readiness to take her show on the road after Broadway, Hepburn made *Coco* into a financial success. But most one-shot musical stars were not able to make their solitary vehicle into a hit.

Because of the degree of Lucille Ball's fame and popularity, **Wildcat** (Alvin; Dec. 16, '60; 172) is perhaps the best remembered one-shot star flop. It was Ball's Broadway debut, her only previous stage experience having been in a touring company of Elmer Rice's *Dream Girl* in 1948. In 1960, Ball's marriage to Desi Arnaz was falling apart; in an effort to escape Los Angeles, Ball, who might have waited a few years and starred in *Hello, Dolly!* or some other first-class musical, signed on for eighteen months of *Wildcat*.

Ball played Wildcat Jackson, determined to strike oil in the Southwest in 1912 and help her lame sister find a husband. The book was by N. Richard Nash, who had authored *The Rainmaker* but had never written a musical before; he would later adapt *The Rainmaker* into *110 in the Shade* and also do the books of *The Happy Time* and *Sarava*. Sammy Cahn and James Van Heusen were going to write the score, but instead it was done by Cy Coleman, in his Broadway book musical debut, and Carolyn Leigh, who had written lyrics to Moose Charlap's *Peter Pan* music. The show was fortunate to have Michael Kidd as director and choreographer, and his staging of "El Sombrero," "What Takes My Fancy," and other numbers helped greatly.

After a tryout during which the character of Wildcat became more and more the Lucy audiences expected from television, the show opened to praise for Kidd, designer Peter Larkin's split-second transformation of a

○ ○ ○ ○ ○

The divine Lucy in two Wildcat numbers. Above, "What Takes My Fancy" with
Don Tomkins; below, "El Sombrero" with Swen Swenson and Al Lanti. Lucy appears to be having a better time than she actually was.

shack into an oil derrick, and Ball. Three reviews were favorable, but it was obvious that the show was not worthy of its star. While the score was good and included one hit song, "Hey, Look Me Over!," *Wildcat* had a clumsy book, with plot similarities to the Annie Oakley–Frank Butler relationship in *Annie Get Your Gun* and to Nash's own *Rainmaker* (a blowhard, here promising oil instead of rain, finally makes good). Nash and Kidd were also the producers, so there was no one around to insist that the show be made better. They correctly believed that the mere presence of Ball would guarantee an audience and didn't try for much more.

Audiences wanted to see Lucy live instead of behind glass, and *Wildcat*, disappointing as it was to everyone—including its star—opened to strong business; there can be little doubt that it would have gone on to run for the duration of Ball's contract and return its investment. Ball had worked hard throughout rehearsals and the Philadelphia break-in, and she was still committed to the show when it arrived in New York, adding a "third act" at the curtain call in which she spoke to the audience, danced, and did an encore of "Hey, Look Me Over!" But on February 7, an exhausted Ball suspended the show for two weeks and flew to Miami Beach. By the time she returned, she had lost interest in *Wildcat* and wanted only to go home to California. In the next weeks, Ball fractured a finger and injured her back. Then, in early May, her divorce from Arnaz became final, and she collapsed on stage during a performance. It was announced that the show would suspend again, from June 5 through August 7, so that Ball could recuperate, then reopen; Betty Jane Watson played the lead for the remainder of the week after Ball, under doctor's orders, withdrew.

But *Wildcat* never reopened, the excuse given out to the press being the musicians' union demand for full pay during the layoff period. But the real reason was Ball's disenchantment with a vehicle into which she had rushed headlong; she later said, "Nobody told me how bad it was. Except the gypsies in the chorus. They knew everything." If Ball was responsible for closing *Wildcat*, however, no one could really hold it against her: the entire $300,000 cost of the show had been supplied by Desilu Productions. And Ball must ultimately have been glad that she did the show: one night after a performance of *Wildcat*, she was introduced to Gary Morton, who became her husband for the rest of her life.

Our second one-shot star never even reached Broadway in her only book musical. In the early seventies, Richard Halliday called Joshua Logan

○ ○ ○ ○ ○

and asked him to find a new show for his wife, Mary Martin. The property Logan came up with was Emlyn Williams' autobiographical 1938 play, *The Corn Is Green*, which had already served as a vehicle for Sybil Thorndike, Ethel Barrymore, Eva Le Gallienne, Blanche Yurka, and Bette Davis, the latter in the 1945 film version. Logan discovered that Williams had written the book and lyrics for a musical version of his play in 1964, shifting the story of a spinster teacher's effect on her prize pupil from a Welsh mining town to the cane fields of the American South, making his hero, Morgan, a black field hand. Logan brought in Albert Hague to compose the score and decided to direct, coproduce and coauthor the book with Williams for the show that came to be known as **Miss Moffat** (Philadelphia; Oct. 7, '74; closed on the road).

The team auditioned the show for Martin, but when Halliday died, Martin lost interest in returning to the stage. Katharine Hepburn, who later played Moffat in a television version of the play, turned the show down, one musical apparently having been sufficient for her. Logan's choice for his star, a choice that would prove fatal, was Bette Davis, who had been the screen's Moffat at age thirty-six. Davis had starred in the musical revue *Two's Company* in 1952, and during its tryout, musical stager Jerome Robbins had, at Davis's request, called Logan in for help. But a bone disease had led to Davis's abrupt departure from *Two's Company*, and its subsequent closing after three sold-out months; Logan and others believed the disease was a sham. Davis had also left Tennessee Williams' *The Night of the Iguana* early in its Broadway run. All signs indicated that the film star's commitment to stage vehicles was shaky at best, but Logan went ahead and signed Davis for a cross-country tour of *Miss Moffat* to last forty-four weeks, culminating in a Broadway opening in the fall of 1975.

During rehersals, Davis limped around in pain, and was hospitalized in late August 1974, canceling the scheduled Baltimore premiere. Published reports maintained that Davis was using a back ailment as ammunition in her clashes with Logan. When *Miss Moffat* opened in Philadelphia, the critics greeted the show coolly, and Davis admitted to Logan, "I'm too big a star to be giving a poor performance, which I'm now doing." On Thursday of the second week in Philadelphia, Davis announced that she was in pain and unable to continue. The fifteenth performance of the show was its last. The producers had wisely taken out insurance against Davis's absences to cover the show's $500,000 cost.

But *Miss Moffat* wasn't quite over yet. In 1975, Davis told Rex Reed,

○ ○ ○ ○ ○

"It was a mistake. The audiences stood up cheering and screaming every night, but I knew it wasn't what they wanted. They wanted me to be a bitch, not a middle-aged school teacher . . . I had to carry the burden of the re-writes . . . Joshua Logan finished me off in two weeks . . . They wanted me to learn 40 pages in four days! . . . I will never go near the stage again as long as I live!" Logan, incensed by these comments, told his side of the story in 1978, in his second volume of autobiography, *Movie Stars, Real People, and Me*. When he did, Davis sued him for libel, a suit that was later dropped. Logan, refusing to give up on the show, directed it again at the Indianapolis Civic Theater in 1983 with a mostly non-Equity cast headed by Ginger Rogers. It played two weeks, then vanished.

Undoubtedly the show would have been far better off with Mary Martin as its star; at sixty-six, Davis was too old for the part and appeared visibly uncomfortable onstage. She would interrupt herself in midsong to ask where she was, and her singing was even more problematic than it had been during *Two's Company*. There was nothing wrong with the idea of resetting the story in the South, but while there were some attractive melodies, Williams' lyrics were frequently awkward, and the score added little to the original play. *Moffat* felt like a sixties project whose time had passed. Logan and Williams were quick to blame Davis for the swift closing, but *Moffat* might have continued on its tour with another star had it evidenced any signs of life in Philadelphia. It didn't; what could have been a touching, conventional musical obviously wasn't working, the wrong star notwithstanding. What is most curious, in retrospect, about *Miss Moffat* is that anyone involved could ever have imagined that, given her stage record, Davis would carry on with a year's tour and an extended Broadway engagement. Interested buffs and camp followers rushed to Philadelphia, well aware of something the show's creators didn't seem to know: Bette Davis as *Miss Moffat* was never going to make it to Broadway.

One of Broadway's most popular and awarded actresses, Julie Harris was the best thing in her one and only musical, **Skyscraper** (Lunt-Fontanne; Nov. 13, '65; 248), based on Elmer Rice's 1945 play, *Dream Girl*. Betty Field had created the lead in the original production of *Dream Girl*; Lucille Ball, as mentioned, had done the national tour; and Judy Holliday starred in a New York City Center revival. *Dream Girl* was first to be musicalized for Nanette Fabray. Rodgers and Hammerstein became

IN TIMES LIKE THESE

PAULA STONE and MIKE SLOAN present

EDDIE FOY · GRETCHEN WYLER · STEPHEN DOUGLASS

In the Musical Comedy

RUMPLE

Lyrics by **FRANK REARDON** · Music by **ERNEST G. SCHWEIKERT**

Book by **IRVING PHILLIPS**

Production Directed by

JACK DONOHUE

Rumple made it to Broadway but is utterly forgotten. Bette Davis as Miss Moffat only played Philadelphia, but it's notorious.

interested in the property, then producers Feuer and Martin announced that Cy Coleman and Carolyn Leigh would write the score for a *Dream Girl* musical to star Carol Channing. It was ultimately written by Peter Stone, with a score by James Van Heusen and lyrics by Sammy Cahn. Feuer and Martin produced *Skyscraper* simultaneously with another show, *Walking Happy*, that opened the following fall. Both were directed by Feuer and had Cahn–Van Heusen scores.

Harris played Georgina Allerton, a daydreamer reluctant to sell her brownstone to a contractor who wants to put a skyscraper in its place. While in Detroit, the show was heavily rewritten and began to resemble Rice's play less and less. Leading man Victor Spinetti was replaced by Charles Nelson Reilly, thus beginning Reilly's long friendship with Harris which later saw him directing her in play after play.

The show postponed its Broadway opening to preview three weeks in New York, during which time *Journal American* columnist Dorothy Kilgallen caused a furor when she attended a preview and, breaking an unwritten rule, commented negatively upon the show in her column. After much additional work, however, *Skyscraper* opened to generally good reviews, with most of the praise going to Harris and to Michael Kidd's reliably expert musical staging.

But *Skyscraper* qualifies as one of the weakest shows ever to receive favorable reviews. Georgina's daydreaming in the musical was no longer used organically; there was no connection between the main story— whether or not Georgina would give up her home—and her flights of fancy. The final version of *Skyscraper* borrowed only the heroine's name and the idea of her daydreaming from Rice's play, and the daydreaming was now just a gimmick to pad out a thin evening.

The songs were too obviously aimed at the hit parade, with an often dim connection to the characters singing them, and Cahn's lyrics were actively annoying. *Skyscraper* was a charmless, clunky contemporary musical, one of numerous losers of the sixties set in present-day New York (*How Now, Dow Jones, Bajour, Breakfast at Tiffany's, Subways Are for Sleeping, The Fig Leaves Are Falling*). The show relied on tributes to such New York institutions as the Gaiety Delicatessen, the New York Film Festival, and construction workers to camouflage its dull love story and silly plot. Perhaps Kilgallen, who died just before *Skyscraper* opened, helped the show: her prediction of doom may have led critics to expect the worst, which *Skyscraper* was not. *Skyscraper* survived for eight months and was

o o o o o

nominated for the Best Musical Tony against *Sweet Charity*, *Mame*, and *Man of La Mancha*. *La Mancha*—not *Skyscraper*—was the winner.

One-shot musical star Maureen O'Hara had a singing voice superior to that of Ball, Davis, or Harris, but her vehicle was no better. For her Broadway debut after a successful career in films, O'Hara chose **Christine** (46th Street; Apr. 28, '60; 12), throwing in her lot with the same producers that had mounted *The Vamp* for Carol Channing. Sammy Fain wrote his penultimate flop score for the show, and the book was coauthored by Pearl S. Buck and Charles K. Peck, Jr., Buck qualifying as the only Nobel Prize winner ever to write the libretto for a Broadway musical.

Christine, based on Hilda Wernher's novel *My Indian Family*, was about an Englishwoman who arrives in India to discover that her daughter, married to a native doctor, has died in childbirth. Christine blames India for the tragedy but is gradually drawn to her daughter's husband.

When the tryout began, Buck announced to the press that she barely knew her alleged coauthor and insisted that Peck's name be removed from the credits. It emerged that Peck had written an outline and treatment which Buck claimed she never used. After the Philadelphia reviews, however, Peck was called back to rewrite Buck. Cy Feuer replaced director Jerome Chodorov, but neither wanted credit and the show's Broadway Playbill listed no director at all. To make O'Hara more comfortable, Christine was transformed from English to Irish during the tryout.

Christine was an overt rip-off of *The King and I*. There was again a lovely widow from the United Kingdom who arrives in an exotic locale, the conflict of Eastern and Western cultures, a young female thwarted in love, and cute children who charm the heroine. The dialogue was stilted, and the audience was told rather than shown that Christine and Dr. Rashid had fallen in love. An unconvincing floperetta, *Christine* had several pretty tunes, especially the lovely duet for Christine and Rashid, "My Little Lost Girl." What *Whoop-Up* had done for the actress named Asia, *Christine* did for its lead dancer, Bhaskar, who walked away with the reviews.

Christine's original director, Chodorov, wrote the book for **I Had a Ball** (Martin Beck; Dec. 12, '64; 199), about a matchmaking Coney Island fortune-teller named Garside, and nightclub comedian Buddy Hackett was persuaded to make his sole musical appearance in the lead. The show was the idea of its producer, Joseph Kipness, and featured a score by

○ ○ ○ ○ ○

Jack Lawrence and Stan Freeman; Lawrence had already cowritten the score for the unsuccessful *Courtin' Time*, and Freeman would later coauthor the score for the flop *Lovely Ladies, Kind Gentlemen*. Lloyd Richards, later dean of the Yale School of Drama, artistic director of Yale Repertory Theatre, and director of the plays of August Wilson, was hired to direct Hackett but was replaced in Detroit by John Allen after a dispute with Kipness. Richards, who would direct one more musical flop the following year—*The Yearling*—retained program credit.

I Had a Ball's Detroit reception was highly encouraging, with Variety informing its readers that the show "seems destined to give everyone a ball who sees it in the coming years on the stage and in films." But the New York critics, who praised Onna White's dances and leads Hackett, Richard Kiley, Karen Morrow, and Luba Lisa, were far more divided. The undisciplined Hackett soon began to fool around onstage; after two months, he inserted a ten-minute stand-up routine into the first scene (after which he told the audience "Now I gotta go 'n' act") and offered another lengthy monologue at the curtain call.

I Had a Ball harked back to the vehicles built around clowns like Bert Lahr and Ed Wynn, as well as to such for-laughs-only forties musicals as *Follow the Girls* and *Are You With It?* The show's absurd plot was nothing more than an excuse for jokes and numbers, and its often enjoyable score was only lightly integrated into the story. *Ball* could easily have opened twenty-five or thirty years earlier and not been out of place.

While his son David was playing Dorothy Loudon's son in *The Fig Leaves Are Falling*, Jack Cassidy was playing opposite his wife, Shirley Jones, in her one Broadway musical lead, in **Maggie Flynn** (ANTA; Oct. 23, '68; 82). Based on fact, it was set in Lower Manhattan in 1863 during draft protests and told of an Irish woman (Jones) running an orphanage for the children of runaway slaves. Maggie, about to wed a colonel, is once again drawn to the ne'er-do-well husband (Cassidy) she believed dead.

Maggie Flynn had book, music, and lyrics by Hugo Peretti, Luigi Creatore, and George David Weiss. The first two were pop record producer–writers, while Weiss seemed to like doing things in threes, having already been one of three composers of both *Mr. Wonderful* and *First Impressions*. The show's director, Morton Da Costa, helped out with the book.

There was more than a hint of *The Sound of Music* in *Maggie Flynn*. Maggie, surrounded by cute children in a time of local unrest, was not unlike the indomitable Maria Von Trapp, and the "Thank You Song" was a blatant imitation of "Do Re Mi." While well-tailored to its stars (both of whom, however, missed performances frequently), the show was relentlessly mediocre, and its plotting was heavy-handed. There was also something cheap about the show's attempt at contemporary relevance; it seemed to be exploiting its Civil War period in order to raise parallel contemporary issues (the Vietnam War, draft protests) that it could then drop for the next pretty ditty. The score was the most pleasant thing about this unwieldy stew. Peretti, Creatore, and Weiss later collaborated on a musical called *Comedy*, which closed in Boston in 1972.

Broadway also has its two-shot musical stars. Lauren Bacall appeared in only two new musicals, but both had long runs and won her Tonys. Opera star Cesare Siepi, on the other hand, was a double loser. In 1963, bass-baritone Siepi, famous for his Don Giovanni, played another Giovanni, one whose little restaurant in Rome is threatened by competition from the new restaurant next door, Uriti, one of a chain that undersells in mass quantities. The show was **Bravo Giovanni** (Broadhurst; May 19, '63; 76), based on a novel by Howard Shaw called *The Crime of Giovanni Venturi* and directed by Stanley Prager. Prager directed four musicals (*Let It Ride* earlier, *Minnie's Boys* and 70, *Girls,* 70 later), all flops.

The main problem of *Bravo Giovanni* was obvious: its plot was extremely farfetched. Would Giovanni and his cohorts really have been able to dig a tunnel between the two restaurants and contrive a system to steal food from Uriti without anyone discovering it until the final curtain? Then, too, the romantic relationship between Giovanni and Miranda (Michele Lee) consisted of a series of artificial conflicts designed to keep them apart until the end. Giovanni kept saying that he was too old for Miranda, but the fortyish Siepi was still dashing; there was really nothing standing in the way of the romance except the contrivances of the libretto. Siepi wasn't ideally cast here, too attractive and self-assured to be convincing as a little man fighting big business. But *Giovanni* had its charms, especially Siepi's singing of some lovely songs by Milton Schafer and Ronny Graham ("Rome," "If I Were the Man"), Carol Haney's staging of an Act Two kitchen ballet, and Maria Karnilova's demonstration of a dance craze called the Kangaroo to the exhausted companions who are entertaining her so Giovanni can complete his tunnel. Karnilova's husband, George S. Irving, was saddled with his usual complement of cheesy, embarrassing songs ("Uriti," "Virtue Arrivederci") that could only come from a flop musical.

○ ○ ○ ○ ○

As *Hazel Flagg* had done some years earlier, *Bravo Giovanni* suspended performances for the summer; it reopened after Labor Day and closed for good a week later, losing $550,000, one of the costliest flops of its period. Two weeks before *Giovanni* opened, another musical set in Rome—ancient Rome this time—opened on Broadway. When the Tony nominations came out the following spring, Stephen Sondheim's superbly inventive score for *A Funny Thing Happened on the Way to the Forum* was not nominated, but *Bravo Giovanni's* was.

Siepi returned to Broadway during the 1978–79 Broadway season, one rich in big-scale flop musicals. The show was **Carmelina** (St. James; Apr. 8, '79; 17), and this time Siepi was involved with a more illustrious creative team. The score was by Burton Lane and Alan Jay Lerner, who had already collaborated on film scores for *Royal Wedding* and *Huckleberry Finn* (the latter unproduced) and the Broadway musical *On a Clear Day You Can See Forever*. The book was begun by Lerner, but when he hit a snag he asked Joseph Stein to join him. *Carmelina* was to be one of several flops (*Lolita, My Love, 1600 Pennsylvania Avenue, Dance a Little Closer*) with which Lerner closed his career. If *Carmelina* was less ambitious, lighter, and more overtly commercial than the other late Lerner flops, it was no more successful.

Lerner, Stein, and Lane later denied that their musical was based on the 1968 movie *Buona Sera, Mrs. Campbell*, in which Gina Lollobrigida played an Italian woman who for seventeen years has pretended to be the widow of a fictional American war hero, Lieutenant Eddie Campbell. Impregnated by one of three American soldiers who romanced her during wartime, Lollobrigida has been collecting monthly checks from all three ever since, in order to give her daughter a better life. When the soldiers return to the little town of San Fiorino, Italy, for a reunion, the heroine is confronted with her deception. *Carmelina's* creators claimed they read about the real-life Mrs. Campbell and began writing their show unaware that a movie was also being made about the same story. But while the musical's credits never mentioned the movie, *Carmelina*, if less farcical and more focused on the heroine and her daughter than the film, was quite obviously based on *Buona Sera, Mrs. Campbell*.

Georgia Brown, who has had nothing but Broadway flops since her debut in *Oliver!*, played the title role, and Jose Ferrer directed his third and final flop musical. Lerner and Lane had not gotten along on *Clear Day*; this time around, almost no one got along.

Siepi had an even weaker role than he had in *Bravo Giovanni*, spending the entire evening pining for and chasing after Carmelina. The show

○ ○ ○ ○ ○

underwent almost no change during its two tryout engagements and promptly closed on Broadway at a loss of over $1 million. A recording was made after the show closed, but Siepi declined to appear on it; his part was taken by Paul Sorvino.

If one reads the script and plays the album of *Carmelina* today, one might think that *Carmelina* was a better show than it appeared to be at the St. James in 1979. The show had its share of textual problems: the one-joke story, sufficient for a mildly enjoyable film, was too skimpy for a major musical, and the romantic comedy suggested by the opening number was slighted in favor of sitcom plotting. But the score was quite fine, Lerner's usual literate lyrics complementing Lane's elegant melodies beautifully. Siepi's opening number, "It's Time for a Love Song," Brown's "Why Him?," and the nostalgic trio "One More Walk around the Garden" for Carmelina's soldiers were all strong, but "Someone in April" (its melody written for *Clear Day*) was outstanding, relating all the necessary exposition and setting up the rest of the story with great skill. *Carmelina's* real problem was its production: on an unattractive set by Oliver Smith, Ferrer staged a lifeless production that never provided the invention that might have disguised the thinness of the plot. Done in by its uninspired staging, *Carmelina*—which might have been more warmly received in the fifties or sixties but was decidedly out of place by the late seventies—was a competently written show.

Unlike Siepi, our second two-shot star, Alexis Smith, scored a triumph in her first Broadway musical outing, *Follies*, winning raves even from the critics who disliked the show. She returned to Broadway during the same season as *Carmelina*, playing Lila Halliday, forties movie-musical star, now reduced to touring in *Dolly!* and *Mame*, in the musical **Platinum** (Mark Hellinger, Nov. 12, '78, 33). Lila, attempting a comeback in a recording studio, meets declining rock star Dan Danger, who writes her a hit song and with whom she begins a relationship.

Platinum began life in Buffalo under the title *Sunset*, with Smith starring, direction by Tommy Tune, a score by Will Holt and Gary William Friedman, and a book by Louis LaRusso II. For Broadway, only the songwriters were retained; Joe Layton directed and choreographed, and the new book was by Will Holt and Bruce Vilanch. Paramount Pictures supplied part of the financing and allowed the show to rehearse on one of its old soundstages. As in *Follies*, Smith received raves, but the show closed after a month's run at a loss of $1.743 million. A revised version, reverting to the title *Sunset* and starring Tammy Grimes, opened off-Broadway at the Village Gate in 1983. Managing to destroy anything that was good about *Platinum*, the new *Sunset* closed in one night.

Indeed, there was some gold in *Platinum*. Its basic concept of a clash of generations and styles—rock versus forties swing, crass versus class—was an intriguing one that was never fully exploited. An unconventional show, *Platinum* nevertheless failed to live up to its stunning opening, in which Lila, standing in a recording studio where her old soundstage used to be, drifted from the song she was trying to record into a personal statement of what it took to be a movie star "back when" in the number "Nothing But." But there was a pervading implausibility to the events of *Platinum*'s book, and the show tended to make forties nostalgia far more attractive than seventies heavy-metal rock. Smith was ideally cast and excellent, but she was not a big enough draw to carry the show; the failure of *Platinum* meant that producers stopped searching for musical vehicles for her. The action of *Platinum* had eerie parallels to Smith's own plight; in between and after her two Broadway musicals, Smith, just like Lila Halliday, took to touring in stock.

Like Channing, Fabray, Grey, Loudon, and most of the others in this chapter, Smith was more than willing—and able—to set an audience on its ear. But where were the shows? The changing economics of Broadway in the last three decades means that performers have to look to film and television if they wish to work with any regularity. There simply are not enough musicals produced anymore to maintain a career like Martin's or Merman's, a continuous career as a Broadway musical star. It is unlikely that the next forty seasons on Broadway will see that many new Broadway musical star flops; nowadays, there are more opportunities to flop out in Hollywood.

Three

MAJOR WRITERS

"[G]reenwillow] makes Glocca Morra look like a teeming slum . . . it is barely credible that this simple-minded extravaganza is the work of the man who created *Guys and Dolls*."—Kenneth Tynan, *The New Yorker*, on *Greenwillow*

"As we all should probably have learned by now, to be a Stephen Sondheim fan is to have one's heart broken at regular intervals . . . Mr. Sondheim has given this evening a half-dozen songs that are crushing and beautiful—that soar and linger and hurt. But the show that contains them is a shambles."—Frank Rich, *The New York Times*, on *Merrily We Roll Along*

William Johnson, Judy Tyler, and Helen Traubel in Pipe Dream *(above)*

As we have seen, star flops may be remembered chiefly because of who was billed above the title, but they do not, for the most part, fail because of that headliner. The flops in this section, while they may have involved big-name stars and directors, tend to be remembered for one or more of their writers. Many of these writers were, at least as far as the credits go, concerned only with the show's score. Others had a hand in both score and book, a few also directed, and one wrote only the book.

Were these writers entirely to blame for the failures of their shows? Surely they must be more culpable than the stars of the previous chapter, who, with the exception of Newley, had little control over the quality of their material. It is already apparent that the score is seldom the main cause of a show's failure, so the writers in this chapter who are credited only with the show's score may appear to be less guilty than those who also wrote the book or directed. But musical theatre is one of the most collaborative of art forms, and even if one is listed only as the composer of the highly acclaimed music of a show which is otherwise condemned, one must share in the responsibility for the show's failure. Every member of a show's team, be it the librettist, lyricist, composer, director, or designer, cannot help but be involved in every element of the show. If asked why the shows in this chapter flopped, many of their writers would blame an actor, a director, even a designer, rather than take responsibility upon themselves. Whose fault was it anyway?

By the 1950s, Richard Rodgers and his partner, Oscar Hammerstein II, had not only revolutionized musical theatre in terms of the integration of book, score, and dance but had also created expectations for each new project they announced that were not easy to live up to. If the controversial *Allegro* (1947) and the disappointing *Me and Juliet* (1953) were not as universally satisfying as *Oklahoma!*, *Carousel*, *South Pacific*, and *The King and I*, Rodgers and Hammerstein had never had a show that didn't run over three hundred performances, show a profit, and tour after Broadway. Not until 1955, that is, and **Pipe Dream** (Shubert; Nov. 30, '55; 246).

It began when Feuer and Martin purchased the musical rights to John Steinbeck's 1945 novel, *Cannery Row*, and asked Steinbeck to write the book, Frank Loesser to write the score, and Henry Fonda and Julie Andrews to star. As Steinbeck struggled with the libretto, he worked on a new novel, eventually called *Sweet Thursday*, using the same characters and setting as *Cannery Row*. Changing their minds, Feuer and Martin decided to use the new book as the basis for their musical, but after a year, they

○ ○ ○ ○ ○

turned the whole thing over to Rodgers and Hammerstein, who had decided to adapt *Sweet Thursday* and produce the show themselves. Rodgers and Hammerstein supplied the entire $250,000 cost, and Feuer and Martin were promised twenty percent of the ultimately nonexistent profits. Russell Nype and then David Wayne were announced for the role of Doc, who experiments in his biological lab in Monterey, California, without benefit of an MD certificate, but the part went to William Johnson, playing Alfred Drake's *Kismet* role on Broadway at the time of his hiring. For the part of the tough, insecure drifter, Suzy, to whom Doc is drawn, Rodgers and Hammerstein chose Judy Tyler, best known as Princess Summer-Fall-Winter-Spring on the "Howdy Doody" television show. And as Metropolitan Opera star Ezio Pinza had done wonders for *South Pacific*, Rodgers & Hammerstein hired Helen Traubel, the Wagnerian diva who had left the Met for television, films, and nightclubs, to play Fauna, the owner of the local bordello. Harold Clurman, who had never staged a musical before, took on the direction. While working on *Pipe Dream*, Rodgers was operated on for cancer, and he was still in discomfort throughout the tryout and Broadway run.

The reviews in Boston were favorable if subdued. Two songs, "The Happiest House on the Block" and "How Long?," were written on the road. When Clurman faltered, Hammerstein stepped in, and Joshua Logan did some doctoring as well. *Pipe Dream* arrived in New York with the largest advance sale in Broadway history, $1.2 million. Perhaps indicating some doubts about their new show, Rodgers and Hammerstein had lifted their ban, in effect since 1946, on theatre parties, and *Pipe Dream* opened with more than seventy performances sold to groups. The New York critics were more divided than those in Boston, with Brooks Atkinson in the *Times* and two others moderately favorable, and Walter Kerr in the *Herald Tribune* and three others negative. Steinbeck predicted the show would become one of Rodgers and Hammerstein's "two-year flops," and the show underwent revision in late March, with several numbers shifted. Traubel missed a number of shows and withdrew when her contract expired three weeks before the show closed (she was succeeded by Nancy Andrews). *Pipe Dream* was nominated for the Best Musical Tony (it lost to the only other nominee, *Damn Yankees*) and eight other Tonys. But its run was the shortest of any Rodgers and Hammerstein show, it sustained a small loss on its investment, and there was no post-Broadway tour. An announcement that *Pipe Dream* would go into the Drury Lane Theatre in London (where *Oklahoma!*, *Carousel*, *South Pacific*, and *The King and I* had

○ ○ ○ ○ ○

Pipe Dream: *The Rodgers and Hammerstein score was strong, but there were problems.*

played) in the fall appeared to be wishful thinking. Two strange postscripts to the *Pipe Dreams* saga: within a year of its closing, William Johnson died of a heart attack, and Judy Tyler was killed in an automobile accident, and many years later, a film version was proposed, then shelved—it was to have starred the Muppets.

Pipe Dream contains a generally fascinating score. There's a gorgeous ballad of yearning for Suzy, "Everybody's Got a Home but Me"; Doc's opening statement of the show's theme, "All Kinds of People"; the flat-out hit ballad "All at Once You Love Her"; a rueful duet for the no-longer-dewy-eyed lovers, "The Next Time It Happens"; the unconventionally structured "Suzy Is a Good Thing," "A Lopsided Bus," and "Bum's Opera"; and other good songs like "The Man I Used to Be" for Doc and "Sweet Thursday" for Fauna.

The show's problem was clearly not its score. So what were the problems? First, there was the matter of audience expectation. *Pipe Dream* was a quiet, relatively uneventful show by a team from which the public had come to expect the serious, the monumental, the deeply moving. Then, there was the question of sex: Steinbeck believed that one of the show's problems was that the character of Suzy was cleaned up and no longer specifically a prostitute before her arrival on Cannery Row and at Fauna's Bear Flag Cafe. Rodgers and Hammerstein may have been uncomfortable with handling sex openly; it's never made clear whether Suzy is a hooker or not, and the other denizens of the neighborhood have also been sanitized. For once in their careers, the celebrated team may have been playing it safe.

But the biggest problem with the show was not the character of Suzy, or even Traubel, whom many, including Rodgers, blamed for its failure. Rodgers and Hammerstein were aware that the characters of this story were unlike those they had dealt with in their recent shows. In a Sunday advance piece they wrote for the *Herald Tribune*, they said of the show's characters: "They stimulate us because we haven't met them before in our work. Their problems are simple . . . We find pleasure that their worries, this time, are not concerned with the future of a kingdom or with miscegenation . . . Just like other beasts, we need desperately to have change in our lives." But the team was best when they had something to say, as in *The King and I, South Pacific*, and *Carousel*; except for the idea that "It takes all kinds of people to make up a world," *Pipe Dream* had little substance. While the characters had charm, they were never especially interesting, and the story was devoid of conflict and suspense. Laya-

○ ○ ○ ○ ○

bouts—people who don't really do anything—are not the stuff of drama, it would seem. *Pipe Dream*'s failure can be attributed to the choice of material itself compounded by an overly tasteful treatment of potentially raffish characters.

After Hammerstein's death, Rodgers wrote the music for five more Broadway musicals. One, with his own lyrics, was a distinctive success (*No Strings*), one ran mainly because of its star (*Two by Two*), and the other three were flops. The most inexplicable was **Rex** (Lunt-Fontanne; Apr. 25, '76; 49), which was coproducer Richard Adler's idea. The book, originally to have been by Jerome Lawrence and Robert E. Lee, was instead written by Sherman Yellen, who wrote a much better one for the earlier *The Rothschilds*. For his lyricist, Rodgers chose one of the best, Sheldon Harnick. Edwin Sherin, whose principal musical-theatre credit was being fired from *Seesaw*, was hired to direct. Tempestuous British actor Nicol Williamson was cast as Henry VIII, Penny Fuller was to play both Anne Boleyn and Anne's daughter, Elizabeth, and an as yet unknown Glenn Close was chosen for Princess Mary.

During the show's second tryout engagement in Boston, Harold Prince, who had produced Adler's two hit musicals, *The Pajama Game* and *Damn Yankees*, and four of Harnick's shows, agreed to take over the direction, although Sherin stayed on and Prince was not credited. *Rex* opened to a unanimously negative New York press, and its run of six weeks was the shortest of Rodgers' career. *Rex* was momentarily awakened on May 13 when during curtain calls, Williamson—who had not endeared himself to either the cast or the creative team—slapped dancer Jim Litten in front of a shocked audience. Litten had said, "That's a wrap" during the bows, but Williamson seems to have heard it as "That was crap."

Rex raised a question that was never answered: what made Adler, Rodgers, and Harnick think Henry VIII a good subject for a musical? While Henry was indeed a fascinating figure, how does one make sympathetic a man who kills his wives because they give birth to daughters rather than sons? Henry's reason for insisting on a son for the throne (a woman there would provoke chaos and civil war) was not made believable, and his sexism was particularly unpleasant for a seventies audience well into the women's movement. While the material would have benefited from a darker treatment than it received, it is doubtful that it could ever have worked: Henry, who by that time had been amply covered on stage, screen, and public television, should have been left alone.

○ ○ ○ ○ ○

Nicol Williamson, before he started acting up, looks over Richard Rodgers' shoulder as Rodgers plays a tune from his penultimate score, Rex.

Rex had other problems in addition to its fundamental one. First, it was of necessity episodic: one wife replaced another—Henry went through two during the intermission—and there was no way to develop each one. Second, the book was literate but heavy, the only humor being the unfunny bawdy jokes given to the court jester. And third, it only caught dramatic fire in the second-act confrontation between Henry and Elizabeth.

Again, Rodgers provided very attractive music. "No Song More Pleasing" (the last of many great Rodgers waltzes) and "Elizabeth" for court minstrel Smeton, "Away from You" for Henry, "As Once I Loved You" for Catherine, and "Time" for Elizabeth were all strong, with Harnick contributing simpler lyrics than was his wont.

When the disastrous movie-musical *Lost Horizon* was released, Bette Midler told a reporter that she intended to see it anyway, quipping, "I never miss a Liv Ullmann musical." Midler couldn't have known then that six years later the solemn film star would be starring in her very own Broadway musical, a show that would be Rodgers' last. Rodgers and Hammerstein had produced John Van Druten's play *I Remember Mama*, based on stories by Kathryn Forbes, on Broadway in 1944. It told of the Hansens, struggling Norwegian immigrants in San Francisco in the early twentieth century, and in particular of Mama—who pretends to her children that she has a bank account to give them a sense of security— and her eldest daughter, Katrin, an aspiring writer. *Mama* worked beautifully on stage, on film in 1946, and as a TV series from 1949 to 1956. In 1956, Rodgers and Hammerstein contemplated turning the play into a musical, to star Charlotte Greenwood and Shirley Jones, but stopped because of the property's recent exposure. (It did become a musical, called *Mama*, at the Studio Arena Theatre in Buffalo in 1972, written by John Clifton and Neal Du Brock and with Celeste Holm in the title role.)

But by 1979, Rodgers, seventy-six and seriously ill, responded when Martin Charnin suggested *I Remember Mama* to him again. By this time, Charnin had had his one big hit, *Annie*, so producer Alexander H. Cohen put *Annie's* book writer (Thomas Meehan), director–lyricist (Charnin), and set designer (David Mitchell) together with Rodgers and Ullmann, who had worked for Cohen in a revival of *Anna Christie*. It took 323 investors to come up with the necessary $1.25 million, half of which was supplied by Universal Pictures, which had recently dropped $700,000 when the musical *Alice* closed in Philadelphia the year before.

○ ○ ○ ○ ○

In contrast to *Rex*, **I Remember Mama** (Majestic; May 31, '79; 108) had one of the stormiest tryout/New York preview periods ever. The day after poor reviews appeared in Philadelphia, Charnin was fired; Cy Feuer assumed control within a week. After his dismissal, Charnin sent a telegram to his three *Annie* companies, stating, "As you may or may not know, artistic differences have been responsible for my stepping aside as director of *I Remember Mama*. Ms. Ullmann and I do not see 'I to I' about how musicals are made. To make a long and ugly story short, there's no longer a fjord in my future." Charnin later added that he was let go because of his desire to replace Ullmann: "Singing frightened her, and she couldn't memorize her lines . . . It was my idea to ask Liv Ullmann. However, where I had thought of it as an ensemble piece, she thought of it as a vehicle for her." There were also rumors of a romance between Ullmann and Charnin.

Many musical-theatre fans are capable of coming up with the first six names in the answer to the trivia question, "Who were Richard Rodgers' seven lyricists?": Lorenz Hart, Oscar Hammerstein II, Rodgers himself, Stephen Sondheim, Martin Charnin, and Sheldon Harnick. They may be pardoned for stumbling over the last name: Raymond Jessel. As Charnin was fired as director, he was obviously not going to be around to write new lyrics, so Jessel, whose only other credit was producer Cohen's earlier musical *Baker Street*, was brought in to write the lyrics for five new songs.

In Philadelphia, there were two Katrins: an older one looking back and narrating (Kate Dezina) and a younger one appearing in the scenes (Kristin Vigard). Dezina was dismissed, the two roles were combined for Maureen Silliman, and a new part was created for Vigard. Justine Johnston, who was playing authoress Florence Dana Moorhead, was replaced by Myvanwy Jenn, now playing authoress Dame Sybil Fitzgibbons.

The Shuberts pushed Michael Bennett's *Ballroom* to an early death to bring the ailing *I Remember Mama* into the Majestic Theatre. The show played forty previews, postponing its opening twice. In New York, Graciela Daniele was succeeded as choreographer by Danny Daniels, one more child was replaced, the role of Mama's boarder, Mr. Hyde, was cut, and more songs came and went. *Mama* opened to only one good review (Clive Barnes in the *New York Post*) but stayed open, at a loss, until Labor Day. Although the show's postponements had rendered it ineligible for the 1979 Tony Awards, Cohen, then producer of the Tony telecast, managed to get a number from *Mama* on the show by presenting Rodgers with a special award. An unintentionally comic television commercial, in

○ ○ ○ ○ ○

which Ullmann told viewers that as a child in Norway she had fallen in love with the music of Rodgers and was now fulfilling her dream of singing his music on Broadway, ran frequently. When Charnin suffered a severe heart attack in June and attributed it to his *Mama* firing, Ullmann fired back with, "I hope that Martin Charnin will start doing something more constructive than blaming his failures and illnesses on other people." The show lost $1.5 million and was not recorded until five years later, with only George Hearn and George S. Irving of the original cast appearing on the album.

The idea of a musical *Mama* seemed like a sound one, but a closer examination of the original play proves otherwise. The play was episodic, with several plots but no overall dramatic through-line. In order to provide one, Meehan made the musical's plot hinge on Papa's inability to find work and his decision, at the end of the first act, to leave the family and take up a shipyard job in Norway. A severe mistake, this served to make the kindly father into a villain and slighted the relationship between Mama and Katrin, the play's most touching aspect.

Ullmann was also a problem. She had lovely moments but was not fully at ease as a musical leading lady, coming to life only in the "Fair Trade" number with Dame Sybil where mama offers her prized recipes in exchange for the authoress's opinion of Katrin's stories. *Mama* might have worked better in the sixties with Mary Martin or Inga Swenson heading the cast, and Florence Henderson was briefly considered as a replacement for Ullmann.

Rodgers' score contained only traces of the musical theatre's greatest melodist: best were "A Writer Writes at Night"; Papa's expression of love for his wife, "You Couldn't Please Me More"; and "When?," the latter cut on the road but restored on the recording and in the acting edition. As Uncle Chris, George S. Irving once again had his usual "I am in a flop" numbers—even the song *about* him was a dud—and David Mitchell's lovely sets were the biggest asset. Rodgers lived only four months after *Mama's* closing.

Owing to his own ill health and changes in the musical theatre, Cole Porter's career had flagged by the mid-forties, when Rodgers and Hammerstein were dominating Broadway. Porter's career was revived by his greatest hit, *Kiss Me, Kate*, in 1948. Porter wrote three more shows after *Kate*; the final two (*Can-Can, Silk Stockings*) were successful, but the one that followed *Kate* was not.

○ ○ ○ ○ ○

Out of This World (New Century; Dec. 21, '50; 157) was based on the Amphitryon legend, in which the god Jupiter assumes the form of the mortal general Amphitryon in order to spend the night with the general's wife. It had already served as the basis for the Alfred Lunt–Lynn Fontanne vehicle *Amphitryon '38*, by Jean Giradoux as adapted by S. N. Behrman. The book for the Porter musical was first written by Dwight Taylor, who had done Porter's *Gay Divorce*, but Porter, not happy with it, asked Betty Comden and Adolph Green to write a new one. Theirs went unused, Reginald Lawrence reworked Taylor's material, and Lawrence and Taylor shared the credit. Agnes de Mille was hired to direct, but not to choreograph (Hanya Holm was choreographer), and *Kate*'s producers, Lemuel Ayers and Saint Subber, also presented *Out of This World*, with Ayers, who had designed *Kate*'s stunning sets, doing equally dazzling work here. For the star part of Juno, Jupiter's jealous wife, Carol Channing was first choice (she turned it down to do *Gentlemen Prefer Blondes*), followed by Judy Holliday, Hermione Gingold, and Martha Raye. Finally, the role went to veteran actress Charlotte Greenwood, who hadn't been seen on Broadway since 1927.

Early in the first tryout stop, Philadelphia, de Mille was replaced by George Abbott, who received only an acknowledgment in the back of the Playbill. Abbott brought in F. Hugh Herbert for further book doctoring; star Greenwood was not happy with Abbott or Herbert. Abbott cut what would prove to be the show's most famous song, "From This Moment On," probably because the show's leading man, William Eythe, was not much of a singer.

In Boston, the local censors forced certain risqué material to be dropped (Porter's dirty lyrics had Mercury singing about "Pandora, who let me open her box"). Then, Eythe was arrested in a subway men's room having sex with another man just before the opening in New York and only got to appear at the opening through payoffs.

Out of This World forced *Kate* to move from the New Century to the Shubert. The critics raved over the physical production but found the book creaky and sex-obsessed. William Hawkins in the *World-Telegram & Sun* noted that "the male dancing chorus is almost as unhampered by raiment as the customers in a steam bath." While it only lasted five months on Broadway, *Out of This World* had a life afterward. It was revived off-Broadway at the Actors' Playhouse in 1955, then presented by Equity Library Theatre twice, the second time with a new book by George Oppenheimer. In 1978, it got another new book, by Lawrence Kasha

○ ○ ○ ○ ○

Above, Lemuel Ayers' dazzling design for the finale of Cole Porter's Out of this World. Pictured on the Playbill cover below are Sydney Chaplin and Carol Lawrence, both of whom would like to have gotten out of Jule Styne's Subways Are for Sleeping.

and David S. Landay, and was called *Heaven Sent* when Charlotte Rae, then Jo Anne Worley, starred in it in California. In 1982, it was announced that Howard Ashman was writing yet another new book, but none ever materialized.

It would appear to be evident, then, that *Out of This World* suffered from book trouble. Porter himself said, "The book was bad. The scenery was so spectacularly great that the audience looked at it and neither heard nor saw the performers." But the problem was more complex: the show's book was a standard, thirties-style farce, competent but old hat, and by this time audiences had experienced the Rodgers and Hammerstein shows and Porter's own *Kate*. *Out of This World's* libretto, which might have gotten by ten years earlier, no longer sufficed. What made writers in the seventies and eighties want to create new books for the show was Porter's score, which is glorious; rarely has there been such a discrepancy in quality between a show's script and its songs. Ranking with Porter's best, but underrated by the first-night critics, *Out of This World's* score includes such delights as "Use Your Imagination," "I Am Loved," "Where, Oh, Where," "No Lover for Me," and "Nobody's Chasing Me." One might assume from playing the cast recording that the show was heavenly, but audiences at the time found it a distinct letdown after the fresher, more sophisticated *Kate*.

Frank Loesser wrote the scores for six book musicals, four of which, *Where's Charley?*, *Guys and Dolls*, *The Most Happy Fella*, and *How to Succeed in Business without Really Trying*, were major hits and demonstrated Loesser's astonishing versatility. Loesser had two flops, however, one before and one after *How to Succeed*, and for these he must take greater responsibility than Rodgers or Porter should for theirs: he was colibrettist for both.

Greenwillow (Alvin; Mar. 8, '60; 97), based on B.J. Chute's novel, took place in a mythical village, a place of superstition and quaint ritual in which residents used words like " 'tis" and " 'twould." The Briggs family has long been afflicted by a devil's spell that causes the eldest son of each generation to heed a call to wander. Young Gideon resolves to end the curse by not marrying or fathering children. And for comic relief, there are two contrasting reverends, one lean and severe, the other round, sweet, and forgiving; and Gideon's Gramma, who spends much of the evening attempting to get back a cow from the man she once almost married.

It was a show of firsts: Anthony Perkins made his musical theatre debut

○ ○ ○ ○ ○

as Gideon, and to accommodate the star, George Roy Hill, who had directed Perkins in *Look Homeward, Angel*, was hired to direct his first musical. Though Loesser began work on the show alone (after it was turned down by Lerner and Loewe, perhaps because of similarities to *Brigadoon*), he was later joined by Lesser Samuels, a screenwriter making his stage debut. *Greenwillow* was also to be Loesser's first flop.

On the strength of the Loesser and Perkins names, the financing was raised in three weeks, and things proceeded smoothly except for the replacement in Philadelphia of the original leading lady, Zeme North, by Ellen McCown. When *Greenwillow* opened at the Alvin Theater (forcing *Once Upon a Mattress* out of the first of its four Broadway houses), the critics, all of whom loved Perkins, were evenly divided on the show. Brooks Atkinson was enthusiastic, but *Greenwillow* is another show that demonstrates that a strong *Times* review can't always save a show. Unlike the male members of the Briggs family, audiences had no trouble resisting the call of *Greenwillow*, which used up its advance sale in three months.

Loesser always tried something entirely different in each of his musicals, but perhaps this was material for which he was fundamentally unsuited. It's hard in retrospect to figure out what attracted the sharp, sophisticated Loesser to Chute's characters and setting. Unlike *Brigadoon* or *Finian's Rainbow*, *Greenwillow* lacked any sophisticated element: it was entirely too quaint and precious for its own good. The only subplot, that concerning the disputed cow, was feeble, and there was virtually no second act. The wind-up was most unconvincing: after worrying for two hours about when his call to wander will come, Gideon finally hears it. But this time, the voices call him to stay home, and he does, with sweetheart Dorrie. Loesser's score, however, is often gorgeous, and the original cast album of *Greenwillow* is a classic example of how misleading recordings of flop musicals can be. Listening to it, one finds it hard to believe that the whole show wasn't wonderful and forgets that the album preserves the only good thing about the show. The recording might lead one to want to revive the show, but *Greenwillow* is best left undone.

If Loesser had not chosen wisely with the material of *Greenwillow*, he made an even more curious choice when he approached Sam Spewack in 1965 about musicalizing a play Spewack had written called *Once There Was a Russian*, which had run one performance on Broadway four years earlier. But Spewack, who felt that the original play had failed because it was a big story reduced to one setting, agreed to open it up as a lavish

○ ○ ○ ○ ○

PLAYBILL

a weekly magazine for theatregoers

Alvin
Theatre

GREENWILLOW

ALLEN B. WHITEHEAD
IN ASSOCIATION WITH
FRANK PRODUCTIONS INC.
PRESENTS

pleasures
aNd palaces*
A NEW MUSICAL COMEDY

MUSIC AND LYRICS BY FRANK LOESSER
BOOK BY SAM SPEWACK AND FRANK LOESSER
BASED ON A PLAY BY SAM SPEWACK
DIRECTED AND CHOREOGRAPHED BY BOB FOSSE

STARRING ALFRED MARKS   PHYLLIS NEWMAN
HY HAZELL   JOHN McMARTIN

WITH LEON   MORT   ERIC   SAMMY   WOODY
      JANNEY   MARSHALL   BROTHERSON   SMITH   ROMOFF
              JOHN ANANIA   BARBARA SHARMA   MICHAEL QUINN

SCENERY & LIGHTING BY   COSTUMES BY   MUSICAL DIRECTOR   ORCHESTRATIONS BY
ROBERT RANDOLPH   FREDDY WITTOP   FRED WERNER   PHILIP J. LANG

ORIGINAL CAST ALBUM ON UNITED ARTISTS RECORDS

*"Mid pleasures and palaces though we may roam,
Be it ever so humble, there's no place like home.
OLD RUSSIAN PROVERB

Entire contents © 1965 by Frank Productions Inc.
All rights reserved.

The great Frank Loesser came to grief with Greenwillow *and* Pleasures and
Palaces. *Photo features Hy Hazell and Alfred Marks, the latter soon to be replaced
by Jack Cassidy, in* Pleasures and Palaces, *Loesser's last show.*

musical. Spewack and Loesser collaborated on the book for **Pleasures and Palaces** (Detroit, Mar. 11, '65, closed on the road), and they got Bob Fosse, who had taken over the musical staging from Hugh Lambert on Loesser's last show, *How to Succeed*, to direct and choreograph.

Set in Russia in 1780, *Pleasures and Palaces* tells of Potemkin's attempt to woo and wed Catherine the Great and rule through her. He is threatened when Catherine invites Admiral John Paul Jones to help the Russians in their war against the Turks. At the final curtain, Potemkin escapes to America, taking on the name Benedict Arnold and planning to capture Washington, then return and conquer Russia.

The show was a series of mistakes. First, it was clearly not a good idea to make a play that had been roundly panned a few seasons earlier the basis for a major Broadway musical. It is rarely workable to portray historic figures like Catherine the Great and Potemkin onstage, particularly when they receive the unfunny, cardboard treatment they got in *Pleasures and Palaces*. The part of Potemkin, which cried out for a Bert Lahr, was given to a rich-voiced but subdued British actor named Alfred Marks. Marks was replaced by Jack Cassidy; Cassidy was much better, but the critics had already covered the show. And the score was far from top drawer Loesser, with one beautiful song, "Truly Loved," later recycled in a London stage version of Loesser's film *Hans Christian Andersen*. About the only one who had any fun was Phyllis Newman as the much-married Countess Sura, a nymphomaniac who has just shot yet another husband when Potemkin meets and falls for her.

The Boston engagement and the scheduled May 10 opening at the Lunt-Fontanne Theatre were both cancelled, and the loss was $450,000. It was the second tryout closing for Hy Hazell, a highly amusing British performer, who was saddled with the thankless role of Catherine. When her biggest London success, *Lock Up Your Daughters*, had been imported a few years earlier, she had come with it, but it, too, shut down prior to New York. Hazell died a few years after *Pleasures and Palaces*, never having made it to Broadway.

If Rodgers and Loesser often initiated ideas for their musicals and were involved in every aspect of them, Jule Styne was more the old-school songwriter. While Styne always wrote music appropriate to the show at hand, he rarely conceived of or developed those shows. He just loved to write music and depended on collaborators like Comden and Green to come up with the ideas. Styne's work for the musical theatre reached

○ ○ ○ ○ ○

its peak with *Gypsy* in 1959; he was clearly inspired by collaborators Stephen Sondheim, Arthur Laurents, and Jerome Robbins to outdo himself, and he never again attained quite that level. There were other major hits before (*Gentlemen Prefer Blondes, Bells Are Ringing*) and after (*Funny Girl*) *Gypsy,* plus some borderline shows, not exactly flops but, for one reason or another, not hits either (*Say, Darling, Fade Out—Fade In, Hallelujah, Baby!*). And then there were the outright flops, the first of which was the Helen Gallagher vehicle, *Hazel Flagg.*

One show Styne did initiate is **Subways Are for Sleeping** (St. James; Dec. 27, '61; 205) when he bought the rights to a collection of ten stories by Edmund G. Love, based on real experiences but unconnected and essentially plotless. Styne brought the book to Comden and Green who, perhaps sensing that what Styne had purchased would require considerable invention to become the basis of a musical, only wanted to write the lyrics. When Ketti Frings, Arthur Laurents, and Abe Burrows all passed, Comden and Green agreed to do the book as well. It was the fourth collaboration between Styne, Comden, and Green, and yet another Comden and Green musical (*On the Town, Wonderful Town, Bells Are Ringing, Do Re Mi*) set in New York. David Merrick, who had produced the team's *Do Re Mi* the year before, took the project on and hired Michael Kidd to direct and choreograph. While the names Rosalind Russell, Phil Silvers, Ray Bolger, and Comden and Green themselves were all bandied about as possible casting, Sydney Chaplin, who had been in the team's *Bells Are Ringing* and would later do *Funny Girl* with Styne, was hired for the male lead. Carol Lawrence was given the female lead, and Phyllis Newman, married to Green, and Orson Bean were cast as the secondary comic pair.

Subways underwent a drastic rewrite during its first stop in Philadelphia. In the original version, Lawrence played Angie, personal secretary to the advertising whiz responsible for making E-Z Cola into an empire, who was preparing to marry her boss. Groggy from shots she's taken for her honeymoon trip, Angie wanders into the subway, where she encounters Tom Bailey (Chaplin), a dropout from society who helps others like himself find odd jobs and places to sleep. The rest of the original version involved Tom's falling for Angie and attempting to help her start a new life while preventing her fiancé from finding her. In the new version, Angie's fiancé is gone, and she is a staff writer for *Madame* magazine, working on a feature story about the well-dressed bums of Manhattan. She pretends to be a stranded out-of-towner to get her story, and when Tom finds out the truth, he is furious. At the end, Tom, reunited with

○ ○ ○ ○ ○

Angie, decides to write a book about his life as a drifter, to be called *Subways Are for Sleeping*.

An examination of the two versions reveals that the writers seriously weakened their project in revision. The first version was a satire of the rat race, reminiscent of Comden and Green's screenplay for *It's Always Fair Weather*. Angie was a part of the big-business world Tom was fleeing, and her escape from her fiancé dovetailed nicely with her growing interest in Tom and his life-style. In the final version, Angie was merely running away from being a magazine writer, and there was little at stake for her or Tom.

One reason why the central story was rewritten was that the audience was far more interested in the Newman–Bean relationship than in the Lawrence–Chaplin one. Newman, clad in a towel for most of the evening, played Martha Vail, a former beauty pageant contestant stranded in her hotel room because she can't pay her bill, and Bean played Tom's friend, Charlie, who comes to her aid. It was clear that the show had to be about Tom and Angie, but the only scenes that were playing well were those between Martha and Charlie.

Merrick's publicity machine went immediately into gear. Before the show arrived in New York, Merrick had thousands of "teaser" posters bearing only the show's title placed in trains and on platforms. Transit Authority officials insisted they be taken down, however, when bums began interpreting the posters as permission to spend the night on the subway. When the New York reviews were mixed to negative, Merrick attempted perhaps his most legendary publicity stunt, one he had wanted to pull for years but had been unable to carry off as long as Brooks Atkinson was the *Times'* critic. Looking through local phone books, Merrick found seven men whose names were the same as the seven major New York drama critics and invited them to a preview and dinner. Securing their permission to be quoted, Merrick and his press agent, Harvey Sabinson, invented the ecstatic paeans ("John Chapman" called *Subways* "the best musical of the century") that would be attributed to them. They devised an ad with photos of each of the phonies next to his quote, and a headline reading "7 Out of 7 Are Ecstatically Unanimous About *Subways Are For Sleeping.*" The *Times* and the *Post* killed the ad, but it ran in early editions of the *Herald Tribune* on January 4. While the show's creative team despised such antics, they had to admit that it helped the show stay open.

Two songs in the show on opening night (and preserved on the album),

○ ○ ○ ○ ○

"I Said It and I'm Glad" and "How Can You Describe a Face," were dropped within weeks. As the run wore on, there was no love lost between Lawrence and Chaplin, who had been greatly dissatisfied with their parts since Philadelphia. In April, the *Journal American* ran this item: "I think the director ought to sit out front some night, without warning, and then suggest to Carol Lawrence and Sydney Chaplin that their love scenes would play much better if they didn't look as if they were on the verge of homicide." *Subways*, thanks to theatre parties, Merrick's stunts, and the theatre economics of the time, lasted over six months and returned eighty-five percent of its investment, an achievement unthinkable today given the show's reviews and quality.

Subways' problems went beyond the imbalance in interest between the two love stories. There was a serious predictability problem (it's obvious that Tom will discover Angie's true identity before long and that she will ultimately prove she's interested in him for himself and not just as story material) as well as a serious believability problem (would Angie really give up her successful career to live in the streets with Tom?). The book, while professional, shows an unwillingness on the part of the writers to come to grips with the dark side of the material, sugarcoating the dropout life-style throughout. With homelessness a far more visible problem now than it was thirty years ago, *Subways* is more topical today than it was originally. But, with its presentation of the homeless as well-dressed citizens indistinguishable from executives, living of their own volition a pleasant alternative to the daily grind, *Subways* would now seem shockingly dated and dishonest.

In addition to Newman and Bean, *Subways* had two other assets. The choreography, especially for the "Be a Santa" number, displayed Kidd's usual invention and vigor (Valerie Harper and Michael Bennett were two of the gypsies who danced it). And the score was good, especially an unusual-sounding opening; Chaplin's ballad, "I'm Just Taking My Time"; the production number "Ride through the Night"; the catchy duet "Comes Once in a Lifetime"; and two comedy numbers, "I Was a Shoo-In" and "I Just Can't Wait."

Arnold Bennett's novel *Buried Alive*, which had already been adapted to the stage and screen, might have been the basis for a decent musical, but **Darling of the Day** (George Abbott; Jan. 27, '68; 31), another Jule Styne flop, was one of the most ill-starred projects in Broadway history. Bennett's story was about Priam Farll, a celebrated painter in early twentieth-century

○ ○ ○ ○ ○

England, who loathes the phoniness of art-world society. When his butler dies, he takes the opportunity to trade places with him and "get out of this world alive." Complications ensue when sweet widow Alice Chalice, who has been corresponding with the butler, meets Farll in his butler guise, and when Farll's dealer discovers evidence that his most successful client is still alive.

The book for *Darling of the Day* was first written by Keith Waterhouse and Willis Hall; Peter Wood was set to direct and Geraldine Page to star. But E.Y. Harburg, the lyricist, did not see eye to eye with that team, so S. N. Behrman wrote a new book, and Albert Marre was hired to direct. That grouping didn't work out either, and it fell to Nunnally Johnson to write yet another new book, Steven Vinaver to direct, and Vincent Price (whose passion for art gave him a personal connection to the role) and Patricia Routledge to create the leads.

Before rehearsals started, Vinaver was fired, replaced by Marre, and then rehired. After bad reviews in Toronto and Boston, Noel Willman was brought in to replace Vinaver, Roger O. Hirson was brought in to revise the book, and Johnson removed his name from the credits; there was no author listed when the show opened on Broadway. Johnson announced to the press that he would never again write for Broadway, as he had only made ten thousand dollars from his books for *Breakfast at Tiffany's* (unused), *Henry, Sweet Henry,* and *Darling of the Day.* The show's title, which was *The Great Adventure* before rehearsals and *Darling of the Day* in Toronto, was changed to *Married Alive* in Boston, then back to *Darling of the Day* for New York.

The most interesting thing about *Darling of the Day* is that it was a flop that got good reviews—but the good reviews came too late. Because first-string *Times* critic Clive Barnes wished to cover a dance event, the *Times* assigned its second-stringer, Dan Sullivan (the man who had reviewed *Tiffany's* on Broadway), to cover it. Watts in the *Post* and Chapman in the *News* liked it, but Sullivan didn't. A few days later, Barnes wrote about the show favorably in his dance column, and in the Sunday *Times,* Walter Kerr also approved; but the damage was done, and business never picked up. *Darling of the Day* closed as the costliest Broadway failure to date, losing over $750,000 on an initial investment of $500,000.

The big question is: Would *Darling of the Day* have succeeded if Barnes or Kerr had reviewed it in the *Times* upon its opening? The answer is: probably not. Styne considered *Darling* his "Lerner and Loewe show" and later said it had "one of the best scores I'd ever done." Harburg, always

○ ○ ○ ○ ○

One of Broadway's most unfortunate shows, Darling of the Day. Above, stars
Vincent Price and Patricia Routledge. Below, Playbills from Boston and New York
illustrate one of the show's several title changes.

one of the theatre's wittiest lyricists, did good if overloaded work here, and Styne's music is sometimes very lovely. Routledge had a beguiling waltz called "Let's See What Happens," a beauty called "That Something Extra Special," and one bona fide showstopper, "Not on Your Nellie." Better than the score was Routledge herself, an abundantly gifted singer— comedienne from England. Ideal as the warm and understanding widow who helps Farll to a happy ending, she received nothing but love letters from the critics and won a Tony for the role. After *Darling of the Day*, Routledge went on to an unusually ill-fated musical career in America, being wonderful in such bombs as *Love Match*, *1600 Pennsylvania Avenue*, and *Say Hello to Harvey*.

The biggest problem was not the book or score, but simply that *Darling of the Day* played like a flop, lacking in energy and stodgy in the extreme. There was a noticeable lack of directorial invention, and the show simply laid there, with only Routledge to activate it from time to time. But the fundamental story is sound, and, using most of the score and revising the book a bit, a talented director might be able to make *Darling of the Day* into a decent evening.

Styne's next show was no more successful and also suffered from an enervated production. **Look to the Lilies** (Lunt-Fontanne; Mar. 29, '70; 25) was safely based on the novel *Lilies of the Field* and the screenplay of the successful 1963 film for which Sidney Poitier won an Oscar. Styne chose his *High Button Shoes* collaborator, Sammy Cahn, for the lyrics, Leonard Spigelgass as librettist, and Joshua Logan as director. Styne wanted Ethel Merman to play Mother Maria, who induces on-the-lam Homer Smith to build her a chapel in New Mexico, but Logan wanted and got Shirley Booth, who made her return to Broadway after six years of her TV series "Hazel." Everyone wanted Sammy Davis, Jr., for Homer, but Davis wanted too much money, so Al Freeman, Jr., whom Logan would later call difficult and antagonistic, got the part.

Lilies skipped a road tryout and played a month of New York previews, opening on Easter Sunday to raves for Booth and mixed reviews otherwise. There have been shows that ran with reviews that were no better, but *Lilies* did not, and moderately pleasant as it was, it didn't really deserve to. The story was familiar from the hit movie, and even if one hadn't seen the movie or read the book, it was all too predictable: one knew from the beginning that Homer, despite continued refusal, would build the chapel. There was also a calculated quality about the evening, with

○ ○ ○ ○ ○

its nuns out of *The Sound of Music* (which had played the same theatre) and its black hero. 1970 was a time of protest and upheaval, and *Lilies*, with its tastefully good black man, was too late, lacking the edge that might have made the story seem current. But the biggest problem was Logan's staging, which was static and uninspired and made a mild, gentle story that much milder and gentler.

Cahn was not as good a theatre lyricist as Styne collaborators like Comden and Green, Sondheim, or Merrill, but the score had several nice numbers, including "I, Yes Me, That's Who" for Booth, "First Class Number One Bum" for Freeman, and a duet for two whores called "Meet My Seester." In Freeman's songs, Styne used some pop-rock sounds for the first time, mixed with his otherwise standard Broadway sound. Freeman lacked Poitier's charm, but Booth had charm in abundance, even though the role never really allowed her to cut loose. It was Booth's last appearance in a musical.

Styne's next show to make it to Broadway, *Sugar*, based on the film *Some Like It Hot*, was undistinguished, but with Gower Champion to direct it and Merrick producing, it ran. After an eight-year absence, Styne returned with a musical about a successful stage and film composer who invites the audience to an evening of entertainment which will be followed by his suicide at 10 P.M., the songs and dances preceding the suicide to explain what went wrong. If seventy-five-year-old Styne wasn't ready to kill himself, **One Night Stand** (Nederlander; Oct. 20, '80; closed in previews) showed how desperate he was to work.

Styne had gone to Herb Gardner to discuss the possibility of musicalizing Gardner's *A Thousand Clowns*, but Gardner presented Styne with the idea for *One Night Stand*, and Styne somehow went along with it. Gardner wrote his first musical book and lyrics for the show, and John Dexter was asked to direct. Jack Albertson and Elliott Gould were sought for the leads, but instead the less-than-stellar company was headed by Jack Weston and Charles Kimbrough. *One Night Stand* played eight previews, then closed down forever; coproducer Joseph Kipness told the press, "Gardner and Dexter could not agree on one thing, and there was nothing the producers could do about it." Miraculously, a cast album was released.

One Night Stand was quite obviously not a musical. While individual monologues and scenes in Gardner's bizarre script have the offbeat Gardner wit and would be fine for acting class exercises, it was simply not a musical book, and there was no good reason for songs to be included. Gardner's lyrics were poor, and Styne's music was erratic and often unnecessary. While *One Night Stand* was clearly unconventional, it was also a hopeless idea that never began to entertain an audience. It looked like the work of people with no experience in musicals, making Styne's involvement all the more surprising. Styne later wrote the music for a version of *Treasure Island* which played in Canada, but *One Night Stand* represents the last new Styne score heard on Broadway to date.

Although Arthur Schwartz's musical-theatre career was—unlike Rodgers', Loesser's, or Styne's—revue-oriented, Schwartz still ranks as one of the major Broadway composers from the twenties through the fifties. In the fifties, Schwartz wrote two musicals with Dorothy Fields for Shirley Booth, then rejoined his long-time partner Howard Dietz for two final shows. The last was Mary Martin's *Jennie*, but the one before it, **The Gay Life** (Shubert; Nov. 18, '61; 113) was better. Fay and Michael Kanin took Arthur Schnitzler's episodic play *The Affairs of Anatol* and imposed a through-line on it with the character of Liesl, a shy girl in love since childhood with the rake Anatol; Anatol, like Gaston in *Gigi*, finally abandons his wild life when he realizes he is in love with the innocent child he has known for years but never thought of romantically.

Kermit Bloomgarden, producer of such hit musicals as *The Most Happy Fella* and *The Music Man*, hired Gerald Freedman, who had assisted Jerome Robbins and others with earlier musicals, to make his directing debut, and Herbert Ross to choreograph. While the show was in Detroit (as the first show ever at the Fisher Theatre), Bloomgarden had Ross take over the entire production, though Freedman retained credit as director. *The Gay Life* opened on Broadway to a mixed response, with more good reviews than bad. The show was substantially revised shortly after the opening. One fine song, "Why Go Anywhere at All?", was lost when it was decided not to tell the story as a flashback. But competition from *How to Succeed, Carnival, Camelot, My Fair Lady, The Sound of Music, Irma La Douce, Do Re Mi, The Unsinkable Molly Brown*, and *Milk and Honey* proved too much for it, and it expired after four months.

What everyone loved about *The Gay Life* was its Liesl: Barbara Cook was ideally cast and demonstrated that she was capable of carrying a show all by herself. *The Gay Life* also had one of the best Dietz and Schwartz scores ever, and Cook's renditions of two of the loveliest songs, "Magic Moment" and "Something You Never Had Before," were unfor-

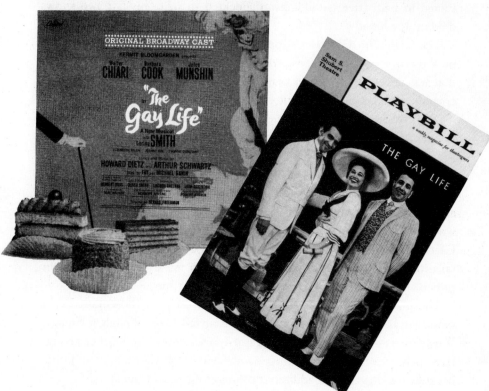

Barbara Cook was not the only one involved in The Gay Life who wanted to hurl a chair at leading man Walter Chiari. Those are authentic Viennese pastries in The Gay Life record ad.

gettable. And the turn-of-the-century Vienna setting inspired gorgeous sets and costumes, the latter earning Dietz's wife, Lucinda Ballard, a Tony.

It's now fashionable—and too easy—to blame the show's failure on its Anatol, Italian film comedian Walter Chiari. Dietz does, in his auto-biography, *Dancing in the Dark*: "Our leading man couldn't act, dance, sing or speak English, which was a handicap." But Chiari, if a little hard to understand, was charming, and the show would have been no more successful with another Anatol. Its real problem was the so-so book, adequate but insubstantial, and lame in its attempts at humor. When the show was published for the first time in 1986, it was retitled, for perhaps obvious reasons, *The High Life*.

Noel Coward—playwright, composer, lyricist, director, and per-former—had great success with musical revues and operettas in the twen-ties and thirties. Beginning with *Pacific 1860* in 1946, however, Coward wrote five unsuccessful book musicals. The first three were dismissed by British critics and never reached New York; feeling that he was under-valued in his native land, Coward decided to write his last two shows directly for Broadway.

The Girl Who Came to Supper (Broadway; Dec. 8, '63; 112) was to be the last show with a Coward score and the only one of his musicals that was never performed in London. It was based on Terence Rattigan's comedy *The Sleeping Prince*, written in 1953 in honor of Queen Elizabeth II's coronation. The play had been staged in the West End with Laurence Olivier and Vivien Leigh, on Broadway (for only sixty performances) with Michael Redgrave and Barbara Bel Geddes, and made into a movie (as *The Prince and the Showgirl*) with Olivier and Marilyn Monroe. Set in 1911 London just prior to and during the coronation of George V, the play and musical both were about chorus girl Mary Morgan from Milwaukee, who meets the prince regent of Carpathia and is invited to dine at the Carpathian embassy. The Regent, seeking a one-night stand, eventually falls in love with Mary after she manages to make peace between the prince and his estranged son, the king of Carpathia.

The play took place entirely in the royal suite at the embassy; the musical was opened up to include St. Martin's Lane, Trafalgar Square, Westminster Abbey, and backstage at Mary's show. In another change from play to musical, the prince's wife became his mother, the prince became a widower, and adultery no longer figured in the story.

Herman Levin made *The Girl Who Came to Supper* his first musical pro-

○ ○ ○ ○ ○

duction since *My Fair Lady*. He signed Harry Kurnitz to do the adaptation, then discovered to his surprise that Coward was willing to write only the score, leaving the staging to Joe Layton, who had choreographed Coward's *Sail Away* the year before. As it had done for *My Fair Lady*, CBS provided most of the financing. Rex Harrison and Christopher Plummer were early choices for the part of the regent, which ultimately went to Jose Ferrer, and Florence Henderson got her first—and last—star lead on Broadway as Mary.

Girl opened to raves in Boston, then less good reviews in Toronto. Coward wrote in his diary, "Harry Kurnitz, who had been taking several bows in New York, went into deep shock. Personally I was delighted. Everyone concerned was far too complacent." The reviews in Philadelphia were favorable, but during the Philadelphia run, President Kennedy was assassinated. Ferrer's first song, "Long Live the King (If He Can)" was dropped immediately, and Coward reworked "Countess Mitzi" from his 1938 *Operette* into "My Family Tree" to take its place.

On Broadway, the reviews were great for Henderson and Tessie O'Shea, who stole the show with her peripheral fifteen-minute cycle of cockney songs. Otherwise, most critics approved, but the two most important ones—Taubman in the *Times* and Kerr in the *Tribune*—did not. A furor arose when Ferrer, without permission, flew off to Puerto Rico one Saturday night to visit his wife, Rosemary Clooney, and was unable to get back because a blizzard had closed the New York airports. Ferrer's understudy, David Brooks, was stranded in transit, and Levin had to cancel the show, at a cost of ten thousand dollars, which he attempted to charge to Ferrer. *Girl* soon succumbed to such new competition as *Hello, Dolly!* and *Funny Girl;* an announcement that the show would open at London's Drury Lane in mid-August proved to be mere whistling in the dark.

Kurnitz's adaptation of Rattigan's slight but charming piece is competent if lacking in warmth, but it was a thin story for a huge musical, and the musical centerpieces—O'Shea's medley and Henderson's capsule, one-woman presentation of the entire *Coconut Girl*, Mary's show—were extraneous. Coward's score, which divides into integrated character numbers (Henderson had the better ones, like "Here and Now") and typical Coward revue-style songs, was pleasant, but Coward never really musicalized the characters.

The real problem with *Girl*, however, was that it was a blatant attempt to copy *My Fair Lady* and never equaled its predecessor's quality. For *Fair*

○ ○ ○ ○ ○

Look to the Lilies (*pictured above, stars Al Free-man, Jr., and Shirley Booth*), The Girl Who Came To Supper, *and* Kwamina. *All involved major writers, all had their good points, but none really worked.*

Lady's flower girl and professor, *Girl* had its chorus girl and prince. Stanley Holloway became O'Shea, Robert Coote became Roderick Cook, and Cathleen Nesbitt became Irene Browne as the Grand Duchess. The Ascot scene from *Fair Lady* became the coronation scene here, and the embassy ball turned into the foreign office ball. Even the show's leads, a not sufficiently appealing Ferrer and an enchanting Henderson, were echoes of the nonsinging Rex Harrison and soprano charmer Julie Andrews.

If Coward was only partly to blame for the failure of *Girl*, classically trained composer–lyricist–librettist Marc Blitzstein must take full responsibility for **Reuben Reuben** (Boston; Oct. 10, '55; closed on the road), easily the most difficult work ever presented to an audience under the guise of a Broadway-style musical. Blitzstein's *The Cradle Will Rock* (1937) was a success, but his operatic version of Lillian Hellman's *The Little Foxes* failed on Broadway under the title *Regina* (1949). *Reuben Reuben*, for which Blitzstein was sole author, came immediately after his greatest success, his English-language adaptation of the Brecht–Weill *The Three-penny Opera*.

Reuben took place from 9:30 P.M. to dawn on the Lower East Side of Manhattan, and its hero (Eddie Albert) was a victim of aphonia, unable to speak unless approached with warmth and love. The son of a circus performer known as the Human Dart who, as the show begins, has recently jumped to his death because of world tension, Reuben is encouraged to do likewise by a shady barkeeper who has taken out an insurance policy on Reuben's life. With the help of a girl (Evelyn Lear) he meets, Reuben learns to communicate and ultimately realizes that he is free to avoid his father's fate.

This synopsis makes the show sound much clearer than it ever was. *Reuben*, an almost through-sung opera, comprised a dissonant, fragmented score punctuated with occasional lyrical passages of extraordinary beauty, and dialogue spoken over constant underscoring. While Broadway had already seen and acclaimed Gian Carlo Menotti's operas *The Medium* and *The Consul*, those works had strong narratives; *Reuben* never offered a clue to its significance.

Cheryl Crawford produced the show, hiring Robert Lewis, who had directed *Brigadoon* for her and *Regina* for her and Blitzstein, to stage it. *Reuben* probably holds the all-time walkout record; on its opening night at the Shubert Theatre in Boston, at least three hundred bewildered customers were gone before the second act, and many who stayed talked

○ ○ ○ ○ ○

Two scenes from Marc Blitzstein's impenetrable but fascinating Reuben Reuben. Above, Kaye Ballard, as the Countess, takes Eddie Albert, as Reuben, under her wing. Below, Reuben gives Evelyn Lear, at left, cause for concern at the San Gennaro Festival.

back. One patron, on his way out, asked Blitzstein if he had anything to do with the show; when Blitzstein said that he'd written it, the man socked him in the jaw.

The critics were equally shocked and bewildered; clearly, Crawford had made a mistake by advertising the show as a musical and not as a contemporary opera. Blitzstein was unable to make significant changes, and Crawford closed the show ten days later, cancelling its November 8 opening at the ANTA Theatre.

As director Lewis himself later said, *Reuben* was a show about noncommunication which never communicated itself to the audience. The libretto problems were far too severe to be corrected on the road; indeed, the show was probably unfixable. When heard today—a complete, live tape exists—*Reuben* emerges as a fascinating work to which the only possible reaction is: How did Crawford and company ever dream they would get away with it or that an audience would enjoy it?

Blitzstein only wrote one more musical for Broadway, the unsuccessful but vibrant *Juno*, four years later. For that show and for the first time in his career, Blitzstein let someone else write the book. Crawford went on to produce other musicals, but she passed on *West Side Story*; *Reuben* had apparently scared her away from anything different for a while. *Reuben Reuben* and *Kelly* would seem to offer definitive evidence that musicals involving jumps from bridges are inadvisable.

A new generation of Broadway talent emerged in the fifties and sixties, and Richard Adler and his partner, Jerry Ross, burst upon Broadway with two smash hits, *The Pajama Game* in 1954 and *Damn Yankees* one year later. Ross, who shared music- and lyric-writing chores with Adler, died soon after *Yankees* opened, and Adler's musical-theatre career was never the same. Adler wrote three more shows, all failures.

Only two of them made it to Broadway. The first was **Kwamina** (54th Street; Oct. 23, '61; 32), which contained Adler's first independently written score. It was conceived for his wife, Sally Ann Howes; at a party, Adler had discussed African nationalism with Adlai Stevenson, then ambassador to the United Nations, and then told television writer Robert Allan Aurthur of his conversation: *Kwamina* would be Aurthur's first and only musical book. Tony Richardson was to direct but was replaced by Robert Lewis; Agnes de Mille handled the choreography. The entire $420,000 cost was provided by John S. Schlesinger, a South African industrialist.

∘ ∘ ∘ ∘ ∘

Kwamina (which means "born on Sunday") takes place in a West African nation that is about to gain independence from British rule. Kwamina (Terry Carter), the son of a tribal chief, returns home from medical training in London and soon clashes with the white, African-born doctor Eve Jordan (Howes). Kwamina, who wants to free his people from ancient barbaric practices and superstitions, is soon drawn to Eve against his will. Kwamina finds that tribal rituals are not easily replaced by modern ideas. When his father dies, three others must die with him, according to custom. Kwamina tries desperately to prevent this but cannot, and he is voted out of his tribe, his clinic destroyed by tribe members. On Independence Day, Eve and Kwamina decide to work together to teach a new way of life to the young people of the tribe.

With a turntable set which revolved to show the clinic or the village, *Kwamina* opened in Toronto, where reviews were promising (and where Adler caught his wife in a dalliance with her leading man). It moved to Boston, where Adler and Howes reportedly clashed over the show's problems. The New York reviews were mixed but mostly negative; there was much praise for de Mille and her dancers and for the physical production, less praise for the book. Shortly after the reviews came in, the show's African drummer led a voodoo ritual backstage, aimed at destroying the critics who had not liked *Kwamina*. *Kwamina* closed after only a month's run.

Adler's score, which was recorded the day after the closing, was far more serious and dramatic than anything he had done before. While it stuck mainly to the Broadway idiom, the ensemble song "Welcome Home" was very close to genuine African music. "Nothing More to Look Forward To," a duet for the girl betrothed to Kwamina and the man she loves, was beautiful, and Adler's work on the whole was interesting and colorful.

Kwamina deserves points for ambition, its willingness to deal with an important contemporary theme, much of its score, and its dances. When *Kwamina* stuck to the natives, it worked well, and its picture of a village struggling for freedom from both outside rule and its own witch doctors was often gripping. What did not work was the love story, which was formulaic. Kwamina and Eve were mouthpieces for ideologies rather than individually drawn characters, and the conflict between Kwamina and the head witch doctor was far more compelling than the Kwamina–Eve conflict and romance.

As was the case with *Christine*, there were also unfortunate but pronounced similarites to *The King and I* in *Kwamina*. Both dealt with the

○ ○ ○ ○ ○

tension between barbarism and democracy in a country on the verge of change. *Kwamina's* secondary pair of doomed lovers who cannot be together and must meet in secret were replays of Tuptim and Lun Tha from the Rodgers and Hammerstein classic. Both shows featured a clash of cultures represented by the leading male and female characters, and in both, these characters are eventually drawn to each other.

The creators came to realize that there was another reason for the show's failure, this one beyond their control: *Kwamina* was a black musical (albeit created entirely by whites), and Broadway audiences were not yet very interested in seeing black musicals (unless, like *Jamaica*, they had Lena Horne headlining)—*Kwamina* had only two whites in its cast. Moreover, while audiences would have no trouble later the same season accepting a romance between a white man and a black woman in *No Strings*, they were not ready in 1961 for one between a white woman and a black man.

Adler's last Broadway show to date was far less interesting than *Kwamina*. For **Music Is** (St. James; Dec. 20, '76; 8), Adler wrote only the music, leaving the lyrics to Will Holt, and coproduced. The show was another of George Abbott's late-career flops, and it was Abbott's idea. Perhaps because he had had a hit in 1938 by adapting Shakespeare's *Comedy of Errors* into *The Boys from Syracuse*, Abbott turned to *Twelfth Night* this time, doing both the adaptation and the staging. The show was a bittersweet reunion, for Abbott had directed and cowritten both of Adler's smash hits.

Music Is, with a typical Abbott cast of talented unknowns, was one of the first musicals to premiere at a regional theatre (the Seattle Repertory Theatre) before going on to Washington, D.C., and Broadway. The New York reviews were entirely negative, and the show promptly lost $757,000.

In 1968, the off-Broadway musical *Your Own Thing* had found a way to musicalize *Twelfth Night* while also commenting on late sixties fads and feelings by exploiting the link between Shakespeare's story and contemporary sexual confusion and unisex styles. But *Music Is* had no point of view or conception whatsoever and was content to rehearse the bare bones of the original plot, minus most of Shakespeare's dialogue. The romantic side of the story worked better than the comic in both book and score, and the score was rather good, Adler synthesizing a sound in between standard show music and contemporary styles. Catherine Cox, as Viola, delivered a ravishing ballad called "Should I Speak of Loving

○ ○ ○ ○ ○

You?," there was an oddly attractive song for Sherry Mathis as Olivia called "Sudden Lilac," and several others of the show's songs are worthy of investigation by cabaret performers. But the score, a pleasant company, and some clever musical staging by Patricia Birch were unable to disguise the fact that *Music Is* was pointless, an unfortunate end to Adler's Broadway career.

Perhaps because composer–lyricist Stephen Sondheim has had the most distinguished career in contemporary musical theatre, his flops tend to be more interesting and better known than other people's. Sondheim has probably had more shows that ran but lost money than any other major artist: *Follies*, *Sweeney Todd*, *Sunday in the Park with George*, and *Into the Woods* all had substantial runs but failed to pay back in their original productions. Those shows cannot really qualify as flops, but Sondheim has two shows to his credit that surely can, *Anyone Can Whistle* and *Merrily We Roll Along*, which together lasted a total of twenty-five performances. (His 1991 show, *Assassins*, played two months at the non-profit Playwrights Horizons, but did not go on to Broadway.)

Sondheim arrived on Broadway in the late fifties as the lyricist of *West Side Story* and *Gypsy*. In 1962, Broadway heard its first full Sondheim score in *A Funny Thing Happened on the Way to the Forum*. Two years later, Sondheim wrote the score for **Anyone Can Whistle** (Majestic; Apr. 4, '64; 9)— originally called *The Natives Are Restless*, then *Side Show*—which reunited him with his *West Side Story* and *Gypsy* librettist Arthur Laurents, who wrote *Whistle's* book and also directed.

George S. Kaufman once said that satire is what closes on Saturday night; *Anyone Can Whistle*, a satire on conformity and the insanity of the so-called sane, opened *and* closed on successive Saturday nights. It took place in a town which, because it manufactured a product that never wore out, is in the depths of depression. The corrupt mayoress, Cora Hoover Hooper, and her henchmen cook up a fake miracle—water from a rock— to attract tourists. Meanwhile, frigid Nurse Fay Apple, who can only let herself go when disguised in a red wig as "Ze Lady from Lourdes," meets J. Bowden Hapgood, ostensibly a doctor but actually the latest addition to her "Cookie Jar," the local asylum "for the socially pressured." With Hapgood's encouragement, Fay destroys the asylum's records and sets her cookies free as the townspeople realize the miracle is fraudulent. At the end, Fay summons up her first whistle, and Hapgood returns for her as a genuine fountain springs from the rock.

○ ○ ○ ○ ○

Producer Kermit Bloomgarden had trouble raising the money for such a bizarre project, but insiders like Irving Berlin, Frank Loesser, Richard Rodgers, and Jule Styne, well aware of how talented Laurents and Sondheim were, all invested. Increasing the show's risk, the three stars hired, Lee Remick, Harry Guardino, and Angela Lansbury, had no previous experience in musicals. Billed as "a wild new musical," the show received mixed to negative reviews in Philadelphia, where actor Henry Lascoe had a heart attack and was replaced by Gabriel Dell. *Whistle* couldn't afford to go to another tryout town, so it went directly to the Majestic near the end of a strong musical season, with *Hello, Dolly!* across the street and *Funny Girl* newly arrived a few blocks uptown. Critics John McClain, Norman Nadel, and Martin Gottfried raved, John Chapman was mixed, but pans from Howard Taubman, Walter Kerr, and Richard Watts sealed the show's fate. The authors paid for a full-page *New York Times* ad which listed the titles of famous musicals that did not open to unanimous acclaim, but it didn't help, and *Whistle* expired after a week. Sondheim, who wrote just the lyrics for another unsuccessful Laurents musical the following year (*Do I Hear a Waltz?*), kept a low profile for the rest of the sixties, reemerging at the beginning of the seventies with three extraordinary shows.

Because of Sondheim's takeover of the musical in the seventies and Lansbury's later triumphs as a Broadway musical comedy diva, *Anyone Can Whistle* is the flop that more fans lie about having seen than any other. Indeed, it has become much more chic to have seen *Whistle* nowadays than it was at the time. It has also become fashionable to say that *Whistle* was ahead of its time—but was it?

Deliberately anarchic, it was a decisive break from realism and from conventional musicals of its period. The characters and events were not meant to be real, and it went so far as to end the first of its three acts with its company appearing as an audience in theatre seats, laughing at and applauding the supposedly "insane" real audience. But *Whistle* may have suffered because its author was also its director: another director might have done something about the fact that the show's satire is scattershot, with too many targets; *Whistle* is simply not funny enough and not enough fun.

Whistle may have vanished quickly, but what's most important about it is that it showed Sondheim working for the first time in a style that would reach fruition in his later masterworks. In *Whistle*, he created unorthodox numbers, complex musical scenes, and pastiche numbers, all of which he

∘ ∘ ∘ ∘ ∘

In Anyone Can Whistle, *Angela Lansbury* (pictured above with *Arnold Soboloff and Henry Lascoe*) *made a smashing debut as a Broadway musical diva. Below, Lee Remick takes her curtain call; it was both Remick's Broadway musical debut and her farewell.*

would develop further in *Company, Follies,* and *Sweeney Todd.* The "Simple" scene, in which Hapgood, impersonating a doctor, attempts to divide a crowd into two groups, the "Cookies" and the "Sane," if not wholly successful, was one of the longest continuous sequences of music, dialogue, and staging ever seen in a musical, and Sondheim's next shows would contain similar sequences.

Whatever its shortcomings, *Whistle* was one of a kind, not amusing enough to succeed but too fascinating to dismiss. Most of the score is wonderful, and except for Herbert Ross's dazzling choreography, the cast album, recorded the day after the show closed, preserves the best of the show. The mix of terrible and laudatory reviews was precisely what the show merited: *Whistle* is both wonderful and awful, unsatisfying in and of itself but glorious for its foolhardy thumbing of its nose at convention and its pointing the way toward the innovations of the next decade.

Since *Whistle* premiered on Broadway, it has undergone little revision and has had only a few small-scale revivals. **Merrily We Roll Along** (Alvin; Nov. 16, '81; 16), on the other hand, is the show that refuses to die, undergoing constant revision and restaging in the decade since its New York opening. Its creation began when Harold Prince's wife suggested to her husband that he consider doing a show about teenagers. Prince thought of a forgotten 1934 play by George S. Kaufman and Moss Hart called *Merrily We Roll Along* and decided to take from it its title, its themes of integrity and loss of ideals, and its structural device of moving backward in time. In the musical, the playwright of the original play became a composer, the painter became a lyricist, and most of the original dialogue was discarded.

It's easy to see what attracted Prince to the play: its theme of disillusionment and dreams betrayed was not far from that of other shows on which he had collaborated with Sondheim. What's harder to understand is how Prince connected the play to the idea of a show about teenagers. Ultimately, it was Prince's conceit to enhance the ironies of the story, which begins with jaded adults who have sold out and follows them back to their idealistic beginnings, by having it performed by young, unspoiled actors. So Prince wound up with a show not about but instead *performed* by teenagers, a concept that would prove better in theory than in practice.

For *Merrily,* the team responsible for the landmark *Company*—Prince, Sondheim, and librettist George Furth—was reunited. Furth's largely original book follows three friends—composer Franklin Shepard, lyricist

○ ○ ○ ○ ○

Charles Kringas, and novelist Mary Flynn—from their first meeting in the mid-fifties through 1980, by which time Frank has betrayed his talent by becoming a film producer and recording executive, Charley has become a Pulitzer Prize-winning playwright to whom Frank is no longer speaking, and Mary has turned into a dipsomaniacal film critic. But of course, this tale is presented in reverse: the show opens in 1980, with the mature Frank advising the graduating class of Lake Forest Academy, from which he and Charley had graduated in 1955, to face life's realities and accept compromise. Ten scenes follow the graduation, each set earlier than the last and each showing the changes undergone by the central trio. The show ends in 1955 at Frank and Charley's graduation, as Frank offers his classmates Polonius' advice: "To thine own self be true."

Perhaps because the previous Sondheim–Prince musical, *Sweeney Todd*, had succeeded without benefit of a tryout, it was decided to do likewise with *Merrily*. What ultimately turned into six weeks of previews was held at the Alvin Theatre; the hit *Annie* was evicted so that *Merrily* could play where *Company* had triumphed a decade before. The first public preview is now legendary for the bewilderment with which it was greeted by an audience largely made up of Sondheim–Prince freaks. Unable to follow the plot or even figure out who some of the characters were, many walked out, and the walkouts continued throughout previews. Soon, reports creeped into the press about the show's disastrous reception, and rumors spread that previews might be suspended.

They continued without break, but *Merrily*'s preview period is now regarded as the classic example of the dangers of previewing in New York with no prior tryout. The poisonous word of mouth did irreparable damage to the show, in spite of the fact that by the time it opened, *Merrily* had undergone an almost unprecedentedly radical revision. James Weissenbach, the original Frank, was replaced by Jim Walton, who had been playing a small role. Choreographer Ron Field was replaced by Larry Fuller. Virtually every scene was rewritten, especially those in Act One, and three songs ("Darling," "The Blob," and "Honey") were dropped. Solo speeches for the main characters, directed to the audience, were added to help spectators understand who everyone was. Late in previews, one mature actor, Geoffrey Horne, joined the otherwise youthful cast to play the older Frank in the opening and closing graduation scenes. The endless and confusing "Rich and Happy" party scene, which got laughs instead of gasps when Frank's wife, Gussie, was pushed into a pool (filled with paper rather than water) was trimmed and clarified, and the pool was

○ ○ ○ ○ ○

eliminated. Mary's undying torch for Frank, who marries two other women during the course of the show, was emphasized in both dialogue and song.

For all the changes, the critical reception *Merrily* was greeted with when it opened after two postponements was as poor as if no work had been done at all. Only Clive Barnes in the *Post* felt the show was not to be dismissed. *Merrily* was allowed to continue for two weeks, and its score was recorded the day after the closing. Its failure put what may be only a temporary end to the Sondheim–Prince collaboration, and *Merrily* became the first in a string of Broadway flops (*A Doll's Life*, *Grind*, and *Roza* followed) directed by Prince. The show's failure was made all the more poignant by its having been performed by young people whose expectations of a hit were like the radiant hopes of Frank, Charley, and Mary on the rooftop looking forward to the appearance of Sputnik and the lives ahead of them in the "Our Time" scene. As the characters' hopes were betrayed, so were those of the kids in the company.

After *Merrily* closed, Sondheim told Stephen Farber in the *Daily News*, "I was very happy with the New York production by the time it opened. The show *was* in extremely poor shape in the early previews. It was too cluttered, and that's when a lot of the bad word of mouth started. But we did a lot of work on it, and the audiences who saw it during the two weeks of its official run loved it. I don't want to comment on the reasons for the bad reviews, but I don't think they had much to do with the intrinsic quality of the show."

Though *Merrily* was indeed a much better show by the time it opened, numerous problems remained. It was hurt by its unattractive, gymnasium setting, with Erector-Set bleachers and lockers, and its costumes, with the cast in sweatshirts identifying the characters by their relation to Frank to combat audience confusion. Prince later admitted that he was never able to come up with a satisfying visual concept for the show; his original instinct—to have had no sets at all—would have been a better solution.

Telling the story backward, which worked for Harold Pinter in his enigmatic, deliberately clinical play *Betrayal*, tended to confuse and alienate *Merrily* audiences; it was difficult to get interested in or care about the characters. The audience was never shown how Frank got to be where he was at the beginning of the evening; many of the changes in the characters took place offstage, announced but not dramatized. Then too, it was never made clear what Frank had done to his friends that was so terrible; is deserting Broadway musical theatre to work in Hollywood an unforgivable sin?

The performers seemed far more at ease in the final scenes, when they were playing their own age, than when they were attempting to portray hardened forty-five-year-olds; Furth's arch, brittle quips sounded positively weird emanating from the lips of teenagers. And *Merrily*'s theme— selling out versus integrity—was not a particularly fresh one; when Sondheim dealt with artistic integrity again in his next show, *Sunday in the Park with George*, it was in a far more imaginative context and treatment.

What was unquestionably right about *Merrily* was almost all of Sondheim's score, which featured complex interconnections of melodies, and "reprises" which, because of the show's reverse chronology, preceded the actual songs. There was the heartbreaking plaint for Mary, "Like It Was," and her clear-eyed "Now You Know"; the beautiful "Our Time"; the clever spoof of sixties revue material, "Bobby and Jackie and Jack"; "Opening Doors," a song which was actually a complete scene covering two years in the lives of the central characters; and two effective and overtly commercial ballads, "Not a Day Goes By" and "Good Thing Going."

For all its problems, *Merrily* exerted an emotional pull that transcended any flaws. The image of three young people on a rooftop, with the promise of infinite possibility ahead, was one of the most haunting in contemporary musicals.

As with *Whistle*, *Merrily*'s cast album preserved most of what was best about the show, and within months of its release, colleges across the country began producing the show. After productions in Los Angeles and at the Guildhall School of Music and Drama in London, *Merrily* got its first major revival, at the La Jolla Playhouse in the summer of 1985. Directed by James Lapine, Sondheim's collaborator on *Sunday in the Park with George*, this *Merrily* featured a heavily revised book by Furth and was performed by more mature, seasoned performers capable of playing older or younger versions of their characters as required. The graduation scenes were dropped, and what motivated Frank's changes was spelled out more specifically. Two new songs—"That Frank" in the first party scene, and "Growing Up," in which Frank pondered the nature of friendship—were added, and there were countless changes in dialogue, song, and characterization throughout. Sondheim and Furth continued to revise, and another major production took place at Arena Stage in Washington, D.C., in 1990, honoring most of the La Jolla changes, adding some new ideas, and even restoring some old lines. The show began on the rooftop, and

○ ○ ○ ○ ○

the book made the backward action easier to follow by supplying clues to what's going to happen in "later" scenes (which, of course, take place earlier).

For all the innumerable changes, *Merrily* is still a problematic show with a wonderful score. It's still somewhat confusing, and Franklin Shepard is still not a very sympathetic or interesting hero around whom to build an evening. Furth's book, filled with witty lines and insightful moments, still contains too much arch dialogue: no one talks quite the way the characters in *Merrily* too often do. But there is no doubt that the show will continue to be performed on both an amateur and professional level, where it will continue to frustrate, fascinate, and strike profound chords in its audiences.

No other major Broadway composer of recent years has had as many flops as Charles Strouse. While there have been hits, and big ones—*Bye Bye Birdie, Applause, Annie*—Strouse has had six consecutive flops beginning with *A Broadway Musical* in 1978. Strouse is one of the few composers left who likes to go up to bat again and again, and if the projects aren't always worthy of his talent, Strouse seems to enjoy exercising it nonetheless.

His first flop was the Ray Bolger vehicle *All American,* which was followed by the successful Sammy Davis vehicle *Golden Boy.* But then came another flop, **It's a Bird . . . It's a Plane . . . It's Superman** (Alvin; Mar. 29, '66, 129), the fourth Strouse–Lee Adams collaboration. It was produced and directed by Harold Prince: with *Cabaret* next, *Superman* was to be the last conventional, old-style show with which Prince was ever involved.

Produced at a time when "Batman" was all the rage on TV and pop art and comic-book heroes were popular, *Superman's* book, by David Newman and Robert Benton, told of its hero's being threatened by the jealous Dr. Abner Sedgwick, a ten-time Nobel Prize loser seeking revenge by attempting to destroy the world's symbol of good, and Max Menken, a columnist on the *Daily Planet* who resents Lois Lane's attraction to Superman.

Patricia Marand replaced original leading lady Joan Hotchkiss in Philadelphia, and Prince tried to promote advance ticket sales by offering lower prices for mail orders sent in before the box office opened. Prince also designated three prices for orchestra seats and two-dollar seats at the top of the balcony. *Superman* was another failure that the *New York Times'* critic, then Stanley Kauffmann, loved, and there were some other good

○ ○ ○ ○ ○

reviews too, but even with four matinees a week, the show was forced to close after four months, losing its entire $400,000 investment. There was a dreadful ABC-TV production of the musical in 1975.

Newman and Benton, who went on to become major screenwriters, did not give up on the idea, though, and later collaborated on the screenplay of the wildly successful *Superman* movie. The popularity of that film and its sequels indicates that there was potential in a Superman musical, but this one was not, as some later claimed, ahead of its time. *Li'l Abner* and *Annie* were successfully adapted from comic strips into musicals because genuine sentiment and warmth were added to the one-dimensional originals. *Superman* was nothing but a cartoon: there was no way to care about any of the characters or what was happening to them, and the script was not funny enough to make up for the lack of emotional involvement. The particular plot invented for the musical was uninspired, with the romance between Lois and Dr. Sedgwick's lab assistant particularly weak. While the show, to its credit, played it straight and avoided camp, it didn't come up with much that was imaginative in any style. *Superman* was noticeably lacking in suspense or wit.

The Strouse–Adams score had enjoyable numbers but was not distinguished, and the best thing about *Superman* was its cast, especially Jack Cassidy as self-adoring Max and Linda Lavin as his secretary Sydney, and Robert Randolph's designs. One number was performed, comic-book style, on an eight-panel, double-tiered set.

Strouse's **A Broadway Musical** (Lunt-Fontanne; Dec. 21, '78; 1) was an original backstage show about a white producer putting together a musical based on a serious play by a black author. With a book by William F. Brown, author of the then still-running *The Wiz*, it attempted to spoof tasteless producers, show-biz lawyers, idealistic writers, schlocky Vegas stars, theatre-party ladies—*and* the craze for black musicals. Strouse, with *Annie* still a new smash, rejoined Adams—they hadn't worked together since *I and Albert* in London in 1972—and the team drew on its experiences with *Golden Boy* (the star of *A Broadway Musical*'s musical, *Sneakers*, bore a strong resemblance to Sammy Davis) to explore the situation of a black star in a show created by whites. George Faison, who had choreographed *The Wiz* and taken over the direction of *1600 Pennsylvania Avenue*, was hired to direct and choreograph. The show was produced by Garth H. Drabinsky, then just beginning his Cineplex Odeon movie-theatre empire, and Norman Kean, the producer of *Oh! Calcutta!*, who some years later

Three of the many flops of the talented Charles Strouse. The Playbill below right was for Sneakers, the musical within the musical A Broadway Musical; it was a prop in that show.

killed himself and his wife, the actress Gwyda DonHowe, who, as it happened, played the producer's wife in *A Broadway Musical*.

Billed as "A musical about a Broadway musical," *A Broadway Musical* played an unorthodox workshop tryout at the Theatre of the Riverside Church on Manhattan's Upper West Side. During that run, things got sticky when the white producers of this show about whites producing a black musical fired the black Faison and replaced him with the white Gower Champion. The leads at Riverside, Helen Gallagher and Julius LaRosa, were both replaced by the time the show opened, with a no-star cast, on Broadway. Champion took only "production supervised by" credit in the final Playbill, feeling he hadn't had enough time to work on the show. The reviews were terrible—Julius Novick of the *Village Voice* called it "the best Broadway musical since *Platinum*" (which had opened just a month earlier)—and the show lost $1 million in one night. *A Broadway Musical* and Strouse's next five Broadway musicals were to run a combined total of twenty-seven Broadway performances.

What might have made a good revue sketch did not make a good musical. *Sneakers'* producer was so obviously a crass, theatrically ignorant boor that there could be no doubt that the show he was assembling would be lousy—yet the audience was expected to like him and root for his success. The characters were all cliches, the script far too obvious in its satire. What's worse, it was never very funny. A shallow treatment of a theme with potential—the exploitation of blacks by whites—was capped with an absurd ending, in which the *Sneakers* author, who never wanted to turn his play into a musical in the first place, steps into the lead to save the show.

The score was not up to Strouse and Adams' standard. Strouse recycled *A Broadway Musical's* "Let Me Sing My Song" into the title tune of *Dance a Little Closer* (the melody had already been used in the London production of *Golden Boy*), and "Together" became "Dumb Dog" in the movie version of *Annie*.

Strouse followed *A Broadway Musical* with **Charlie and Algernon** (Helen Hayes; Sept. 14, '80; 17), based on the novel *Flowers for Algernon*, which had become the successful film *Charly* in 1968. The book and lyrics were by David Rogers, who had already written a nonmusical version of the novel. *Charlie and Algernon* was an attempt at a small musical at a time when economics were beginning to dictate that producers find intimate musicals.

○ ○ ○ ○ ○

Novel, movie, and musical all told of Charlie, who has an IQ of 68 and makes his living sweeping at a bakery. Through an experimental operation, he becomes so intelligent that, for instance, he can read *War and Peace* in one night. Unfortunately, the result of the operation is only temporary, and Charlie begins a process of regression which proves irreversible.

The show was first done in Edmonton, Canada, then, under the title *Flowers for Algernon*, in London. But even with Michael Crawford winning raves as Charlie, the London production, directed by Peter Coe, only lasted a month. It then went to the Folger Theatre in Washington, where it was directed by Louis W. Scheeder, and that production eventually came to Broadway, where it was billed as "A Very Special Broadway Musical" and was performed in one act. Critics liked only the title number, in which Charlie and a spotlit mouse danced out their anger at being exploited.

Such gloomy material was ill-suited to a musical: doctors and retarded men just don't sing. And as was the case with the movie, the basic story was hard to believe: would the scientists, after performing their experimental operation on a mouse, use a grown man in their next attempt? Could Charlie really read *War and Peace* just weeks after his operation? It was also predictable: just as surely as Charlie becomes smarter, we know he's soon going to begin reverting. Strouse came up with a few pretty tunes—to Rogers' weak lyrics—but *Charlie* is his least interesting score.

Strouse's music was the best thing about **Dance a Little Closer** (Minskoff; May 11, '83; 1), the last of Alan Jay Lerner's string of late flops, and a show for which Lerner must take the blame. It was his idea to adapt Robert E. Sherwood's 1936 Pulitzer Prize-winning play *Idiot's Delight* (a vehicle for the Lunts on Broadway, Clark Gable and Norma Shearer on film), updating its story from the eve of World War II to "the avoidable future," during a confrontation between NATO and Soviet forces that could lead to World War III. The lead female character was transformed from an American showgirl pretending to be a Russian countess into one pretending to be a British lady, and the man she was traveling with was changed from a munitions maker to a Kissinger-like, Austrian-born American diplomat. In *Dance a Little Closer*, lounge entertainer Harry Van is stranded on New Year's Eve in the Austrian Alps when the conflict begins and the border is closed. In the same hotel is Cynthia Brookfield-Bailey, whom Harry recognizes as a girl he slept with in a Ramada Inn in Omaha

∘ ∘ ∘ ∘ ∘

ten years earlier. The border is finally opened, and when Cynthia is left stranded by her diplomat lover, she finally ends the game of cat and mouse with Harry as planes of uncertain origin circle ominously overhead.

Lerner wrote the book and lyrics and conceived the show for his eighth wife, Liz Robertson, and perhaps to protect her, he also chose to make his official directorial debut—he had taken over *Camelot* and *Gigi* without credit—with the show; this decision was also influenced by his dissatisfaction with the direction of his *1600 Pennsylvania Avenue* and *Carmelina*. *Dance* had a workshop at 890 Broadway, then went directly into previews at the Minskoff Theatre. In spite of bad word of mouth during previews—the show was dubbed *"Close a Little Faster"*—Lerner was not willing to do much revision. *Dance* opened to unanimous pans, with good words only for the score; in anticipation of the reviews, a huge opening-night party to which five hundred people had been invited was canceled the day before the opening. The show ran one night, and it might have been wise to cut Robertson's line, in a flashback to her days as a singer in Omaha, "Thank you for coming to my closing night."

Dance actually played better at 890; an old-style book musical, and an intimate one at that, it was dead on arrival at the Minskoff, with its huge stage laden with David Mitchell's uninviting set, which resembled an airport lounge more than a ritzy hotel in the Austrian Alps. Leading man Len Cariou was in bad voice from too much *Sweeney Todd* and was not well cast; Robert Goulet might have been fine in the role. And it probably would have been better to keep the story in its original period, which might have at least provided some nostalgia and color. The attempt at topicality was a mistake, and the story was unconvincing when set in contemporary times. Other mistakes: first-act flashbacks told us that Harry and Cynthia had once had an affair, so there was no suspense about whether or not Harry really knew her years earlier (there were no such flashbacks in the play), and the musical made a pair of newlyweds from the original into a pair of gay airline stewards, who were married in an awkward scene in the second act. A good deal of very elegant music by Strouse went down with a show that steadfastly refused to come to life. As usual, Strouse was not to blame.

Everyone must start somewhere: for the team of Jerry Bock and Sheldon Harnick, one of the most talented to emerge in the late fifties and early sixties, it was with the mediocre *The Body Beautiful*. For John Kander, who

○ ○ ○ ○ ○

when teamed with lyricist Fred Ebb became one of Broadway's most successful composers, it was with the slim, Ebb-less *A Family Affair.*

Bock had written revue material and shared the score for *Mr. Wonderful* with two other writers when he met Harnick, who had also contributed to Broadway revues (including *New Faces of 1952* and Bette Davis's *Two's Company*). **The Body Beautiful** (Broadway; Jan. 23, '58;, 60), one of the few original musicals of its period, had a book by *Mr. Wonderful* librettists Joseph Stein and Will Glickman which told a lightly comic story set in the prizefighting world; because it introduced to Broadway the team that would go on to write *Fiorello!*, *She Loves Me*, and *Fiddler on the Roof*, it is significant beyond its actual value. It was a mild, adequate, and starless show, with the then standard love story, subplot, and comic relief—not terrible, but ordinary and too weak to withstand competition from better shows.

The Bock and Harnick score was not great either, but it contained a couple of outstanding songs which showed what they were capable of. Especially good was the sophisticated "A Relatively Simple Affair," in which the two principal ladies, in the dressing rooms of their fighter boyfriends, compare life-styles. Bock's music, though pleasant, was not yet up to Harnick's witty lyrics. (An example of the latter: *Girl, I have the key to what Jean-Paul Sartre meant. Boxer, And while you're at it here's the key to my apartment.*) It is to the credit of producers Robert Griffith and Harold Prince that they saw through a so-so show to the talent of its songwriters. They hired Bock and Harnick to write *Fiorello!* the following season, and Prince was to do three more shows with the team.

John Kander's only Broadway show without Fred Ebb was his first, **A Family Affair** (Billy Rose; Jan. 27, '62; 65). It had a book by James and William Goldman, and Kander and James Goldman contributed the lyrics. Set in Chicago, it began with a boy asking a girl to marry him and ended with the pair marrying. In between, mostly, were arguments between the mother of the groom and the uncle of the bride; because personalities like Eileen Heckart, Shelley Berman, Morris Carnovsky, and Bibi Osterwald were among the leading players, it played amusingly. Highlights included a number in which a football game was used as a metaphor for the two families pitted against each other, and Berman, as the bride's uncle, plotting revenge against Heckart's takeover of the wedding plans on the telephone. But *A Family Affair* does not read well today; if revived, it might cross over the borderline of taste with respect to its portrait of middle-class Jews.

A Family Affair, originally optioned by Leland Hayward, who had Jerome Robbins to direct it and Gertrude Berg interested in starring, is best remembered as the first directorial job of Harold Prince. When it opened in Philadelphia, Word Baker, who had recently had a big off-Broadway success with *The Fantasticks*, was the director. Prince, who had originally turned down the show, agreed to take over, cleaning up a messy production, getting rid of a hideous set, and bringing out what was good in the book and score. But because of poor business, the tryout could not be extended, and Prince was aware that while the show had been improved, it wasn't good enough to make it. He reluctantly put his name on it, and it opened to mixed reviews, including a favorable one from Walter Kerr. But even after ticket prices were reduced, there was little business, and the show closed after two months, losing $420,000 on an original investment of $350,000.

Kander's talent was obvious in such songs as the romantic ballads "Anything for You" and "There's a Room in My House" and in the raucous toe-tapper "Harmony." Prince remembered Kander's work in *A Family Affair* and hired Kander (and his new partner, Fred Ebb) to write their first Broadway score for his production of *Flora, the Red Menace* three years later. The team would do three more shows (*Cabaret, Zorba*, and *Kiss of the Spider Woman*) with Prince. James Goldman also worked for Prince again, writing the book for *Follies*.

If *A Family Affair*'s original director, Word Baker, was never able to capitalize on the success of *The Fantasticks*, the authors of *The Fantasticks*, lyricist–librettist Tom Jones and composer Harvey Schmidt, had an original and distinctive voice which guaranteed that Broadway would soon come calling. And it did, first with *110 in the Shade* in 1963, then *I Do! I Do!* in 1966. If the latter had traces in its staging of the intimate, experimental style of Jones and Schmidt's off-Broadway origins, both were written in conventional Broadway fashion and were decidedly uptown shows. With their next Broadway show, **Celebration** (Ambassador; Jan. 22, '69; 110), Jones and Schmidt, writing their first completely original musical, attempted to do an experimental, off-Broadway–style show on Broadway. Cheryl Crawford, always one for unusual musicals, coproduced, and Jones directed.

○ ○ ○ ○ ○

After *I Do! I Do!*, Jones and Schmidt had opened their Portfolio Studio in a converted brownstone on Forty-seventh Street. Their plan, to develop shows in a workshop setting, was not unlike what Michael Bennett did with *A Chorus Line* a few years later. *Celebration* was first performed at Portfolio, then went directly to Broadway, where it opened after two weeks of previews to mixed-to-negative reviews. Because *The Fantasticks*, which also received mixed reviews, had taken a while to catch on, the producers of *Celebration* had taken the precaution of raising $250,000 for a show that only cost $125,000 to open. The reserve kept *Celebration*, which could easily have closed in a couple of weeks, open for almost four months. It was revived at the Portfolio in 1975, in a season of four shows that included the team's acclaimed *Philemon*, after which the Portfolio ceased to exist.

But *Celebration*, which deserves credit for originality and daring, was not a very interesting show and often a downright irritating one. Suggested by an editorial in the *New York Times* about the meaning of the winter solstice, *Celebration* described itself pretentiously as "a fable based upon ancient ceremonies depicting the battle between Winter and Summer." Taking place on "a platform" at New Year's Eve, it was about an orphan who does battle with Edgar Allen Rich, the wealthiest man in the Western World and a manufacturer of things artificial, over a girl named Angel (played by Susan Watson, who had created the role of Luisa in *The Fantasticks* when it was first performed at Barnard College). It was also a metaphoric retelling of the Garden of Eden story, ending with Rich defeated and the orphan and Angel leaving their garden. But *Celebration* was obscure, and few cared enough to attempt to figure it out.

As Jones himself later admitted, "All of the seasonal underpinnings which were inherent in *The Fantasticks* but disguised, although sensed by me, became so up-front in *Celebration* that they became overbearing and pretentious . . . The symbols crashed too loudly." *Celebration* obviously meant more to its authors than was communicated to its audiences, who were simply not sufficiently entertained. The show also contained an unpleasant equation of old age with all that's bad, and youth with all that's free and good, a concept that is now extremely dated.

The score, reminiscent of *The Fantasticks* and other Jones and Schmidt pieces, contains, like all of the team's work, many good things, especially the title song, the hero's "Orphan in the Storm," and a duet for the hero and Angel, "I'm Glad to See You've Got What You Want." Shockingly,

○ ○ ○ ○ ○

Celebration is the last new Jones and Schmidt musical to make it to Broadway, in spite of two tries since: *Colette* in 1982 and *Grover's Corners*, a musical version of *Our Town*, in the late eighties.

Cy Coleman, a versatile composer whose background as a jazz pianist gives his work a distinctive sound, arrived on Broadway in the sixties with Lucille Ball's *Wildcat*, then did five shows (*Little Me, Sweet Charity, Seesaw, I Love My Wife, On the Twentieth Century*) which were hits or at least had decent runs. He had his first outright disaster with **Home Again, Home Again** (Stratford, Connecticut; Mar. 12, '79; closed on the road), which, like *One Night Stand*, saw a couple of Broadway pros—Coleman and director Gene Saks—dabbling in the sub–avant–garde with other writers who had no experience with musicals. *Home Again*, with lyrics by Barbara Fried and a book by *New York Times* columnist Russell Baker, was a revuelike saga of one man's fifty-year search for values and the American dream. But there were no real characters, and the show was incoherent and obvious in its satire. It had strong thematic similarities to an infinitely better show, *Allegro*, which, like *Home Again*, concerned a search for values in America, affirmed home as the ultimate destination, and featured Lisa Kirk. In *Home Again*, Kirk had a ridiculous part, the mother of the hero's wife, and was given only one appearance and one musical number in each act, both at wedding celebrations. Kirk was written out during the show's first stop in Connecticut.

The musical went on to Toronto, where its title, originally a single *Home Again*, was doubled, but it shut down there and did not meet its April 26 date at the Mark Hellinger. It was the second consecutive out-of-town closer for director Saks, whose last musical had been *The Prince of Grand Street*. *Home Again* lost $1.25 million. The authors later wrote a backstage musical, not unlike *A Broadway Musical*, based on their experiences with *Home Again*. Entitled *13 Days to Broadway*, it used several of the jauntier songs from *Home Again*, but after being announced for imminent production season after season, it quietly disappeared.

Coleman's next show was the hit *Barnum*, which he coproduced. He didn't return to Broadway until the end of the 1988–89 season, the worst for musicals ever. But even after *Carrie, Legs Diamond*, and *Chu Chem*, **Welcome to the Club** (Music Box; Apr. 12, '89; 12) was no bargain. A.E. Hotchner—the author of biographies of Ernest Hemingway, Doris Day, and Sophia Loren—and Coleman were clearly the guilty parties: Coleman suggested that an unproduced play of Hotchner's be made into the book for a musical the pair coproduced, and they even shared the lyric writing, although neither had had much experience in that area.

Under the title *Let 'Em Rot*, the show was first read at the Actors Studio in New York, then directed by Morton Da Costa at the White Barn in Westport and by Frank Corsaro at the Coconut Grove Playhouse in Miami. For Broadway, Peter Mark Schifter, who had staged operas, but not musicals, was hired to direct. *Welcome to the Club* was mounted on Broadway for $1.5 million, dirt-cheap for a musical in the late eighties, but it probably would never have made it to New York at all had Coleman and Hotchner not invested in it themselves.

During previews in New York, when the show came to be known as *"Welcome to the Load-Out,"* Frank Corsaro was invited back to help with the direction, while Larry Gelbart, who was working on the book for Coleman's next show, *City of Angels*, contributed too. Featured performer Sharon Scruggs was replaced during previews by Sally Mayes, who as country-western queen Winona Shook proved to be the evening's sole bright spot.

Because of its size and cost, the creators of *Welcome to the Club* gave interviews saying that their show was an intimate, unpretentious throwback to the old-fashioned values of character, song, and comedy, not a modern mammoth relying on spectacle and hydraulics. But with writing like this, bring on the spectacle! The idea and setting doomed the show to failure: it concerned four husbands, two divorced and two separated, in a minimum-security alimony jail in what was supposedly present-day New York. Their wives appeared in real visits, flashbacks, fantasy sequences, and as backup singers, but there was no real plot, and the script was simply a series of song cues. Coleman came up with a few good tunes, but this was not to be a flop saved by a good score, and Coleman and Hotchner's decision to do their own lyrics was unwise.

The ugly set typified the whole cheesy project, which was incredibly dated in its attitudes towards women and male–female relationships. The show's hideous logo, with a man's legs dangling half-devoured from a pair of rouged female lips, said it all.

Larry Gelbart wrote the books for only three Broadway musicals, all of which played on West Fifty-second Street. The second, which he wrote with Burt Shevelove, was for *A Funny Thing Happened on the Way to the Forum* at the Alvin; the third was for Coleman's *City of Angels*, across

∘ ∘ ∘ ∘ ∘

the street at the Virginia—Gelbart won Tony Awards for both of these. But first came **The Conquering Hero** (ANTA; Jan. 16, '61; 8), which played at the same theatre as *City of Angels*. (The ANTA Theatre, originally called the Guild Theatre, was renamed the Virginia in 1981.) The score was by Moose Charlap and Norman Gimbel, who had done *Whoop-Up*. Gimbel, apparently discouraged by two flops in a row, stopped writing Broadway musicals after *The Conquering Hero*, but Charlap went on to *Kelly*.

Both the musical and the film on which it was based, Preston Sturges' 1944 comedy, *Hail the Conquering Hero*, were about a young man who, because his father had been a war hero, has always dreamed of being a marine. He enlists in the war, but his chronic hay fever causes him to be discharged immediately. Ashamed to go back home, he hooks up with some marines who see to it that he returns a hero, convincing his town that he was wounded in battle. Tom Poston played the lead, heading a nonstellar company.

The Conquering Hero had a chaotic tryout which inspired Gelbart's oft-quoted quip, "If Hitler is alive, I hope he's out of town with a musical." When the show received negative reviews in its second tryout town, producer Robert Whitehead fired the show's director–choreographer, Bob Fosse, who had directed only one previous musical (*Redhead*, a hit). The producers took the foolhardy step of replacing Fosse with Albert Marre, fired the leading lady, and asked Dick Shawn to replace Poston (Shawn declined). Meanwhile, Fosse took the show's producers to arbitration to protect his choreography; though he eventually won the case (after the show closed), the producers had still enjoyed the use of Fosse's two big dance sequences, which got the best of the reviews on the road and in New York.

Several shows have opened on Broadway with no director or choreographer billed in the program. *The Conquering Hero* has the distinction of being the only show ever to open on Broadway without a director's or choreographer's credit *and* without a producer's above-the-title credit— only a line at the bottom of the Playbill title page which read, "produced under the management of Robert Whitehead and Roger L. Stevens." They were indeed the reluctant producers, along with ANTA, a nonprofit organization which fronted most of the money and wound up in disastrous debt as a result.

Gelbart's book is generally sharp and funny, and the property was well-suited to his style. And as was the case with their score for *Whoop-Up*, Charlap and Gimbel did come up with a few catchy tunes. Actually, *The*

Conquering Hero was a passable show that might have made it had Fosse (whose Broadway career eventually comprised seven musicals, six of which were hits) been allowed to remain.

Meredith Willson burst upon the Broadway scene in 1957, at the age of fifty-five, with a huge hit, *The Music Man*. He wrote three more musicals, each less successful than the one before. His second, *The Unsinkable Molly Brown*, made money; his next, *Here's Love*, did not, but ran too long for inclusion here. His final show never made it to Broadway at all.

1491 (Los Angeles; Sept. 2, '69; closed on the road), with a book by Willson and Richard Morris, who also directed, was another Edwin Lester–Civic Light Opera epic. It was a speculation on the events leading up to Christopher Columbus's acquiring three ships and sailing to the Indies, spiced up with a triangle between Columbus (John Cullum), Queen Isabella (Jean Fenn), and Beatriz (Chita Rivera), Columbus's true love. At the end, Isabella gives Columbus his ships to revenge herself on Beatriz, whom Columbus would not give up. The authors claimed they wrote the show to parallel recent developments in space exploration, but there was no discernible connection.

1491 played four months in Los Angeles and San Francisco, but except for the sets, costumes, and leads, no one liked anything about it. Willson remade Columbus into *The Music Man*'s Harold Hill, here conning the Spanish king and queen into giving him what he wanted, throwing in a touch of *Man of La Mancha*'s Quixote for good measure. While the idea of speculating about Columbus's activities in 1491 was not necessarily a bad one, it was carried out without wit or excitement; the show was one of the last gasps of the floperetta, with appropriately ponderous dialogue: *Isabella*: "State affairs become more pressing every year." The score, while it did not sound like standard floperetta schlock, was surprisingly lacking in good tunes, and Columbus and Isabella were saddled with rhythm numbers in Willson's "speak song" style from *The Music Man*. Rivera, exploited for her usual spitfire talents, had one showstopper called "Why Not?," choreographed by Danny Daniels.

The team of Richard Maltby, Jr., a lyricist who also directs, and composer David Shire has few peers in contemporary musical theatre. But they are perhaps best known for two compilations of their songs, *Starting Here, Starting Now* and *Closer Than Ever*. Among the most talented music-theatre writers of the last thirty years, Maltby and Shire have made

○ ○ ○ ○ ○

Dorothy Chandler Pavilion • Beginning Tuesday, September 2, 1969

LOS ANGELES CIVIC LIGHT OPERA

GEORGE B. GOSE, president   EDWIN LESTER, general director

presents

The World Premiere of a new musical!

JOHN CULLUM
as Columbus

JEAN FENN
as Isabella

in

MEREDITH WILLSON'S

"1491"

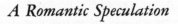

also starring

CHITA RIVERA
as Beatriz

A Romantic Speculation

Music and Lyrics by **MEREDITH WILLSON**

Book by **MEREDITH WILLSON** and **RICHARD MORRIS**

with collaboration by **IRA BARMAK**

featuring

GINO CONFORTI

BRUCE GORDON   JOSEPH MELL

KATHRYN HAYS

and introducing

STEVEN ARLEN

•

Produced by **EDWIN LESTER**

Dances and Musical Numbers staged by **DANNY DANIELS**

Scenery by **OLIVER SMITH**

Costumes by **MILES WHITE**

Lighting by **PEGGY CLARK**

Dance and Choral Arrangements and Musical Direction by **JULIAN STEIN**

Orchestrations by **IRWIN KOSTAL**

Associate Producer: **EDWARD M. GREENBERG**

Directed by **RICHARD MORRIS**

"1491" is based on an idea by Ed Ainsworth

Ya got trouble, Meredith Willson, with this one. Yet another Edwin Lester folly.

it to Broadway exactly once, with *Baby* in 1983. But there were several attempts before that: after writing musicals at Yale and an off-Broadway musical called *The Sap of Life*, they collaborated in 1967 on a show about computer dating called *How Do You Do, I Love You*; it had a fine score, but its book wasn't strong enough to carry it from a stock tour to Broadway.

The following year, they were brought in to replace the original song-writer of **Love Match** (Phoenix; Nov. 3, '68; closed on the road), a musical about the courtship and marriage of Queen Victoria and Prince Albert. Christian Hamilton had written the book, and the staging was by Danny Daniels, supervised by Noel Willman. Max von Sydow had agreed to play Albert and then changed his mind; the part went to Laurence Guittard. Opposite Guittard was the ever-wonderful Patricia Routledge, fresh from *Darling of the Day* (also taken over by Willman). *Love Match* opened in Phoenix and closed in Los Angeles, with Routledge winning raves from everyone. Another musical on the same subject, orig-inally called *H.R.H.* and optioned by David Merrick, was competing with *Love Match* to open first, but because Julie Andrews turned *H.R.H.* down, *Love Match* won the race. (*H.R.H.* eventually became *I and Albert*; with a score by Strouse and Adams, it ran four months in London in 1972.)

Love Match had a very fine score, highlighted by "I Hear Bells" (sung by a river "mudlark" who otherwise had little reason for being in the show) and Victoria's breathless "I Think I May Want to Remember Today," her reaction to her first meeting with Albert. If the music and lyrics were on a par with Sondheim's sixties work, the book, while literate and sometimes charming, was undramatic and failed to capitalize on its con-cept of Victoria remembering the past selectively. *Love Match*, *I and Albert*, and *Rex* demonstrate the problems inherent in basing musicals on the lives of kings and queens. For that matter, be they Queen Victoria or Marilyn Monroe, legendary real-life figures aren't easily made to sing.

Dear World (Mark Hellinger; Feb. 6, '69; 132) certainly qualifies as a catastrophe and as a star flop, but it appears in this section because of the particular place it holds in the career of its composer–lyricist, Jerry Herman. After writing a couple of off-Broadway revues, Herman began his Broadway career with the moderately successful *Milk and Honey*. He next did the scores for two of the biggest hits of the sixties, *Hello, Dolly!* and *Mame*, and for a time it looked as if Herman had only to create a vehicle for a series of menopausal stars to have a smash. The rude awak-ening came with *Dear World*, the first of three successive Herman flops.

Jean Giraudoux's *The Madwoman of Chaillot*, as adapted by Maurice Valency, ran almost a year on Broadway in 1948. Herman, who had played the part of the deaf-mute as a University of Miami student, had long sought the rights to musicalize *Madwoman*, but they were held by Michel Legrand and Richard Wilbur, who had written a musical version of the play with Valency as librettist. With the clout he possessed after two gigantic hits, Herman was finally able to get the rights away from that team. As he would later reassemble the *Annie* team for *I Remember Mama*, producer Alexander H. Cohen reunited Herman with *Mame*'s star (Angela Lansbury), librettists (Jerome Lawrence and Robert E. Lee), featured star (Jane Connell), musical director (Donald Pippin), and orchestrator (Philip J. Lang) in a blatant attempt to cash in on that still-running show's success. *Dear World*'s heroine, Countess Aurelia, driven mad when she let the love of her life get away, takes on the chairman of the board of the world's largest corporation, who is attempting to get at the oil underneath Paris, and wins, saving the world and then going off to conquer a new "tomorrow morning." With an unconventional philosophy and an ability to conquer the establishment and solve all problems, even Aurelia herself had striking similarities to Mame Dennis.

The original play had only two settings, the cafe and Aurelia's apartment. The musical opened the play up to include the Parisian sewers, a flea market, and some streets. The play's ragpicker and sewerman were combined into one character, and the play's three other madwomen became only two.

Lansbury, very hot after *Mame*, signed a two-year contract, and Cohen splashed a glamour photo of her, swathed in white fur, across full-page newspaper ads eliciting mail orders before the show even went into rehearsal. *Dear World* then embarked on an extremely troubled period of development. Lucia Victor, longtime assistant to Gower Champion, was hired to make her Broadway directorial debut. After a few days, Lansbury and others were not happy, and Victor soon "resigned," "artistic differences" with Lansbury and the authors given out to the press as the reason for her departure. Peter Glenville, who had directed Lansbury in *Hotel Paradiso* on Broadway, came in. The reviews in Boston were mostly negative, and Cohen instigated a suit against *Women's Wear Daily* when it printed an item stating that Lansbury wanted the show closed in Boston. Glenville, who had signed on in between commitments as a favor to Lansbury, withdrew, and Joe Layton became the show's third director, also replacing choreographer Donald Saddler.

○ ○ ○ ○ ○

Above, a theatre-party audience about to be disappointed by Dear World. *But they were not disappointed by Angela Lansbury, here telling Kurt Peterson that one must begin again* "Each Tomorrow Morning."

Even a flop can have four different Playbill covers. In order, they were the melancholy Boston pose; the "Bette Davis" photo; the logo cover; and the desperation cover, with an eight-by-ten glossy of Lansbury sans her Countess Aurelia drag.

At record-high ticket prices, *Dear World* played forty-nine New York previews, canceling its opening several times while critics threatened to review it. Joe Masteroff worked on book revisions, but Lansbury was by now aware that the show was getting worse, not better: "I promise you that the show we opened with in Boston had far more quality in the first five minutes than we ever achieved with all the changes," she later said.

Dear World finally opened in early February, to mostly poor reviews containing praise for Lansbury, Miguel Godreau as the mute, Connell and Carmen Mathews as Aurelia's fellow madwomen, and Herman's score. Shortly after the opening, the *New York Post* ran this item: "Lansbury wants out. And the rest of the cast is feuding with Angela. They claim she behaved like a virago, insisting on multiple changes in the play out of town. Angela, on her part, insists that the musical, which was faring badly with audiences in Boston, needed them." Whatever the truth, *Dear World* had mostly run out of audiences by the time it opened on Broadway; it lasted about four months on what was left of the advance sale, then closed at a loss of $750,000. Lansbury went on to win her second Tony as Best Actress in a Musical.

Dear World was a classic mismatch of material and authors. The bombastic style so suited to *Mame* was wrong for Giraudoux's delicate piece, which was blown up into a big musical quite alien in spirit to the original. The heroine of the play was far more complex than the one in the musical, who was pretty much the standard Broadway musical heroine of the period. The show was so overproduced from the beginning that it was not really fixable on the road or in previews.

There were other problems built into the source. In 1969, it's doubtful that even the original play itself would have worked—a film version released the same year with Katharine Hepburn and an all-star cast also bombed. Like Giraudoux's *Madwoman*, *Dear World* was virtually plotless: it established a situation at the beginning—there's oil under Paris, and the Establishment wants it—and abruptly resolved that situation at the final curtain. Nothing really happened in between.

Herman's score contained lovely things like Aurelia's "And I Was Beautiful" and the tea-party sequence for the three madwomen, but also some things that were damaging. The title song, moved on the road from late in the second act to the first act finale, was a very destructive number, completely foreign to Giraudoux, and with a poor lyric to boot.

For all of the show's flaws, those who saw it may never be able to forget the sight of Lansbury, draped in a nine-foot feather boa, confront-

○ ○ ○ ○ ○

ing a lost lover in her sleep—hers was a stunning performance. In later years, Lansbury chose to blame the failure of *Dear World* on her very presence in it, maintaining that her public had not wished to see her playing an old and unglamorous lady. But she was wrong: Lansbury was the one great thing about the show. Make that Lansbury and the logo.

Why didn't Jerry Herman realize that his style was not suited to Giraudoux? Why didn't Richard Rodgers see that *Pipe Dream* would not be another *South Pacific*? What made Frank Loesser, the composer of *Guys and Dolls* and *How to Succeed*, write *Pleasures and Palaces*? How did Charles Strouse get involved in six musical flops in a row? That the writers discussed in this section are talented men is beyond question. But a musical's road from original conception to finished production involves so many variables that there is often no way of knowing in advance that no matter how much serious thought and hard work are put in, some ideas just won't work. And as we have seen, the writer is often at the mercy of producers, directors, even other writers, who may not share the same conception of the show as he does. The most promising projects can go awry, and even the most talented artists are not immune to failure. That's what makes theatre so unpredictable, so fascinating to follow season after season. That's showbiz.

Four

THE MOVIE
WAS BETTER

" 'I had the strangest feeling,' remarks Dennis King shortly after his arrival, 'that the world had stopped turning on its axis.' And so, as the evening wore on, did I. "—Walter Kerr, *Herald Tribune,* on *Shangri-La*

"Utter disaster . . . seems likely to be remembered among such legituner fiascos as *Buttrio Square, Cafe Crown* and *Kelly.*"—Hobe Morrison, *Variety,* on *Pousse-Café*

" *Gantry* opened Saturday night with its cast practically reading the closing notice on stage . . . a mess. "—Martin Gottfried, *Women's Wear Daily*

Dolores Gray in Carnival in Flanders (*above*)

Many properties, even if they were originally novels or plays, are best known and loved in their film versions. And many films were made into successful musicals: *A Little Night Music, Sweet Charity, Zorba, Applause, La Cage aux Folles, Little Shop of Horrors, Nine,* and *Carnival* were all inspired by popular films. But inevitably there are Broadway musicals which fall short when compared with their famous film sources. Some of the musicals in this section were based on material that first appeared as a novel or play, but which achieved greatest or most lasting renown in the movies; some were based on original film scripts. In all cases, the musical failed to live up to the source.

At least five Broadway musicals were based on movies that were already musicals. Only one of these, *42nd Street,* provided a really new theatrical experience; its director–choreographer, Gower Champion, transmuted the original through his own choreographic sensibility, and with many new songs added, the show was stylistically dissimilar to its source and so felt like a new musical, even though its story was the same old clichéd one from the picture. But the other stage musicals taken from movie musicals were so lacking in creative impulse that it might have been better to simply lower a screen and show the film than take the trouble to mount a production doomed to suffer by comparison to its source.

Gigi was a 1944 novel by Colette, a French film, and a 1951 Broadway play, adapted by Anita Loos and starring Audrey Hepburn, before it reached its most successful incarnation, the 1958 movie musical written by Alan Jay Lerner and Frederick Loewe as their first project after *My Fair Lady.* Lerner and Loewe had split after writing *Camelot* in 1960, but reunited to write the songs for the film *The Little Prince.* Because they enjoyed working together again, in 1973 they finally accepted the offer Edwin Lester had been making for years to present a stage version of their **Gigi** (Uris; Nov. 13, '73; 103).

Lerner and Loewe wrote five new songs for the stage production, which premiered at the Los Angeles and San Francisco Civic Light Operas, then toured, with Lerner unofficially replacing Joseph Hardy as director. It received mixed reviews on Broadway, closing after less than four months and, even after its long pre-Broadway tour, losing more than half of its investment of $800,000. The Lerner–Loewe score, because it had never been sung on Broadway before, won the Best Score Tony Award.

There were several problems with this stage *Gigi.* While it offered enjoyable performances from Alfred Drake, Agnes Moorehead, Daniel Massey, and Maria Karnilova, the Gigi, Karin Wolfe, unlike her film

○ ○ ○ ○ ○

predecessor, Leslie Caron, was not able to hold her own with her fellow stars: Wolfe was adequate but bland. Further, though the show's book was basically faithful to the film script, with bits of new dialogue here and there, its story of the selling of a young girl to a man proved more distasteful to seventies sensibilities than it had to fifties filmgoers. Then, too, the film of *Gigi* had always borne striking similarities to *My Fair Lady*; putting *Gigi* onstage only called attention to them. Moreover, the stage version lacked style, so the thinness of the plot became more obvious.

But producers would not give up on a stage *Gigi*. In 1984, a new American tour went out, with Louis Jourdan, the film's Gaston, playing Honore (the Maurice Chevalier part) and lip-synching to prerecorded tracks. In 1985, John Dexter directed a London stage version which turned the piece into an intimate chamber musical very much unlike the huge Broadway version. It too failed: all stage versions of the movie were ultimately pointless, as none could equal the film's cast or its stylish evocation of Paris in 1900. With the film readily available on television and later on videotape, what was the point?

Equally pointless was the stage version of another celebrated movie musical, **Seven Brides for Seven Brothers** (Alvin; July 8, '82; 5). Joshua Logan had acquired the stage rights to Stephen Vincent Benét's 1928 short story "The Sobbin' Women" in 1949, but they lapsed, and MGM took over the property, turning it into the acclaimed 1954 film *Seven Brides for Seven Brothers*. Not content to leave well enough alone, Lawrence Kasha and David S. Landay decided to produce and write a stage version, following the screenplay very closely; Kasha also directed. Al Kasha (Lawrence's brother) and Joel Hirschhorn, who had won Oscars for disaster-movie songs, wrote six new songs, dropping four from the film's fine Gene de Paul–Johnny Mercer score.

The stage *Seven Brides* first toured during the 1978–79 season with the film's stars, Jane Powell and Howard Keel, who, twenty-five years later, were simply too old. A new tour began in 1982, with Debby Boone playing opposite first Laurence Guittard, then David-James Carroll. During the road tour, Boone starred in an unintentionally hilarious television special called "One Step Closer," in which she appeared with the show's gypsies and tried desperately to look like one of the kids.

Perhaps it would have been wiser to leave this *Seven Brides* on the road, but it arrived on Broadway to become the fifth consecutive musical bomb at the Alvin Theatre (preceded by *Merrily We Roll Along, The Little Prince*

○ ○ ○ ○ ○

and the Aviator, a revival of *Little Johnny Jones* with Donny Osmond, and *Do Black Patent Leather Shoes Really Reflect Up?*). The cast (minus Boone, who, according to the TV special, was inseparable from the company) picketed the *New York Times* for two days to protest Frank Rich's review, carrying placards declaring that Rich was "killing family entertainment." The Broadway *Seven Brides* closed in three days, but another stage version was presented in London in 1985; this time a recording was made which preserved the stage version's new songs.

The problems of *Seven Brides* on stage were similar to those of *Gigi*. The stage choreography could not hope to measure up to Michael Kidd's in the film, considered a high point in screen dance. The stage *Seven Brides*, even more than *Gigi*, looked like a touring package, suitable in New York only for out-of-towners. And as with *Gigi*, there was a pervading point-lessness about the whole project. The film was delightful, and there was no good reason to attempt a stage version that could only lose by com-parison. *Gigi* and *Seven Brides* were followed on Broadway by stage versions of *Singin' in the Rain* (1985) and *Meet Me in St. Louis* (1989). The last two had longer runs than the first two, but all were artistically bankrupt projects, financial failures, and entirely unnecessary.

By the mid-sixties, it is likely that Sinclair Lewis's *Elmer Gantry*, John Steinbeck's *East of Eden*, and Marjorie Kinnan Rawlings' *The Yearling* were more familiar to the public through film versions than through the im-mediate experience of reading the novels. The film versions of these novels worked well, but were these books suitable material for Broadway mu-sicalization?

Gantry (George Abbott; Feb. 14, '70; 1), based on Lewis's 1927 novel, which had been successfully adapted to the screen in 1960, had a book by Peter Bellwood and music by conductor Stanley Lebowsky, neither of whom had ever written a Broadway show before. The lyricist, Fred Tobias, had already collaborated on the lyrics for the disastrous *Pousse-Café*. *Gantry* was to be the only Broadway musical officially directed by choreographer Onna White. Like the film, the musical used less than half of the novel's plot, concentrating on the episodes involving Gantry and revivalist Sister Sharon Falconer.

Producer Joseph Cates decided on a month of New York previews instead of a tryout, but wanting to have it both ways, he announced plans to invite twelve out-of-town critics to New York during previews to offer their views on the show. This idea naturally enraged the New York critics

○ ○ ○ ○ ○

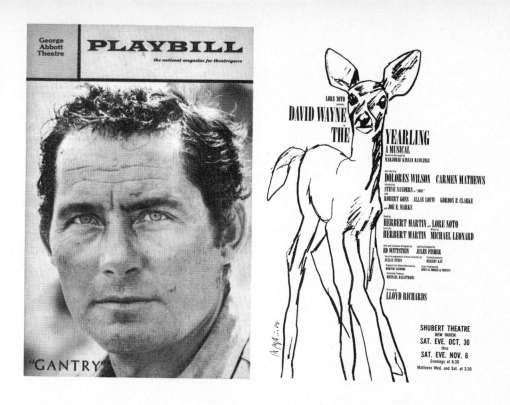

Three bombs that had been screen successes. Note the Lucite mountain in the Shangri-La photo below (left to right: Harold Lang, Joan Holloway, Jack Cassidy, Dennis King, Alice Ghostley, Martyn Green).

and was promptly dropped. The last show to open at the George Abbott Theatre before it was torn down, *Gantry* received negative reviews and closed in one night.

When the audience arrived at *Gantry*, it was greeted with a show curtain painted to resemble the side of a worn revival tent. It bore the inscription "Where Will YOU Spend Eternity?"—the answer turned out to be, at *Gantry*. Its book was a mere sketch of the novel's plot, with weak songs plunked, often aimlessly, into it. The book softened the less pleasant aspects of Lewis's hero and eliminated the girl Elmer had seduced who later became a prostitute (Shirley Jones won an Oscar for the part in the movie). Leading man Robert Shaw, making his musical debut (and fare-well), could sing a little, but it wasn't pleasant to hear. There was one fine gospel song, "He's Never Too Busy," but it was otherwise a poor score.

Cates didn't give up on musicalizing Lewis's novel, and in 1988 he presented another musical version, this time called *Elmer Gantry*, at Ford's Theatre in Washington, D.C., with an all-new writing team. The second *Gantry* musical was seen again at the La Jolla Playhouse in 1991. Lewis's novel had definite musical possibilities, but with its extravagant characters, outsized emotions, and tragic ending, it would have been more at home as an opera than as a musical.

Steinbeck's novel *East of Eden*, successfully filmed in 1955 with memo-rable performances by James Dean and Julie Harris, was considerably less suited to musicalization than *Elmer Gantry*. But Mitch Miller, of "Sing Along" fame, got United Artists to put up $500,000 to produce a musical version of *East of Eden* called **Here's Where I Belong** (Billy Rose; Mar. 3, '68; 1). The music was by Robert Waldman, the lyrics by Alfred Uhry; the team would later write a far superior musical, *The Robber Bridegroom*, and Uhry would win acclaim for his Pulitzer Prize-winning play, *Driving Miss Daisy*. The book was by Terrence McNally, who would go on to write another musical book (for *The Rink*) in which the young protagonist also mistakenly believes that one of his or her parents is dead. Michael Kahn made his Broadway debut as director, the most important roles were played by talented unknowns (Walter McGinn and Heather MacRae), and the above-the-title "stars" were nonmusical nonstars Paul Rogers (who sang pleasantly and spoke without a trace of his English accent) and Nancy Wickwire.

The show opened in Philadelphia, where a fire among the spotlights

○ ○ ○ ○ ○

proved to be the only moment of excitement on opening night. After bad reviews, choreographer Hanya Holm, just about the only person involved in the show who had any experience with Broadway musicals, was replaced by Tony Mordente, as if Holm's work were the problem with the show.

The musical, while eliminating major portions of Steinbeck's story, followed the novel and film's story of the Trask family in the Salinas Valley in the early 1900s, in particular brooding son Cal's rivalry with his father's preferred son, Aron. As in the other versions, Cal finds out that his mother, whom he believed dead, runs a nearby cathouse, and Aron's girl Abra is ineluctably drawn to the "bad" brother.

When book changes went in that were not his own, McNally asked to have his name removed from the credits. Miller claimed that McNally had not made the changes requested and refused to remove McNally's name, stating that eighty-five percent of the book was still McNally's. Finally, Miller relented, and the Broadway Playbill listed "Alex Gordon," a nom de plume for novelist Gordon Cotler, as the author of the book. In spite of the rewrites, much of McNally's original work remained.

On opening (and closing) night, nineteen members of an assocation known as the Oriental Actors of America picketed the theatre to protest the presence in the show of James Coco, a McNally favorite, absurdly cast as Lee, the Chinese houseboy who raised Adam Trask's sons. The reviews were terrible.

Steinbeck, whose *Sweet Thursday* had not succeeded as *Pipe Dream*, once again resisted musicalization. Much of the plot hinged on Adam's plans to ship frozen lettuce east and Cal's dabbling in bean futures, material unsuited to song and dance. A ballet and song in the show about the packing and shipping of lettuce was expectedly awful, as were all the production numbers. As long as *Here's Where I Belong* concentrated on Cal, Aron, and Abra, things were better, and there was a pretty ballad called "Waking Up Sun" and a nice duet for the brothers called "No Time." But the score didn't help sufficiently, and Steinbeck's story proved too dreary for a musical.

If *Here's Where I Belong* was a bleak, dullish show, it was a lark compared to **The Yearling** (Alvin; Dec. 10, '65; 3), adapted from the Pulitzer Prize-winning 1939 novel. *The Yearling* tripled the runs of one-nighters *Gantry* and *Here's Where's I Belong*. Gregory Peck and Jane Wyman had starred in the successful 1946 film version of the story of a boy in Northern Florida

o o o o o

in the late nineteenth century who comes of age through his experiences with a pet fawn. The musical, produced by Lore Noto, who had presented *The Fantasticks*, had a score by Michael Leonard and Herbert Martin and a book by Martin and Noto; none of them had written a Broadway musical before (Leonard and Martin would later write five songs for a flop Broadway comedy revue called *How to Be a Jewish Mother* in 1967).

Once again, Lloyd Richards was hired as director of a musical, and once again he was replaced (by Herbert Ross) without losing his directorial credit. The company included a fawn, two deer, two beagle hounds, a redbird, a raccoon, and Carmen Mathews in her latest musical flop. After two tryout dates, *The Yearling* arrived in New York; the Broadway opening was postponed from December 14 to January 3, then moved up to December 10 (significantly, a Friday), on only four-days' notice, when the money ran out. The company, headed by David Wayne as the father, played its opening-night performance with the closing notice posted backstage. *The Yearling* closed the next day, losing $375,000, $100,000 of it provided by Mercury Records.

Martin later said that he should never have attempted the book and that Noto should have hired an experienced librettist. Noto later claimed that Lloyd Richards was the problem. The truth was that *The Yearling* was highly unsuited to the musical stage. With a severe mother who had seen several of her babies die, the death of twelve-year-old Jody's best friend Fodder-Wing, and the shooting of Jody's beloved fawn at the end, *The Yearling* was almost unrelieved gloom, a very depressing evening. It also involved deer, snakebites, and bear hunting, the kind of thing best left to the movies. As with *Gantry*, *The Yearling* might have been possible as an opera, where constant misery is often the bill of fare.

Unlike *Gantry* and *Here's Where I Belong*, however, *The Yearling* had several wonderful songs in a generally fine score. Composer Leonard had once coached Barbra Streisand and was able to get *Yearling* songs to her; she recorded "I'm All Smiles," "My Pa" (cut prior to Broadway), "Why Did I Choose You?," and "The Kind of Man a Woman Needs," and *The Yearling* became one of the few disasters which, while they may never produce a cast recording, contain a couple of songs that lived on.

Probably because of the score, *The Yearling* was revived in 1985 at Atlanta Theater of the Stars, with a book solely by Martin and direction by Lucia Victor (of *Dear World* fame). John Cullum was the father this time, but in spite of considerable rewriting, this *Yearling* was even less effective than the original production.

○ ○ ○ ○ ○

James Hilton's novel *Lost Horizon*, which told of a group of travelers hijacked to a land where time does not exist and people live very long lives, was a big success on film in 1937 with Ronald Colman as Conway, the leader of the group, who has been brought to Shangri-La to succeed its High Lama. Although he died during the early stages of the subsequent stage production, Hilton shared book credit with Jerome Lawrence and Robert E. Lee for **Shangri-La** (Winter Garden; June 13, '56; 21), the Broadway musical based on his novel.

An initial pair of producers intended to musicalize *Lost Horizon* by using unpublished songs from the trunk of the late Vincent Youmans and wanted Walter Kerr (who later panned the show) to direct. The second pair of producers hired Harry Warren, the veteran film composer, to write the music to lyrics by Lawrence and Lee. *Shangri-La* was another show that experienced a tortuous tryout: in Boston, film star Lew Ayres withdrew from the role of Conway and was replaced by Jack Cassidy (who had been playing a smaller role in the show) until longtime operetta star Dennis King was ready to take over. (King's son John Michael was playing Freddy Eynsford-Hill across the street in *My Fair Lady* when *Shangri-La* arrived at the Winter Garden). Shirley Yamaguchi, a Japanese film and stage star who had been the original choice for the female lead, replaced Susan Cabot in Boston. And when he opened a Boston newspaper, *Shangri-La*'s director, Marshall Jamison, found out he was being replaced by Albert Marre. The show shut down for a couple of weeks in Boston for additional rehearsal.

The New York critics had good words for Irene Sharaff's costumes, Yamaguchi, Harold Lang and Joan Holloway as a pair of USO hoofers, and Alice Ghostley as a comic missionary. Singled out for the highest praise were Peter Larkin's sets, which featured mountains made of Lucite and a translucent, tilted floor with colored lights beneath.

Hilton's story, which had made for an enjoyably campy nonmusical film, was turned into a stage musical lacking in magic and entirely too placid; the tranquility of Shangri-La was taken too literally by the show's creators. The score sounded rather like one of Wright and Forrest's adaptations of classical themes, with a few pretty tunes prettily sung by Cassidy and Yamaguchi.

The authors may not have realized that musicalizing Hilton's novel would point up the story's similarities to *Brigadoon*. Both are about "lost" towns with a secret; at the end of the first act of both, an outsider learns

o o o o o

the truth about the town; and both had almost the same ending, with the outsider hero managing to return to the town from civilization through willpower and belief. But *Brigadoon* had a wonderful score, superb choreography, and considerable charm and humor. *Shangri-La* did not.

Shangri-La is one of very few flop musicals that was later presented on television, in a Hallmark Hall of Fame presentation in October 1960. Richard Basehart, Marisa Pavan, Claude Rains, Gene Nelson, Helen Gallagher, and Alice Ghostley, in her original role, had the leads. In 1973, Burt Bacharach and Hal David made a new attempt to musicalize Hilton, which turned into the movie-musical disaster *Lost Horizon* (the one Bette Midler couldn't wait to see). Harry Warren's old film-songs came to Broadway twenty-four years after *Shangri-La* in the long-running *42nd Street*, which opened at the Winter Garden Theatre, erstwhile home of *Shangri-La*.

Unlike most of the properties discussed thus far in this chapter, *The World of Henry Orient* should have made a wonderful musical. Nora Johnson's autobiographical novel about the farcical escapades of two teenage girls who inadvertently terrorize their idol, a concert pianist, was inspired by Johnson's own crush on Oscar Levant. The property achieved much greater fame when Nora and her father, Nunnally Johnson, adapted her story of adolescence, growing up, and learning to accept life's hard knocks into the screenplay for a 1964 film, also called *The World of Henry Orient*. For the musical stage, the elder Johnson wrote the book, and Bob Merrill, whose most recent project was *Breakfast at Tiffany's*, provided the score for **Henry, Sweet Henry** (Palace; Oct. 23, '67; 80). George Roy Hill, who had directed the film so well, directed his second unsuccessful Broadway musical; *Greenwillow* was his first.

The show first played Detroit, then was greeted with unanimous praise in Philadelphia. But it arrived on Broadway one week after *New York Times* critic Clive Barnes had been overcome by *Hair* at the Public Theatre and decided that Broadway musicals must have scores reflecting the sounds of contemporary music. *Henry, Sweet Henry* did not, and Barnes was extremely displeased with the show and with Merrill's score in particular. Walter Kerr liked the show in the Sunday *Times*, and there were other good reviews, but *Henry* never recovered from Barnes' pan and lost its $400,000 investment in less than three months.

In *Henry*, the scenes, songs, and dances for the adolescent girls were far better than those for the mature characters like Henry, transformed

○ ○ ○ ○ ○

for the musical from a pianist into an avant-garde composer, and Mrs. Boyd, the adulterous mother of Val, the show's central character. Merrill successfully musicalized the feelings of a neglected, sensitive young woman in "Here I Am," "Do You Ever Go to Boston," and "I Wonder How It Is to Dance with a Boy," dealing with these emotions more directly (if less subtly) than they had been presented in the movie. But Merrill had a much harder time musicalizing the adults, Henry and Mrs. Boyd sharing a notably embarrassing duet called "To Be Artistic." Moreover, Don Ameche's Henry and Carol Bruce's Mrs. Boyd, owing to their material, were no match for Peter Sellers and Angela Lansbury in the same parts in the movie.

Michael Bennett contributed imaginative choreography to the girls' fantasy in "I Wonder How It Is to Dance with a Boy" and to a hippie scene in Washington Square Park. But the show never quite captured the charm and humor of the film; the story was not told as well in the musical; and some of the songs (including the hippie number and two amusing outcries for Alice Playten as Val's demonic nemesis, Kafritz) actually took up time that should have been devoted to plot development. But because the movie had been a fine choice for musicalization, the musical wasn't awful, as long as it stuck to the young people.

There were two successful films called *Seventh Heaven:* a 1927 silent movie with Charles Farrell and Janet Gaynor and a 1937 sound remake with James Stewart and Simone Simon; both were based on a play by Austin Strong. It was perhaps inevitable, then, that someone would try to musicalize the story of Diane, a girl of the streets, and Chico, the "king of the Paris sewers" who aspires to be a street cleaner, and of their bliss in Chico's seventh-floor garret.

John C. Wilson, director of *Kiss Me, Kate* and *Gentlemen Prefer Blondes,* staged the musical **Seventh Heaven** (ANTA; May 26, '55; 44), and Hollywood composer Victor Young composed the music. The book was by Victor Wolfson and Stella Unger, with lyrics by Unger. Designer, painter, and illustrator Marcel Vertes was hired to create the scenery and costumes. The show had been planned as a vehicle for Edith Piaf and her husband, Jacques Pills, but instead it provided Broadway debuts for Gloria De Haven and Ricardo Montalban. Chita Rivera received a great deal of attention as one of a trio of prostitutes.

In New Haven, Paul Hartman, who played Boule, the rascally taxi driver who narrated the show, was replaced by Kurt Kasznar. Fifi D'Orsay,

○ ○ ○ ○ ○

who played the hookers' madam, held on through New Haven and Philadelphia but was replaced by Beatrice Arthur in Boston.

Seventh Heaven had a mixed-to-pleasant score; particularly good were the opening "C'est la Vie," Montalban's "A Man with a Dream," and the numbers for the prostitutes. Peter Gennaro, fresh from dancing "Steam Heat" with Carol Haney in *The Pajama Game*, choreographed two good ballets, the carnival number ending the first act and the "White and Gold" ballet, Chico's dream, just before he leaves to fight in WWI, of his wedding to Diane. (Gennaro's assistant was Lee Becker; two years later, Gennaro would co-choreograph Becker and Rivera in *West Side Story*.) And everyone loved Vertes' colorful designs.

But Diane and Chico tended to get lost among all the local color, and the effective schmaltz of the play and film versions was bungled. The material became much more explicit—Diane, formerly a street thief, was now specifically a prostitute—and the frail charm was gone. Moreover, the lack of a substantial plot, a fault somehow less noticeable in the film versions because of the glamorous stars, was more evident in the musical. A late May opening and mixed-to-negative reviews killed *Seventh Heaven* off in six weeks.

Two acclaimed British film comedies, *The Captain's Paradise* and *Georgy Girl*, were the basis for unsuccessful Broadway musicals; the first made a rather better musical than the second. Alec Coppel's screenplay for the 1953 Alec Guinness film *The Captain's Paradise* was turned into **Oh Captain!** (Alvin; Feb. 4, '58; 192), which told of Captain Henry St. James, who, when at home in Surrey, is the model of the proper Englishman. But the captain sails from London to Paris every week (in the movie, the voyage is between Gibraltar and North Africa), and in Paris, Henry becomes an animal, full of joie de vivre, with Bobo, a singer at Le Club Paradis. When Henry's proper English wife, Maud, surprises him—and Bobo— in Paris, pandemonium breaks loose.

Richard Adler and Jerry Ross, Sammy Cahn and James Van Heusen, and Bob Merrill were variously announced for the score, but it was eventually written by Jay Livingston and Ray Evans, Academy Award-winning Hollywood songwriters making their Broadway debut. Danny Kaye was the first choice for the role of Henry, then David Wayne, Dennis King, George Sanders, Sid Caesar, and even Laurence Olivier considered it. When Jose Ferrer was signed to direct and cowrite the book with Al

Abbe Lane (on Playbill cover with Tony Randall) looks every bit as saucy as the logo for Oh Captain!, at right. Below, the wonderful Susan Johnson goes into action in Oh Captain!. Having already appeared in Buttrio Square, Johnson left the hit Most Happy Fella for Oh Captain!; Whoop-Up followed nine months later.

Morgan, he considered playing Henry, but the part went to stage and television actor Tony Randall.

Abbe Lane got the role of Bobo, and her husband, bandleader Xavier Cugat, was hired to play Manzoni, the Captain's first mate. Cugat received third billing in the early advertisements but withdrew just before the tryout and was replaced by Edward Platt. Reviews in Philadelphia were good, and *Oh Captain!*, probably because of its source, Lane, and its sexy logo, arrived on Broadway with an advance sale of over $2 million. The New York critics were evenly divided, all of them praising Randall and the other principals. (Somehow, RCA Victor considered Abbe Lane so important to the success of its record catalogue that it would not risk allowing her to appear on the Columbia Records cast recording; Eileen Rodgers took her place, and Lane recorded a couple of *Oh Captain!* songs on one of her RCA recitals. Ferrer and wife Rosemary Clooney, who was mentioned in the show's script, recorded an LP entirely devoted to the score of *Oh Captain!*) Dorothy Lamour replaced Lane a week before the show closed.

Shortly after the closing, co-producer Donald H. Coleman was slapped with two law suits for misappropriation of funds; in spite of a run of over six months, the show had lost almost all of its $300,000 investment. The charges against Coleman included allowing Ferrer to put on the show's payroll his brother Raphael (as assistant stage manager) and his lawyer.

Oh Captain! was a return to the tired-businessman girlie show, but with musicals like *West Side Story, My Fair Lady, New Girl in Town,* and *The Music Man* nearby, it seemed a little out of place. The Livingston and Evans score was an enormous help, though, well above average and containing several excellent numbers. There was also a delightful if irrelevant scene in which Henry, just arrived in Paris, encounters a flower seller named Lisa, played by the celebrated Russian ballerina Alexandra Danilova. Choreographer James Starbuck's dance for Randall and Danilova, describing a Paris night on the town, was the best five minutes in the show. There was also the unfailing Susan Johnson, who as Mae, proprietress of Bobo's club, sported purple tresses and introduced her showgirls to the audience with the line, "Now folks, on with the show and the ladies of the ensemble. That's a French word for, like, broads."

But the musical opted for a sitcom plot instead of the film's subtler, cleverer story. In the movie, the captain's two wives never meet; instead, each decides she wants the life the other one is leading, and both ultimately leave Henry for men who will give them what they want. And

Oh Captain!'s writers made a serious strategical error: they had Henry sing a song about his "Three Paradises" (the ship and his two homes) too early in the show; it let the audience in on the big secret before they were allowed to discover it for themselves.

Overall, *Oh Captain!* was silly, dirty, and amusing. A borderline fifties musical—not great, not bad, but good for a season's run—it lacked the charm and class of the movie. Three years later, Livingston and Evans contributed a less interesting score to *Let It Ride*, a botched musicalization of *Three Men on a Horse* which starred George Gobel and Sam Levene and ran two months.

If *Oh Captain!* didn't quite live up to its film source, **Georgy** (Winter Garden; Feb. 26, '70; 4) was a far more unnecessary adaptation of the hit 1966 British film comedy *Georgy Girl*, which told of Georgy, a dowdy teacher; her bitchy roommate, Meredith; and Jos, who impregnates Meredith and then falls for the warmly lovable Georgy. The book for the musical, based on a novel by Margaret Forster and the screenplay by Forster and Peter Nichols, was by Tom Mankiewicz, the music by George Fischoff, and the lyrics by Carole Bayer (later, as Carole Bayer Sager, the lyricist for the Broadway hit *They're Playing Our Song*). Peter Hunt, hot from the previous season's *1776*, was hired to direct.

Georgy was not terrible, but it never provided a reason for being. At the time, it was typical for even the most conventional book musicals to be outfitted with trendy, pop-style scores, and *Georgy*'s was modestly attractive. But the movie was a small story that focused on four people, and attempts to open it up and to bring on an ensemble for production numbers were forced and damaging. The musical's leads—nonstars Dilys Watling, John Castle, Stephen Elliot, and Melissa Hart—were good but easily outclassed by the star power of the film's Lynn Redgrave, Alan Bates, James Mason, and Charlotte Rampling. Without a scintillating personality in the title role, there really was no justification for repeating what had been done so well on the screen only four years earlier. Watling, rather too attractive for Georgy, was, at season's end, the forlorn third nominee for the Best Actress in a Musical Tony Award against Lauren Bacall in *Applause* and Katharine Hepburn in *Coco*.

Four substantial musical flops were inspired by popular French-language movies. The earliest was **Carnival in Flanders** (New Century; Sept. 8, '53; 6), a benighted project from its inception. Based on a flawless 1934

○ ○ ○ ○ ○

film comedy called *La kermesse heroique, Carnival in Flanders* took place in 1616. A Spanish duke descends on a peaceful Flemish town, and the mayor decides to play dead, hoping the Spanish will leave. But the duke decides to stay when he sees the mayor's wife, Cornelia, so the mayor must continue to play dead and watch as the duke pays court to his "widow."

Harold Arlen was to have written the score, but the task ultimately fell to James Van Heusen and Johnny Burke, who had collaborated on the disastrous *Nellie Bly* in 1946. The scenic production, inspired by Flemish painters like Breughel (Breughel's son appeared in the script as the young romantic lead), was by Oliver Smith and Lucinda Ballard. As Cornelia, Dolores Gray had her first starring part in a book show in New York, and John Raitt was the duke. It was Raitt's third consecutive flop, after *Magdalena* and *Three Wishes for Jamie*, but he was rewarded with *The Pajama Game* at the end of the same season. Much of the show's financing was supplied by Bing Crosby, many of whose hit songs were written by Burke and Van Heusen.

The book was originally by George Oppenheimer and Herbert Fields. Oppenheimer withdrew in Philadelphia, and Fields' sister, Dorothy, came in to help with rewrites. During the Philadelphia engagement, Edwin Lester tried to back out of presenting *Carnival in Flanders* at his California Civic Light Operas that summer, claiming it was too salacious; he attempted to book *Hazel Flagg*, then on its summer hiatus, instead. Lester was forced to take the show, but Preston Sturges, who had fled *Make a Wish*, took over the direction (from Bretaigne Windust) and rewrote the book, taking credit for both, before the show got to Los Angeles. The original choreographer, Jack Cole, was replaced by Helen Tamiris, and Walter Abel, who took on the role of the mayor when William Gaxton withdrew before rehearsals, was also replaced for Broadway.

The show that limped into the New Century was panned, with raves only for Gray and lead dancer Matt Mattox, still performing much of Cole's choreography. Gray received a Tony Award as Best Actress in a Musical—her Cornelia ranks as the shortest-lived Tony-winning performance ever—then headed straight back to Los Angeles to begin a four-picture contract with MGM.

La kermesse heroique had musical possibilities, but *Carnival in Flanders'* flat, plodding book, full of lame jokes, destroyed them. The score was considerably better, with a lot of opportunities for Gray to unfurl one of the theatre's best voices. One song, "Here's That Rainy Day," went on to have a life after the show. But with its book written and rewritten by Oppenheimer, H. Fields, D. Fields, and Sturges, and its personnel changed again and again, *Carnival in Flanders* might best have been left on the road.

A flop that in the last decade has gained an undeserved reputation as an undervalued gem, **King of Hearts** (Minskoff; Oct. 22, '78; 48) was based on the screenplay of the 1967 French film directed and coauthored by Philippe de Broca. The film had not initially made a big impression in this country, but it developed a large cult following mostly among college students, who found its theme—that lunatics are saner than so-called "sane" people—suitable to their world view.

The musical was first performed at the Westport Country Playhouse, with music by Peter Link, lyrics by Jacob Brackman, a book by Steve Tesich, direction by A. J. Antoon, and Robby Benson in the lead. For Broadway, Joseph Stein wrote a new book, Ron Field directed and choreographed (it was the last show he directed on Broadway), and Don Scardino, who had recently headed the cast of the flop musical *Angel* at the same theatre, played the lead (and later married the show's ingenue, Pamela Blair). The Broadway version tried out in Boston, not far from the Cambridge movie house in which the *King of Hearts* movie had played for years, then came into the Minskoff—a theatre far too large for a show like this, which required intimacy—ran six weeks, and lost $1.8 million. The acting version now distributed features Tesich's original book.

The theme of *King of Hearts* was already well-worn, not to mention meretricious. And the story was far too thin for a musical: in 1918 in a small French village, the Germans have planted bombs set to go off in time for the arrival of American troops. The town is evacuated, except for the inmates of the local asylum, and one American soldier is sent ahead to defuse the bombs. Taking refuge at the asylum, he leaves the gates open, and the inmates wander into the deserted town and live out their fantasies by assuming roles of prominent townspeople. Not a bad little idea, but all of that took place in the show's first fifteen minutes, and nothing really happened again until the soldier located the bombs and decided to remain with the lunatics at the very end. Stein's book was short on humor, and in the absence of a plot, the evening was padded out with a lengthy circus sequence, a coronation, and other diversions. The score, including a pleasant romantic duet called "Nothing Only Love," was not good enough to make a difference.

○ ○ ○ ○ ○

Ron Field later claimed that Santo Loquasto's eye-popping sets were the cause of the show's failure: "They destroyed the show . . . I wanted rubble . . . instead, he gave me a clean little clockmaker's village, all very quaint." But overwhelming as they were, Loquasto's sets were the best thing in the show.

Similar problems beset our next musicalization of a French film, **Roza** (Royale; Oct. 1, '87; 12). The show was actually adapted from Romain Gary's 1974 novel *La vie devant soi*, but that story was far better known as the Academy Award-winning 1977 film *Madame Rosa*, which had starred Simone Signoret. The musical was the idea of the French pop composer Gilbert Becaud, who brought the show to Harold Prince. Prince turned the show down a few times, then took it on, bringing in Julian More to write the book and lyrics. It was to be Prince's fourth consecutive New York flop (*Merrily, A Doll's Life,* and *Grind* preceded it), although his production of the blockbuster *The Phantom of the Opera* had its premiere in London just before *Roza* went into rehearsal.

Roza, set in 1970 in Belville, an immigrant quarter of Paris, told of a Polish-born former prostitute, a survivor of the concentration camps, who makes her living by taking care of the children of prostitutes, among them Momo, an Arab boy seeking his real parents. The musical had actually secured a date (June 26, 1984) and a theatre (the Adelphi) for a London opening, but the financing fell through days before rehearsals were to begin. Perhaps because of the failure of *A Doll's Life* and *Grind,* Prince chose to develop *Roza* in two regional theatres, the Center Stage in Baltimore and the Mark Taper Forum in Los Angeles. Audiences seemed to like it in both cities; Prince was aware that it wasn't strong enough for Broadway, but he allowed it to go in anyway. The New York critics condemned the show for its calculated sentimentality, and it ran less than two weeks. Prince later said that had *Roza* not gone to Broadway, it might have had a life in regional theatres.

Georgia Brown delivered an all-out star performance; if the actress best remembered for her Nancy in *Oliver!* now seemed to be playing Fagin, and if the musical Roza sometimes sounded like Zorba or Tevye in drag, it wasn't Brown's fault. Becaud's score, employing French, Jewish, African, Arabic, and Caribbean styles, at least reflected the ethnic mix of the show's setting. But it leaned too heavily in the direction of soft Euro-pop, with Brown's opening song, "Happiness," the only totally successful number.

○ ○ ○ ○ ○

But *Roza*'s biggest problem was the same one that plagued *King of Hearts*: lack of a plot. The musical set up its situation and introduced its characters in the first few minutes; then, except for one encounter between Momo and his father, little happened for the rest of the evening. Rich atmosphere carried the show for a while, but the second act was virtually all padding, marking time until Roza's death with street performers, voodoo rites, and other interludes.

As with *King of Hearts*, the set, by Alexander Okun, was stunning. Showing the apartments of Roza and many of her neighbors with disorienting levels and angles, and staircases that went down to go up, it conveyed better than anything in the script the vivid tumult and color of life in Belville. *Roza*'s assets were Brown and a palpable sense of an entire community onstage, teeming with life. But *King of Hearts*, *Roza*, and our next show, *The Baker's Wife*, all demonstrate that mood pieces with little story can—thanks to location color, star presences, and close-ups—work on screen, but they don't often adapt well to the musical stage.

The failure of **The Baker's Wife** (Los Angeles; May 11, '76; closed on the road) was much sadder than that of *Flanders*, *King of Hearts*, or *Roza* because it had one thing that those other three French-film adaptations didn't: a wonderful score. Marcel Pagnol and Jean Giono's play and 1938 film *La femme du boulanger* was first announced for musicalization in 1952 by Feuer and Martin, who had in mind Bert Lahr for the title role, Frank Loesser for the score, and Abe Burrows for the book. Over the years it was discussed as a possible vehicle for Zero Mostel. Ultimately, David Merrick took on the property; it was something of a homecoming for him, as his first major musical hit had been *Fanny*, also based on Pagnol and also featuring a young heroine who marries an older man. For the book, Merrick hired Joseph Stein, then in his period of decline which had already produced *So Long, 174th Street* and would go on to include *King of Hearts*, *Carmelina*, and *Rags*. The music and lyrics were by Stephen Schwartz, who had enjoyed an unbroken string of hits (*Godspell*, *Pippin*, *The Magic Show*) before *The Baker's Wife*. Topol, the Israeli star who had won acclaim in *Fiddler on the Roof* in London and on screen, was signed to make his American stage debut. *The Baker's Wife* also featured the last set by Jo Mielziner, who died just before the show hit the road.

Merrick sent *The Baker's Wife* out on a lengthy tour, commencing with a Civic Light Opera engagement in Los Angeles. During the tour, original director Joseph Hardy was replaced by John Berry, choreographer Dan

○ ○ ○ ○ ○

La Strada

Lilo was glorious—in Can-Can. She was far less effective in Pousse-Café (photo above, with Theodore Bikel). Pousse-Café, La Strada, and The Baker's Wife were all based on far superior foreign-language films.

OPERA HOUSE AT THE KENNEDY CENTER

TOPOL

in

THE BAKER'S WIFE

Siretta was succeeded by Robert Tucker, and leading lady Carole Demas was followed by Loni Ackerman, who was herself replaced by Patti LuPone. Jerome Robbins came in to "advise" in San Francisco, where Herschel Bernardi was mentioned as a possible replacement for Topol, who wasn't working out. But Topol stayed until two weeks before the show closed in Washington, D.C. Paul Sorvino played the last two weeks of the run and would have gone on to the Martin Beck Theatre for the scheduled November 21 opening. But Sorvino, much better than Topol, was too late; Schwartz and Stein were so dissatisfied with what had happened to their show by that time that they requested it be shut down. *The Baker's Wife* had played six months and lost $1 million.

Like *Merrily We Roll Along* after it, however, *The Baker's Wife* stayed alive thanks to a recording, made on a shoestring with only the four leads, of ten of the show's songs. The songs, especially "Chanson," "Merci, Madame," "Gifts of Love," and "Meadowlark," were so ravishing that companies across the country took up the show, and Schwartz and Stein actively involved themselves in revisions. *The Baker's Wife* was given its New York premiere by the York Theatre Company in 1985, and though the original book had been considerably improved, a miscast Jack Weston in the lead and uninspired direction by Schwartz did not help the show's cause.

Trevor Nunn, director of such megahits as *Cats* and *Les Misérables*, kept hearing songs from *The Baker's Wife* (particulary "Meadowlark," which Merrick had decided was too long for a ballad and had eliminated for a time by going into the pit and tearing up the music) being sung by performers at his auditions. Nunn became interested in the show, worked with the writers, staged a workshop, and then directed and coproduced a large-scale West End production of *The Baker's Wife* in 1989. With a superb performance by Alun Armstrong as the baker, and Nunn's wife, Sharon Lee Hill, in the title role, the London production featured several new songs, all fine if not as wonderful as the ten on the American recording retained for London, and restored a few from the initial tryout. The book used much of the York Theatre revision, but with many additional changes. For all of the improvements, the London version swelled the show to almost three hours by creating too much new material for the supporting characters. The length only served to emphasize *The Baker's Wife*'s main problem, and the London production closed quickly.

That main problem, from Los Angeles to London, is simple and irreparable: the show has one of the thinnest plots ever. A new baker arrives in town with his young wife; the wife runs off with the attractive chauffeur of the local marquis; the baker stops baking, causing a local catastrophe, until the wife, contrite and wise, returns to her husband. It's significant that Merrick's *Fanny* combined three Pagnol plays and films to make a single successful musical book. All the songs and scenes involving the colorfully comic locals are so much padding, and the fine score is ultimately let down by the tenuousness of the material. There are other problems: the story is predictable, with little doubt that the wife will return to her baker, and the chauffeur is an unsympathetic character. But all the rewrites and improvements which *The Baker's Wife* has undergone from 1976 to 1989 are really beside the point because of its wispy story, which worked in the film (thanks to colorful personalities like Raimu as the baker and authentic local color). When people hear the score of *The Baker's Wife*, though, they want to produce the whole show, so if this particular flop is never likely to work completely, it is surely likely to be done again.

One film directed and cowritten by Federico Fellini and starring Fellini's wife, Giulietta Masina—*Nights of Cabiria*—had been made into a successful Broadway musical (*Sweet Charity*). But success was not to happen a second time when Fellini's 1954 film *La Strada* was unwisely adapted into a Broadway musical. The show was produced and had a book by Charles K. Peck, Jr., who had coauthored the Maureen O'Hara vehicle *Christine* with Pearl S. Buck. Alan Schneider, who had won his reputation by directing Albee, Pinter, and Beckett, was hired to direct his first musical (he directed another one the following year, *Blood Red Roses*, which lasted one night), and Alvin Ailey was the choreographer.

In terms of musical theatre, the only major name **La Strada** (Lunt-Fontanne; Dec. 14, '69; 1) boasted was its composer–lyricist Lionel Bart, whose *Oliver!* had been a big success on Broadway and who had several other distinguished London musicals (*Blitz!*, *Maggie May*) to his credit by the time of *La Strada*. But Bart was also beset by personal demons, and after one big London flop (*Twang!!* in 1965), he was never to be the same.

La Strada followed the film's screenplay quite closely: Zampano, who travels through southern Italy with his strong-man act, buys the simple-minded Gelsomina as his latest concubine–assistant. Her clowning makes her the star of the act, and she falls in love with Zampano in spite of his brutal treatment. When the two join a circus, Gelsomina finds a confidant in acrobat-clown Mario, but the jealous Zampano kills him. Zampano

○ ○ ○ ○ ○

ultimately leaves the inconsolable Gelsomina to die on the road, and continues on.

During the tryout, the musical's Zampano, Vincent Beck, was replaced by Stephen Pearlman. In a far more extreme move, however, Bart's score was gradually removed, until on opening night, only three of his songs remained. The program carried a singular insert: "At this performance, additional music and lyrics by Martin Charnin and Elliot Lawrence." In fact, Charnin and Lawrence had written an entirely new score, although Charnin took no credit in the program proper and Lawrence, a musical director and orchestrator, was credited in the back of the program as "orchestra personnel supervisor."

La Strada seemed to have abandoned all hope by the time of its Broadway opening, so the negative reviews and one-night run were not a surprise. It lost $650,000. *La Strada* suffered even more acutely from the problem built into *The Yearling*: because it followed a relentlessly bleak, tragic screenplay, it emerged as one of the most depressing musicals ever. What it lacked was the beauty, compassion, and poetry Fellini was able to impart to this brutal, unpleasant story. The only hope for a musical *La Strada* would have been in the opera house.

Bernadette Peters, in her first Broadway lead, did not let the show down; if *La Strada* had worked, Peters might not have had to wait a few more years before becoming a top-level musical-theatre star. The score was not bad, particularly Peters' haunting opening "Seagull, Starfish, Pebble," written by Lawrence and Charnin but sounding uncannily like Bart, and "Sooner or Later" for the unlucky Larry Kert as Mario.

The celebrated 1930 German film *The Blue Angel*, based on a 1905 novel by Heinrich Mann called *Professor Unrath*, should have made a better musical than *La Strada*, but it didn't. French singer Lilo had been brought to Broadway to star in Cole Porter's *Can-Can* in the fifties; good as she was, her appearance in that show is perhaps best remembered for her insistence that featured performer Gwen Verdon's role be abbreviated. Lilo's husband, the marquis Guy de la Passardiere, arranged his wife's return to Broadway after a decade in a musical adaptation of *The Blue Angel*. To accommodate its leading lady, the action of the musical, originally called *Sugar City* and finally **Pousse-Café** (46th Street; Mar. 18, '66; 3), was shifted from the novel and film's Berlin to New Orleans in the twenties. Following the basic outlines of the original, *Pousse-Café* told of a stern Latin professor at a military school who confronts a club performer/

○ ○ ○ ○ ○

prostitute named Solange, who has been corrupting his best student. Bewitched by the lady's charms, the professor marries her and winds up performing a humiliating clown number in her show. He attempts to return to his school but is ultimately destroyed by his passion.

The book for *Pousse-Café* was written by Jerome Weidman, who had already cowritten *Fiorello!* and *Tenderloin* and, on his own, had written the fine book for *I Can Get It for You Wholesale* and the libretto for an utter horror called *Cool Off*, a musical starring Stanley Holloway and Hermione Baddeley which closed out of town in 1964. The music for *Pousse-Café* was by the distinguished jazz composer Duke Ellington, who never had much success with Broadway musicals, and the lyrics were by Marshall Barer—who had written the lyrics and coauthored the book for *Once Upon a Mattress*—and Fred (*Gantry*) Tobias. Walter Slezak was the first choice for the professor, but the part went to Theodore Bikel. Because of his connections, the marquis was able to get Henry Ford 2nd and Mrs. Barry Goldwater to invest in the show.

During the tryout, the show's director, Richard Altman, was replaced by the celebrated interpreter of Eugene O'Neill plays, Jose Quintero, in his only appearance as a Broadway musical director. By the time the show got to New York, neither the novel, which was credited as the musical's source on the road, nor the film was mentioned in the program; *Pousse-Café* arrived on Broadway pretending, in spite of its familiar story, to be an original musical. With the exception of Travis Hudson as a club singer/madam, the critics disliked everything about *Pousse-Café*; it was another Friday-to-Saturday show, and it lost $450,000. Bikel had starred two years earlier in the musical version of *Café Crown*, which also ran three performances; it was now clear that Bikel needed to choose his cafés with greater care. Following the closing, the marquis was brought up on charges of violating financing regulations and was temporarily barred from producing other shows.

Pousse-Café was a show in which everything—the book, the score, the direction, even the leads—was wrong. Lilo, too old for her role, was described by George Oppenheimer in *Newsday* as "a non-infectious diseuse." The book never convincingly explained what attracted the professor to Solange, or what made him marry her. Ellington came up with a surprisingly weak score; there was one pretty song for the professor called "Thank You, Ma'am," but there were far more onstage songs than plot numbers. Neither Ellington, Lilo, Bikel, Weidman, or Barer ever returned to Broadway after *Pousse-Café*.

○ ○ ○ ○ ○

At least *The Blue Angel, La Strada, Carnival in Flanders,* and *The Baker's Wife* were great films. The musical **Sarava** (Mark Hellinger; Feb. 23, '79; 140), by choosing a mediocre Brazilian film called *Dona Flor and Her Two Husbands* (which was first a novel) for its source, was on shakier ground from the start. *Sarava* (the Brazilian equivalent of *shalom* or *ciao*) took place in Brazil during carnival time, and was about Flor, whose husband, Vadinho, with whom she shared a very full sex life, is suddenly killed while helping a philandering friend defend himself from an angry husband. Through voodoo, Vadinho comes back to life, visible only to Flor and ready to wreak havoc on her new marriage to Teo, a quiet pharmacist.

Sarava involved two seminames, N. Richard Nash, who wrote the book and also made his debut as a lyricist, and Mitch Leigh, who composed the score. The show was billed as "the Mitch Leigh production," although Eugene V. Wolsk was listed as the producer. Otherwise, it was a substandard production, with the unknown Rick Atwell directing and choreographing (*Sarava* was the only Mitch Leigh musical not directed by Albert Marre) and a less-than-top-flight cast. The star, Tovah Feldshuh, sounded uncannily like Leigh's favorite leading lady, Joan Diener, when she sang.

Sarava became a Broadway legend, not for anything in the show itself, but because of its attempt to get people into the theatre during previews by means of a sexy television ad campaign. The ads ran constantly and were, for some reason, effective; the management, happy with the way business was building, kept on postponing the opening. The press became resentful that the ads were selling the show to the public and at the instigation of *New York Times* critic Richard Eder took matters into its own hands and reviewed *Sarava* on February 12, prior to the show's third scheduled opening eleven days later. (Much the same thing would happen to *Merlin* at the same theatre four years later.) The critics were all negative, except for Eder, who quite enjoyed it. His *Sarava* review appeared on the same page with his negative review of the hit *They're Playing Our Song,* and this, along with his recent obtuse and dismissive *Ballroom* review, hastened his assignment elsewhere in the pages of the *Times.* Business declined after the reviews, but the TV ads kept running, and *Sarava* managed to move to the Broadway Theatre before ending its run of five months. While *Dona Flor and Her Two Husbands* was quaintly sexy as a film, it lost most of its ethnic charm and turned vulgar in the musical version.

○ ○ ○ ○ ○

Leigh's score was his least interesting, and the whole show had an amateurish feel about it.

Of all the movies ever adapted to the musical stage, perhaps none cried out to be left alone as much as *Gone with the Wind*. Several talented people were foolhardy enough to try to musicalize what was probably the most popular movie of all time, one based on an equally popular novel by Margaret Mitchell. What is surprising about the musical version of **Gone with the Wind** (Los Angeles; Aug. 28, '73; closed on the road) is that it was rather good.

The musical had a unique history, beginning in Tokyo, where a nine-hour non-musical version of Mitchell's novel had inaugurated the Imperial Theatre in 1966. Because of the enormous success of that production, Kazuo Kikuta and the Toho Company, which owned the stage rights to the novel, decided to mount a musical version at the same theatre. Kikuta wrote the book and hired Americans Harold Rome and Joe Layton respectively to write the score and stage the musical, which was called *Scarlett* when it opened in Japan in January 1970. The show's designers, conductor, orchestrator, and dance arranger were also experienced Broadway talents.

Instead of going on to Broadway, the musical went to London, where it was cheaper to present and where the critics could not destroy it as easily as the New York critics could. For London, Horton Foote wrote a new book, but most of the Japanese team remained when the show opened, under the title *Gone with the Wind*, at the Drury Lane Theatre in May 1972. The reviews were mixed, with several excellent, and the show ran a year, playing mostly to "coach parties" and tourists. The original London horse, Charlie, who had become a star on opening night when in the middle of the tense burning of Atlanta sequence he relieved himself onstage, suffered a backstage accident eight months into the run. He was put to sleep and was replaced by Nellie, his understudy.

It probably would have been better not to brave the United States with the musical; it had already been panned by New York critics like Clive Barnes, Richard Watts, and Rex Reed, who covered it in London. But its American premiere, originally scheduled for Atlanta, took place under the auspices of the Los Angeles and San Francisco Civic Light Operas and was produced by the show's West End presenter, Harold Fielding. Lesley Ann Warren was Scarlett and Pernell Roberts played Rhett Butler in the American edition, which was to have played a ten-city, forty-four

○ ○ ○ ○ ○

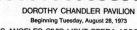

DOROTHY CHANDLER PAVILION
Beginning Tuesday, August 28, 1973

LOS ANGELES CIVIC LIGHT OPERA ASSOCIATION
Oscar T. Lawler, president

HAROLD FIELDING
presents
JOE LAYTON'S
production

LESLEY ANN   PERNELL
WARREN   ROBERTS

in

Margaret Mitchell's
Gone
with the
Wind

with

TERENCE   UDANA
MONK   POWER

ANN HODGES   THERESA MERRITT   CHERYL ROBINSON
and
ROBERT NICHOLS

Music & Lyrics   Book
HAROLD ROME   HORTON FOOTE

Scenery Designed by   Costumes Designed by
DAVID HAYS   PATTON CAMPBELL

Associate Scenic Designers   Lighting by
TIM GOODCHILD and ROMAIN JOHNSTON   H. R. POINDEXTER

Dance & Choral Arrangements by   Music Advisor
TRUDE RITTMANN   RAY COOK

Orchestrations by KEITH AMOS

Production Stage Manager LARRY DEAN   Production Assistant LYNN SUMMERELL

the Director   Assistant Choreographer
RUSSELL   HARRY NAUGHTON

Musical Director JAY BLACKTON

Entire Production Directed and Choreographed by
JOE LAYTON

U.S. National Tour of GONE WITH THE WIND produced by
le High Enterprises, Inc., in association with Jove Enterprises, Inc.

Memorable movies, less memorable musicals.

week tour and to have opened on Broadway on April 7, 1974. But the West Coast reviews were brutal, and the Fielding production stopped there. Another American production, mounted in Dallas in 1976 under the direction of Lucia Victor, toured to three cities, then the musical *Gone with the Wind* was seen no more. The ideal American venue for the musical, the Jones Beach Marine Theatre in Long Island, was never contemplated.

In London, Layton's fluid, continuous-action staging was remarkable, telling a sprawling story in eight sequences (four to an act) which combined song, dialogue, dance, and movement and propelled the action forward without a break. June Ritchie's West End Scarlett was stunning, a performance to rival Vivien Leigh's (and repeated eight times a week). Rome's score, his last for the theatre to date, was underrated; it too favored lengthy sequences over individual numbers, although Rhett's "Two of a Kind" and a tongue-in-cheek duet for Rhett and Scarlett, "How Often," were very attractive separate songs. Some of Rome's lyrics, however, were most peculiar: of marriage, Rhett sang, "But sometimes it's so miracle, full of strange and wonderful."

The musical *Gone with the Wind* faced several insurmountable problems. The movie ran 222 minutes, and in Japan, the musical *Scarlett* lasted four hours. But the London and American versions ran two and a half hours— an hour of that songs—and there was a tremendous amount of plot to cover. The script relied too often on the audience's prior knowledge of the story and characters; people and scenes that had been richly portrayed in the book and movie were only sketched in in the musical. And as was the case with *Breakfast at Tiffany's*, the movie of *Gone with the Wind* had a famous musical theme for which nothing in the score of the staged version could quite substitute.

Anyone attempting a musical version of *Gone with the Wind* would have to be a lunatic or a genius. Rome and Layton were neither, but their *Gone with the Wind* was far from the embarrassing disaster that legend has made of it. But if it was perhaps as good a stage-musical version as could have been made from the book and film, it left the same question hanging in the air that virtually all the film adaptations in this section failed to answer: Why bother to do it at all?

○ ○ ○ ○ ○

Five

DON'T LET THIS HAPPEN TO YOU

"So awful it makes *Holly Golightly* look like a nostalgic work of art and no I'm not kidding."—Kevin Kelly. *Boston Globe*, on *Sherry!*

"*Raggedy Ann*, I gather, was a great hit in Russia, and although I can see how not understanding a word of it must be genuinely helpful, I would not have guessed the extent. But perhaps it was all merely relief at discovering how ineffectual U.S. bombs could be."—John Simon, *New York Magazine*

"If the show's creators had any respect for the dead, they would not give the defenseless Mr. Lerner partial artistic 'credit' for a show that makes his own unsuccessful Presidential musical, *1600 Pennsylvania Avenue*, seem like *My Fair Lady* by comparison."—Frank Rich, *The New York Times*, on *Teddy and Alice*

Leslie Uggams in Her First Roman *(above)*

In the "I Love Lucy" episode entitled "Lucy Writes a Novel," Lucy Ricardo learns that her novel, *Real Gone with the Wind*, has found a publisher. But she is crushed when she discovers that the publisher wishes only to include excerpts of her work in a book called *How to Write a Novel*—in the chapter entitled "Don't Let This Happen to You."

Certain mistakes seem to recur again and again in the making of musicals, mistakes that might be avoided if the creators thought about similar projects and why they failed. Herewith are nine "don't"s, all of which, if followed, might discourage similarly misguided future projects.

#1: *Don't musicalize works which can't be musicalized.*

Some people think any novel, play, or movie can be made into a successful musical, and if you have a Sondheim or the next Michael Bennett at your disposal, perhaps it can. But there are certain works which defy musicalization, and five flop musicals, three of which closed on the road and all of which were based on novels, illustrate that handily.

Leon Uris, with no experience writing musicals, took the first half of his 1958 novel *Exodus*, already made into a movie by Otto Preminger, and fashioned it into the book for **Ari** (Mark Hellinger; Jan. 15, '71; 19), another unsuccessful attempt to tap the Jewish theatre-party market. *Ari* told the story of its title character's fight to get a group of German concentration camp survivors, mostly children, into Palestine, then under British blockade. Uris got his equally inexperienced friend Walt Smith to write the music, and probably for want of someone better, Lucia Victor was hired to direct. Both stars were on their second flop musical: David Cryer, who had made a strong impression in *Come Summer*, was Ari, and Constance Towers, in what might be dubbed the "Sally Ann Howes" role—a cool shiksa ultimately drawn to the exotic leading man—had already starred in *Anya*. After two chances, neither performer was ever asked to create a lead in a Broadway musical again.

Was *Exodus* suitable material for a musical? With its detention camps and shipboard hunger strikes, it was the kind of relentlessly gloomy story far more appropriate to film, which could at least offer real locations and realistic action. If the theme was potentially stirring, it did not lend itself to song and dance well. To compound the initial mistake, the treatment the story received here was wooden, the score lifeless (Something called "Steady Records" was to have recorded the show, but it passed). Every-

○ ○ ○ ○ ○

thing important in a song lyric tended to be contained in the title. Clearly, Uris and Smith were not the ones to musicalize *Exodus*, but even if greater musical-theatre talents had been involved, *Exodus* was probably not material for a Broadway musical anyway.

James Clavell's 1976 novel *Shōgun*, set in early seventeenth-century feudal Japan, had a bit more going for it as potential musical material— forbidden romance, exoticism, local color—than *Exodus*. Clavell himself decided that the novel, already transformed into a hugely successful television miniseries, should be a musical, and Clavell also wound up providing a good deal of the show's $7 million cost when the musical languished unproduced for almost eight years.

Unlike Uris, who wrote not only the book but even the lyrics for *Ari*, Clavell accepted the fact that he had no experience with musicals and hired writers—mediocre ones who had never worked on a successful musical before. But if Clavell did not repeat Uris's biggest mistake, he still failed to realize that his novel was unsuitable material for musicalization. The plot of the enormous book and the twelve-hour miniseries was far too complex and convoluted to be boiled down into two and a half hours of theatre, particularly when most of the evening was sung. The musical that arrived on Broadway with the official title of **James Clavell's Shōgun: The Musical** (Marquis; Nov. 20, '90; 72) was virtually impenetrable to all except diehard fans of the book or movie. The Playbill contained a lengthy plot synopsis, but even that was not easy to follow.

With a cast of thirty-eight and over three hundred costumes, *Shōgun* was an obvious attempt at a Broadway version of a London pop opera spectacle; *Les Misérables* was the clearest model. To further the resemblance, Peter Karrie, a Colm Wilkinson sound-alike who had taken over Wilkinson's role in *Les Miz* as well as the title role in *The Phantom of the Opera* in the West End, was hired to play the central role of a shipwrecked English sea captain who becomes embroiled in a Japanese political power struggle while carrying on an affair with a married noblewoman.

When it opened a tryout in Washington, D.C., *Shōgun* was almost entirely sung; music was cut and dialogue gradually added to enable the baffled audience to follow the action. This revision upset composer Paul Chihara (an American of Japanese descent), and his objections led to his prompt dismissal from the production. (Chihara later told *Theater Week* magazine that the show, with the score as he had originally written it, was "the best musical since *Porgy and Bess*.") Around the same time, Karrie was fired when it was discovered that he was hopeless with the newly added dialogue.

Shōgun's troubles continued during New York previews when Philip Casnoff, Karrie's replacement, was knocked to the floor by a falling screen during the performance attended by most of the major critics. The show was halted in the middle of the second act, obliging those critics to return a few days later. The reviews were unanimously negative, and *Shōgun* survived for two months until Japanese tourism, which had been keeping the show alive, dried up when war broke out in the Persian Gulf.

Shōgun was often visually striking. It began with a shipwreck, complete with green laser-beam lightning, and also included an earthquake and a battle on horseback in the snow. The grandly elegant scenery (Loren Sherman) and costumes (Patricia Zipprodt) were not enough, however, to offset the tepid score, which contained a few attractive melodies in the Andrew Lloyd Webber vein but no style of its own. Because the show's director, Michael Smuin, hailed from the world of ballet and was more comfortable choreographing than attempting to clarify the plot, *Shōgun* featured a great deal of extraneous dance: the show's camp highlight was the Act Two opener, "Fireflies," in which scantily dressed dancers swirled about among black-clad figures waving lighted wands. But for the most part, *Shōgun* was not bad enough to be camp. It was merely remote and uninvolving, failing utterly to make one care about the events transpiring onstage. *Shōgun* was the kind of show that fans and members of the theatre community peg as a sure loser well in advance of its tryout; here, as usual, they were right.

The three other musicals that illustrate the same lesson were far more interesting shows, but each was done in by its source. Bruce Jay Friedman's 1964 novel *A Mother's Kisses* was a hilarious portrait of a vulgar, outrageous, destructive mother who follows her son to camp and to college, embarrassing him until he finally rebels. But it was not good source material for a musical: it didn't really have a plot, and the terrifying Meg was a lot easier to laugh at on the page than when brought to life, particularly in the unflinching performance by Beatrice Arthur in the musical of **A Mother's Kisses** (New Haven; Sept. 21, '68; closed on the road).

Initially, Jerome Chodorov wrote a book for the show to lyrics by Bob Merrill, but after Friedman's play *Scuba Duba* became a hit, Friedman decided to do the adaptation himself. Richard Adler wrote both music

○ ○ ○ ○ ○

and lyrics (it was one of his three flops after *The Pajama Game* and *Damn Yankees*), and Gene Saks, who had just directed wife Arthur in a supporting role in *Mame*, now directed her in her first musical star part. *Mame's* choreographer, Onna White, was hired for the dances. Bernadette Peters, who had a small role, was written out in rehearsal.

A Mother's Kisses was hated by audiences in New Haven and Baltimore and was practically forced to cancel its scheduled October 29 Broadway opening at the 46th Street Theatre. The problem was simple: there was no way of making Meg into an acceptable musical heroine, certainly not when she was being made the center of a conventional musical in the *Mame* mold. Meg was not lovable like the eccentric Mame Dennis, or Rose in *Gypsy*, whom we somehow can't resist for all her unpleasant qualities. Because of the source material and Arthur, *A Mother's Kisses* was frequently a riot, but it was unpleasant in the extreme, never came up with a real story, and except for a couple of Meg's songs, had an undistinguished score. Arthur was marvelous, making no attempt to soften the unpalatable character. She would have made the leap from supporting to star performer had the show worked; instead, she drifted into television, where she was soon playing Maude, a lovable version of Meg.

Prettybelle (Boston; Feb. 1, '71; closed on the road) had one of the hottest teams ever to collaborate on a flop: Gower Champion, Angela Lansbury, Jule Styne; and Bob Merrill. The wild card in the deck was Alexander H. Cohen, and it's remarkable that so soon after her *Dear World* experience Lansbury chose to work for Cohen again.

Prettybelle, based on a droll 1970 novel by Jean Arnold, tells of alcoholic–schizophrenic Prettybelle Sweet, widow of Sheriff Leroy Sweet, confined when the curtain rises to the Piciyumi State Asylum in Louisiana, where she is working on her memoirs, entitled *Rape and Resurrection*, as therapy. Prettybelle, addressing the audience directly, narrates the events that have caused her to be institutionalized: after Leroy's death, she discovered that her husband, a redneck bigot, had been responsible, in the line of duty, for the unlawful deaths of several members of minority groups. Prettybelle decides to expiate her husband's guilt, first by writing checks to the NAACP, then by allowing herself to be "defiled" by a Mexican delivery boy and a black houseboy. Prettybelle ultimately gets revenge on Leroy's deputy, with whom she once had an affair, by accusing him of raping her, then takes permanent refuge in the asylum.

The musical had book and lyrics by Merrill, and Styne, in a slump

○ ○ ○ ○ ○

The Prettybelle team (top photo, left to right: Jule Styne, Gower Champion, Angela Lansbury, Alexander H. Cohen, Bob Merrill). Which one was the wild card? Below, an album of vocal selections from a show that never reached Broadway.

period (*Darling of the Day, Look to the Lilies*), rejoined his *Funny Girl* partner for the score. The show opened and closed at the Shubert Theatre in Boston (*Follies* was trying out around the corner at the Colonial), canceling its March booking at the Majestic Theatre. Most of the original cast reunited eleven years later to record the score.

Arnold's novel was extremely difficult to transfer to the stage without its story becoming ugly. How does one make scenes like the flashback showing why Prettybelle's son was institutionalized at age thirteen— encouraged by his father to learn to shoot, he shot dead three people, all of whom resembled his father—workable in a musical? *Prettybelle* suf- fered further from a problem similar to that of *A Mother's Kisses*: wildly unconventional material used as the basis for a conventional musical. If the story was ever to succeed as a musical (which is unlikely), it would have needed a far more original, wacky style than director–choreographer Champion ever provided. Further, Styne and Merrill were simply the wrong team for the adaptation: what was meant to be wildly comic played uneasily, and the score, which had its moments, was nevertheless not eccentric and unusual enough for the story. Styne and Merrill were simply not comfortable writing songs for Louisiana rednecks in search of "poon" or for genteel Southern ladies singing of their defilement at sleazy motels. Lansbury, however, was never better, and a heavily made-up Charlotte Rae was a hoot as her ancient mother, constantly accusing young men of undressing her with their eyes. *Prettybelle* was a daring attempt at some- thing different, something dealing with real-life issues, and with Lans- bury's incandescent performance and the wild goings-on, it was the kind of show that flop collectors boast about having caught. But even if the wrong team tackled *Prettybelle*, it was still material that tended to defy musicalization.

Prettybelle was near-impossible material uneasily adapted for the musical stage. **Lolita, My Love** (Philadelphia; Feb 16, '71; closed on the road) has the singular distinction of being both a complete mistake *and* a superb adaptation, with a marvelous score and perfect leads, of one of the great novels of the twentieth century. Vladimir Nabokov's *Lolita* had already been transferred to the screen by Stanley Kubrick and Nabokov, but in a considerably bowdlerized version. Alan Jay Lerner decided to make Nabokov's tale of a middle-aged professor's passion for a preteenage nym- phet into a musical, and it was to become the first of the five flops with which Lerner ended his stage career. John Barry, who would later write

○ ○ ○ ○ ○

Billy for the West End and *The Little Prince and the Aviator* for Broadway, was the composer.

The show opened in Philadelphia to terrible reviews and shut down for repairs. Director Tito Capobianco (who had directed Beverly Sills in many of her operatic triumphs) was replaced by Noel Willman, who had done *Darling of the Day* and *Love Match,* neither of which was mentioned in his *Lolita* program bio. Danny Daniels, who had replaced Jack Cole during rehearsals, was replaced by Dan Siretta, and the original Lolita, considered too ripe at fifteen, was replaced by a thirteen-year-old.

The show reopened in Boston, but while the critics there appreciated the show's strengths, business was nonexistent. *Lolita, My Love* canceled its scheduled opening at the Mark Hellinger Theatre, where Lerner's *My Fair Lady, On a Clear Day You Can See Forever* and *Coco* had played. Its original cost, $650,000, had, with all the changes, ballooned to $900,000.

When Nabokov first rejected the idea of a movie based on his novel, he said: "It was perfectly all right for me to imagine a twelve-year-old Lolita. She only existed in my head. But to make a real twelve-year-old play such a part would be sinful and immoral, and I will never consent to it." Nabokov foresaw exactly what the musical's main problem would be: the events of the novel are far more palatable when imagined than when acted out onstage, where, without Nabakov's powerful writing, they become distasteful and unappealing.

But *Lolita, My Love* had a great deal going for it. Shakespearean actor John Neville—in a role rejected by Richard Burton—was a marvelous hero, even singing well, and Dorothy Loudon, still in the midst of her flop period, was ideal as the vulgar Charlotte Haze; one of the show's problems was that audiences missed Loudon terribly after she was killed off at the end of the first act. Lerner's lyrics were frequently dazzling, and Barry's music indicated genuine talent as a theatre composer only hinted at in his other stage scores. "In the Broken Promise Land of Fifteen" for Humbert, a showstopper for Loudon called "Sur les Quais," a nightmarish, cross-country sequence called "How Far Is It to the Next Town," and most of the other songs demonstrate how well Lerner and Barry succeeded in musicalizing the characters.

When granting his blessing to the project, Nabokov said, "Mr. Lerner is most talented and an excellent classicist. If you have to make a musical version of *Lolita,* he is the one to do it." Indeed, *Lolita, My Love* was as good a musical as could have been made from the novel, and Humbert was allowed to be as vivid and tragic a hero as he was in the book. But

○ ○ ○ ○ ○

the musical was a distinguished work that could never have succeeded, a grand attempt at the impossible. Ten years later, Edward Albee adapted the novel to the stage, and the result, with Donald Sutherland as Humbert, closed after twelve performances. An extremely ill-conceived and awkward adaptation, it made one appreciate what fine work Lerner had done in a lost cause.

#2: Don't musicalize works that don't need music.

This is related to but different from mistake #1. There are certain works that are so tightly constructed that the addition of music can only weaken them, while there are others that simply do not need music. One of the reasons why Tom Jones and Harvey Schmidt have not been able to get their well-executed musical version of *Our Town* (called *Grover's Corners*) to Broadway is that Wilder's play is lyrical enough to sing without music. Six other musicals, all based on successful plays, demonstrate the need to examine whether or not musicalizing your source will add to it or detract from it.

One of the musicals Maltby and Shire had written at Yale was an adaptation of Edmond Rostand's 1897 play, *Cyrano de Bergerac*. In the sixties, David Merrick announced a musical *Cyrano*, to star Christopher Plummer and have a score by Leslie Bricusse and Anthony Newley. The reason why *Cyrano* has never made it as a Broadway musical may be that Rostand's play, one of the most romantic and lyrical in dramatic literature, is practically a musical all by itself. Only musical-theatre geniuses would be able to add enough in a musical adaptation to make it worth doing, but talents of that caliber would probably be too smart to attempt it in the first place.

Anthony Burgess, author of *A Clockwork Orange*, had translated and adapted Rostand's play for the Guthrie Theatre in Minneapolis, where it was directed by Michael Langham. When Burgess later wrote the book and lyrics for a musical version of the play, with film composer Michael J. Lewis writing the music, Langham decided to mount it at the Guthrie. It was taken up for Broadway, but Langham was replaced as director by Michael Kidd, and the Broadway book credit was ambiguous, indicating that Burgess's work had been tampered with.

Cyrano (Palace; May 13, '73; 49) received raves in Boston but mixed reviews in New York. In the title role, Plummer, who had played the nonmusical Cyrano as early as 1962, was brilliant, many maintaining that

○ ○ ○ ○ ○

he was the best Cyrano ever, musical or nonmusical. But there was little audience interest, and the show closed after eight weeks, losing all of its $500,000 cost. After the closing, A&M Records, which had supplied half the financing, released an elaborate double-LP recording of the show, and Plummer won the Tony Award as Best Musical Actor. When the Royal Shakespeare Company brought Rostand's play to Broadway in 1984, it was in Burgess's nonmusical adaptation.

The *Cyrano* that played the Palace was basically Burgess's translation cut down and with songs added. Leigh Beery as Roxana had three ravishing numbers, but the other characters were not musicalized as well. Cyrano's "From Now Till Forever" and "No Thank You" sounded like songs from *Man of La Mancha;* indeed, the success of *La Mancha,* with another public-domain romantic hero fighting convention, may have been responsible for the musical *Cyrano's* getting to Broadway.

But Rostand's play did not really need songs, and the score would have had to have been far better to equal the musicality of the play's dialogue. Another problem was that the action of the perfectly plotted, lengthy original was slowed down by the songs; even when the songs were good, they brought the evening to a halt. One year after *Cyrano,* Wright and Forrest wrote another musical version of the play, called *A Song for Cyrano,* which played a summer-stock tour, then vanished. It starred José Ferrer, the most famous nonmusical Cyrano, to whom Plummer had played Christian in a televised *Cyrano* in 1951.

The other four plays adapted into musicals under our second heading were not of the caliber of Rostand's, but they were all accomplished and successful examples of their respective genres, and all were diminished, if not destroyed, in their translation to the musical stage.

At the beginning of the second act of **Sherry!** (Alvin; Mar. 28, '67; 65), a musical version of the 1939 George S. Kaufman–Moss Hart comedy success, *The Man Who Came to Dinner,* playwright Bert (Jon Cypher) protests seductive actress Lorraine Sheldon (Dolores Gray)'s plan to turn his play into a musical. Bert says, "But it's a play," to which Lorraine replies, "Of course. So was every musical—once." When Bert goes on to say that his play is a tragedy and doesn't require songs, Lorraine says, "Broadway's been waiting for a really tragic musical comedy." If *Sherry!* was not exactly tragic, it was a distinct mistake.

James Lipton, author of the book and lyrics for our earlier flop *Nowhere to Go but Up,* wrote *Sherry!* to music by film composer Laurence Rosenthal.

○ ○ ○ ○ ○

Above left, Dolores Gray serenades Clive Revill in Sherry! The photo was obviously taken after the sheet music (above right) was printed with George Sanders'
name on it. The Playbills below also reflect the switch from Sanders to Revill.

It was another tryout beset by change: Director Morton Da Costa and choreographer Ron Field (Field had triumphed with *Cabaret* earlier the same season) were replaced by Joe Layton, who took a "staging and direction supervised by" credit in the final program. For the part of Sheridan Whiteside (the character based on Alexander Woollcott), who terrorizes the Stanleys of Ohio when he is forced to stay at their home after suffering an accident on their property during a publicity tour, George Sanders seemed like an ideal choice and was even able to sing. But the Boston critics were not convinced by his performance, and when Sanders' wife became critically ill, he lost heart and withdrew. Clive Revill took over, joining a cast which included Eddie Lawrence (as Banjo, a character modeled on Harpo Marx), who did not mention in his program bio that he had written *Kelly*.

Revill was fine, as were Elizabeth Allen as Whiteside's secretary and, above all, Dolores Gray. If ever a performer woke up a sleeping show, it was Gray, who entered forty minutes into the first act and delivered the exuberant title song. The songs for Allen and Gray were fine, but the composers never came up with a decent number for Whiteside, only warmed-over Henry Higgins imitations.

Even with the same cast and a better score, however, *Sherry!* would not have worked. Kaufman and Hart comedies are models of airtight construction, with no fat on them whatsoever, and *The Man Who Came to Dinner's* taut hilarity was diluted by the songs, which added nothing to the original script and were sometimes awkwardly dropped in. While *Sherry!'s* book stuck closely to its source, it was foolhardy to attempt to open up the one-set original while cutting it down to make room for songs. Moreover, the original play was an unsentimental one, and Whiteside was not a very pleasant character around which to build a musical.

So *Sherry!* was doomed by its choice of material, though its creation probably happened because such still-running hit musicals as *Hello, Dolly!* and *Mame* had been based on successful comedies. But *Auntie Mame* had always played like a musical comedy without songs anyway, and *The Matchmaker* was a warmly sentimental farce made even more effective by the addition of songs and dances. *Sherry!* was a forced musical adaptation of a play that would have been better left unmusicalized.

Leslie Bricusse, who after writing two hit musicals with Anthony Newley never had much success in the theatre, compounded the problem of *Sherry!* in his **Say Hello to Harvey** (Toronto; Sept. 14; '81, closed on the road), for which he wrote book, music, and lyrics. Mary Chase's comedy *Harvey*, about Elwood P. Dowd, whose best friend is an imaginary, six-and-a-half-foot-tall white rabbit, won the Pulitzer Prize (over *The Glass Menagerie*) in 1944, ran over four years, and was made into a successful film. But it was another of those superbly constructed character farces which could only be weakened by adding songs. Bricusse went the song-writers of *Sherry!* one better (one worse, actually) by creating songs that were almost uniformly poor and which, like some of those in *Sherry!*, interrupted rather than advanced the action. The musical numbers in *Say Hello to Harvey* either repeated what was already established in dialogue or stopped the action dead. It was a musical in which one dreaded the beginning of the next song; Bricusse never really musicalized *Harvey*, just interrupted it with lousy and entirely extraneous songs.

The musical *Harvey* was produced by Canadians and mounted in To-ronto, where it closed prior to scheduled Washington and New York engagements. Elwood was played by Donald O'Connor, who had made his Broadway musical debut earlier the same year in another mistake, *Bring Back Birdie*. As Elwood's sister, Veta, Patricia Routledge gave another superb performance in a bomb; after *Harvey*, she washed her hands of the American musical theatre.

Resetting the action in the present was another mistake, as Chase's story, in effect a tribute to staying drunk, was less appealing when set in the eighties. *Say Hello to Harvey* opened up a two-set play to include scenes in the bar only described by Elwood in the play and brought on an extraneous chorus for numbers like the opening "Smalltown U.S.A." In between the songs, Chase's original play still shone through; while *Harvey* didn't need music, it could have been musicalized far better than it was by Bricusse.

Joseph Stein wrote a successful Broadway comedy in 1963 called *Enter Laughing*, based on a novel by Carl Reiner, and subsequently wrote the book for a musical version of *Enter Laughing* called **So Long, 174th Street** (Harkness; Apr. 27, '76; 16). Both play and musical were about David Kolowitz, who worked as a druggist's assistant while taking the first awkward steps to his real goal, to be an actor. The score was by Stan Daniels, a television writer—producer making his Broadway debut, and Burt Shevelove directed.

To enlarge the slight but funny original, the authors came up with the concept of making most of the songs David's fantasies, punctuating the

○ ○ ○ ○ ○

realistic book scenes. So there were numbers in which David had a *Tom Jones*–like lunch with a pretty older secretary or attended his own funeral as he worried about facing his first audience. An imaginary butler sang to Garbo on the phone that she'd have to be patient about being fitted into David's busy sex schedule. But the fantasies were for the most part charmless and not very funny, and they added little to the original play. Since Stein wrote both play and musical, *So Long* was basically a "chop and drop" job, with the original play cut down to make way for the fantasy numbers. The sweet original became overblown and vulgar with the fantasies, which ultimately damaged the original instead of helping it.

To accommodate the show's leading man, Robert Morse, who was rather too old to play David, a frame was added to the story in which the mature David was seen in a dressing room, preparing to go onstage. This allowed for a silly surprise ending, with David going onstage not as a star actor but to accept the award as Pharmacist of the Year. There were two amusing numbers, "Men" (for David's girlfriend Wanda) and "The Butler's Song" (for George S. Irving, here given uncharacteristically funny material), and a nice opening, but the score was otherwise weak. Nor was the obviously goyish Morse ideal casting for the obviously Jewish David. *So Long, 174th Street* closed after two weeks, the same two weeks which also saw *Rex* and *1600 Pennsylvania Avenue* open and bomb. The Harkness Theatre was never used again as a legitimate house, but the marquee for *So Long* stayed up for quite a while, in spite of Morse's protests.

Joshua Logan directed and coproduced William Inge's 1953 Pulitzer Prize-winning Broadway play, *Picnic*, and directed the 1956 film version of it as well. He should not have pressed his luck by directing a musical version of *Picnic* called **Hot September** (Boston; Sept. 14, '65; closed on the road). David Merrick, who had recently had success with musical adaptations of Broadway plays of the fifties (*Hello, Dolly!*, *110 in the Shade*), joined forces with Leland Hayward, with whom he had produced *Gypsy*, to present the musical. Paul Osborn, author of *Morning's at Seven* and *On Borrowed Time*, wrote his first musical book (although he had done the screenplay for *South Pacific*). For the score, the producers hired the new team of Kenneth Jacobson and Rhoda Roberts, who later wrote an off-Broadway musical called *Show Me Where the Good Times Are*, the title song of which was lifted from *Hot September*. With the exception of Eddie Bracken, the cast consisted of newcomers as well.

In Boston, leading lady Kathryn Hays was replaced by Sheila Sullivan

○ ○ ○ ○ ○

HOT SEPTEMBER

Four bad shows, mistakes all.

(Logan felt this hurt the show), and Betty Lester replaced Patricia Roe as Hays's mother. Many musicals that came into New York from the road received far worse reviews out of town than *Hot September*, but Merrick and Hayward chose to cancel the show's October 20, 1965, opening date at the Alvin Theatre. (*Hot September* folded in Boston the same week Louis Jourdan left *On a Clear Day You Can See Forever*, which was also trying out there.) The cast, minus Bracken, recorded the score with a small-combo accompaniment; an LP of this tape was issued more than twenty years after *Hot September* closed. Unsuccessful attempts were later made to adapt two other Inge hits into musicals: *Cherry*, based on *Bus Stop*, was supposed to open in London in 1972 with Bernadette Peters but never did, and *Sheba*, based on *Come Back, Little Sheba*, starred Kaye Ballard in Chicago in 1974.

Picnic did not have much plot: it was a study of sexuality, emotion, and character, tricky to musicalize. For *Hot September*, the original one-set play was blown up to include scenes in a locker room (which allowed for Logan's requisite beefcake sequence), around a swimming pool, and at picnic grounds, a pizza joint, and a parking lot. A full dance ensemble was brought on for a couple of numbers. Much new dialogue was added to cover all the scene changes, and several scenes in the play were softened; *Hot September* diluted an already fragile play at every turn. The score was totally inadequate to the seething sexuality and heated emotions of Inge's original, a play that didn't really require music to begin with.

As a play, Hy Kraft's 1942 comedy, *Cafe Crown*, doesn't rank with *Picnic*, *The Man Who Came to Dinner*, or *Harvey*, not to mention *Cyrano de Bergerac*, so the producers of the musical **Cafe Crown** (Martin Beck; Apr. 17, '64; 3) were at a disadvantage to begin with. Kraft did his own adaptation, and Albert Hague wrote the score (*Cafe Crown* would be the first of three flop musicals which ended Hague's Broadway career). Theodore Bikel was Samuel Cole, a character based on Yiddish theatre star Jacob Adler, Brenda Lewis was his wife, Tommy Rall led Ron Field's dances, and Sam Levene was Hymie, the busboy at Cafe Crown, modeled on the Cafe Royale, where Yiddish theatre performers congregated. Alan Alda was featured as a Buffalo dentist who tries unsuccessfully to marry into the theatrical clan.

In a year that saw the openings of *Hello Dolly!*, *Funny Girl*, and *Fiddler on the Roof*, *Cafe Crown* opened on a Friday with its closing notice already up. The original play, moderately amusing at best, had very little plot,

○ ○ ○ ○ ○

only an abundance of amusing characters (like Mendel, the critic who writes his reviews before he sees the shows) and a lot of local color. It was too thin to musicalize, and the weak score helped not at all. Once again, a play that took place entirely in one setting—the cafe—was opened up to include scenes on streets, onstage, and in dressing rooms, all of which diminished the charms of the original. And casting the overwhelming Levene as Hymie, an important part but not the central character, unbalanced the story. *Cafe Crown's* bizarre "King Lear" ballet in the second act was one of the low points of sixties musicals.

#3: Don't start with a bad/impossible idea.

Many of the shows already discussed in this book began with less than wonderful ideas. But the five in this section started off with ideas that could not possibly have succeeded. The first three were poor shows, the other two fascinating failures.

Gertrude Berg had played her supreme creation, Molly Goldberg, on the radio, on Broadway, on screen, and on television. It was probably inevitable that someone would attempt a Broadway musical about the Goldbergs, and it fell to four writers with no Broadway experience to do the adaptation. **Molly** (Alvin; Nov. 1, '73; 68) featured Eli Mintz, repeating the role of Uncle David which he had played in all previous *Goldberg* incarnations; Kaye Ballard starred as the title character. At the advice of a numerologist, Ballard dropped the *e* from her first name for the show, but she was to have no more luck with *Molly* than she had already had with such bombs as *Reuben Reuben, Royal Flush,* or *The Beast in Me.* The show had an unusual "backers' audition," with Ballard going on Carol Burnett's TV show and, in costume and makeup, singing "Go in the Best of Health" (a song which remained only vestigally by the time the show opened on Broadway) to raise money for the production. The producers also arranged a product tie-in, and those who bought advance tickets at the box office received a free bottle of Yoo Hoo chocolate drink in honor of Molly's signature greeting.

Jewish theatre-parties eagerly bought seats, but from the first performance in Boston, it was clear that *Molly* was not a good show. Director Paul Aaron (who had already been dismissed from 70, *Girls,* 70) was replaced by Alan Arkin after Michael Bennett, Morton Da Costa, and Burt Shevelove declined to take over. Choreographer Bert Michaels was replaced by Grover Dale (Michaels took his wife, who was playing the

○ ○ ○ ○ ○

ingenue lead, with him), and Murray Schisgal did some book rewrites. *Molly* played five weeks of previews in New York, during which it went through much of its advance sale. It survived for two months after the opening, losing $600,000 on an investment of $400,000.

The problem was that Molly Goldberg *was* Gertrude Berg, and vice versa. There really was no character without her, and it was foolhardy to attempt a musical about the Goldbergs without Berg at least writing it, as she had most of the other versions. Moreover, the authors relied too heavily on the audience's familiarity with and fondness for the characters and failed to supply a real story or even a character for Ballard to play. The plot was very weak: most of the first act concerned husband Jake's plan, after losing his job as a cutter of ladies' dresses, to move the family to California, a plan rendered meaningless when Jake's brother arrived from California just before intermission. Ballard, a sophisticated comedienne, worked hard at playing an unsophisticated woman, but the last-minute addition "I See a Man" was the only number that gave her something to play and allowed her to be herself. Danny Fortus, playing Molly's son Sammy, had a pretty ballad called "In Your Eyes," modeled on his pretty ballad "Mama a Rainbow" in *Minnie's Boys*, in which he played Minnie's son Adolph, but otherwise the score was weak. Trying to resuscitate the Goldbergs without Berg was just not a good idea.

If Henry VIII and Queen Victoria weren't great subjects for musicals, Queen Nefertiti and King Akhnaton of Egypt were even less likely. Christopher Gore, author of the book and lyrics of *Via Galactica*, wrote **Nefertiti** (Chicago; Sept. 20, '77; closed on the road), which told of Akhnaton's unsuccessful attempt to take religion away from corrupt priests and give it to the people, aided by his queen, who refuses to save herself from execution, believing that what she and her husband stood for would live on.

Nefertiti, with music by David Spangler and direction by Jack O'Brien, who had staged an acclaimed *Porgy and Bess* for *Nefertiti*'s producer, Sherwin M. Goldman, opened at a time when interest in ancient Egypt was strong thanks to the touring Treasures of Tutankhamen exhibit. Andrea Marcovicci had the title role, and Robert LuPone was the pharaoh. LuPone, who created the role of Zach in a *A Chorus Line*, followed that show with leads in two musicals, *Nefertiti* and *Swing* (1980), which closed out of town, and one, *Late Nite Comic* (1987), which should have.

After a 1976 production at La Mama under the title *Brothers*, *Nefertiti*

o o o o o

opened in Chicago, where members of a black arts organization picketed the theatre, maintaining that Nefertiti was black and should have been portrayed by a black actress. Joe Masteroff came in to rewrite the book, but the producers pulled the plug, canceling the scheduled November 10, 1977, opening at the Minskoff.

While *Nefertiti* possessed a theme with a certain grandeur, there was no way, short of brilliant writing, to bring such a story and characters to life onstage. The result was plodding and stilted, and the score was too heavily tinged with pop rhythms. "Someone Is Here" was a striking song for Nefertiti, but others had titles like "Egypt Is Egypt Again."

Now consider this premise for a show: Kate, the "voice of Dow Jones," whose job it is to announce the latest stock market averages, is engaged to Herbert but becomes pregnant by the suicidal Charley. When Herbert tells Kate he will marry her when the Dow Jones average hits 1000, Kate takes microphone in hand and announces that it has. Her lie causes a hurricane of buying, followed by a near crash. Charley saves the day by getting the oldest man on Wall Street to buy everything, causing everyone else to buy, and winds up with Kate.

Was there a dumber plot in postwar musicals than that of **How Now, Dow Jones** (Lunt-Fontanne; Dec. 7, '67; 220)? Why does everyone believe Kate's lie? Doesn't anyone on the stock-market floor realize she's lying? Why is Charley trying to kill himself at the beginning? Why was there no second act at all? Given the absurd plot, not credible for a moment, there was no way *How Now, Dow Jones* could ever have succeeded.

Max Shulman wrote the book, based on an idea of the show's lyricist, Carolyn Leigh. Elmer Bernstein wrote the first of his two Broadway scores. The producer was David Merrick, whose *Dow Jones* program bio read, in its entirety, "Mr. Merrick is best known as the distinguished producer of the musical *Breakfast at Tiffany's*."

Reviews were good in New Haven, but less than favorable in Philadelphia, where the original director, Arthur Penn, withdrew after "artistic differences" with Merrick and was replaced by George Abbott. Merrick also brought in Michael Bennett to redo Gillian Lynne's choreography, and Bennett brought Tommy Tune with him to assist and to dance in the show. Madeline Kahn, playing a supporting role and understudying the show's comedienne, Brenda Vaccaro, was written out on the road.

New York reviews were mixed to negative, but the show's advance sale, which could only have been due to its title and to Merrick's name,

○ ○ ○ ○ ○

kept *Dow Jones* running for seven months. It was nominated for the Best Musical Tony as well as for five others, and Hiram Sherman won his Tony as the Wall Street tycoon who sets Vaccaro up as his mistress and then neglects to visit her.

How Now was another weak, cheesy sixties musical set in contemporary Manhattan. The script was filled with references to current products, television commercials, and celebrities, always a sign of desperation. There were, however, compensations: Vaccaro was very amusing, and her number "He's Here" was the show's highlight. "Walk Away" was a strong ballad, and "Step to the Rear," with Tony Roberts leading a group of marching Jewish widows, was the requisite showstopping production number. The score also had its share of floppo numbers, but given the show's initial idea, no score or stager could have made *How Now, Dow Jones* work.

In 1943, Oscar Hammerstein II transformed Bizet's *Carmen* into the Broadway hit *Carmen Jones*, resetting it in the South during wartime and giving it an all-black cast. Charles Friedman, who had directed the book of *Carmen Jones* (he'd also directed Kurt Weill's *Street Scene*) conceived the idea of adapting another opera, this time Verdi's *Aida*, to the musical stage. He decided to transplant the story from ancient Memphis, Egypt, to Memphis, Tennessee, in 1861, the first year of the Civil War. Pharaoh became General Farrow; Amneris somehow became Farrow's daughter, Jessica; Radames became Raymond Demarest; Amanasro, Aida's father, became Adam Brown, a runaway slave; high priest Ramfis became plantation owner Rumford; and Aida was still Aida, now Jessica's half-black slave. The opera's famous Triumphal Scene became a celebration of the Southern victory at Bull Run.

Friedman spent five years writing the bad idea that came to be called **My Darlin' Aida** (Winter Garden; Oct. 27, '52; 89). It arrived on Broadway as the most lavish spectacle since *The Great Waltz* in 1934, costing over $300,000. There was no tryout because of its size, just two weeks of previews in New York; it was one of the first times a show ever had more than a night or two of performances in New York prior to the opening. The Coordinating Council of Negro Performers protested the hiring of Elaine Malbin and her alternate, Eileen Schauler, for the role of Aida, but the show's producer claimed he could not find a suitable black performer for the role.

The New York critics were unanimous in their praise for Malbin's Aida

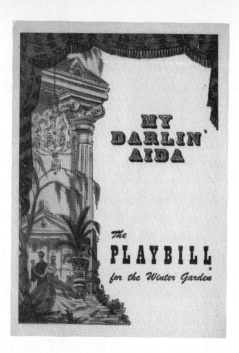

Dorothy Sarnoff and William Olvis celebrate the Bull Run Victory near the end of
Act One of My Darlin' Aida. Lemuel Ayers designed the Memphis square.

and Dorothy Sarnoff's Jessica Farrow, and they raved over Lemuel Ayers' sets and costumes. Otherwise, they were evenly divided, although the music critics who covered it found more to like than their drama colleagues.

For *My Darlin' Aida*, Friedman found a perfect equivalent for the Egyptian–Ethiopian conflict of Verdi's opera in the North–South conflict, and all the original plot elements dovetailed with the new setting. But Friedman had not taken into account the major difference between *Carmen* and *Aida* which made one easy to translate to Broadway and the other impossible. *Carmen* was an opéra comique, with individual arias very much like songs, relatively simple melodies, and spoken dialogue in between the songs—it was not all that dissimiliar to a musical. *Aida*, a grand opera with no dialogue, had complex arias without simple, hummable tunes, and its score proved intractable. Despite Friedman's efforts, Verdi's arias did not work as songs in a Rodgers and Hammerstein–style musical play, which was what Friedman was aiming for, and Friedman's melodramatic dialogue played awkwardly beside Verdi's music. Stunningly designed and very well played, *My Darlin' Aida* was a worthy mistake, and it had its admirers. But most preferred their Verdi straight.

Fascinating mistakes naturally bring us to Harold Prince, for with the exception of *Roza*, Prince's flop musicals are often more interesting than the hits of other directors. The second in the string of Prince flops that began with *Merrily We Roll Along* was **A Doll's Life** (Mark Hellinger; Sept. 23, '82; 5). In addition to directing, Prince was also one of eight producers, and the show had a book and lyrics by Betty Comden and Adolph Green, working in a totally atypical style, and music by Larry Grossman. Prince took his leads, George Hearn, Betsy Joslyn, and Edmund Lyndeck (who replaced Giorgio Tozzi during rehearsals) from his recent production of *Sweeney Todd*.

The authors introduced the published text of *A Doll's Life* with this note: "A Doll's Life is the story of what happened to Nora, the heroine of Henrik Ibsen's *A Doll's House*, after she slammed the door leaving eight years of domestic married life behind her. It is a romantic odyssey of self-realization in the difficult world of 1879, in which she rises from the depths of poverty and hopelessness to the heights of glamour, wealth, and achievement. Along the way she learns that men as well as women are trapped in the traditions of the world they are born into, and that each person must have the inner strength to stand alone."

○ ○ ○ ○ ○

This description makes the theme of the show much clearer than it was to audiences at *A Doll's Life*. The arbitrary action proceeds as follows: After leaving husband Torvald and her children, Nora, laboring as a dishwasher, meets lawyer Johan (played by Hearn, who also played Torvald), who helps her while falling in love with her. She moves in with Otto, a composer, but walks out when she realizes that Otto does not see her as an equal partner. She educates herself, then leads a workers' rebellion in a cannery and is jailed. When Johan introduces her to the cannery owner, Eric, she decides to trade her favors for better conditions for her fellow workers. Pawning the jewels Eric gives her, Nora begins to acquire the kind of wealth and power known at the time only to men. With Johan's help, she soon heads a perfume empire, but she declines Johan's offer of marriage, choosing to return to the children she deserted. Having made it alone in a man's world, Nora has come to believe that she and Torvald are ready to meet as equals and talk.

Prince told this bizarre story in a production that repeated many of his staging trademarks: dim lighting, chorus members observing and commenting upon the action, a bridge spanning the stage, a dearth of choreography. There were four dancing characters, a man and three women, who were supposed to represent the three phases of a woman's life and were reminiscent of the ballroom couples in *Evita* and *Follies*. The show's visual look was inspired by the work of the painter Edvard Munch, Ibsen's contemporary.

If talents like Prince, Comden, Green, and Grossman could not make *A Doll's Life* work, it was because the idea they started with was doomed to failure. Why ask what happened to Nora after she slammed the door at the end of *A Doll's House?* Ibsen's play deliberately ended there, having made its point without needing to go any further. To compound the initial mistake, Comden and Green never made Nora a real human being, just an overloaded symbol, burdened with fighting every feminist battle imaginable. Her four-year adventure was not made credible—even with Johan's help, Nora's accomplishments are unbelievable—or sufficiently interesting, and the statement of the show was never clearly put forth. As Nora, Joslyn worked hard and often well, but the show needed a more sympathetic, bewitching performer if it hoped to make audiences care about an often unmotivated and inconsistent character.

The opening frame of the show also proved unhelpful. *A Doll's Life* began with a present-day rehearsal of the final scene from Ibsen's play, after which the actress playing Nora (whom the director of the scene, *also* played by Hearn, called "Betsy") disappeared into a time warp and became the Nora of 1879. This added an unnecessary layer, especially since the show never returned to the rehearsal again, and proved confusing to audiences. Why not just begin with the last scene of *A Doll's House*, rather than a contemporary rehearsal of it?

In spite of all its problems, *A Doll's Life* had a cockeyed fascination about it, and there was one marvelous element, Grossman's music, operatic in breadth and one of the most original and interesting scores of the eighties.

A Doll's Life and Prince's next flop, *Grind*, would both have benefited from workshop productions. But Prince never used them, and he tried *A Doll's Life* out in Los Angeles, where it received mostly negative reviews and lost money during its ten-week run. In spite of the reviews, *A Doll's Life* was not changed very much during the L.A. run. It was greeted in New York with much harsher reviews than it deserved: what should have been considered an ambitious failure was treated like an utter horror. It closed instantly, losing $4 million, the original $3 million investment increased to cover the L.A. losses.

Fortunately, the score was preserved on disc. An ambitious community theatre group, one with strong voices and musical forces at its disposal, should consider rethinking *A Doll's Life*. It might play better—and more clearly—than it did in Prince's enormous, dark production.

#4: Don't attempt to musicalize a major work if you're not up to it.

Whether or not Henry James's *The Ambassadors*, Herman Melville's *Billy Budd*, Charles Dickens's *David Copperfield*, or George Bernard Shaw's *Caesar and Cleopatra* was ever likely to make a good Broadway musical is a fair question. But that question was beside the point when all four works were made into Broadway musicals by writers not remotely up to the task.

The Ambassadors is one of James's most difficult and complexly written novels, and while a Sondheim or a Lerner might have tackled it interestingly, Don Ettlinger (book), Don Gohman (music), Hal Hackady (lyrics), and Stone Widney (direction) did not. Hackady had already done *Minnie's Boys*, and Widney was an assistant director on such Lerner shows as *My Fair Lady*, *Camelot*, and *Coco*. Ettlinger and Gohman were one-shots, and this was the one.

The musical, which shortened James's title to **Ambassador** (Lunt-Fontanne; Nov. 19, '72; 9), told of Lambert Strether, a Massachusetts "man you can set your watch by," sent to Paris by his employer and fiancée, Amelia, to extricate her son, Chad, from the clutches of a Frenchwoman. In Paris, Lambert is transformed, acting on impulse for the first time in his life and enjoying the company of the middle-aged Marie de Vionnet. He is shocked to learn that it is Marie herself who is having the affair with young Chad. Ultimately, though, realizing that he has never actually lived, Lambert, "the ambassador," chooses to stay in Paris with Marie, while Chad returns home to a safer life.

Naturally, James's novel needed to be simplified for the musical stage, but all that was really left of it in *Ambassador* was a situation and some of the characters. Lambert, Marie, Chad, and Amelia are potentially rich musical characters, but the authors supplied only an ordinary, unimaginative, Civic Light Opera–style treatment. *Ambassador* was stodgy and stiff, and its Paris was the Paris of dozens of musical comedies—all artists, champagne, nightclubs, and l'amour. The musical was also far more predictable than the novel: it is clear from the time Lambert meets Marie that he is going to fall for her. Several of the tunes were attractive, but the lyrics were earthbound, and the treatment as a whole never approached what was required to adequately musicalize James.

Ambassador was actually twice a flop. With Danielle Darrieux an ideal Marie and Howard Keel just right for Lambert, the show was first produced in London, where it cost $265,000 as compared with the $800,000 it would have cost to mount on Broadway. The producers were American, and over one hundred American investors flew over for the opening at Her Majesty's Theatre. After a run of only three months in the West End, the authors (Anna Marie Barlow joined Ettlinger on the book) rewrote *Ambassador* for New York, dropping several songs, adding some new ones, and making one major miscalculation: they eliminated the opening scenes set in Massachusetts, depriving the audience of the chance to learn who Lambert was. Using the London stars, sets and costumes, *Ambassador* opened to worse reviews in New York than it received in London and lasted a week. Composer Gohman committed suicide after *Ambassador*'s failure.

Ambassador was not hard to sit through, but **Billy** (Billy Rose; Mar. 22, '69; 1) was. Herman Melville's short novel *Billy Budd* had already been made into an unsuccessful but admired Broadway play in 1951 and a film ten years later. It had already been musicalized, and brilliantly, by Ben-

○ ○ ○ ○ ○

jamin Britten in his 1951 opera, and it was not a good idea to drag the novel out again, this time converted into a fashionably intermissionless, ninety-minute rock musical.

What was worse, though, was that it was done by writers who didn't seem to realize what made Melville's novel tick. None of those who received final credit for *Billy*—Stephen Glassman (book), Ron Dante and Gene Allen (score), and Arthur A. Seidelman (direction)—had ever created a Broadway musical before or would after.

The executors of the Billy Rose estate would not allow the show to be booked into the Billy Rose Theatre under its original title, *Billy-Be-Dam'*, so it was shortened to *Billy*. There were words of praise for Ming Cho Lee's set and Grover Dale's choreography (it was Dale's choreographic debut), but nothing else. *Billy* retained the characters and plot outline of Melville, but Melville's allegorical richness and mystical atmosphere were more important than his story. In *Billy*, all that was left was the bare bones of that story, with a noisy folk-rock score and some robust dancing added; the result was a pointless, lifeless show. *Billy*, opening during the war in Vietnam, also attempted to use Melville's story as an antiwar tract, and the lyric of its big song, "It Ain't Us Who Make The Wars," followed the title with the words "But it's us who's got to fight 'em." In its opening sequence, *Billy* managed to get one woman, supposedly the girl Billy left behind, on board the Man-of-War. But its flogging scenes seemed aimed more at *After Dark* readers than tired businessmen. Amazingly, *Billy* was staged in New York before Britten's *Billy Budd*, which was subsequently presented with great success by the Metropolitan Opera.

There have been successful musical adaptations of the work of Dickens (*Oliver!*, *The Mystery of Edwin Drood*), but Al Kasha and Joel Hirschhorn, who wrote the less-than-wonderful new songs for the stage version of *Seven Brides for Seven Brothers*, had little success musicalizing Dickens' *David Copperfield*, reducing the title to **Copperfield** (ANTA; Apr. 16, '81; 13), with, surprisingly, no exclamation point. The authors followed the basic outlines of the novel but were forced to eliminate huge chunks of the plot, including the characters of Steerforth, Little Emily, Ham, Barkis, Mrs. Gummidge, and Rosa Dartle.

Directed by Rob Iscove, who had been credited with the Sandy Duncan revival of *Peter Pan* (although his work had been fixed by Ron Field), *Copperfield* opened on Broadway to dreadful reviews. It was not quite as terrible as all that, with several catchy if derivative ditties, but it lacked

○ ○ ○ ○ ○

any real inspiration as far as rethinking the novel in terms of musical theatre. *Copperfield* was simply sequences from the novel, halted for simple little tunes, and played against Tony Straiges's handsome scenery. It might have gotten by as a regional-theatre holiday musical but was acutely out of place in the Broadway of the eighties. And *Copperfield* tended to announce itself as a flop throughout, aided by the presence of key flop-performers George S. Irving and Carmen Mathews.

If Kasha and Hirschhorn weren't up to Dickens, there was never a mismatch quite equal to Bernard Shaw and Ervin Drake. Drake, basically a pop composer, wrote the score for *What Makes Sammy Run?*, which had a long if unprofitable run. But he was unwise to attempt to adapt Shaw's *Caesar and Cleopatra*, writing not only the score but the book as well for **Her First Roman** (Lunt-Fontanne; Oct. 20, '68; 17). *The Chocolate Soldier* and *My Fair Lady* seemed to make Shaw viable for musical adaptation, but no one ever really succeeded in doing it again, least of all Drake.

Michael Benthall, who had once directed Laurence Olivier and Vivien Leigh in the Shaw original, was hired to direct, shortly after he had finished directing *I'm Solomon*. Leslie Caron was Benthall's first choice for Cleopatra, but when he saw Leslie Uggams in *Hallelujah, Baby!*, he changed his mind. He hired Richard Kiley, fresh from *Man of La Mancha*, for Caesar. Both leads had just won Tonys and were coming off the greatest success they would ever have in musical theatre; valiant performers, they were in no way the problem with *Her First Roman*.

In Boston, Dania Krupska replaced choreographer Kevin Carlisle, and Derek Goldby, who would be fired from *The Rothschilds* two years later, replaced Benthall. The score was changed radically during the tryout, with Jerry Bock and Sheldon Harnick contributing three songs to the final version.

Her First Roman's New York reviews were so bad that even an advance sale could not keep it open: it lost $575,000. Drake's book was the main problem: a Cliffs Notes version of the original play, it followed the highlights of Shaw's plot, retaining occasional passages of Shaw's dialogue, but simplified and watered down its source throughout. And what Drake failed to realize was that Shaw was less interested in telling the story of Caesar and Cleopatra than he was in using their story to comment satirically on contemporary morality. All that was left in the musical was the plot, with Shaw's all-important philosophical musings absent. To make matters worse, Drake, unlike Shaw, made the relationship between Caesar

○ ○ ○ ○ ○

Kiley and Uggams may have used the song title at top as their excuse after the disastrous Her First Roman *closed.*

and Cleopatra explicitly that of lovers; Caesar was indeed "her first Roman" in the musical. Drake also added a stupid ending, in which Cleopatra joined Caesar on his voyage home instead of remaining in Egypt and awaiting Mark Antony, whom Caesar had promised to send her.

A score by Lerner and Loewe might have helped, but except for two charming songs for Cleopatra at the beginning, "Many Young Men from Now" and "Save Me from Caesar," Drake's melodies were pedestrian and his lyrics worse. The title of the first song, "What Are We Doing in Egypt?," set the tone, and Cleo had an up-tempo number in which she sang, "The wrong man's the right man for me." In the middle of Cleopatra's dramatic eleven o'clock number, "Just for Today," the dead body of her servant Ftatateeta (played by the enormous Claudia McNeil) was exposed, after which Uggams had to pick up the song again. The production featured beefcake sufficient unto a Josh Logan musical.

#5: Don't write shows without an audience.

One of the most bizarre musicals ever to reach Broadway, **Raggedy Ann** (Nederlander; Oct. 16, '86; 5) was based on stories written by Johnny Gruelle for his sickly daughter, Marcella. The musical had a book by William Gibson, the playwright who had rewritten the book for *Golden Boy*, and a score by Joseph Raposo, best known for his "Sesame Street" songs. Raposo had already written the songs for an animated film called *Raggedy Ann and Andy*, and he recycled some of them for this, his only Broadway musical. Patricia Birch, the choreographer whose only previous solo directorial credit was for *Truckload*, a musical produced by Adela Holzer which closed in previews at the Lyceum Theatre in 1975, directed and choreographed.

First produced under the title *Rag Dolly* in Albany, the show was sent to Moscow for a cultural exchange, CBS underwriting the cost. The Russians seemed to love it. Later the same year, it arrived on Broadway, received terrible reviews, and closed immediately.

Raggedy Ann had strong similarities to *The Wizard of Oz* and *Peter Pan*, but it was difficult to follow and never managed, as those musicals did, to come up with a coherent plot. The entire show was the fever dream of a sick child, called Marcella in the musical as in real life, whose father is a drunk and whose mother has run off. The father gives Marcella a doll, which comes to life, and Raggedy Ann and her friends, to show their gratitude to Marcella for bringing them to life, help her stay alive

○ ○ ○ ○ ○

by outwitting General Doom and bringing Marcella to the Doll Doctor in Los Angeles. The Doll Doctor turns out to be Marcella's father; Raggedy Ann makes the supreme sacrifice and gives her heart to Marcella; and Marcella wakes from her dream, healthy, although her doll's heart seems to have disappeared.

It was even harder to figure out for whom the show was meant than to follow the action. *Raggedy Ann* was far too grim and humorless for children and offered little to entertain adults. The story brought up deep-seated childhood fears, with Marcella's illness the embodiment of a child's rage over her broken home. Certain images, especially that of Marcella's mother attempting to hang herself in a forest of skeletons, were particularly scary. There was a heavy Freudian overlay to everything—General Doom even attempted to date Marcella at one point. Raposo came up with a few tuneful songs, but *Raggedy Ann* was a perverse curiosity suitable neither for adults nor children.

The same was true of the superior **Wind in the Willows** (Nederlander; Dec. 20, '85; 4), which had played the same theatre as *Raggedy Ann* one year earlier. Kenneth Grahame's beloved 1908 book had already been dramatized by A.A. Milne as *Toad of Toad Hall*, frequently performed as a Christmas pantomime in England. The musical was entirely the work of newcomers, and it was one of leading man David Carroll's (formerly David-James Carroll) numerous flops (*Spotlight, Seven Brides for Seven Brothers, Chess*). Edward Berkeley was replaced as director by Tony Stevens during previews.

The biggest change made in the adaptation from book to musical was making Mole a woman and adding a near-romance between her and Rat, who enjoys "messing about in boats" on the river. Admirers of the original objected, and this change also contradicted the gay subtext of the novel. Book musicals with actors playing animals (here they looked like people, but bore suggestions of animal appearance) are rarely a good idea and tend to suggest children's theatre; *Cats*, one of the biggest hits ever, has no dialogue and is essentially a revuelike series of numbers. Once again there was not enough for either adults or children. But most of the critics failed to notice that the show had some fine songs (especially "The World Is Waiting for Me" and "I'd Be Attracted") for Mole and Rat, although the ones for the evil weasels were dire. And Carroll (as Rat), Vicki Lewis (as Mole), and Nathan Lane (as Toad) were quite good. The musical *Wind in the Willows* was first done at the Folger Theatre in Washington,

D.C., and, like *Copperfield*, might have been acceptable fare as a holiday show at regional theatres. Even though it was almost Christmas when the show arrived on Broadway, bringing *Wind in the Willows* in was extremely misguided.

#6: Don't fool around with a good source.

Vicki Baum wrote her novel *Menschen im Hotel* in the late twenties, then adapted it to the stage; the play, under the title *Grand Hotel*, was seen on Broadway in 1930 with Sam Jaffe. The property achieved its greatest fame two years later as an all-star (Greta Garbo, John Barrymore, Lionel Barrymore, Wallace Beery, Joan Crawford) MGM movie. It became a musical twice: the second musical stuck very close to the novel, while the first made substantial changes which were to prove its downfall.

In his book for the musical **At the Grand** (Los Angeles; July 7, '58; closed on the road), Luther Davis switched the action of Baum's story from Berlin in 1928 to present-day Rome. He made the novel's ballerina, Grusinskaya, into American opera diva Isola Parelli, clearly modeled on Maria Callas (Parelli's rival was named "Rena Saldi"). This change was made to accommodate the show's leading lady, Joan Diener, whose husband, Albert Marre, was directing for producer Edwin Lester. *At the Grand* featured the second original score by Wright and Forrest (their first was for *Carefree Heart*, which had closed on the road the year before). The show was a reunion of *Kismet* veterans Lester, Diener, Marre, Davis, and Wright and Forrest.

The biggest change Davis made from the original was in his treatment of Kringelein. A bookkeeper for the corrupt businessman Preysing in the original, Kringelein became a scullery worker at the Grand Hotel Roma who, learning he has only a short time to live, decides to take a room at the Grand, secretly living in luxury until he is exposed. Preysing was eliminated altogether, and two deported American gangsters were added for a comedy scene in which Kringelein, set up as a dupe in a poker game, beats the pros at their own game.

The reason why Kringelein's role was altered and expanded was that Paul Muni, who had performed in musicals on the Yiddish stage early in his career, agreed to play it. Muni took the part only because his wife longed to see him singing and dancing in white tie and tails onstage once more.

At the Grand received mixed reviews but did good business in Los Angeles

○ ○ ○ ○ ○

Above, two flops based on classic novels. Below, Paul Muni gets the royal treatment at Grand Hotel in At The Grand.

and San Francisco. It is likely that it would have proceeded to the 46th Street Theatre, where it was scheduled to open on September 25, 1958, had not Muni refused to continue. Muni, suffering from paranoiac fears that Marre and Diener were against him, barely slept a wink during the run, and when his preliminary contract was up, he refused to sign a new one. As reported by Jerome Lawrence in his book *Actor: The Life and Times of Paul Muni*, the cast of *At the Grand* did not take well to Muni's closing the show and decided to avenge themselves on the last night. Muni had an intense dislike of cleavage and scantily clad chorus girls; during the final performance, a chorus girl deliberately slapped a bare breast in his face. Diener topped that during her curtain call by turning upstage to Muni and opening her full-length mink coat to reveal herself naked but for a long-stemmed rose between her legs.

Pushing Kringelein to the fore at the expense of Isola, the Baron, and Flaemmchen—the ambitious stenographer from the original renamed Sophia in *At the Grand* and made into a dancing soubrette—unbalanced the ensemble story, and cutting Preysing eliminated much of the drama and the dark side of the story. *At the Grand* was a pleasantly old-fashioned variation on *Grand Hotel*, sweetly sentimental rather than grim or tragic. Although geared to Muni's whims and to Civic Light Opera audiences used to mindless operettas, it was not badly done.

Grand Hotel had to wait thirty-one more years to make it to Broadway as a musical, and when it finally arrived, it was, surprisingly, once again the work of Davis, Wright, and Forrest. In place of Marre, however, was Tommy Tune, who while remaining faithful to Baum's plot and characters transmuted the story through his own unique theatrical sensibility. Tune made his *Grand Hotel* a two-hour, nonstop ballet of spoken dialogue, song, dance, movement, and underscoring, with musical numbers fragmented and several things to watch at any given moment. *Grand Hotel '89* did not skirt the dark side of the story and period, and Tune was careful to give all the principal characters equal weight. This state-of-the-art, splintered *Grand Hotel* was truer to Baum's theme of money and love driving people to the brink while life goes on. Seven songs from *At the Grand* ("Table with a View," "What You Need," "I Waltz Alone," "We'll Take a Glass Together," "Crescendo," "Never Before," and "Alone," the last with a different lyric and renamed "How Can I Tell Her") found their way into *Grand Hotel*, although two of them were heard only in Boston. During the tryout, Tune dismissed Wright and Forrest, bringing in Maury Yeston to compose several new songs and revise others, and asked Peter Stone to

○ ○ ○ ○ ○

do some book revisions. So while Wright, Forrest, and Davis finally made it to Broadway with a successful *Grand Hotel* musical, it was a mixed victory for them. Perhaps they still prefer *At the Grand*.

#7: *Don't do the same thing twice.*

In 1959, *Little Mary Sunshine*, a spoof of *Rose-Marie* and other operettas, opened off-Broadway and went on to run for almost three years. The book, music, and lyrics were entirely the work of Rick Besoyan, who also directed. In 1963, Besoyan arrived on Broadway with another operetta spoof, **The Student Gypsy, or The Prince of Liederkranz** (54th Street; Sept. 30, '63; 16), and demonstrated the perils of repeating oneself.

The Student Gypsy spoofed *Naughty Marietta*, *The Student Prince*, and even *Il Trovatore*, and was more scattered in its satirical targets than *Little Mary*. It represented a reunion of friends from *Little Mary*, with Besoyan again writing and directing, Ray Harrison choreographing, and several performers back on board, including leading lady Eileen Brennan. Edward Padula, who was at the same time working on another musical about gypsies, *Bajour*, was unable to raise the money, so one of Padula's investors, insurance man Sandy Farber, took over, with Besoyan coproducing without credit. There was not enough money for a tryout, so the new show played two weeks of Broadway previews, then opened. The reviews were preponderantly negative, and the show lasted two more weeks; Brennan went into *Hello, Dolly!* immediately after the closing. Farber produced Besoyan's next musical, *Babes in the Wood*, off-Broadway a year later; it also failed. Besoyan died in 1970.

When read today, Besoyan's *Student Gypsy* script is rather amusing, with its war between Singspielia and Liederkranz, a prince disguised as a royal grenadier, a shy virgin transformed into a gypsy, and gypsy queen Zampa, who years before stole the heir of Liederkranz and put her son in his place. But was it wise for Besoyan, after establishing himself off-Broadway with a hit operetta spoof, to make his Broadway debut with another one? Then, too, *Little Mary* had been done on a shoestring, its cheapness adding to its sense of informal fun; *Student Gypsy* was as elaborate as some of the shows it was spoofing, and the sense of harmless fun was gone. The songs tended to sound less like spoofs and more like the real thing, although Besoyan was an adroit parodist. And there was the nagging feeling that "I Love Lucy" had done the mythical kingdom—handsome prince—gypsy

○ ○ ○ ○ ○

queen–innocent maiden operetta spoof as well—or better—in half an hour.

#8: *Don't use old music.*

Wright and Forrest had great success adapting old music in *Song of Norway* and *Kismet*, but they were developing themes, not simply recycling old tunes. Tommy Tune's *My One and Only* demonstrated that a show could succeed with old songs (by the Gershwins) as the entire score. But in general, audiences like to feel they're going to hear something new when they go to a "new" musical.

It was perhaps its use of old music that caused **The Happiest Girl in the World** (Martin Beck; Apr. 3, '61; 97) to fail after only three months. Loosely based on Aristophanes' *Lysistrata*, in which the women of Athens join forces to withhold sex from their husbands until the men stop making war, *Happiest Girl* used the music of Jacques Offenbach, most taken directly from opera and operetta arias. E.Y. Harburg conceived the show and wrote the lyrics, and Fred Saidy (who had already written four musicals with Harburg) and Henry Myers did the book. It was directed by its star, Cyril Ritchard, who had directed two Offenbach works for the Metropolitan Opera and appeared in one of them. Carol Lawrence was first announced for the female lead, which went to Janice Rule. The publicity declared that the show had the heaviest scenery and lightest-weight female costumes in years; the male costumes were equally scanty.

Reviews in New Haven and Philadelphia were good, but the Broadway notices were mixed; audiences enjoyed it, but potential ticket buyers may have been turned off when they heard that the show had music by Offenbach. And unlike in the Wright and Forrest adaptations, Offenbach's melodies were heard here in pretty much the same form as they had already been heard on operatic stages. Harburg's lyrics, as always, were witty. Ritchard, playing Pluto and seven other roles (Pluto's various disguises), was most amusing, and Rule in her musical debut was entrancing. But *Lysistrata* was an overly familiar story, and the show's level of humor did not rise much above burlesque. Broad, bawdy, and obvious, it was moderately entertaining, but the combination of an old story and an old score may have done it in.

One year later, a musical called *La Belle*, loosely based on Offenbach's *La Belle Helene*, with William Roy adapting Offenbach's music, opened and closed on the road. It was directed by Albert Marre and starred Joan

○ ○ ○ ○ ○

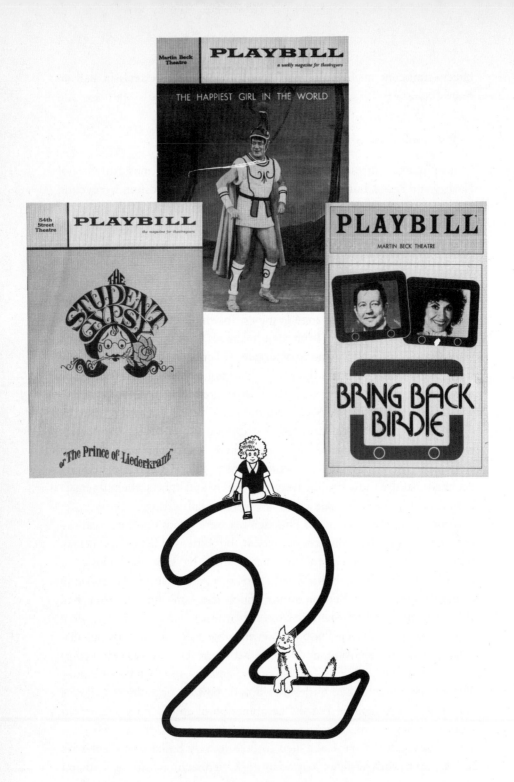

The Student Gypsy *illustrated the inadvisability of repeating oneself,* Happiest Girl *the inadvisability of using old music. The failure of* Bring Back Birdie *and* Annie 2 *may mean that Charles Strouse won't be doing any more sequels.*

Diener opposite Menasha Skulnik. In 1972, a dreadful semimusical version of *Lysistrata* was presented on Broadway, starring Melina Mercouri and with songs by Peter *(King of Hearts)* Link.

Every so often, producers and writers decide that what audiences want is an old-fashioned slice of musical Americana. Audiences usually don't, and when they're given old music as well, they're even less interested. **Teddy and Alice** (Minskoff; Nov. 12, '87; 77) was a flop derived from an earlier flop: when Stone Widney (the director of *Ambassador*) was researching Teddy Roosevelt for Alan Jay Lerner's disastrous *1600 Pennsylvania Avenue*, he and Lerner concluded that there was enough material for another musical about Teddy, one which might focus on his obsession with his flamboyant daughter Alice. Lerner advised on *Teddy and Alice*, and when it was produced after his death, Lerner received program credit as "artistic consultant."

Teddy and Alice had a gestation period of about seven years, during which time Robert Preston was sought for the lead and a backers' audition was presented on cable television. With a book by Jerome Alden, who had already written a solo play about Teddy called *Bully*, and lyrics by Hal Hackady (his fourth Broadway flop), it finally got on. It was first tried out in Tampa, where Widney, who had been with the project since its inception, was replaced as director by John Driver. On arrival in New York, the critics were not kind and audiences stayed away.

For the score, Richard Kapp adapted the work of John Philip Sousa, who wrote operettas in addition to his famous marches. Kapp also wrote some new tunes: the final count was Kapp 4, Sousa 4, Sousa mixed with Kapp 6. While Beth Fowler, as Teddy's second wife, Edith, and Ron Raines, as Alice's suitor Nick Longworth, had one very nice number apiece, Teddy's political cronies had floppo numbers, and the attempt to fit words to "Stars and Stripes Forever" was not successful.

The problems of *Teddy and Alice* went beyond its lack of a completely original score. The book was shallow and humorless, never really telling the audience very much about Teddy except that he could not let Alice go. The audience was often told what a madcap eccentric Alice was supposed to be but was never shown much evidence. The political aspect of the show was reduced to a cartoon, and there was no suspense, as it was obvious that Teddy would have to allow Alice (who went down in history as Alice *Longworth*) to marry Nick eventually. And after a long evening, there was no clear reason provided for Teddy's sudden change

○ ○ ○ ○ ○

of heart. The show's camp highlight was its Act One finale, "Wave the Flag," with Teddy projected out over the audience on the guns of a convention float shaped like a battleship. Len Cariou worked hard as Teddy, but the show was his second Lerner-related musical flop at the Minskoff. Even with an original score and a better book, *Teddy and Alice* would probably not have found acceptance on Broadway in 1987.

Our third and final flop with old music was based on Philip Barry's 1928 play *Holiday*, the story of Johnny Case, who wants to go off and explore the world and himself before settling down as a member of the wealthy Seton family into which he is about to marry. *Holiday* might have made a good musical, although like *Harvey* and *The Man Who Came to Dinner*, it was tightly constructed and didn't really need songs. But it was a distinct mistake to musicalize it the way Burt Shevelove, who should have known better, did when he adapted the play into **Happy New Year** (Morosco; Apr. 27, '80; 17). Shevelove, who wrote the script and directed, decided to use Cole Porter songs for the score. When the show was first performed at the Stratford Festival in Canada, the Porter songs were of the rarer variety; by the time *Happy New Year* got to Broadway, Porter standards ("Night and Day," "Easy to Love," "You Do Something to Me") had crept in alongside lesser-known songs like "Let's Make It a Night" and "Once Upon a Time."

While Porter's style was a good match for Barry—Porter himself musicalized Barry's *The Philadelphia Story* in the film *High Society*, which was in turn later adapted to the stage—songs not written specifically for the characters in a story can't musicalize them properly, even if the songs have a vague connection to the mood or idea of a scene and were written in the same period as the original play. Such Porter songs as "Ridin' High" and "Let's Be Buddies" had nothing to do with the characters singing them here; the songs in *Happy New Year* became intrusions, stopping the story dead.

To make matters worse, much of the original play was hacked away to allow time for these songs that didn't fit (and weren't particularly well performed). Two important couples from the play, the insufferable Crams and the salt-of-the-earth Potters, were eliminated. A narrator (who turned out at the end to be the older Johnny Case) was added, a lazy device to cover over the parts of the play that were missing. And as the film versions of both *Holiday* and *The Philadelphia Story* attest, Barry works better with star personalities; with the exception of John McMartin, who was the

○ ○ ○ ○ ○

narrator, *Happy New Year* had a cast of unknowns who have remained so. But the show was dead from the moment its creators decided to take the easy way out to musicalize Barry.

#9: Don't do sequels.

No one has ever satisfactorily answered the question of why sequels have always been popular in the world of film but don't work well in the theatre. In loosely written musicals of the twenties and thirties, a star would often play the same character in more than one show; but in contemporary musical theatre, there has never been a successful sequel (William Finn's Marvin musicals function as a trilogy rather than as an original and its sequels), and most successful musical-theatre writers wouldn't dream of writing a sequel to one of their hit shows. But the devil-may-care Charles Strouse did it—twice.

Bring Back Birdie (Martin Beck; Mar. 5, '81; 4) picked up the action of *Bye Bye Birdie* twenty years later. The first *Birdie* ended with music publisher and aspiring English teacher Albert and his girlfriend-secretary Rose marrying, and Albert leaving show business when his one client, rock 'n' roll singer Conrad Birdie, is drafted. In the sequel, Albert is offered twenty thousand dollars if he can find Conrad and persuade him to perform on a television show. Albert takes a leave of absence from his job teaching English and locates Conrad, now overweight and the mayor of Bent River Junction, Arizona. The action is complicated by the rebellion of Rose and Albert's teenage children, one of whom runs off to join a cult while the other joins a punk-rock group, and by the reappearance of Albert's long lost mother, Mae, whom Albert also finds in Arizona.

For *Bring Back Birdie*, the team that wrote the original—Michael Stewart, Strouse, and Lee Adams—was brought back, as was original star Chita Rivera, who had recently done *Bye Bye Birdie* in stock. Gower Champion, who had his first big Broadway triumph with *Bye Bye Birdie*, was dead; Joe Layton conceived and directed the sequel. Donald O'Connor made his Broadway debut opposite Rivera, and Elvis impersonator Marcel Forestieri played Conrad. The producers booked the Martin Beck, where the first *Birdie* had opened twenty-one years earlier. Probably because of the elaborate (and hideous) design concept, which featured dozens of working television monitors, the show had no tryout, just a series of chaotic New York previews during which it became obvious to all that there was no hope. Layton and Stewart skipped the opening night performance, and at one of the final performances a few days later, O'Connor forgot the words to his song "Middle-Aged Blues," asked the boys in the band for help, and then said, "You sing it! I hated this song anyway!" to gasps from the audience. Rivera received her customary Tony nomination.

Bring Back Birdie may rank as the worst Broadway musical ever to be created by top-level professionals. The book was tasteless and ridiculous: Albert's mother, Mae, a highly amusing character in the original, became vulgar, nasty, and unfunny (through no fault of actress Maria Karnilova); in the absurd conclusion Mae revealed that she, like Rose, was Spanish, too. The book eliminated the likable Kim and her boyfriend Hugo from the original. And despite a nice opening song called "Twenty Happy Years" and a couple of others which Rivera forced into showstoppers, there were also grotesque gospel and punk songs, retreads of numbers from the original ("The Telephone Hour" became "Moving Out"—with cordless phones—and "Spanish Rose" became "Well, I'm Not!"), and a desperate curtain call reprise of "Rosie" from *Bye Bye Birdie*. There is no question that a revival of the original, with Rivera, would have been a much better idea. One sat through the sequel wondering how the authors ever thought they would get away with it.

Even if *Bring Back Birdie* had been better, it might not have made it, for audiences did not seem particularly interested in finding out what had happened to Albert, Rosie, and Conrad twenty years later. But everyone seemed eager to return to the story of orphan Annie, billionaire Oliver Warbucks, and the hilariously evil Miss Hannigan when it was announced that a sequel to the 1977 smash hit musical *Annie* was in the works. Much of the creative team from *Annie* was reassembled for **Annie 2: Miss Hannigan's Revenge** (Washington, D.C.; Jan. 4, '90; closed on the road): director–lyricist Martin Charnin, librettist Thomas Meehan, original Hannigan Dorothy Loudon, original FDR Raymond Thorne, set designer David Mitchell, costume designer Theoni V. Aldredge, one producer (Lewis Allen), and in spite of his experience with the *Birdie* sequel, composer Charles Strouse. Harve Presnell, who played Warbucks in *Annie* on tour and at the end of the Broadway run, returned to the role for the sequel. A nationwide talent search produced eleven-year-old Danielle Findley for the part of Annie, and for the part of Annie's dog, Sandy, Beau was hired (the original Sandy was deemed too old for the part and died the year *Annie 2* opened).

The original *Annie*, one of the last successful conventional fifties-sixties–

○ ○ ○ ○ ○

style book musicals, had a beautifully constructed libretto, an always suitable and appealing score, a lovely physical production, and Loudon, making a great deal out of what was essentially a comic-relief supporting role. But the chief reason why the original show was such a hit was its emotional underpinnings. In *Annie*, the eponymous orphan believes that her parents are still alive and will one day retrieve her from the orphanage in which they deposited her. When she is brought to Warbucks' mansion for Christmas, she transforms the life of the gruff businessman, who falls in love with her and wants to adopt her. But Annie insists that her parents intend to come for her, and reluctantly, Warbucks sets in motion all his forces to find the parents who he knows will take Annie away from him. After foiling the scheme of Hannigan and her brother to get Annie— and a considerable reward—for themselves, Warbucks, having learned that Annie's parents are truly dead, adopts the orphan. Annie, in true Cinderella fashion, ends *Annie 1* with everything she could want: a new father (who's also the richest man in the country), a home, and a surrogate mother in Warbucks' devoted secretary, Grace.

And therein lay the problem as far as a sequel was concerned: Annie was no longer in any jeopardy and no longer needed anything. The emotional through-line of *Annie* had been brought to a satisfactory conclusion; *Annie* was self-contained, and its plot did not allow for further development. But *Annie* also made a profit of $20 million during its almost six-year run, and its creators, particularly Charnin, couldn't resist doing what Charnin refused to call a sequel, but instead dubbed a "continuation." Indeed, Charnin announced the sequel from the stage of the Gershwin Theatre at the conclusion of the final performance of *Annie* in January 1983. Realizing the problem inherent in attempting to continue a story that already had the perfect ending, the team decided to center *Annie 2* around Hannigan's revenge; this decision, more than anything else, doomed the new show to failure from the start.

When *Annie 2* began previews on December 22, 1989, at Washington, D.C.'s Kennedy Center (where *Annie* had become an instant hit prior to Broadway), the story went like this: It's 1934, six weeks after the end of *Annie*, and Miss Hannigan takes advantage of a fire to escape from the Women's House of Detention, where she was sent for her involvement in the scheme to defraud Warbucks. Meanwhile, Warbucks, having adopted Annie, is visited by Congresswoman Marietta Christmas (Marian Seldes), who as head of the United Mothers of America orders Warbucks to find a mother for Annie within ninety days, or the child will be

∘ ∘ ∘ ∘ ∘

withdrawn from his home. Warbucks is fond of Grace (Lauren Mitchell), who is obviously all the mother Annie needs, but feels he's too old to marry her. So he asks Grace to draw up a press release describing the kind of woman he's seeking for Annie's mother and announcing a nationwide contest.

The escaped Hannigan is consumed with a desire to revenge herself on Annie; she hooks up with ex-con Lionel McCoy (Ronny Graham), who falls for her and, to further the revenge scheme, secures a job as one of Warbucks' chauffeurs. It is Hannigan's scheme to become Warbucks' wife and Annie's mother, then get rid of both of them and become the world's wealthiest widow. McCoy takes Hannigan to his former cellmate Maurice's Brooklyn beauty shop (prison has obviously turned Maurice into a stereotypical sissy), where she is more or less transformed into something resembling Warbucks' ideal mate.

At an overflowing Yankee Stadium, Warbucks is interviewing candidates when Hannigan arrives, dolled up and calling herself Charlotte O'Hara—from the deep South. Thanks to McCoy's inside knowledge, Hannigan is chosen as one of the finalists. But her elation turns to despair when Mrs. Christmas insists that Annie judge the contest along with Warbucks; Hannigan is certain Annie will recognize her.

Later, outside the Fulton Fish Market, Hannigan discovers a tough street-kid named Kate (also played by Findley), who is a dead ringer for Annie. Hannigan decides to train Kate to impersonate Annie and take her place. As the curtain falls on Act One, Hannigan exults to Kate, "You, you, you could be Annie, too (2)!"

In the second act, Hannigan and her cohorts kidnap Annie and substitute the imposter at Coney Island, where Warbucks has brought Annie for an evening out. At last, Hannigan wins the contest, but just as she and Warbucks are about to be married, Grace figures out the plot and rescues Annie from death by drowning. Warbucks suddenly decides he's not too old for Grace and chooses her to be Annie's mother.

This description of the *Annie 2* plot may sound better than it played: it was greeted by *Annie 2*'s first preview audience in stunned silence—rarely has an audience hated a show so much. Charnin immediately decided to postpone the Washington D.C. opening and get to work, while Mike Nichols (producer of *Annie*), Tommy Tune, and Peter Stone came to Washington, D.C. to offer suggestions. When the show opened on January 4, the reviews were horrendous, but work continued, and by the end of its month-long Washington run, *Annie 2* had been radically altered. The opening scene in the House of Detention had been dropped, along with Hannigan's first song; Warbucks had now sent Hannigan off to Australia to punish her, and she now jumped ship and took refuge on McCoy's tugboat. A line of orphans, vital to the spirit of the original, was added, but there wasn't time to give them much to do. The scene in Yankee Stadium was moved to a hotel room, and the opening of Act Two—Annie cheering up FDR with the show's big song, "When You Smile"—was moved from Wall Street to Yankee Stadium, with Annie cheering up Babe Ruth. The effeminate Maurice became the butch Charlie Spinoli, and lines like Maurice's "Are we men or are we hairdressers?" were dropped. An attempt was made to make Annie more than just a prop by giving her new songs; Hannigan no longer intended to kill Annie, only to send her away; McCoy was no longer Hannigan's love interest but just her accomplice, and he lost his duet with Hannigan; and Hannigan, no longer masquerading as a Southern belle, disguised herself as the dead-serious Frances Riley, a hard-knock lady from Connecticut. Hannigan-as-Riley was given a grim new showstopper called "But You Go On," in which she sang out the horrors of her life. The decision to change Hannigan's impersonation from the giddy O'Hara to the tragic Riley meant that Loudon was deprived of virtually all of the opportunities for the kind of comedy at which she excels.

For all the changes, the problems of *Annie 2* were too severe to be corrected in a few weeks. Aside from the basic problem—*Annie* didn't call for a sequel—the creators had made matters worse with a series of miscalculations. The premise of the new plot was shaky—would Warbucks, friend to the president of the United States, simply accept Mrs. Christmas's order to find a wife, and wouldn't he be able to find one for himself, instead of having to advertise and have a contest? Wouldn't Warbucks be able to see through Hannigan's disguise and tell the difference between the fake Annie and the real one? And why was he too old for Grace, who obviously loved him anyway as far back as *Annie 1?*

A more serious problem was the decision to make the show about Hannigan and her revenge. There was no real reason why Hannigan should want to get back at Annie—Annie never did anything to her. The original Hannigan was not really evil, just a miserable old maid who took out her frustrations on her orphan charges. And she was only an accomplice to her brother's scheme in *Annie;* it wasn't her idea. Making the show about Hannigan's search for revenge eliminated the possibility of any real feeling—or any suspense, for that matter: no one in the audience

∘ ∘ ∘ ∘ ∘

could seriously entertain the belief that Warbucks would actually marry Hannigan. Like the first *Annie*, the show needed to be about Annie. It wasn't, and by the time it closed in Washington, it wasn't about much at all.

Was there anything good about the *Annie 2* that so disappointed holiday audiences in D.C.? David Mitchell again came up with very attractive sets, and as usual, composer Strouse proved himself incapable of writing a totally uninteresting score. Borrowing one cut song from *Annie* and a few melodies from one of his unproduced musicals, *Bojangles*, Strouse provided catchy tunes for "When You Smile" and a big production number called "Coney Island," a lovely ballad for Warbucks called "A Younger Man," and a good song for Annie called "Changes."

Annie 2 might have continued on to another tryout town for more work or come into New York and postponed its opening while revision continued. To be sure, New York audiences had already demonstrated their interest in revisiting Annie by coughing up $4 million in advance sales. But the producers of *Annie 2* instead took the radical step of announcing that their show, which had already cost $7 million, would close, abandoning its scheduled March 1 opening at the Marriott Marquis Theatre. *Annie 2*, they said, would receive a workshop production at the Goodspeed Opera House, where *Annie* was first produced, in the summer, and the D.C. *Annie 2* would become a revival of *Annie 1*. Producer Roger Berlind estimated that sixty percent of the sets and eighty percent of the costumes for *Annie 2* could be rolled over for the revival, an extremely unlikely assertion.

The closing of the Broadway-bound *Annie 2* made headlines all over the country; immediately, it became one of the most famous fiascoes in Broadway history, and even Johnny Carson made a joke about it on *The Tonight Show*. The last D.C. performances were heavily attended by New Yorkers who had missed Bette Davis in *Miss Moffat* and Angela Lansbury in *Prettybelle* and weren't going to make the same mistake a third time. Loudon, who had a bronchial infection, missed several shows the last week; then Charnin, perhaps annoyed at Loudon's announcement that she would not appear in the proposed *Annie* revival, forbade her from playing the final matinee; she returned for the last show on January 20.

The proposed revival of *Annie* did not happen, but the Goodspeed production did; *Annie 2* received a bare-bones production at the Goodspeed's Norma Terris Theatre in Chester, Connecticut, from May 17 through July 8, during which enormous changes in book, score, and cast

○ ○ ○ ○ ○

were made. With the original subtitle gone, Hannigan was gradually eliminated too, and Seldes, now playing Commissioner Margaret Stark, became the villain, using her knowledge of Warbucks' likes and dislikes to put her sister (named Fran Riley) in Warbucks' bed. With Hannigan gone, there was no longer any need to have two Annies either. A serious attempt was made to make the show more about Annie: in the new version, Grace quits her job in frustration, and Annie, blaming herself for breaking up what was a happy household, runs away from home, ultimately returning after an on-the-road encounter with a father and daughter teaches her a lesson in values. Two strong numbers were added for the orphans, and it was one of the orphans who figured out the villains' plot. Gone were Yankee Stadium, the Fulton Fish Market, Coney Island, the beauty parlor, and the tugboat. Loudon, Graham, Lauren Mitchell, and poor little Findley, who had had her face splashed across the cover of *Life* magazine, were all gone; Presnell, Seldes, and Thorne remained; and Helen Gallagher was added, first as Hannigan, then, when that part was completely eliminated, as Fran Riley. Very few songs from *Miss Hannigan's Revenge* survived intact. Perhaps the ultimate humiliation: Beau was replaced by a new dog, Chelsea, who more closely resembled the original Sandy, and Beau swallowed his pride and became Chelsea's understudy.

By the time it had concluded its Goodspeed run, there was no question that *Annie 2* was a better show. The story was more believable; the dialogue, woefully deficient in laughs in Washington, was frequently amusing; the new Annie, Lauren Gaffney, was far more appealing than Findley. Almost everything about the show was different, but the initial, less-than-credible premise—Warbucks must find a mother for Annie in ninety days or lose her—remained, and so, for all the improvements, *Annie 2* still had a shaky foundation.

After Goodspeed, Charnin announced that the show would resume around Labor Day, perhaps go out of town again, and reach Broadway during the 1990–91 season. None of that happened. In March 1991, the show's producers held backers' auditions in an attempt to raise money and finally get *Annie 2* on Broadway. When no money was forthcoming, the producers gave up and returned the rights to *Annie 2* to its writers. While Meehan, Charnin, and Strouse may eventually find new producers for *Annie 2*, it might be better if they don't: *Annie 2*, like all the other shows in this section, was, quite simply, a mistake.

Six

MISSED OPPORTUNITIES

"In spite of the fact that *Anya* is an old-fashioned musical, it isn't any good . . . no matter who the real Anastasia was I am going to cling to my blind conviction that the George Abbott who is listed as co-librettist and director is not the real George Abbott."—Walter Kerr, *Herald Tribune*

"Looks like a dinner theater's homegrown answer to *Hello, Dolly!* . . . You want a good night's sleep? Pay your money and rest in peace . . . The book and lyrics battle to a stand-off as they attempt to top each other in witlessness."—Frank Rich, *The New York Times*, on *Onward Victoria*

Bob Dishy, Liza Minnelli in Flora, The Red Menace (*above*)

Even with better handling, it is doubtful that many of the shows in the last section could ever have become successful musicals. But what is even sadder to behold in the theatre than a mistake is a musical that is quite obviously not good, but just as obviously could have been. This chapter surveys a group of shows that, in one way or another, represent missed opportunities. To varying degrees, they all might have made wonderful musicals.

Edna Ferber's novel *Show Boat* was the basis for one of the greatest musicals of all time, and her novel *Saratoga Trunk*, made into a movie starring Gary Cooper and Ingrid Bergman in 1945, offered characters and a story with equally rich possibilities for a colorful, exciting, serious musical. *Saratoga Trunk* was a hot property among musical-theatre writers for several years: Ferber had asked Moss Hart and Rodgers and Hammerstein to collaborate on the show with her, but Rodgers and Hammerstein chose to do *Pipe Dream* instead. Lerner and Loewe promised Ferber they would do the adaptation, and Ferber was furious when, after *My Fair Lady* opened, they too opted to pass.

Ferber, eager to get the musical version of her book on, finally allowed the property to go to Morton Da Costa, whose recent string of hit musicals and comedies was to be broken by **Saratoga** (Winter Garden; Dec. 7, '59; 80). Da Costa wrote his first book for the show and also directed and coproduced. When Ferber read Da Costa's script, she decided to do a rewrite of it herself; she was ignored by the show's team, however, and bowed out, aware that *Saratoga* was not turning into the musical she envisioned.

Saratoga was more fortunate in its songwriters. Harold Arlen wrote the music: it was to be his fifth major book musical with a strong black element, his biggest flop, and his last Broadway show. Johnny Mercer, who wrote *St. Louis Woman* with Arlen, did the lyrics, but when Arlen became ill and grew discouraged with the show on the road, Mercer wrote both music and lyrics for three songs ("Gettin' a Man," "The Men Who Run the Country," and "Why Fight This?").

Saratoga was a much anticipated show and racked up an advance sale of $1.5 million. Rock Hudson and Jeanmaire had been mentioned for the leads, but they went to Carol Lawrence, who had already done *Shangri-La*, *Ziegfeld Follies*, and *West Side Story* at the Winter Garden, and Howard Keel, creating his first role on Broadway. Cecil Beaton provided the sets and costumes, and the show's $400,000 cost was mostly provided by NBC and RCA Victor Records.

○ ○ ○ ○ ○

During the tryout, Jane Darwell quit and was replaced in the part of Mrs. Bellop by Edith King. The New York critics raved over Beaton's sets, with a turntable and fifteen changes of locale, and his more than two hundred costumes, and they liked the leads. But it was clear to all that *Saratoga* was a disappointment, and the advance sale kept it open for less than three months.

One problem may have been that audiences at the time were not especially taken with a show in which both leading characters were out for vengeance and nothing else. Lawrence played Clio Dulaine, an illegitimate Creole girl who returns home to New Orleans, vowing to be respectable and to revenge herself on the Dulaine family which exiled her mother from town. Posing as an American countess raised in France, Clio meets Clint Maroon (Keel), a Montana cowboy who's come to New Orleans to settle his own score with the railroad men who took away his family's property. Clint persuades Clio to accompany him to Saratoga, where he can use her to entice railroad millionaire Bart Van Steed. Clio, determined to be rich, tries not to succumb to Clint's growing affection for her, but she fails. At the ball where her engagement to Bart is to be announced, Clio makes a shocking appearance dressed as a black servant girl, then tells Clint she loves him and doesn't care about being rich. But Clint, having helped Bart in his struggle with railroad thugs, is now rich and can give Clio the respectability—and love—she wants.

Clio and Clint, falling in love against their will as they scheme to settle old family scores, were marvelous central figures for a musical. But one problem was perhaps built into the story: the shift from New Orleans to Saratoga late in the first act brings on a whole new set of characters and drops many others. And Da Costa was an even bigger problem: Ferber's story required a far more skilled librettist, and he was unable to bring the central romance to life. His staging may have been even more at fault than his script; *Saratoga* reads better than it played because Da Costa contented himself with a cumbersome, slow-moving production. Rarely has such potentially red-hot material been given such ponderous treatment. *Saratoga* was billed as "The Morton Da Costa Production," and apparently there was no one else around strong enough to demand improvements.

The lyrics are quite good and much of the music is attractive, but the songs for the leads were rather bland and generic, and much good musical material was cut during the tryout due to the show's length. Ralph Beaumont's slow motion "Railroad Fight" ballet was a highlight, and Beaton's

○ ○ ○ ○ ○

Above, Carol Lawrence rehearses her songs for Saratoga, accompanied by the show's composer, Harold Arlen. Below, Lawrence, in blackface, makes a shocking entrance into the ballroom of the United States Hotel.

sets, which contributed to the heaviness of the evening, were nonetheless dazzling. Lawrence held on to her title of Queen of the Winter Garden by resuming the part of Maria when *West Side Story* returned to the theatre immediately following the closing of *Saratoga*.

Flora, the Red Menace (Alvin; May 11, '65; 87) is another show for which the director–librettist was most responsible for a project's falling short of its potential.

Flora was a show of beginnings and endings. It marked the Broadway debuts of nineteen-year-old Liza Minnelli, who won a Tony Award for it, and the team of John Kander and Fred Ebb. It was the beginning of a life-long relationship between star and songwriters, which saw Minnelli later appearing in the team's *The Act, The Rink, Chicago, Cabaret* (on film), and others, and singing countless Kander and Ebb songs in her concert performances. *Flora* was the last book musical Harold Prince ever produced that he did not also direct, and it was the last collaboration between Prince and George Abbott, *Flora*'s director, who coauthored (with Robert Russell) the book, based on Lester Atwell's novel *Love Is Just Around the Corner*.

Contrary to popular assumption, *Flora* was not written for Minnelli. Russell began writing the show by himself as a vehicle for Barbra Streisand; when Abbott joined the project, he in turn saw it as a vehicle for Eydie Gorme. But Minnelli won the role of Flora Meszaros, who, in the depths of the Depression, is drawn into the Communist party by her boyfriend and fellow artist, Harry Toukarian. As was the case with many earlier Abbott shows, the cast was filled with talented young performers, here including Bob Dishy, Mary Louise Wilson, and Cathryn Damon. *Flora* received such promising reviews in New Haven and Boston that it was recorded two days before its Broadway opening. But the New York critics were far less enthusiastic, and the show collapsed during the summer, losing almost all of its $400,000 investment.

Prince later believed that he should have directed the show himself, and he admitted that he did not have the courage to demand better of Abbott. While *Flora* was pleasant and amusing, it never came to grips with its provocative subject matter. It used its potentially serious subject, a young woman's attraction to communism, as an excuse for a typical Abbott-style farcical romp, ducking most of the possibilities offered by the period and situation. Moreover, Flora was never allowed to become a committed Communist; she only flirted with the party as part of her

○ ○ ○ ○ ○

*Three might-have-been musicals: Above, Flora, the
Red Menace star Liza Minnelli gets a backstage
hug from mom.*

flirtation with Harry. Kander later said, "Abbott couldn't understand why anybody could ever have been Communist," and the show suffered by having a heroine who almost—but never quite—throws herself into the party. There can be little doubt that *Flora* would have been better had Prince conceived and directed it, and the result with Abbott in charge was exactly the kind of experience that would soon cause Prince to abandon conventional musical theatre forever.

Flora's score, however, demonstrated that Broadway had found a team that was there to stay. Kander and Ebb showed that they could handle ballads, comedy numbers, belting showstoppers, and novelty songs with equal facility. Even though *Flora* failed quickly, Prince was smart enough to hire the team immediately for *Cabaret*, with Prince directing and conceiving a production which, unlike *Flora*, never flinched from the seriousness of its subject, while providing entertainment sufficient for those who admired the old-style, Abbott-school musical.

Because of its songs, it was inevitable that *Flora* would be tried again, and it was, in a new version first presented by the off-off-Broadway Vineyard Theatre in November 1987. With a new book by David Thompson, a cast of nine, a tiny orchestra, several new songs added and a few old ones cut, *Flora* was performed as a play within a play being presented by the Federal Theatre Project. Thompson's book, particularly its second act, made communism far more integral to the action and grappled with the issues more seriously. In the new book, it's the party itself that comes between Flora and Harry, rather than the revenge of a jealous other woman in Harry's life. But the new *Flora*, now available for stock and amateur productions, still failed to fully satisfy, and while groups may find the show worth trying, *Flora* may still be most enjoyable as an RCA Victor original Broadway cast recording.

Anastasia, the play by Marcelle Maurette which was seen on Broadway in 1954 in an adaptation by Guy Bolton and on film with Ingrid Bergman and Yul Brynner, might have made a wonderful musical; George Abbott was, again, at least partly responsible for its becoming less than it should have been. **Anya** (Ziegfeld; Nov. 19, '65; 16) was originally written by Bolton, Robert Wright, and George Forrest, with Wright and Forrest this time adapting the music of Sergei Rachmaninoff for their score. Abbott joined the project as colibrettist and director, and the show became the last musical at the Ziegfeld Theatre, which had opened in 1927 with *Rio*

○ ○ ○ ○ ○

Rita, also coauthored by Bolton. During rehearsals, Metropolitan Opera baritone George London withdrew from the part of Bounine, once general of the Cossacks in Czarist Russia and now a taxi-driver in Berlin, which was taken by Michael Kermoyan. Constance Towers played the girl whom Bounine finds in a Berlin psychiatric institute in 1925, a girl who claims to be the czar's supposedly slaughtered youngest daughter.

The show was dismissed as a dated operetta by the critics, and $415,000 was lost in two weeks. The play and movie had done well by a clanky but hard-to-resist story, with an enjoyable enigma at its center; the musical did not. *Anya* opened up a one-set play and invented new characters that got in the way of the main action. A romance between Anya and Bounine was added, which, if perhaps helpful for a musical, was handled weakly. A silly romantic triangle made things worse, with Bounine's romance with Anya complicated by his mistress, Genia. At the end of the first act, Anya announced to the guests that she is an impostor. In the play, she did this to protest Bounine's exploitation of her; in the musical, it was out of jealousy when she thinks Bounine has gone off with Genia. A new character, Katrina, who ran the local café, was added so that Irra Petina could provide some comic relief. In general, the tautness of the original was dissipated, and much of the play's best dialogue was eliminated to make way for the corny romantic complications. In *Anya*, *Anastasia* was given the floperetta treatment—two of the essential floperetta ingredients, the team of Wright and Forrest, and Petina, were present—and the possibilities for an exciting musical were left largely unexplored.

As was the case with their *Grand Hotel* musical, Wright and Forrest would not let go of a potentially effective property, and they worked on revisions of *Anya* for the next twenty-five years. These were staged under various titles in South Africa, Florida, and Massachusetts, with a new book by Jerome Chodorov and a heavily revised score. In 1986, the ninety-year-old Edwin Lester, who somehow had not produced *Anya* in the first place, announced it for his California Civic Light Operas, but it didn't happen. The version presented in 1989 by the Merrimack Repertory Theatre in Lowell, Massachusetts, under the title *The Anastasia Game*, returned the story to the play's single setting, eliminated Katrina, Genia, and other distractions, and radically altered the score. While the production, which starred Judy Kaye and Len Cariou, marked an improvement, it still had Wright and Forrest's operetta-level lyrics, and it still schmaltzed up a superior play.

* * *

○ ○ ○ ○ ○

FRED R. FEHLHABER
presents

CONSTANCE MICHAEL LILLIAN
TOWERS KERMOYAN GISH

A New Musical

also starring IRRA PETINA

with GEORGE S. IRVING   BORIS APLON   ED STEFFE
JOHN MICHAEL KING   KAREN SHEPARD   MARGARET MULLEN

Book by **GEORGE ABBOTT** and **GUY BOLTON**
(Based upon "ANASTASIA" by MARCELLE MAURETTE and GUY BOLTON)

Music and Lyrics by **ROBERT WRIGHT** and **GEORGE FORREST**
(Based on themes of S. RACHMANINOFF)

Choreography and Musical Numbers by
HANYA HOLM

Scenery by   Costumes by   Lighting by
ROBERT RANDOLPH   PATRICIA ZIPPRODT   RICHARD CASLER

Musical Direction by   Orchestrations by
HAROLD HASTINGS   **DON WALKER**
Original cast album by UNITED ARTISTS RECORDS

Production
Directed by **GEORGE ABBOTT**

MAIL ORDERS NOW   OPENS MON. EVG. NOV. 29

PREVIEWS NOV. 15 thru NOV. 27—Evenings Mon. thru Sat.: Orch. $7.50
Mezz. $6.90; Balc. $5.75, 4.80, 4.20, 3.80, 3.00
Matinees Wed. and Sat.: Orch. $4.80; Mezz. $4.20; Balc. $3.80, 3.00
REGULAR PERFORMANCES—Evenings Mon. thru Sat.: Orch. $9.90
Mezz. $8.80; Balc. $7.50, 6.90, 5.75, 4.80, 3.80
Matinees Wed. and Sat.: Orch. $6.25; Mezz. $5.75; Balc. $4.80, 4.20, 3.80, 3.00
Please enclose self-addressed, stamped envelope with mail order and
suggest several alternate dates.

ZIEGFELD THEATRE
54th St. and 6th Ave., New York, N. Y.

One of the last gasps of floperetta, Anya. *Playbill (top right) features the essential Irra Petina, at right. Program below is for* The Anastasia Game, *one of several* Anya *revisions.*

In the seventies, director–choreographer Bob Fosse's control over his shows increased by dangerous increments: in *Pippin*, his staging dominated the book and score; in *Chicago*, he became colibrettist, his concept of the show subsuming all the other contributions; and with *Dancin'*, he eliminated collaborators altogether—*Dancin'* was nothing but an evening of choreography. The precedent it set, however, destroyed Fosse's next and last show, **Big Deal** (Broadway; Apr. 10, '86; 70).

Big Deal, the only Fosse flop that made it to Broadway with his name on it, was set on the South Side of Chicago in the Depression. Charley, an unsuccessful boxer, hooks up with four small-time cohorts to rob a pawnshop. After many complications, the good-guy criminals burrow through the wrong wall and give up, and Charley decides to go straight. Fosse's book was based on the 1958 Italian film *Big Deal on Madonna Street* (Fosse had already derived *Sweet Charity* from a fifties Italian film), and he decided to do the show with an almost all-black cast. Fosse originally planned to invite several songwriters, Peter Allen among them, to contribute to the score, but he eventually decided to use standards ("Life Is Just a Bowl of Cherries," "I'm Just Wild about Harry," "Me and My Shadow") rather than have to work with any writers at all.

Reviews in Boston were mixed, but in spite of protests from the Shuberts, Fosse refused to do much with *Big Deal*. Indeed, there was little he could do, so bizarrely had he conceived the $5 million show. It was performed on an almost bare stage, with a skeletal Peter Larkin set of platforms, scaffolding, and staircases, expensively run by computer and very dimly lit. Except for Loretta Devine's amusing performance as the maid who held the keys to the apartment which abutted the pawnshop, there was little effective humor. And *Big Deal* destroyed almost every one of its old songs: they were heard briefly, the melodies buried and distorted by the arrangements, and the lyrics rarely had anything to do with the characters singing them. Totally ineffective as numbers, the songs became mostly stage waits.

But unlike *Teddy and Alice* or *Happy New Year*, which even with original music would probably not have worked, *Big Deal* was a show of real potential. The sweetly charming hoods, reminiscent of the characters in *Guys and Dolls*, and their big dreams were appealing, and their misadventures in Depression-era Chicago could easily have been the basis for a charming, funny musical. One sat through *Big Deal* thinking about what it might have been like with a book by Neil Simon and a score by Kander and Ebb.

○ ○ ○ ○ ○

If *Big Deal* proved that Fosse couldn't do it all, it also ranks as a collectible flop because of some sleek Fosse staging highlights. There was "Ain't We Got Fun," sung and danced by a gang of men with their feet and hands chained together, and the dreamy, exciting ensemble dance, "Beat Me Daddy Eight to the Bar." Fosse's overall staging concept, in which the dancing, led by two narrator figures, was woven in and out of the scenes, was unusual and often effective. But the four big numbers at the end of the second act, in which each member of the gang fantasized about what he would do if the heist came off, were serious disappointments. In *Big Deal*, Fosse let himself down as deployer of music, writer, and even stager, and it was an unfortunate finale to one of Broadway's great careers.

With its blank verse, outsized emotions, Greek-tragedy plotting, and gloomy picture of Irish immigrants fighting to get out of the ghetto and find a better life, William Alfred's 1965 off-Broadway hit play, *Hogan's Goat*, would have made a marvelous American opera. It might have been a good musical too, but it fell into the hands of Mitch Leigh, Albert Marre, and Joan Diener, and while they did not do totally wrong by it, they failed to come up with a musical worthy of the richly dramatic source material.

Marre and Alfred collaborated on the book for **Cry for Us All** (Broadhurst; Apr. 8, '70; 9), which, like the original, was set in 1890 Brooklyn, where the sins and secrets of the past come to haunt Matt, a young Irishman seeking to overthrow the corrupt mayor, and eventually destroy him and his wife. It was Leigh's idea to musicalize the play, and Phyllis Robinson and Alfred wrote lyrics to Leigh's music. Opera singer John Reardon left the show just before rehearsals, perhaps sensing that director Marre might favor wife Diener, miscast as Matt's delicate wife, at the expense of the show's development.

Cry for Us All was a better show when it premiered in New Haven than it was subsequently in Boston (where its title was briefly changed to *Who To Love*) or New York. The part of Josie Finn (and Margot Moser, who was playing it), crucial to the action of the play, was eliminated, and Diener's part got bigger and bigger as material was taken away from such supporting cast members as Helen Gallagher, Tommy Rall, and Dolores Wilson.

Leigh's music occasionally approached the operatic, especially in the title number, but while it was the best thing about the show, it did not go far enough and was too often lightweight when the material demanded

○ ○ ○ ○ ○

genuine grandeur. The biggest contribution Leigh and his lyricists made to the original play was the introduction of three urchins who commented on and reinforced the action by parodying it in their street games, which became songs. Considering that he was colibrettist, it was remarkable that Alfred allowed his inexorable plotting to be pulled apart to build up Diener's role and for the addition of time-wasting comic-relief numbers for Gallagher and Rall. Little of Alfred's verse remained in the show that opened on Broadway, which was intermissionless, relatively brief, and lacking most of the strengths of *Hogan's Goat*. Howard Bay's three-story brownstone mounted on a constantly moving turntable was beautiful but overwhelming.

Victoria Woodhull, who in nineteenth-century New York made a million as a stockbroker and then ran for president advocating equality of the sexes and free love, should have been a terrific subject for a musical. Carol Channing was announced to play her in a musical called *Vicky for President*, which never happened. In 1976, Patricia Morison and Janet Blair starred in a musical about Victoria and her sister, Tennessee Claflin, called *Winner Take All*, which folded on the road. Woodhull eventually made it to Broadway, but it was in the undercast and amateurish **Onward Victoria** (Martin Beck; Dec. 14, '80; 1).

The cast of unknowns was headed by Jill Eikenberry, who went on to success on "L.A. Law" but who in *Onward Victoria* resembled a Seven Sisters graduate rather than the eccentric force of nature the role required. The show, with a wooden book and cardboard characters, followed the outlines of Victoria's life but invented a romance between Woodhull and Reverend Henry Ward Beecher which was not historically accurate. The score was too pop-sounding, although composer Keith Herrmann showed signs of talent which were more pronounced in his later score for *Romance/Romance*. The show had begun off-off-Broadway in 1979, and on Broadway still betrayed its modest origins—period musicals can't be done on the cheap. And the show's finale, in which reformer Victoria decides to take her act to England, was straight out of the musical *Tenderloin*. Throughout, the complex, strong-willed heroine was reduced to a one-dimensional sex scamp.

Onward Victoria was one of those flops which open with the closing notice already posted and which virtually announce themselves as flops from the moment the curtain rises. There were two camp highlights: the number "Unescorted Women," in which Charlie Delmonico refuses to

○ ○ ○ ○ ○

admit Victoria to his restaurant without an escort, and "Beecher's Defense," a burlesque turn for Victoria in which she sings to the jury at Beecher's trial for alienation of affections about how well endowed Beecher was. The whole thing might have been a camp classic had it not been so sad to see a potentially fascinating subject wasted.

It was Joel Siegel, ABC-TV's drama critic, who had the promising idea of musicalizing the life of Jack Roosevelt Robinson and his struggle for acceptance as the first black player in baseball's major leagues. Siegel coauthored the book with Martin Charnin, and Charnin also wrote the lyrics and directed **The First** (Martin Beck; Nov. 17, '81; 37).

During rehearsals, Darren McGavin quit when the part of Branch Rickey, president of the Brooklyn Dodgers, was reduced, and David Huddleston replaced him. The show opened on Broadway without benefit of tryout; for the opening night party, Studio 54 was transformed into Ebbets Field as it had looked thirty years earlier. Because their own drama critic was the show's author, ABC-TV invited Douglas Watt to review the show. Watt taped his unfavorable review, and ABC killed it.

Robinson's fight for dignity was an affecting story, one which should have made a good musical. *The First* boasted excellent scenic design by David Chapman and fine performances from Huddleston, David Alan Grier, and Lonette McKee. But while it related the events of the story clearly, it did so in standard, uninspired Musical Bio 101 fashion. Some of this flatness may have set in because Robinson's widow, Rachel, was a "consultant" to the show; her presence may have stifled the creators, forcing them to create a by-the-numbers libretto. A bigger problem, though, was musicalizing the story. Charnin and first-time composer Bob Brush had some success with the four songs for Jackie and Rachel, but very little with the music for Rickey, Leo Durocher, the Dodgers, or Jackie's black team, the Monarchs.

It is also possible that audiences were just not interested in the idea of a musical about Jackie Robinson; by the eighties, such inspirational stories may have been better left to television. *The First* was rarely a disgrace, but it failed to provide the emotional power its story would seem to dictate.

Michael Stewart had hits with his books for *Hello, Dolly!, Carnival, Bye Bye Birdie* and *I Love My Wife*, but he had less success with his musicals about real-life show business figures, *George M!, Mack and Mabel*, and his

○ ○ ○ ○ ○

last show, **Harrigan 'n Hart** (Longacre; Jan. '31, '85; 5), the story of the team of Edward Harrigan and Tony Hart, who in the late 1800s had the idea of integrating story, song, and dance in musical farces which reflected the melting-pot ethnic mix of New York City. For *Harrigan 'n Hart*, period songs by Harrigan and Dave Braham were augmented by new ones by Max Showalter and Peter Walker. The show was first mounted as the opening production at the Goodspeed Opera House's Norma Terris Theatre in Chester, Connecticut. It was directed there by Edward Stone; Joe Layton took it over for Broadway, and Stone, hired as Layton's assistant, quit during rehearsals for the Broadway production.

Harrigan 'n Hart might have been an interesting musical about musical-theatre history. Its title characters are often given credit for taking the first steps toward popular American musical comedy, yet the musical about them never explained why. It didn't really show what Harrigan and Hart productions were like, settling instead for a standard backstage story with all the clichés of a 1940s Hollywood composer bio and bearing as much relation to the truth as those movies did. (Nor was Stewart courageous enough to take a clear stance on Hart's homosexual attraction to Harrigan.)

Most of the numbers were of the onstage variety, and the old songs were surprisingly uninteresting. The new ones were seamlessly woven into the old, and a couple of them were respectable. There was some nice Layton staging, and the show was never unbearable; but it ducked its subject, never coming to grips with the team's historic importance or personal relationship, and wasted time with one period number after another.

Harrigan 'n Hart also featured a memorably hateful villainess in Gerta Granville, Hart's wife, played to the hilt by Christine Ebersole. Gerta, questioning Tony's manhood and causing a rift between him and Ned, was so outrageously awful she became a hoot. Her late-in-Act-Two change of heart and subsequent attempt to right her wrongs was singularly unconvincing.

The rich characters of Thomas Wolfe's novel *Look Homeward, Angel* offered interesting possibilities for a dramatic musical. Ketti Frings adapted the Wolfe novel into a Pulitzer Prize-winning play, but when she made her 1957 play into a musical, her partners failed to musicalize the story as effectively as she had dramatized it.

For the musical **Angel** (Minskoff; May 10, '78; 5), Peter Udell cowrote

○ ○ ○ ○ ○

242

the book with Frings and contributed the lyrics, Gary Geld did the music, and Philip Rose produced and directed. It was the third Udell–Geld–Rose collaboration, the team having already done the long-running *Purlie* and *Shenandoah*. The musical was announced (under the title *All the Comforts of Home*) for the uptown Circle in the Square Theatre several times but ultimately wound up premiering at the Northstage Theatre Restaurant in Glen Cove, New York, where it was called *Look Homeward, Angel*. It might have made a passable musical for stock, but *Angel* was unwise enough to hazard Broadway, arriving at the Minskoff Theatre, which was far too big for it. The reviews were unanimously negative. A cast album was recorded which was never commercially released but was distributed out of Rose's office.

Set in 1916, *Angel* told of the Gant family, focusing on Eliza Gant (Frances Sternhagen), an acquisitive woman who has made her home into a boarding house and put her investments ahead of her children, and her two sons, Ben (Joel Higgins) and Eugene (Don Scardino). While the musical book eliminated two characters, it otherwise followed Frings' play very closely, and most of the musical's dialogue was taken verbatim from the play. But *Angel* was another case of "chop and drop": the songs added nothing, were not up to the level of the original dialogue, and failed to make the characters vivid or real. What remained was a diluted version of Frings' play, with sometimes pretty songs that were not even on Frings' level, let alone Wolfe's; during the musical numbers, one waited for what was left of the original play to return.

Doctor Jazz (Winter Garden; Mar. 19, '75; 5) was one of the most chaotic productions in Broadway history, and by the time it opened, it was almost impossible to peer into the mess and see that its initial concept was a fine one. *Doctor Jazz* reunited producer Cyma Rubin, musical director and arranger Buster Davis, designer Raoul Pene du Bois, and performers Bobby Van and Lillian Hayman from the successful revival of *No, No, Nanette*. The show was Davis's idea, and he mixed his original compositions with jazz songs of the early part of the century. Davis was also the author of the book (his first); Donald McKayle was hired to direct and choreograph. Freda Payne was supposed to star, but the lead went to Lola Falana instead. Paul Carter Harrison revised the book prior to rehearsal, and Rubin's daughter, Loni Ackerman, left the show during rehearsal when her part was reduced.

There was no tryout, and the New York preview period was one of

○ ○ ○ ○ ○

Four more missed opportunities.

the most disastrous ever. The Davis—Harrison book was rewritten by Joseph Stein, although Davis was the only one who took credit in the final program. John Berry was brought in and took "entire production supervised by" credit. Joan Copeland left when a lot of her part and all of her singing was cut, and the show almost closed in previews when money ran out. To make matters worse, music writer Gary Giddens wrote a semireview (unfavorable) of the show in *New York* magazine which appeared prior to the opening. Critics liked only Falana and the choreography, and Falana received a Tony Award nomination.

Doctor Jazz told the story of a black singer, her boyfriend, and her white friend and manager, a would-be jazz trumpeter, set against the rise of jazz from its New Orleans origins to mass popularity up North. It was an ambitious and interesting idea, but whatever it might once have been, the *Doctor Jazz* that opened on Broadway was a series of production numbers strung together by minimal dialogue. There were few "book" numbers, and as the story disappeared in the second act, the numbers got bigger and bigger, with Falana descending from the flies in an enormous bird cage for her eleven o'clock song.

Comic strip characters Li'l Abner, Charlie Brown, and Orphan Annie had all made it in the musical theatre; Superman had not. Garry Trudeau decided to take a year's leave from creating his comic strip "Doonesbury," about the inhabitants of the off-off-campus Walden Commune at a New England college, to musicalize it. Trudeau made his debut as a writer for the stage with the book and lyrics for **Doonesbury** (Biltmore; Nov. 21, '83; 104), Elizabeth Swados did the music, and Jacques Levy (*America Hurrah, Oh! Calcutta!*) was the director. *Doonesbury* was a small Broadway musical, with a cast of only ten, and most of the $2 million cost was supplied by Universal Pictures.

Trudeau, although he softened the satirical edge of the strip, came up with a rather endearing book, and even revealed a flair for lyrics. *Doonesbury* might have gotten by if it had had better tunes instead of Swados's usual nonmusic, or if the songs had been more organic to the script (they were mostly respites). The show's comic highlight was a sight gag in which Duke, who has bought the commune supposedly to establish a drug rehabilitation center but really to turn it into a vacation condo complex, literally bulldozed his way into the Walden living room. Even with its low operating costs, *Doonesbury* was too slight and mild to catch on; after Broadway, the show attempted a national tour, which collapsed

○ ○ ○ ○ ○

after a month. *Doonesbury* was a pleasant "almost," an opportunity which never caught fire, scuttled by the wrong composer and the musically inexperienced director and writer.

The life and times of New York City's Mayor Jimmy Walker might have made a colorful musical. Indeed, the musical **Jimmy** (Winter Garden; Oct. 23, '69; 84) was set in the same period as the hit *Fiorello!*, which had contained a song in ironic praise of Walker, and *Jimmy*'s inexperienced creators obviously hoped that lightning would strike twice in the same place. It was the first Broadway production for seventy-seven-year-old movie mogul Jack L. Warner, who had been a friend of Walker's and had employed Walker's girlfriend Betty Compton. The book was by Melville Shavelson, based on a book about Walker by Gene Fowler called *Beau James*, which Shavelson had already directed and cowritten as a Bob Hope movie. The score was by a new husband-and-wife team, Bill and Patti Jacob, and Joseph Anthony was the director. *Jimmy* forced *Mame* out of the Winter Garden and into the Broadway Theatre.

The early script of *Jimmy* indicates that the show was intended as a comment on the corruption of the period, but the bite was abandoned, leaving an empty evening with no wit, style, or credibility; a weak score was the final blow. The book never explained what made Jimmy qualified to run a city, and other real-life characters in the script (Texas Guinan, Al Smith) also failed to ring true. As Jimmy, the musical had a second-rate star in impressionist Frank Gorshin; perhaps Jack Cassidy, who had been sought, would have made a difference. The flop-prone Anita Gillette was good as Compton, and poor Julie Wilson, heavily padded to play the thankless role of Jimmy's estranged wife, Allie, sparked her two big numbers, "I Only Wanna Laugh" and "The Charmin' Son-of-a-Bitch." Wilson later starred in *Legs Diamond*, which covered roughly the same period as *Jimmy*; *Jimmy* was better than *Legs*, but not by much. For 1969 audiences nostalgic for then recent flops, *Jimmy* included a speakeasy raid at the hands of Izzy and Moe, the heroes of *Nowhere to Go but Up*, which had played the same theatre seven years earlier. After terrible reviews, the producers took out quoteless ads advertising the show as "The People's Choice." But the advance sale disappeared after three months, and *Jimmy*, dropping about $1 million, became one of the most expensive flops of its day.

*   *   *

○ ○ ○ ○ ○

John Patrick's play *The Teahouse of the August Moon*, based on a novel by Vern Sneider, opened on Broadway in 1953 and went on to run 1,027 performances, win the Pulitzer Prize and the New York Drama Critics Circle Award, and to be made into a successful film. Patrick himself said, "I always felt that *Teahouse* would make a good musical. It always had the flavor of a musical"—and he was right. *Teahouse's* Captain Fisby, sent to American-occupied Okinawa after World War II to teach the natives democracy and to start an industry there, grows to love the culture he is trying to change. The play was comic, sentimental, light, and big, certainly more suitable for musicalization than *Caesar and Cleopatra* or *The Man Who Came to Dinner*. Why, then, did a play that became an international hit last only two weeks when it was turned into the musical **Lovely Ladies, Kind Gentlemen** (Majestic; Dec. 28, '70; 16)?

Patrick wrote the book for the musical; because MGM owned the play's title, Patrick used for the musical's title the first words spoken in the play by the interpreter Sakini. The score was by Stan Freeman (*I Had a Ball*) and Franklin Underwood, and *Lovely Ladies* was to be producer Herman Levin's last A-level musical; Levin's final musical production was the 1973 disaster *Tricks*, a musical imported from Louisville. Lawrence Kasha, who had already staged *Bajour*, directed.

Before the show went on the road, Levin's office was picketed by the Oriental Actors of America, which claimed that Levin had failed to audition a single Asian American actor for the part of Sakini (the white Kenneth Nelson had been hired for it), and had hired too few Asian American actors for a cast of over forty. During the tryout, David Burns replaced Bernie West as the long-suffering Colonel Purdy, six songs were cut, and five new ones added. Burns was a big help, but the quality of the score was pretty much the same even after the changes.

Clive Barnes opened his *New York Times* review with the words, "Oh, dear! I come to bury *Lovely Ladies, Kind Gentlemen*, not to praise it, but there were one or two decent things, and three or four half-decent things, about this strangely dated musical that modestly opened last night at the Majestic Theatre." This sentence set off a storm of protest: the cast picketed the *Times*, the goat playing Lady Astor in the show bearing the sign Clive Gets My Goat; other placards read Get a Critic, Not a Gravedigger, and End Foreign Rule—Clive Go Home. The *Times* published a letter from Levin, stating, "The first line of his review . . . is an expression of animosity so repellent, so insulting, so obnoxious, so unnecessary, so

○ ○ ○ ○ ○

19 PERFORMANCES ONLY! AUG. 19 thru SEPT. 4

HERMAN LEVIN
PRESENTS

KENNETH RON BERNIE ELEANOR
NELSON HUSMANN WEST CALBES

IN A NEW MUSICAL COMEDY

LOVELY LADIES, KIND GENTLEMEN

Based on VERN J. SNEIDER'S book
"THE TEAHOUSE OF THE AUGUST MOON"
and the play by JOHN PATRICK

BOOK BY
JOHN PATRICK

MUSIC AND LYRICS BY
STAN FREEMAN and FRANKLIN UNDERWOOD

WITH
REMAK RAMSAY · JUDY KNAIZ · LOU WILLS

SCENIC PRODUCTION BY OLIVER SMITH
COSTUMES DESIGNED BY FREDDY WITTOP
LIGHTING BY THOMAS SKELTON

MUSICAL DIRECTION & CHORAL ARRANGEMENTS BY   ORCHESTRATIONS BY   DANCE ARRANGEMENTS BY
THEODORE SAIDENBERG   · PHILIP J. LANG   ·   AL MELLO

MUSICAL NUMBERS STAGED BY
MARC BREAUX

DIRECTED BY
LAWRENCE KASHA

A Theatre Guild — A.T.S. Attraction

MAIL ORDERS PROMPTLY FILLED
Please enclose a stamped, self-addressed envelope with check or money order.
MONDAY THRU THURSDAY EVENINGS:
Orch. $9.00; Balc. $8.00, 7.50, 7.00, 6.00; Family Circle $5.00, 4.00, 3.00.
FRIDAY AND SATURDAY EVENINGS:
Orch. $9.90; Balc. $9.00, 8.00, 7.00, 6.00; Family Circle $5.00, 4.00.
MATINEES THURSDAY AND SATURDAY:
Orch. $7.50; Balc. $7.00, 6.50, 5.50; Family Circle $5.00, 4.00.

SHUBERT THEATRE 250 S. BROAD ST., PHILADELPHIA, PA.
Evenings at 7:30 P.M. — Matinees Thurs. and Sat. at 2:00 P.M.

A musical whose time had passed. Billed star Bernie West was replaced by David Burns by the time Lovely Ladies arrived on Broadway.

cruel and so unprofessional that we would be caitiff dogs if we did not express our resentment and rejection of it in every possible way."

But except for Douglas Watt's in the *News*, the other reviews were not much better. Here was another adaptation damaged by a weak score. Sakini's opening number, "With a Snap of My Finger," and the title song were good, and "Simple Words" for Fisby's love interest Lotus Blossom was nice, but otherwise there was little to recommend, including a big, silly showstopper called "Call Me Back." Patrick's script followed the play's very closely (virtually all the musical's dialogue was taken verbatim). Burns was his usual amusing self, and Nelson was fine as Sakini. After *Lovely Ladies*, though, Nelson left New York for London and never returned.

Lovely Ladies, weak score and all, might have been a hit a decade earlier. But it opened when the war in Vietnam had been raging for several years, and the quaint charm of the East-West story of *Teahouse*, in which Americans try to impose democracy on an alien culture, had disappeared. *Teahouse* was a play of its time and would probably not have revived well by 1970 either. It was understandable that its creators waited until 1970, as the play and film of *Teahouse* would have been too recent for musical-ization ten years earlier. But it was an opportunity seized too late, an idea whose time had clearly passed.

The early years of vaudeville and nightclub singer Sophie Tucker's life were the basis for **Sophie** (Winter Garden; Apr. 15, '63; 8). The music and lyrics were by Steve Allen, whose only other produced musical was the 1969 London flop *Belle Starr*, which starred Betty Grable. The book was by Philip Pruneau, and the show was produced by two men who did industrial shows. The original director, Gene Frankel, known for *The Blacks* and *Brecht and Brecht*, was replaced in Detroit by Jack Sydow. For their star, the producers hired Libi Staiger, who had appeared in small parts in a couple of Broadway shows, understudied Dolores Gray in *Destry Rides Again*, and done the Susan Johnson role in *The Most Happy Fella* in London. Had *Sophie* succeeded, Staiger, the possessor of a powerful, creamy belt like Gray's and Johnson's, might have had a major career. Instead, she drifted into obscurity. Male lead Art Lund had already performed with Staiger in *Happy Fella* and *Destry*.

The show received consistently negative reviews in Columbus, Detroit, Philadelphia, and New York, and its problems were obvious: a cliché-ridden, standard show-biz—bio book and an ordinary score with a couple of nice numbers ("When You Carry Your Own Suitcase" and "When I'm

○ ○ ○ ○ ○

In Love"). The score went unrecorded, although several months later Judy Garland sang three songs from *Sophie* on her CBS television series.

The relatively uninteresting *Sophie* becomes fascinating when one compares it to a very similar musical which played in the same theatre less than one year later—the smash hit *Funny Girl*. Both were backstage bios of singing stars. Both Fanny Brice and Sophie Tucker were portrayed as less than beautiful but fiercely determined, both vowing to make the world sit up and pay attention to their talent. In both shows, the central character has a Jewish mother, performs in the Ziegfeld Follies, and is pursued (and married) by an attractive man. Fanny and Sophie were both drawn as dominating personalities, and in both shows, the husband begins to feel emasculated when his wife's success surpasses his own. Both shows were presented as flashbacks and ended with almost identical scenes in which husband and wife admit that their relationship is over. These scenes were followed by the star bravely going out onstage to wow 'em: in *Sophie*, Staiger performed Tucker's actual signature tune, "Some of These Days," while in *Funny Girl*, Barbra Streisand reprised "Don't Rain on My Parade" (Streisand was only permitted to do Brice's "My Man" in the film version).

Why was *Funny Girl* so fine and *Sophie* so dull? *Sophie* had little humor and made its heroine quite unlikable. The musical Fanny Brice, ambitious as she was, tried to make her marriage work, and was lovably pushy and sympathetic throughout. The musical Sophie Tucker was a calculating girl who only wanted to be a star and would not let even a man who loves her stand in her way. Strange, since unlike Brice, Tucker was around when the show about her was done: she even invested in it when it was floundering on the road and sat through the opening in a box seat. *Funny Girl* had a terrific score, and *Sophie* didn't. And fine as Staiger was, she was not the unique, simultaneously gawky and glamorous personality that Streisand was. A comparative study of *Sophie* versus *Funny Girl* is an object lesson in why one show fails and another, strikingly similar one, succeeds. *Funny Girl* grabbed the opportunity that *Sophie* squandered; because *Sophie* was so forgettable, nobody noticed that *Funny Girl* was the same show as *Sophie*, only good.

Seven

NOT BAD

"*The Girl in Pink Tights* has three tremendous assets—a dancer named Jeanmaire, a singer named Jeanmaire and a comedienne named Jeanmaire . . . Chodorov and Fields have told their tale very literally, very baldly and very badly."—Walter Kerr, *Herald Tribune*

"The most serious musical comedy I ever saw . . . Maurice Evans plays a crusading minister who wants to eliminate the production numbers." —Walter Kerr, *Herald Tribune*, on *Tenderloin*

"A big, noisy musical that has everything going for it except style, invention and finesse."—Martin Gottfried, *Women's Wear Daily*, on *Bajour*

Elaine Stritch in Goldilocks (*above*)

In 1964, a musical called *Bajour* arrived on Broadway. Its story went something like this: gypsy king Cockeye Johnny Dembo (Herschel Bernardi) returns to New York, looking to bring new blood to his tribe by buying his son Steve a bride from the richer Newark tribe who, he hopes, can pull off a big *bajour* (gypsy for swindle). Meanwhile, anthropology student Emily Kirsten (Nancy Dussault) is looking for a tribe to study for her Ph.D. thesis and coerces police Lieutenant Lou MacNiall (Robert Burr) into helping her join Johnny's tribe. Johnny puts a down payment on Anyanka (Chita Rivera), but Anyanka, who is very attracted to Steve, reveals to Johnny her plot to pull a *bajour* on her own father to get the money Johnny needs to buy her. The victim of Anyanka's swindle turns out to be Emily's sweet old mother; Anyanka convinces her that her late husband's insurance money is cursed and that she will remove the curse once it is in her possession. Anyanka gets ten thousand dollars from Emily's mother, uses some of the money to buy herself and marry Steve, gives her father an empty purse, then returns the rest of the money to Emily and goes off with Johnny and his tribe.

Bajour (Shubert; Nov. 23, '64; 232), while it was suggested by *New Yorker* stories by Joseph Mitchell, had an original—and extremely convoluted—book by Ernest Kinoy. The show, which was to have reunited the *Bye Bye Birdie* team of Stewart, Strouse, Adams, and Champion, had to settle for music and lyrics by Walter Marks (his first show—he later did the tacky *Golden Rainbow* for Steve Lawrence and Eydie Gorme) and direction by Lawrence Kasha (his first Broadway show). Producer Edward Padula tried to get Carol Burnett to play Emily but settled for Nancy Dussault.

Bajour got consistently mixed reviews in Boston, Philadelphia, and New York. During the Broadway run, the producers set up a telephone number that was advertised in the ads; a call got one a cast member discussing the show and singing a bit of one of the songs. *Bajour* stayed open for almost eight months, even moving from the Shubert to the Lunt-Fontanne, but it closed at a financial loss in excess of its initial investment of $480,000.

No one has ever been able to determine if *Bajour* was actually good or not: it is the quintessential example of the mediocre, in-between sixties musical. *Bajour's* idea was fun, but while the show was not poorly executed, there was little wit; and the story, not terribly credible to begin with, became increasingly tricky to follow as the evening wore on. The score was pleasant to fair, Peter Gennaro's choreography, led by the superb

○ ○ ○ ○ ○

Above, two Playbills for Bajour, *a quintessential mediocrity. Below, the underrated*
Do I Hear a Waltz?

Rivera, was often exciting (Michael Bennett was one of the gypsies who danced it), and the other leads were fine. *Bajour* was a standard, marginal product of its time, good enough to get by for a season, not good enough to be remembered thereafter. The show never lived up to its exciting, colorful opening sequence, in which Johnny Dembo's tribe took over an empty store and then a whole city.

Bajour was neither good nor bad; there *were* flop musicals, however, that actually were rather good—perhaps not exciting, important, or perfect, but good. This section offers twenty-seven examples of unsuccessful musicals that, for all their shortcomings, played well and made for reasonably entertaining evenings. About half of these shows involved major talents; the failure of the other half may have discouraged the writers involved from trying again and becoming better known.

In 1958, Arthur Laurents approached Rodgers and Hammerstein about musicalizing his 1952 play *The Time of the Cuckoo*, which had already been made into the 1955 film *Summertime*. The team felt that the play was too recent to musicalize, but Rodgers, seven years later and after Hammerstein's death, became the composer and producer of a musical version of *Cuckoo* called **Do I Hear a Waltz?** (46th Street; Mar. 18, '65; 220), with Laurents writing the libretto and Stephen Sondheim the lyrics. (Sondheim and Laurents had already collaborated on *West Side Story, Gypsy, Invitation to a March* and *Anyone Can Whistle.*) It was interesting that after writing both music and lyrics for *A Funny Thing Happened on the Way to the Forum* and *Whistle*, Sondheim was willing to write just lyrics, as he had for his first two Broadway shows. But Sondheim was the protégé of Hammerstein, so it was probably inevitable that he would eventually work with Rodgers—and Laurents and Mary Rodgers talked him into it.

Do I Hear a Waltz? followed Laurents' original play very closely. It was again the story of secretary Leona Samish, in her late thirties, who arrives in Venice and is charmed by antique seller Renato Di Rossi. Leona discovers that Di Rossi is married, and when she sees him taking a commission on the necklace he bought her, she believes he never wanted her, only her money. But the biggest obstacle to the relationship is Leona's own distrustful nature: Di Rossi loses his passion for Leona because of her suspicions, and they bid each other farewell, Leona having perhaps learned not to make the same mistakes again. The only significant changes Laurents made in his original were making the Yeagers, fellow guests at Leona's *pensione*, and their problems more contemporary, and altering the

○ ○ ○ ○ ○

original plot device wherein the currency Di Rossi obtained for Leona turned out to be counterfeit.

The original play took place entirely in the garden of the Pensione Fioria, while the musical also took in Di Rossi's shop and the Piazza San Marco. But the musical had the same number of principals as the original play, adding only a small ensemble for a few numbers. Director John Dexter, then associate director of the National Theatre of Great Britain, who had directed the musical *Half a Sixpence* in London but not on Broadway, conceived *Do I Hear a Waltz?* without dancing, but during the New Haven tryout, Herbert Ross was brought in to add choreography (Ross's production of *Kelly* opened and closed on a Saturday, and he joined *Waltz* that Monday). Florence Henderson and Anne Bancroft were sought to play Leona, but the part went to Elizabeth Allen, with Sergio Franchi opposite her as Di Rossi.

The New York reviews were very mixed, and business fell badly in the summer; the show closed after about seven months. There were Tony nominations for Allen and the score, but *Waltz* was Rodgers' shortest run in over two decades, although shorter ones were to come with *Rex* and *I Remember Mama*.

Do I Hear a Waltz?, because its creators had such a bad time collaborating on it, is now viewed by them as a failure best forgotten. No one seemed to get along: Rodgers was nasty to Sondheim, Laurents refused to listen to Rodgers' suggestions, Allen wouldn't speak to Dexter after he insulted her, etc. Because of all this, those involved may not ever be able to acknowledge that *Waltz* was actually a very well done show. The score was excellent, with Rodgers in generally fine form and Sondheim in altogether superb form. Leona's opening song, "Someone Woke Up"; her plaintive reflection alone at a cafe, "Here We Are Again"; "Moon in My Window" for the three principal ladies; the final duet for Leona and Di Rossi, "Thank You So Much"; and the title song have never really received the recognition they deserve. Beni Montresor's sets were lovely, and the cast was excellent. Allen and Franchi were extremely good but also problematic: Franchi, a natural actor, was a bit too young, and Allen, while more conventionally attractive than Shirley Booth on stage or Katharine Hepburn on film, actually played the role as written, without the overlay of warmth and vulnerability Booth and Hepburn added. As a result, Leona became less likable, and Allen's honest performance pointed up Leona's unpleasant qualities, which had been somewhat whitewashed by her predecessors in the part. Rodgers tried to persuade Laurents to alter Leona's

○ ○ ○ ○ ○

most unpleasant scene from the original in which she gets drunk and reveals Yeager's infidelity to his wife, but Laurents correctly retained the scene.

Sondheim later maintained that *Cuckoo* should not have been made into a musical as it was about a lady who, metaphorically, couldn't sing (he had already done a musical about a lady who couldn't whistle, however). If *Cuckoo* was not a play that cried out to be musicalized, *Waltz* was an excellent adaptation of the enjoyably sentimental original, nicely staged and performed, and with a score of a very high order. And it didn't make the mistake committed by such straight-play adaptations of the sixties as *Hot September* of blowing up the original with big ensemble numbers in which locals kicked up their heels. The creators of *Waltz* worked with integrity and were careful to keep the show a chamber musical; the result was small-scale but classy and ultraprofessional. *Waltz* is eminently playable and revivable, although it will perhaps always have more appeal to ladies' matinee audiences than to others.

When people hear the original Broadway cast recording of **House of Flowers** (Alvin; Dec. 30, '54; 165), they can't imagine how the show could ever have failed. The score, with music by Harold Arlen and lyrics by Truman Capote and Arlen, is one of the theatre's most scintillating, with classic songs like "A Sleepin' Bee," "Two Ladies in de Shade of de Banana Tree," "I Never Has Seen Snow," and the title number. Capote, who proved to be an adept lyricist, got the idea for the story while visiting Port-au-Prince, Haiti, in the late forties, and he introduced lovers Ottilie and Royal in a short story that bore only a passing resemblance to the musical's action. Capote decided to write the book for what was intended as a play with incidental music but wound up as a lavish and large Broadway musical. Producer Saint Subber hired an English director (Peter Brook) and designer (Oliver Messel), and Arlen and Capote did a fair amount of their collaboration on the phone or by mail.

Harry Belafonte, opera singer Mattawilda Dobbs, and Eartha Kitt were mentioned for the leads, which went to the unknown Rawn Spearman, Diahann Carroll (referred to as an "eighteen-year-old ebony thrush" by Walter Winchell), and Pearl Bailey. Before the show went into rehearsal, Bailey told the press, "I've been a hit in every flop. Now I'd settle for being a flop in a hit."

Bailey was cast as Madame Fleur, who runs a bordello in the West

○ ○ ○ ○ ○

Indies and faces competition from neighbor Madame Tango (Juanita Hall)'s brothel. Fleur has adopted Ottilie (Carroll) but changed the girl's name to Violet—all of Fleur's girls are named for flowers (Pansy, Tulip, and Gladiola are the others). Fleur has kept Violet a virgin with an eye toward Violet's becoming her chief asset in her old age but agrees to "loan" her to favored customer Monsieur Jamison in exchange for money that will help her import some exotic ladies to compete with Tango's. When Ottilie falls for young Royal, Fleur arranges to have him "removed," using the same device that has proved effective with several of her husbands. Her plan backfires, but she is forgiven, and a happy ending ensues when Tango's girls leave her to go cruising with Captain Jonas, who had been helping Fleur with Royal's removal.

House of Flowers' book was slight but charming, its humor and outlook possessing a decidedly gay sensibility that may not have pleased straight audiences in the fifties. But the show's history was a most rocky one. In Philadelphia, Bailey collapsed, claiming she was given too much new material to learn, and Juanita Hall was forced to go on for her with script in hand. Choreographer George Balanchine was fired, and Herbert Ross was called in; by the end of the tryout, Ross had also replaced Brook—with whom Bailey had clashed violently—as director, although Brook retained program credit. Josephine Premice resigned from the role of Tulip, Ray Walston replaced Jacques Aubudon as Captain Jonas, and Alvin Ailey and Carmen De Lavallade were added to beef up the dancing. Late in the tryout, Otto Preminger did some work on the show, and Johnny Mercer contributed some new lyrics.

The New York reviews were evenly divided: everyone raved over Messel's magnificent sets and costumes, but the score was not fully appreciated. The album was recorded, with Bailey providing a memorable ad-lib at the end of the song "One Man Ain't Quite Enough" and Arlen singing the word "like" in the last line of Carroll's song "I Never Has Seen Snow" when Carroll's voice gave out. During the run, the second act was restructured, and a new song for Bailey with lyrics by Michael Brown called "Indoor Girl" replaced "Don't Like Goodbyes." When Brook was called back to stage the second act revisions, Bailey announced to the press that as Brook had had nothing to do with the show since the middle of its Philadelphia engagement, Ross was her director and she did not intend to cooperate with Brook. *House of Flowers* lingered for five months and lost about $215,000 of its $240,000 investment. By the time it closed,

∘ ∘ ∘ ∘ ∘

Above, Pearl Bailey and three of her flowers in House of Flowers. Below, star Stritch and creator Coward aboard the Cunard Steam-Ship Coronia ready to Sail Away. Coward even drew the logo on the sheet music, below right.

THIS IS A CHANGING WORLD

Bonard Productions
in association with Charles Russell presents

Noël Coward's
new musical comedy
Sail Away

Book, Music, Lyrics and Direction by NOËL COWARD

however, the show had developed a cult following; the last week was a sell-out, and Bailey said to the audience at the final curtain call, "Where were you when we needed you?"

Like *The Baker's Wife* after it, *House of Flowers* was kept alive by its cast recording, and inevitably there was a revival, off-Broadway at the Theatre de Lys in 1968. Before rehearsals, Capote told the press, "I had in mind a play with music. We hired Pearl Bailey for the lead, which is one thing we shouldn't have done. Pearl began kicking up almost right away, as soon as we went into rehearsal. She overpowered poor little Diahann Carroll, who'd not done anything on the stage before, taking away most of her songs. And it wasn't long before Brook and Balanchine were out and I was rewriting and rewriting and getting further and further away from what we'd had in mind. We're going to do it all very simply now. This is not a revival. This is going to be the show we meant to present."

But Capote was wrong: the original production was mostly glorious, with Bailey and Carroll ideal, fine choreography, stunning decor, and the score richly performed. The revival, with Josephine Premice back, this time as Fleur, Saint Subber again producing, five new songs, and direction by Joseph Hardy, actually did the show's reputation a severe disservice. *House of Flowers* proved to be utterly unsuited to a tiny stage and orchestra, the cast and direction were weak, and the revival failed completely to answer the question of the show's quality raised by the recording. It closed after fifty-seven performances, losing its entire investment, although the loss was offset by the sale of film rights (no film was ever made) to United Artists for $200,000.

House of Flowers was briefly seen again in 1991 in a stock revival, with Patti LaBelle as Fleur and direction by Geoffrey Holder, who appeared in the '54 original. Even the miserable synthesizer-laden arrangements employed in this production could not obliterate Arlen's score. Because of that score, *House of Flowers* will no doubt be tried again, but it is doubtful that a new production could surpass the dazzling original. It just may be that *House of Flowers*, like Sandy Wilson's London musical *Valmouth*, based on the work of Ronald Firbank, will always be a bit too special and rarefied for mass appeal.

"The whole thing is quite obviously headed for enormous success," wrote Noel Coward in his diary during rehearsals for **Sail Away** (Broadhurst; Oct. 3, '61; 167). Coward first conceived *Sail Away* as an expansion of his song "The Bar in the Piccola Marina"; it was to be about a wealthy, newly widowed Englishwoman who visits Capri with her children and is swept up in the bohemian atmosphere. This concept was abandoned, and instead Coward decided to attempt an American-style musical, using a British cruise ship (with mostly American passengers aboard) for his setting. Originally called *Later Than Spring*, the show was conceived by Coward for Rosalind Russell; when she turned it down, he considered tailoring it to Irene Dunne, Judy Holliday, or Kay Thompson. Coward wrote the book, music, and lyrics, did the poster art, and was even heard over the loudspeakers as the voice of Captain Wilberforce.

Sail Away played two tryout engagements: in Boston, where the reviews were mostly good, and in Philadelphia, where they were more divided. In both towns, the show had two leading ladies, Elaine Stritch, who was playing the cruise hostess Mimi Paragon, and Jean Fenn, who was playing Verity Craig, an unhappy, confused wife taking a cruise while contemplating divorcing her husband, played by William Hutt. Verity had an abortive shipboard romance with Johnny Van Mier (James Hurst), attempted suicide, and was finally reconciled with her husband.

Coward and others realized by the second stop that the May–December romance between Verity and Johnny was slowing the show up, and that audiences and critics adored and wanted more of Stritch's Mimi Paragon. It was decided during the Philadelphia run to cut Fenn and Verity entirely (Fenn received eight weeks' salary when dismissed) and to build up Stritch's part so that she was not only the comic relief but also Johnny's love interest. The score also changed radically: Stritch kept one of Fenn's numbers, "Something Very Strange," but otherwise the Viennese–*Bitter Sweet* side of the score went, including two songs Coward was recycling from his West End flop *Pacific 1860*, "This Is a Changing World" and "This Is a Night for Lovers." (The title song, which remained, was from another Coward flop, *Ace of Clubs*.) Hurst got two new songs to go with the new love plot, and the score in general became much brassier and more Broadway-sounding. As an opening night present, Coward and choreographer Joe Layton gave company members a recording they had made of two of the cut numbers, pressed onto a seven-inch disk.

Coward was delighted with the final version, which was set aboard the S.S. Coronia, sailing from New York to Europe. Johnny Van Mier, who has just broken off an affair ruined by his mother's meddling, meets Mimi, former actress and divorcée, who explains, "It's part of my job to accost anyone who looks the teensiest bit lonely and make their life a living hell." Although Johnny is younger than Mimi, he is drawn to her, but

○ ○ ○ ○ ○

Mimi, who otherwise spends her time coping with Italian phrase-books and horrid kiddies, tries to end the affair before it turns sour. After a second act which gave Coward the opportunity to spoof European tourist traps (the show's highlight was a contemporary, rock-and-roll Italian wedding which suddenly turns into a clichéd, old-style, Italian ceremony for the benefit of the tourists), Johnny insists on taking Mimi with him as he debarks.

The New York critics, all of whom loved Stritch and Layton's dances, were evenly divided, with a general feeling that *Sail Away* would have been dandy in the twenties or thirties but was too old-fashioned for the sixties. After a solid start, *Sail Away* did not catch on. Capitol Records recorded the show, *Sail Away* being one of three flop musicals (the other two were *The Gay Life* and *Kwamina*) that Capitol had secured recording rights to during the fall of 1961. Coward at first said the closing came about because "a certain section of New York theatre-cum-café-society is spreading the word that the boys in the show are all pansies and the girls are not attractive enough." He later probed deeper: "Perhaps the book is not strong enough, perhaps Stritch, with all her talent and vitality, hasn't enough star sex appeal, perhaps some of the lyrics are just a bit too clever." Some blamed the closing on *My Fair Lady*, which was evicted from the Mark Hellinger and replaced *Sail Away* at the Broadhurst.

If it is true that *Sail Away* would have been the best musical of 1937, it was a highly enjoyable evening that did not pretend to be anything more than light, revuelike entertainment. The book was paper-thin but filled with witty and amusing dialogue, and it was exactly what Coward had set out to write: "Most of the critics seemed to mourn the lack of a 'strong' story without realizing that a 'strong' story was never intended in the first place. I planned a light, musical entertainment with neither overtones nor undertones of solemnity, and this, so help me, is exactly what I have achieved."

The score was delightful, highlighted by "Why Do the Wrong People Travel?" and "Something Very Strange" for Mimi, and the title song for Johnny. Some of the numbers ("Beatnik Love Affair," "The Passenger's Always Right") sounded as if they were written to be sung by Coward in his cabaret act, and there are those who prefer Coward's own recording of the score to the original cast album. Layton's work was excellent, causing Coward to retain him for his last musical, *The Girl Who Came to Supper*. And Stritch was never better, scoring heavily in every one of her numbers and demonstrating her ability to carry an evening. *Sail Away's*

○ ○ ○ ○ ○

biggest problem was simply that it was out of place on 1961 Broadway. Audiences now expected more from musicals than fluff, no matter how clever, well-executed, and fun that fluff might be.

Sail Away did not die with its five-month Broadway run. The show played London's Savoy Theatre in 1962, with Stritch again heading the company and winning raves. The London reviews were worse than the New York notices, however (Coward deemed them personally abusive), and the London run, while about one hundred performances longer than the New York stand, was also disappointing. There was an Australian production shortly after, but since then, no one has attempted *Sail Away*.

After his *Guys and Dolls, Can-Can,* and *Say, Darling,* Abe Burrows appeared to be an unlikely adapter of the work of Jane Austen; nevertheless, he wrote the book of and directed **First Impressions** (Alvin; Mar. 19, '59; 84), an adaptation of Austen's *Pride and Prejudice.* Burrows based his book on the novel (the original title of which was *First Impressions*) and on Helen Jerome's 1935 nonmusical adaptation, which had been the basis for the acclaimed 1940 film. The score was the work of George Weiss, who had already done *Mr. Wonderful,* and two newcomers, Robert Goldman and Glenn Paxton. Gisele MacKenzie was hired to play the leading role of Elizabeth Bennet but withdrew when she became pregnant. She was replaced by another popular singer, Polly Bergen, with Farley Granger cast as Darcy and Hermione Gingold as Mrs. Bennet. The show was presented by "The Jule Styne Organization," and though he had no other credit, Styne is said to have contributed to the score. Fearing a jinx, the producers abandoned the musical's original title, *A Perfect Evening,* before rehearsals.

The reviews were promising in New Haven, more divided in Philadelphia (where, after a difference of opinion with Burrows, Hiram Sherman was replaced as Collins by Christopher Hewett), and least enthusiastic of all in New York. The New York critics were particularly divided about Gingold, who had won raves on the road; some even maintained that she ruined the show. After six weeks, Bergen was rushed to the hospital with a "tubal pregnancy," and supporting performer Ellen Hanley took over the lead for the final weeks. Bergen later admitted that she had been unhappy with the show as early as New Haven, and it was reported that Bergen and Gingold, who had worked together in *John Murray Anderson's Almanac,* were not getting along. *First Impressions* lost almost all of its $300,000 investment.

○ ○ ○ ○ ○

Above: Bingley and Darcy are arriving, and Mrs. Bennet (Hermione Gingold, center) can't wait to spread the news, in First Impressions. Below, The Girl in Pink Tights: *Charles Goldner presents the star of his ballet company, Jeanmaire, who has already caught the eye of David Atkinson.*

Though it is certainly true that *First Impressions* failed to capture the wit and delicacy of the novel, it was tastefully done and could have been a great deal worse. The book told Austen's story reasonably well; what it inevitably lacked was Austen's voice, which greatly enhances the novel's plot with its constant stream of sharp commentary. Peter Larkin's sets were gorgeous, with a front curtain that opened like a fan during the overture, then disappeared into the flies. Bergen was not totally believable as an early-nineteenth-century English maiden, but Gingold's broad performance carried a fair amount of the evening. *First Impressions'* score has a number of attractive things in it, but for the musical to have succeeded at the end of the fifties, it would have had to contain a *My Fair Lady*–level score. Indeed, all musicals with a literary antecedent and set in England that opened after *My Fair Lady* were inevitably compared to it and found wanting. And *First Impressions* faced competition on Broadway not only from the still-running *Fair Lady*, but from *West Side Story*, *The Music Man*, *Gypsy*, *Flower Drum Song*, *Redhead*, and *Destry Rides Again*.

First Impressions was presented by the Birmingham Repertory Theatre in England in 1971, with Patricia Routledge as Mrs. Bennet, and perhaps the show might have been more successful if presented in England in the first place. It was done the following year by Equity Library Theatre in New York and might be worth trying again; unfortunately the show's story and period dictate the kind of scenery and costumes which would probably be beyond the means of most stock and amateur groups.

Far less likely ever to be seen again is **The Girl in Pink Tights** (Mark Hellinger; Mar. 5, '54; 115), which featured the last score by Sigmund Romberg, who had died more than two years before the show opened. One of Broadway's finest orchestrators, Don Walker, developed Romberg's themes and sketches and presumably contributed a fair amount of the music himself (Walker had already done the score for *Courtin' Time*).

The Girl in Pink Tights was a musical comedy about the creation of the first musical comedy in America. In 1866, a fire at the Academy of Music in New York left a ballet company stranded. The company was integrated into the melodrama *The Black Crook* by Charles M. Barras, playing at Niblo's Garden, and the combination made history. The book for *The Girl in Pink Tights* was the work of Jerome Chodorov and Joseph Fields, taking a giant step backward from their book for *Wonderful Town* the year before. Leo Robin wrote the lyrics, and Agnes de Mille was the choreographer. First conceived as an MGM film for Leslie Caron and Gene

○ ○ ○ ○ ○

Kelly, the show was ultimately built around the scintillating Jeanmaire, who had already triumphed on the New York stage in ballet and had been seen in the film *Hans Christian Andersen*. Jeanmaire played Lisette Gervais, a French ballerina dancing in a New York show (exactly like Jeanmaire herself). Maurice and Gregory Hines had a couple of tap specialties. Original leading man David Brooks was replaced in Philadelphia by David Atkinson.

The New York critics composed love letters to Jeanmaire but were mixed on the merits of the show. *The Girl in Pink Tights* had a perfectly acceptable book and score, both unexciting yet competent, but after the musicals of Rodgers and Hammerstein, it was almost impossible for a show that would not have been out of place in the '20s like *Girl* to gain acceptance. The show relied heavily on the charm and talent of its leading lady and on de Mille's choreography for her, and both ladies came through strongly. The show's most obvious flaw was its finale, when the ballet and melodrama companies came together in *The Red Devil*, as the musical's play within a play was called: the musical's *Red Devil* bore little resemblance to *The Black Crook*. But the show was not concerned with historical authenticity; it was intended only as a vehicle for a star personality. Even though "Zizi" Jeanmaire caused a sensation and her vehicle was pleasant, *The Girl in Pink Tights*, like *Sail Away*, arrived too late.

The Prisoner of Zenda had already been a novel (by Anthony Hope), a play, five movies, and an operetta (called *Princess Flavia* and presented by the Shuberts in 1925, with music by Sigmund Romberg), when Edwin Lester decided to recycle it once more as a vehicle for his *Kismet* star, Alfred Drake. The musical **Zenda** (San Francisco; Aug. 5, '63; closed on the road) featured the last score by Vernon Duke, a major composer whose theatrical career, with the exception of *Cabin in the Sky*, was beset by flops (including Bette Davis's *Two's Company* and Ginger Rogers's *The Pink Jungle*); lyrics were by Lenny Adelson (who later did *Molly*), Sid Kuller, and Martin Charnin. The book was by Everett Freeman; Harry Horner, whose credits included *Lady in the Dark*, designed the lavish sets; *Kismet* choreographer Jack Cole did the dances; and George Schaefer directed and coproduced.

For this version of the story, the action was moved to the present, and Richard Rassendyl (Drake) became a British song-and-dance man rather than the gentleman of leisure he had been in earlier versions. Rassendyl and his troupe arrive in Zenda, having been asked to appear at a command

○ ○ ○ ○ ○

performance in honor of the royal wedding of Princess Flavia (Anne Rogers) and King Rudolph. Rassendyl, thanks to his grandmother's dalliances in Zenda years ago, looks exactly like the king (Drake played both parts), so when the king is drugged by a villainous general planning to overthrow the government, Rassendyl is enlisted to take the king's place at the wedding. Rassendyl, still pretending to be Rudolph, is drawn to Flavia, while Rudolph's mistress, Athena (a new character invented for the musical and played by Chita Rivera), is elated when she learns of the impersonation. *Zenda* added a happy ending to the story, with the real king, who never really loved Flavia, going off with Athena, and Rassendyl, in love with Flavia, deciding to stay in Zenda and continue the impersonation for the rest of his life.

During its three months in San Francisco, Los Angeles, and Pasadena, *Zenda* received mixed-to-favorable reviews; the grosses were strong, and the show returned about half its investment. But its scheduled November 26, 1963, opening at the Mark Hellinger Theatre was canceled when author Freeman refused to permit director-coproducer Schaefer to bring Samuel Taylor in to work on the book. Schaefer, stating that the show was not good enough for Broadway, announced that he was washing his hands of it, at which point Alfred Drake quit immediately. Freeman countered Schaefer's story, claiming that Taylor's changes weren't helpful and that Schaefer's staging was the real problem.

In comparison to its screen versions, the musical *Zenda* was less swashbuckling and a good deal less violent. Moreover, Drake could not appear, as his film predecessors had, as Rassendyl and Rudolph simultaneously. And, although Edwin Lester told the press, "we have a light-hearted, modern, humorous approach that will keep [*Zenda*] from falling into the old operetta rut," like all Civic Light Opera productions, *Zenda* still had vestiges of the old school.

But *Zenda* had a great deal going for it; had it been just a little stronger, it would have been more than acceptable on Broadway. The dual lead was ideal for Drake, who was to do only one more show after *Zenda*—*Gigi*, also for Lester. The score was very attractive, especially Drake's solo "Let Her Not Be Beautiful" and the deliciously tongue-in-cheek title-song duet for Drake and Rogers. *Zenda* was one of the better Civic Light Opera–originated musicals; if it wasn't *Kismet* or *Peter Pan*, it also wasn't *Magdalena*, *Gypsy Lady*, *Dumas and Son*, or *1491*. As good as any number of other early sixties musicals, *Zenda* demonstrates the often thin line separating mild success from forgotten failure.

○ ○ ○ ○ ○

Tenderloin (46th Street; Oct. 17, '60; 216) is one of the most clear-cut examples ever of a follow-up, reunion show. *Tenderloin* had the same producers (Robert E. Griffith and Harold Prince), librettists (George Abbott and Jerome Weidman), director (Abbott), composer (Jerry Bock), and lyricist (Sheldon Harnick) as *Fiorello!*, which had opened one year earlier. Both *Fiorello!* and *Tenderloin* were about an earlier New York, both featured Ron Husmann and Eileen Rodgers, and both were about real-life characters—*Tenderloin* was based on a novel by Samuel Hopkins Adams which fictionalized the life of the Reverend Dr. Charles H. Parkhurst, pastor of Madison Square Presbyterian Church.

Tenderloin was set in Manhattan in the 1890s. It concerned the Reverend Brock, crusading to shut down the Tenderloin, the "juicy" downtown district of vice condoned by corrupt police and politicians. Tommy, an ambitious young reporter for the *Tatler*, ingratiates himself with Brock but plays both sides of the street by warning the cops about Brock's plans to raid the brothels. Tommy helps frame Brock, but at Brock's trial, Tommy admits the truth. The Tenderloin is closed down, but the scandal of the trial causes Brock's church to ask for his resignation. Tommy leaves town to escape the crooked cops out to get him, and Brock decides to carry his campaign to the vice pits of Detroit.

Maurice Evans, who had once done a musical (*Ball at the Savoy* with lyrics by Oscar Hammerstein II) in London in 1933, was hired to play Brock, and while Evans sang well and was right for the part, his casting was perhaps the most serious mistake the show's creators made. What was marvelous in *Tenderloin* was everything involving Tommy and his seamy friends; the scenes involving Brock and his parishioners were far less interesting, but because Evans was the show's star, a fair amount of stage time had to be given over to the Reverend's affairs. Making the Reverend's role equal to that of Tommy's meant that *Tenderloin* had to devote as much time to the dull good characters as to the highly enter-taining bad ones.

But that problem was by no means fatal, and *Tenderloin* offered bountiful compensations for its flaws. Above all, it contained one of the finest scores of any unsuccesful musical; *Tenderloin*, like *Merrily We Roll Along*, *Greenwillow*, and *House of Flowers*, is a classic example of a flop whose cast album leads people to believe that the show must have been sensational. After a wonderful overture and one of the best opening numbers ever, "Little Old New York," Bock and Harnick came up with "Artificial

○ ○ ○ ○ ○

Which of the three musicals in the ad, above right, was not a hit? Above left, Maurice Evans, star of **Tenderloin**. Below, the ladies of the Tenderloin are photographed for The Tattler, as Ron Husmann (right) looks on.

Flowers," "The Picture of Happiness," "Dear Friend," and "My Gentle Young Johnny." The composers also musicalized Brock's trial cleverly: in an all-sung sequence, the trial was reenacted center stage: those involved in the trial mouthed the words sung by people reading newspaper accounts on the sidelines. If the book never made Brock as interesting as the evildoers, the composers came up with good material for everyone. *Tenderloin* also boasted excellent choreography by Joe Layton, imaginative sets and costumes by Cecil Beaton, and fine work from Husmann and Rodgers.

Critics on the road and in New York either liked *Tenderloin* or hated it. During its tryout, James and William Goldman, who had received a Ford Foundation grant to follow the show as observers, were recruited to work on the book. *Tenderloin* opened on Broadway (with *Fiorello!* and *West Side Story*, two other Griffith–Prince musicals set in New York, still playing) to far more negative than positive reviews, but lasted seven months because of its advance sale. Closing at a loss of about half its $350,000 investment, it moved immediately to the Dunes Hotel in Las Vegas, where it played for six weeks in an eighty-minute "tab" version, with the original cast minus Evans and Rodgers. Since then, there have been a few small-scale revivals of the show; *Tenderloin* is still worthy of consideration by groups looking for a lesser-known but interesting show.

The musicals of John Kander and Fred Ebb range from major hits (*Cabaret*) to modest successes (*Chicago*) to mild failures (*Zorba, The Happy Time, Woman of the Year*), to outright flops. *Flora, the Red Menace* was one of the latter, but two other Kander and Ebb flops are even more interesting and performable.

70, Girls, 70 (Broadhurst; Apr. 15, '71; 35) was simultaneously set on the stage of a Broadway theatre and in the Sussex Arms Hotel for senior citizens on New York's Upper West Side. Frumpy Ida, who had gone off to die, returns to her friends at the hotel looking like a million bucks and with a new lease on life, owing to her recent discovery that no one notices when an old person steals things. Ida suggests that she and her pals form a gang, their goal being to refurbish the hotel with their criminal earnings and then invite the elderly poor in as their guests. After a few successes, the gang gets a scare and decides to attempt just one more heist, one that, if successful, will provide enough money to enable them to buy the hotel. At the International Fur Show at the Coliseum, the gang is caught; Ida remains behind to take the rap, then dies. At the

o o o o o

wedding of two of the gang members, Eunice and Walter, Ida returns on a crescent moon and tells all those assembled to say "Yes" to life.

The writing credits for 70, *Girls*, 70 were confusing. The source for the show was the 1960 British film *Make Mine Mink*, which owing to a contractual hitch could not be mentioned. So the book by Fred Ebb and Norman L. Martin was listed as being based on Peter Coke's play *Breath of Spring* (the source of the film), as adapted by Joe Masteroff. Ron Field was to have directed, and it was Field who suggested that the show be done on Broadway, rather than off-Broadway as Kander and Ebb originally planned. Paul Aaron was hired to direct, and the cast was filled with veteran performers from vaudeville, burlesque, and musical comedy.

The reviews in Philadelphia were promising, but on March 12, 1971, the sixty-eight-year-old David Burns, who had replaced the ailing Eddie Foy prior to rehearsals, got a big laugh during the number "Go Visit Your Grandmother," then clutched his chest and fell to the floor; he died shortly after the performance concluded. Burns' number was immediately followed by leading lady Mildred Natwick's song about death, and costar Lillian Roth took Burns' lines for the rest of the evening.

Burns' death put a serious damper on a show celebrating what old people were capable of doing. The Philadelphia engagement was halted, and the show returned to New York for recasting and further rehearsal. Paul Aaron was replaced by Stanley Prager (Aaron would later be fired from *Molly*, too), although Aaron retained credit, with Prager taking "supervisor" billing. Hans Conried was brought in to replace Burns; Burns had played an ex-vaudevillian who was the hotel's desk clerk, but Conried was just one of the residents and had none of Burns' vaudeville turns. The New York reviews were generally unfavorable, and 70, *Girls*, 70 was Kander and Ebb's shortest-running Broadway show; it lost $600,000.

For a show that received mostly terrible reviews, 70, *Girls*, 70 was actually quite entertaining. There were two major problems that it never quite overcame. First, it was one show too many in the then current spate of shows about and/or featuring veteran performers; it had the misfortune to open right after the revival of *No, No, Nanette* and *Follies*. And it had a show-within-a-show concept that, because it was not fully thought through, proved confusing. The cast was listed alphabetically in the program as "Ensemble Players," with no character names attached to any performer; the cast members were supposed to be old performers back on a Broadway stage who were putting on a show about old folks. But the show-biz songs sung in between the scenes by the "performers"

○ ○ ○ ○ ○

("Broadway, My Street," "Coffee in a Cardboard Cup") did not relate to the plot; the performance framework ultimately indicated a lack of trust in the strength of the storyline. It was also confusing when a number like "The Caper," a plot song, was done in front of a drop curtain like the "performance" numbers, and when the actors addressed the audience directly both as "performers" and as characters in the book scenes.

But 70, *Girls*, 70 was funny and charming enough to overcome these problems. The score was delightful, Natwick was divine, and audiences loved it. It deserved to be a success—it played as well as or better than many a hit—and did not merit the barrage of critical disapproval which deprived it of ever finding an audience. Dora Bryan starred in a revised London production at the Vaudeville Theatre in June, 1991. 70, *Girls*, 70 is ideal material for groups with older performers, and its production demands are minimal.

The Rink (Martin Beck; Feb. 9, '84; 204) took place entirely in a decaying roller rink on a crime-ridden boardwalk on the Eastern seaboard in the seventies. But the setting was meant to be a symbolic landscape, representing the unhappy past that Anna Antonelli, who has just sold the rink and is preparing to leave for Italy, is running away from, and to which her daughter, Angel, who has attempted to escape it for years, is returning.

The action covered only a few hours but flashed back over more than thirty years. Angel, having been through the communes and protest marches of the sixties, returns home after a seven-year absence just as her mother is preparing to leave the rink to the wreckers. Angel is horrified to learn that the rink has been sold: she wants to reopen it, just as she wants to confront the past and resolve it. As mother and daughter pick up their old arguments, the audience is shown their history: Anna's husband, Dino, deserts her and Angel; Anna becomes promiscuous after Dino's abandonment and is later raped by local hoods; Angel has a brief, unhappy reunion with the father she believes was dead. At the end, the granddaughter Anna didn't know she had arrives, Anna and Angel forgive each other, and Angel is finally able to let go of the rink.

Kander and Ebb began work on *The Rink* with Albert Innaurato, who was writing a book about a roller-skating palace on the Lower East Side of New York about to be converted into a roller disco. They asked Arthur Laurents to direct, and Laurents, although he declined to become involved, suggested Terrence McNally as a librettist. McNally, who would

∘ ∘ ∘ ∘ ∘

Two Kander and Ebb flops that had their partisans. Above right, the great Mildred Natwick in 70, Girls, 70. Below, Playbills for The Rink: At left, profiles of Rivera and Minnelli; At right, high-kicking Rivera with Stockard Channing behind her.

also collaborate with Kander and Ebb on their next musical, *Kiss of the Spider Woman,* wrote the book for *The Rink,* one of only two original Kander and Ebb musicals (*The Act* was the other one), and A.J. Antoon was hired to direct his first musical.

Kander and Ebb conceived *The Rink* as a vehicle for their friend Chita Rivera. When she heard about the project, Liza Minnelli asked to play Angel to Rivera's Anna, the two having already costarred when Minnelli took over Gwen Verdon's part in *Chicago* in 1975. *The Rink* had a workshop production in New York, after which it was announced that the show would be produced off-Broadway, a plan that would have been impractical if only because of the stars' salaries. After a month of previews, during which an intermission was added, *The Rink* opened on Broadway to mostly negative reviews, the book coming in for most of the criticism. *The Rink* allowed Rivera to win her first Tony Award after five unfulfilled nominations and hung on as long as Minnelli was in it to help attract audiences. But Minnelli was suffering from addiction to drugs and alcohol throughout the run and left three days before she was scheduled to depart to enter the Betty Ford Center in California for treatment. Stockard Channing, who succeeded Minnelli, acted the part beautifully but let the score down. *The Rink* was produced in London four years later, where with lesser names in the leads it failed quickly.

Ebb later blamed the show's failure on Minnelli's presence in it: "I think the casting of her was a fatal mistake . . . it's a second lead, it's a very shlumpy girl. She wanted to do a part where she could really be an actress on a Broadway stage. And that was what the public in general hated about it. People who came to see the show with Liza in it did not want to see Liza without spangles."

While some audience members may have been disappointed in the show's drab, padded Minnelli—because the action took place over a matter of hours, there were no costume changes for the stars until the curtain call—it was more the general sourness and unpleasantness of the material that turned audiences off. Minnelli gave a very honest performance and played beautifully against the more all-out star turn Rivera provided. But the book was problematic: it featured constant bickering between its leads, contained what may be the single most unappealing character ever to grace a musical in nasty, lecherous Uncle Fausto, who made a pass at niece Angel, and was far too cliché-ridden (Dino's father actually uttered the line "I have no son" at one point). The script also never satisfactorily explained why Dino deserted his family or why Angel was the only one onstage who never knew that her father was still alive. On the other hand, McNally provided numerous sharp and vivid lines, with Anna very nicely characterized through her sardonic turn of phrase, and the stars helped mightily to make the show compelling.

Kander and Ebb's score was also of enormous help, particularly the first two numbers: "Colored Lights," Angel's wistful recollection of the childhood which is drawing her back to the rink, and "Chief Cook and Bottle Washer," Anna's jubilant cry of freedom. There was also the ambitious "Mrs. A," as well as more standard comic songs for the leads and the wreckers.

The Rink used the clever device of having the six wreckers play all the characters, both male and female, in the flashbacks. And Peter Larkin's dilapidated rink was a knockout, cleverly designed for the show's final (and costly) coup de theatre: the setting which the audience had been looking at for two hours disappeared into the flies, leaving only a horizon and a staircase, on which three generations of Antonelli women were silhouetted. For all its problems, *The Rink* is one of those flops that collectors treasure.

The 1978–79 Broadway season was the last to feature so many major American musicals, most of which involved big-name talents. *King of Hearts, Ballroom, Sarava, Carmelina, Platinum, I Remember Mama, A Broadway Musical, The Utter Glory of Morrissey Hall, Sweeney Todd,* and *They're Playing Our Song* were all part of the season, but only the last two were successful. One of the shows that got lost that season was **The Grand Tour** (Palace; Jan. 11, '79; 61), Jerry Herman's third consecutive flop (after *Dear World* and *Mack and Mabel*) and Joel Grey's second consecutive flop at the Palace Theatre (*Goodtime Charley* preceded it) and last Broadway musical to date.

The Grand Tour was based on a play by Franz Werfel, which as adapted by S.N. Behrman was a Broadway hit in 1944 under the title *Jacobowsky and the Colonel.* The material became a Danny Kaye movie in 1958 called *Me and the Colonel,* and there had also been a German operatic version. The musical's story was roughly the same as those of the earlier incarnations: it is 1940, and Jacobowsky, the eternal refugee and survivor, born in Poland but also a citizen of Berlin, Vienna, and Paris, hooks up with a bombastic, anti-Semitic Polish cavalry officer headed for England. Accompanied by the colonel's girlfriend, they make their way across France, one step ahead of the invading Germans. Jacobowsky comes to the colonel's aid repeatedly, and the colonel comes to admire the bravery and ingenuity of the little refugee. Jacobowsky, drawn to the colonel's lady, finally bids both farewell and decides to begin his own "grand tour" of life as the curtain falls.

A touching tale of survival, displaced persons, and men of different backgrounds learning to respect one another, *Jacobowsky* was promising material for a musical. It was initially to be musicalized by Stan Daniels and Leonard Gershe and to star Alec McCowen and Richard Kiley. When Michael Stewart took up the property, he convinced Herman, still deeply discouraged by the failure of *Mack and Mabel*, to collaborate with him. Stewart, who had done *Hello, Dolly!* and *Mack and Mabel* with Herman, brought in Mark Bramble to collaborate on the book, and Gerald Freedman was hired to direct.

The reviews in San Francisco were of the promising-but-needs-work variety, and Tommy Tune was called in to redo some of Donald Saddler's choreography and to suggest other revisions. The New York reviews were mixed to negative, with Grey's notices ranging from raves to pans; some felt that the show was an attempt to pander to the Jewish theatre party trade, dubbing it *"Fiddler on the Run."*

But *The Grand Tour*, if less than inspired, was a professional show, lacking only a spark that might have ignited it. The book was properly tense and poignant as required, Herman filled the show with his trademark "take-home" tunes, and Ming Cho Lee's sets had an attractive French impressionist flavor. The leads, however, were problematic: Grey was engaging but somewhat cold for the part of Jacobowsky, and Ron Holgate's colonel was too much the buffoon. Still, *The Grand Tour* was a pleasant, conventional show which might have been able to survive for a season or so on Broadway ten or fifteen years earlier. By the end of the seventies, high ticket prices meant that prospective customers were reluctant to risk attending a so-called "audience show" (i.e. one that audiences like more than critics) and *The Grand Tour* closed after two months (Grey tore up an earlier closing notice onstage), losing $1.5 million. It was tried again by the Jewish Repertory Theatre in 1988, where in a bare-bones production the material seemed stronger than it had on Broadway. The intimate production demonstrated that *The Grand Tour* is highly suitable fare for stock and amateur groups, particularly ones which play to a predominantly Jewish constituency.

Tom Jones had the idea of doing a musical about the life and loves of Colette as early as the fifties. When his wife wrote a play about Colette

○ ○ ○ ○ ○

Talented writers were involved in all three of these flops. The two below are particularly worthy of reexamination.

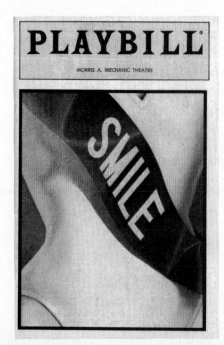

which was presented off-Broadway in 1970 with Zoe Caldwell as star, Jones and his partner, Harvey Schmidt, contributed three songs and incidental music. They then decided to write their own, full-scale Colette musical and spent five years on it, during which time another musical on the subject was presented (unsuccessfully) in London with Cleo Laine as Colette.

The authors were attempting a difficult task, trying to dramatize and musicalize the random and episodic history of a woman's life. Jones said, "The problem in writing the show was to make it cohesive and yet cover her life from age seventeen to eighty, and her diverse, and sometimes not so diverse, relationships with men." The Jones and Schmidt musical **Colette** (Seattle; Feb. 10, '82; closed on the road) begins with a stunning opening number, "There's Another World," in which the aged Colette is transformed into a young girl as her fictional characters call to her to bring them to life. Thereafter, the action followed Colette's relationships with Willy, who signs his name to her novels; Jacques, an aging homosexual who finds her work in the music hall; Missy, a lesbian who draws Colette into her salon; and Maurice, a much younger man whom Colette helps save from the Nazis. At the end, Colette, married to Maurice, is content to grow old, surrounded by the people from her past.

Producers weren't interested in the property until Harry Rigby, who had recently had a big hit with *Sugar Babies*, came along. Rigby was probably the wrong man for this delicate material, which he envisioned transformed into an elaborate star vehicle. In 1980, he announced that Debbie Reynolds would star and Frank Dunlop would direct. A year later, Rigby hired Diana Rigg to star in her first musical: Rigg said she would not sign a contract unless a director was found within a certain time limit; Rigby grabbed Dennis Rosa, who rapidly proved inadequate to the task.

There was almost nothing but misery for the next two months. In rehearsal, the show's cat, Beethoven, was dismissed after chewing off a piece of Rigg's finger. Rosa was fired after the first week, and the reviews in Seattle and Denver were poor. Michael Stewart and Ralph Allen worked on the book, but Rigg refused to rehearse changes when no new director could be found. *Colette*, which was to have gone on to San Francisco, Los Angeles, and Washington before arriving on Broadway in the summer of 1982, folded in Denver at a loss of $1.5 million.

Colette was a class act; had it come to Broadway, there is every likelihood that it would not have succeeded, but it was a lovely piece. The built-in problems were obvious: dramatizing the life of a writer is always

○ ○ ○ ○ ○

difficult, and what was most interesting about Colette was not her affairs but her writing. For all their good work, the authors never totally overcame the fact that there was no real story, a problem which became particularly aggravated in the second act. And Rigby made some producing mistakes that did damage to an already fragile property: the physical production was far too elaborate for the material, and Seattle and Denver may not have been the right tryout cities.

What *Colette* had going for it was its score and its star. With its tinkling vamps and lush melodies, the score sounded typically Jones and Schmidt but was richer and more varied than much of their other work. "Come to Life," "The Room is Full of You," and "There's Another World" are ravishing, and worthy of inspection by enterprising cabaret singers. The Jones and Schmidt songs heard in the 1970 play were not recycled, but some which they had written for it that went unused were included in the musical. Leading lady Rigg, who later mistakenly blamed herself for the show's failure, was terrific, reading the dialogue flawlessly, singing with guts and color, looking sensational, and wisely eschewing a French accent. The supporting cast, which included John Reardon, Martin Vidnovic, Robert Helpmann, Marta Eggerth, and Marti Stevens, was rich-voiced and glamorous.

The authors got another hearing for the show, in a revised version called *Colette Collage*, seen at the York Theatre in 1983 and at Musical Theatre Works in 1991. But *Colette* demands a riveting star, and the casts of these small-scale productions did not begin to compare with Rigg and company. *Colette* is worth trying again, however, and can be done with a minimum of scenery. But it is very much a vehicle, and it must have a distinctive and powerful personality at its center.

The 1975 film *Smile*, written by Jerry Belson and directed by Michael Ritchie, was a wickedly satirical, often vicious spoof of beauty pageants, their contestants, and their creators. It was not a box-office hit but developed a cult reputation. The central problem faced by potential musicalizers of the film was its totally unsentimental nature. Audiences for musicals like to empathize with characters and become involved emotionally on some level, so the nasty and very funny *Smile* screenplay was extremely tricky material to transform into a satisfying musical.

The musical **Smile** (Lunt-Fontanne; Nov. 24, '86; 48) had a very convoluted history, with one constant, composer Marvin Hamlisch, who had already had two hit musicals (*A Chorus Line* and *They're Playing Our Song*)

∘ ∘ ∘ ∘ ∘

and would have his first flop (*Jean Seberg* in London) during *Smile*'s period of development. Originally, Hamlisch wrote his music to lyrics by Carolyn Leigh, and Thomas Meehan was the librettist. Then Jack Heifner wrote another book, which was used in a 1983 workshop production directed and choreographed by Graciela Daniele, with Maureen McGovern, Grover Dale, Trini Alvarado, Jane Krakowski, and Saundra Sauntiago in the cast. Leigh died a few months later, Neil Simon almost wrote a new book, then Howard Ashman, who had had a hit with *Little Shop of Horrors* in 1982 and had been turned down as book writer of *Smile* originally, agreed to make his Broadway debut with the book, lyrics, and direction of *Smile*. Hamlisch threw out the score he had written with Leigh, retaining only the melody of the title number. A new workshop took place in late 1985, after which the Shuberts and David Geffen pulled out as producers of the show.

With new producers, *Smile* tried out in Baltimore. By this time, the top-rated television program "60 Minutes" had, in an almost unprecedented step, begun to follow the show, taping its every move from workshop to tryout to Broadway. By the time it arrived in New York, *Smile* was being looked upon as the great hope for American musicals: such disasters as *Rags*, *Honky Tonk Nights*, *Into the Light*, and *Raggedy Ann* had recently come and gone, and the season's hits were all from London.

But the critics, with a few exceptions, did not buy *Smile*—several pointed out the show's similarity to Hamlisch's biggest hit, *A Chorus Line*—and it was unable to survive for more than six weeks. The failure soured both Hamlisch and Ashman on the theatre, and neither has returned since. (Ashman subsequently had great success as producer and lyricist of the animated film *The Little Mermaid;* the title character's voice was provided by one of *Smile*'s leads, Jodi Benson. Ashman died of AIDS in 1991, the same year Hamlisch announced he was working on two new musicals for Broadway.)

Heifner's book was far more cynical and unsentimental than Ashman's and much closer to the screenplay in its attitude towards it characters. There was not a single truly sympathetic figure, and while it was more consistent in tone than the Broadway book, it was heartless—audiences would not have embraced it. Ashman's book took place over three days, during which contestants for the state finals of the Young American Miss Pageant are put through their paces at Santa Rosa Junior College. Robin Gibson, smart and out of place, rooms with Doria Hudson, a devout beauty-pageant believer from a broken home, a perpetual loser trying to

○ ○ ○ ○ ○

become a winner. As for the adults, Ashman focused on Brenda Di Carlo Freelander, former California "YAM," and her husband, Big Bob, who is also one of the judges. When Doria loses in the preliminaries, she decides to teach Robin how to win, urging her to use her fatherlessness to win points with the judges. Another girl finds the opportunity she's been seeking to humiliate fellow contestant Maria Gonzales, a Mexican girl who won the talent competition, when she finds Brenda's son taking pictures of the girls taking showers. Brenda, under consideration for the position of national spokeswoman for the pageant, saves the day after Maria's humiliation and gets the job; Robin, who succumbs to pressure and uses her fatherlessness to gain sympathy, loses; and Doria is first runner-up. Brenda and Big Bob go home to work on their family problems; Robin, upset by how far she was willing to go to win, goes home with her mother; and Doria goes on to the next pageant, still dreaming of being a winner.

Ashman was quite right in seeking to humanize the story and deemphasize the satire, and he succeeded in making Robin and Doria touching characters. But he was stuck with the residue of satire from the film, and the book is marred by inconsistency and uncertainty in tone. This was particularly true in the treatment of Brenda and Big Bob, whom the audience is at one moment asked to laugh at, at the next to sympathize with, and then to view as embodiments of the false values represented by beauty pageants.

But Smile's shortcomings were outweighed by its strengths. Both Hamlisch scores were good, but the Broadway one was superior: critics failed almost entirely to appreciate it, but their failure was understandable, as the score's quality was obscured on a first hearing by its fragmentation, with long musical sequences instead of simple, isolated songs. The staging by Ashman and choreographer Mary Kyte was extremely fluid, and the entire production was ultraprofessional; as the ad slogan said, Smile had "the look of a winner." But with no names in the cast and unfavorable reviews, Smile was never able to find the audience that would have enjoyed it. Smile was perhaps the most underappreciated musical of the eighties, and it is highly recommended to stock and amateur groups. The version published by Samuel French for subsequent productions differs substantially from what played on Broadway; there is much new dialogue and some new songs, and by reinstating some ideas from the movie, Ashman has made the whole thing tougher.

*　　*　　*

○ ○ ○ ○ ○

The musical **Baby** (Ethel Barrymore, Dec. 4, '83, 241), which finally got the team of Richard Maltby, Jr., and David Shire on Broadway, showed how impending parenthood—or the lack of it—causes three couples on a college campus to reexamine their relationships. As the show begins, all three appear to be expecting: Allan, a dean, and his wife, Arlene, are in their forties and have an empty house for the first time in their marriage now that their three daughters are in college; track coach Nick and wife Pam, in their thirties, have been trying to conceive for two years; and unmarried students Lizzie and Danny have just begun to live together. Arlene decides to keep her baby but confronts her husband with the realization that they've never functioned successfully as a couple, only as parents, an admission that proves beneficial to their marriage. Pam learns that she's actually not pregnant and embarks on a grisly regimen with Nick in an attempt to conceive; their marriage is strained by it, and they come to realize that while they may never become parents they are complete with each other. Lizzie finally agrees to marry Danny, and the curtain falls on Lizzie giving birth, as Danny and the other two couples look on.

Baby's gestation was lengthy: Sybille Pearson did the book after earlier versions by Susan Yankowitz and Ted Tally didn't work out, and the show went through workshops and other auditions to raise money. Directed by Maltby, *Baby* was, symptomatic of its time, a very small Broadway musical that required ten producers to get on. It looked simple, with an orchestra upstage behind a curtain, but it wound up costing $2.75 million, thanks to its design concept, which included computer-operated, shower-type curtains, hung on overhead tracks, on which films showing the development of the fetus were projected.

Unfortunately, *Baby* was up against audience reluctance: people didn't like the idea of a musical about having babies (even though *Baby* was actually about more than just that). When they saw the show, they tended to enjoy it, but it was hard to get them to go. *Baby* was also a starless nonspectacle, requiring much stronger reviews for survival than it received; the reviews actually made the show sound clinical and unappetizing, and gave little indication of its humor or warmth. *Baby* was an adult musical about real life, and it was touching and unfailingly intelligent. Its producers gave it every chance, keeping it open—sometimes at a loss—for eight months. But in spite of strong partisans, it never quite caught on and did not return its investment.

Of course, *Baby* had its problems. The book was schematic in its use

○ ○ ○ ○ ○

of contrasting couples of different age groups; the show might have done better off-Broadway, even though its writing was of Broadway caliber; the "shower curtains" were noisy and distracting; and the show was utterly heterosexual, a problem for some musical comedy fans. But *Baby* is a perfect piece for community theatre and stock productions, with an outstanding score, one of the best heard on Broadway in the eighties. It includes Lizzie's beautiful ballad "The Story Goes On," in which she realizes she is part of a chain of life; an extremely clever duet for Lizzie and Danny called "What Could Be Better?"; two parallel numbers, one for three women ("I Want It All"), the other for the husbands ("Fatherhood Blues"); an honest duet for the older couple called "And What If We Had Loved Like That?"; and other equally well crafted and superb items.

Lesser names were involved in six musicals which were pleasant but too mild to ever achieve substantial success. Two of these, **Courtin' Time** (National; June 13, '51; 37) and **Seventeen** (Broadhurst; June 21, '51; 180), have several things in common: virtually simultaneous openings, turn-of-the-century settings, lots of appealing qualities, and failure— thanks to June openings and strong competition.

Courtin' Time, originally intended as a vehicle for Walter Huston, who died during the show's planning stages, was based on Eden Phillpott's 1924 British comedy, *The Farmer's Wife*. The musical moved the story from England to 1890s Maine and told of Samuel Rilling, a widowed farmer whose daughters are about to leave him to get married. He decides that he, too, should remarry, and without benefit of courting, he proposes to three women, all the while overlooking his lovely and faithful housekeeper, Araminta. Rejected by two of the ladies (and by the father of the third), Samuel naturally winds up with Araminta at the end.

The score was by Jack Lawrence (*I Had a Ball* later) and Don Walker (*The Girl in Pink Tights* later), George Balanchine did the dances, and Alfred Drake directed. It was the second of associate producer Alexander H. Cohen's flops, and the first of Carmen Mathews' string. For the part of Araminta, the producers cast Billie Worth, a talented performer who had replaced Mary Martin in *Annie Get Your Gun* on the road and understudied her in *South Pacific*. Worth went on to star in *Call Me Madam* in London, but the failure of *Courtin' Time* and of her next American show, *Carefree Heart* (a Wright and Forrest musical that closed on the road), meant that she was no longer under consideration for important new parts.

While in Philadelphia, *Courtin' Time*'s leading man, Lloyd Nolan, with-

Courtin' Time *and* Seventeen *opened a week apart. Both had charm, but both were defeated by competition and June heat.*

drew due to vocal problems. Director Drake played the rest of the Philadelphia engagement, then Joe E. Brown took over. The reviews in New York were strong for Brown and Worth but otherwise divided, and Atkinson in the *Times* did not approve. Hoping that business would be better four blocks uptown, *Courtin' Time* moved to the Royale but expired shortly thereafter.

The hit of the show was Mathews, who stopped it cold with "Golden Moment," an operetta-style outburst of ecstasy following Brown's proposal (which was followed by her turning him down). *Courtin' Time* was nice but unexciting, and it could not hope to compete with such other current Broadway attractions as *Guys and Dolls*, *Kiss Me, Kate*, *The King and I*, *South Pacific*, *Call Me Madam*, *Top Banana*, and a return engagement of *Oklahoma!*

These shows also hurt the chances of the worthy *Seventeen*. Based on Booth Tarkington's 1916 novel, the show, set in 1907, was a sweet, charming tale of the pain of adolescence and of the uproar caused in an Indianapolis neighborhood by the summer visit of a flirtatious young woman who speaks in baby-talk and carries her dog, Floppit, with her wherever she goes. *Seventeen* had been musicalized unsuccessfully in 1926, under the title *Hello, Lola*. This new adaptation had a book by Sally Benson and a score by Walter Kent and Kim Gannon, but it was first written by John Cecil Holm, Stella Unger, and Alec Templeton, all of whom received royalties from the Broadway version. Milton Berle, who was being spoofed in *Top Banana* at the Winter Garden, was one of the producers; the staging was by Hassard Short, who had *Lady in the Dark, Carmen Jones*, and the 1946 revival of *Show Boat* to his credit; and the book was directed by Richard Whorf. Kenneth Nelson, who would create the role of The Boy in *The Fantasticks* nine years later, played Willie Baxter, in desperate pursuit of a dress suit he could wear to woo Lola Pratt from St. Louis.

This time, it was Atkinson who gave the show its best review; otherwise, the notices were mixed. *Seventeen* hung on for six months, then began a tour which lasted one week. Its main problem was a quality imbalance between book and score: Benson's libretto captures perfectly the tone of the original and is quite appealing and funny, while the score is pleasant but undistinguished. With stronger music, *Seventeen* might have been a hit. As it was, it was enjoyable but too lightweight to withstand the nearby competition.

A story by Maurice Walsh was the basis of John Ford's 1952 film *The Quiet Man*, which nine years later was turned into the Broadway musical

○ ○ ○ ○ ○

Donnybrook! (46th Street; May 18, '61; 68). The show, set in Innisfree, Ireland, was about American Sean Enright, who returns to his native town to buy a house and falls for the fiery sister of Will Danaher; Will is seeking to buy the same property. The story is complicated by the fact that Enright, a former prizefighter, killed a man in the ring and now refuses to fight anyone for anything, and by Flynn, the local jack-of-all-trades, who negotiates the sale of the house as well as various marriages.

Robert E. Griffith, Harold Prince, and Frederick Brisson were among the backers of *Donnybrook!* because its coproducer, Fred Hebert, had stage-managed several musicals for them. *Donnybrook!*'s score was by Johnny Burke, who had done lyrics for *Carnival in Flanders*, the book was by Robert E. McEnroe, and Irishman Jack Cole made his directorial debut. Art Lund was Enright, Eddie Foy played Flynn, and Susan Johnson played wealthy widow and tavern keeper Kathy Carey. For the female lead, Rhonda Fleming and Joan Diener were both mentioned, but after a talent search, the part went to unknown Kip Hamilton, who was replaced by her understudy Joan Fagan less than a week before performances began in Philadelphia.

Donnybrook! received its share of good reviews; in New York, both Taubman in the *Times* and Kerr in the *Herald Tribune* were favorable. But even the good reviews were too mild to have much impact, and the cast was not particularly stellar. Opening late in the season, and a month after a better musical also based on a hit fifties movie, *Carnival*, arrived, *Donnybrook!* quickly declined and disappeared after two months. But it was a charming and tastefully done show. Its source was a perfectly good one for musical adaptation, and its score, particularly the opening, "Sez I," and two duets for Foy and Johnson, was highly attractive. Cole's staging was fine, most notable for its staged overture, during which the principal characters were introduced (behind a lit scrim) at their daily activities, each appearing and disappearing as an Irish folk dance gradually grew into a stirring ballet. Fagan, who went on to replace Inga Swenson in *110 in the Shade*, then was never heard from again, was superb. For Johnson, wonderful as always, *Donnybrook!* was the last in a bizarre string of Broadway musical roles that invariably had her involved in watering holes of one sort or another. Johnson had been a waitress in *The Most Happy Fella*, the manager of a nightclub in *Oh Captain!*, the proprietress of a roadhouse saloon in *Whoop-Up*, and in her Broadway farewell, the owner of *Donnybrook!*'s pub.

*　　*　　*

○ ○ ○ ○ ○

Harold Brighouse's 1915 play *Hobson's Choice* was set in the late 1800s in an industrial town in Lancashire, England. It told of Henry Hobson, bootmaker, who has three daughters and intends to hold on to the eldest, the intelligent and fiercely capable Maggie, who manages everything for him. But Maggie has other plans: she decides that because she is the best saleswoman around and because Will Mossop, Hobson's illiterate but skilled employee, makes the best boots in town, she and Will should become partners in business—and marriage. Will is engaged to another and has no love for the domineering Maggie, but Maggie, seeing Will as her best and last chance, is determined to make Will into the businessman *and* husband she wants.

Hobson's Choice, a delightfully funny and touching play, had been thought of as a musical on and off for years. Perhaps because the play was triumphantly revived by the National Theatre in London in 1964, producers Cy Feuer and Ernest Martin took it up and, in 1965, announced that Mary Martin had agreed to star in a musical version to be called **Walking Happy** (Lunt-Fontanne; Nov. 26, '66; 161). To accommodate Martin, the play's setting was to be switched from Lancashire to a coal-mining town in Pennsylvania. After several months, the producers announced that because of Martin's commitment to touring in *Hello, Dolly!*, she would be unable to meet the starting date of *Walking Happy*, and that the musical would now proceed without her and revert to the play's original setting. There must have been more to the story than was revealed to the press, however; why didn't Feuer and Martin simply wait until Mary Martin was ready?

Walking Happy became the last Broadway show presented by Feuer and Martin, and they produced it simultaneously with the Julie Harris vehicle *Skyscraper*, which opened exactly one year earlier and shared with *Walking Happy* its director (Feuer) and songwriters (Sammy Cahn and James Van Heusen). The book for *Walking Happy* was by Ketti Frings and Roger O. Hirson, who would go on to revise the book for *Darling of the Day* and write *Pippin*. For the role of Will Mossop, Feuer and Martin hired British star Norman Wisdom, who had played the Ray Bolger role in the London production of their first hit musical, *Where's Charley?*

Walking Happy's reviews were mixed to good on the road and in New York, and the show was nominated for the Best Musical Tony Award, with nominations also going to Wisdom, leading lady Louise Troy, the composers, and choreographer Danny Daniels. The show ran for five months in New York, then moved on to San Francisco and Los Angeles

WALKING HAPPY

THE EDUCATION OF H*Y*M*A*N K*A*P*L*A*N

a New Musical Comedy

Walking Happy *and* Minnie's Boys *weren't hard to sit through, and* The Education of H*Y*M*A*N K*A*P*L*A*N *had its moments.*

for a fourteen-week stand at Edwin Lester's Civic Light Operas. It was supposed to go on to London but never did.

Walking Happy is another one of those shows that demonstrate the fine line between flop and hit. The book stayed close to the original play, except for the scenes at a pub which were added to give George Rose (as Hobson) the opportunity to sing some unnecessary songs. (Rose's number "Such a Sociable Sort," in which he sang and danced with demons of his besotted imagination, was the show's low point.) Cahn's lyrics were not always felicitous, and *Walking Happy* needed a better score to equal the level of its book, choreography, and the performances of Wisdom and Troy.

Still, there have been hits with worse scores (e.g. *Applause*), and *Walking Happy* was a decently entertaining, conventional show that had the misfortune to open at the same time as three superior and more inventive musicals—*Cabaret, I Do! I Do!* (with the elusive Mary Martin) and *The Apple Tree*—arrived on Broadway. Had Martin actually been willing to do *Walking Happy* after *Dolly!*, it might have been a solid hit. And as the original play had always been more popular in England, it is likely that the musical, with British favorite Wisdom, would have fared better in London, where it would have been vastly superior to most home-grown musicals of the sixties.

During the intermission of the opening night performance of **The Education of H*Y*M*A*N K*A*P*L*A*N** (Alvin; Apr. 4, '68; 28), New York's Mayor Lindsay, who was in the audience, was informed that Martin Luther King, Jr., had just been assassinated in Memphis. The news spread rapidly through the theatre, and audience members, hearing rumors that riots were about to start all over the country, could only think about the fastest way to get safely home.

The creators of *H*Y*M*A*N K*A*P*L*A*N* now maintain that the unfortunate circumstances of its opening night caused the show to fail, but pleasant and sweet as it was, *H*Y*M*A*N K*A*P*L*A*N* would probably have fared little better if it had opened on any other night. Benjamin Bernard Zavin's book was based on characters, especially Hyman, the irrepressible Russian tailor studying to become a U.S. citizen at a night-school in Chicago, introduced by Leo Rosten in stories in the *New Yorker* in the thirties. The musical was the idea of Paul Nassau and Oscar Brand, who had already written the flop *A Joyful Noise*, and they contributed the

○ ○ ○ ○ ○

288

score, while eighty-year-old George Abbott directed the show as his 110th Broadway production.

For the musical, Rosten's characters were moved from thirties Chicago to New York in 1919 so that the notorious Palmer Raids of that period—in which alleged radicals and left-wingers were persecuted by the district attorney and often deported without benefit of trial—could be used to give weight to the light story. The musical showed how the overeager Hyman rents a tailor shop, hoping to share it with his smart classmate Rose Mitnick. But Rose is threatened with an arranged marriage to a stranger, Yissel Fishbein, whose family had given Rose and her mother the money to come to America. Hyman is illegally arrested for anarchy, but all ends happily when night-school teacher Professor Parkhill intercedes, Rose refuses to marry the insufferable Fishbein, and Hyman and his classmates are sworn in as U.S. citizens.

With Tom Bosley, whom Abbott had made a star in *Fiorello!*, ideally cast as Hyman, the show opened in Philadelphia, where business was so poor that the tryout had to be cut short. The show arrived on Broadway at the end of one of the weaker musical seasons (*Henry, Sweet Henry, Golden Rainbow, The Happy Time, How Now, Dow Jones, Darling of the Day*, and *Here's Where I Belong*), so there was room for a good new musical on Broadway. The critics were mixed to negative, except for John Chapman in the *News*, who loved it. The most powerful critic, Clive Barnes in the *Times*, was still conducting his crusade for musicals to have contemporary sounds; aware of Barnes' predilections, Brand had written a letter to Barnes, printed in the *Times* two months before H*Y*M*A*N K*A*P*L*A*N opened, in which he expressed his fear that the musical would not be judged fairly since its music was not remotely like that of the pop charts. Barnes gave it one of his typical damning-with-faint-praise notices, saying "it is only when *Hyman* is at its very best that it can suggest *Fiddler* at its very worst."

Actually, *The Education of* H*Y*M*A*N K*A*P*L*A*N was a nice show, with a humorous book, some good choreography by Jaime Rogers, fine performances by Bosley and the other principals, and a mediocre score with at least a few good numbers, particularly Rose's defiant Act Two showstopper, "When Will I Learn?" But the reviews were not strong enough to get audiences to a show without box-office names like Steve Lawrence and Eydie Gorme or Robert Goulet; this was an evening of charm and light humor, rather than a blockbuster. And *Fiddler on the Roof,*

○ ○ ○ ○ ○

then in its fourth year on Broadway, had set a standard for musicals about Russian Jews that was difficult for other musicals to live up to.

In 1989, the American Jewish Theatre brought back *H*Y*M*A*N K*A*P*L*A*N* in a tiny production staged by Lonny Price. The show, a typical Abbott musical with numerous production numbers, did not reduce easily, and with most of the dancing dropped, it played more like a play than a musical. But *K*A*P*L*A*N*, an underrated charmer, is worthy of being tried again.

A little-known sidelight to the history of *H*Y*M*A*N K*A*P*L*A*N* is the show's role in one of the most successful musicals of all time. In 1968, dancer Donna McKechnie found herself at a career and personal low point; she phoned *K*A*P*L*A*N* choreographer Rogers and begged for a chance to work on the show, in any capacity. Rogers, who had choreographed McKechnie and Michael Bennett on the television show "Hullabaloo," created a dancing role for her in *K*A*P*L*A*N*. McKechnie later related this story at the taped talk sessions six years later that were the basis for Bennett's *A Chorus Line*. So when Cassie, the *Chorus Line* character loosely based on McKechnie, begged director Zach for the chance to start again, the situation was at least partly based on McKechnie's 1968 phone call to *H*Y*M*A*N K*A*P*L*A*N*'s choreographer.

Minnie's Boys (Imperial; Mar. 26, '70; 80), a musical about the early show business years of the four Marx Brothers and their meddling but lovable mother, Minnie, was first written by David Steinberg. Then Burt Shevelove and Neil Simon were asked to try their hand at the book, which was finally written by Arthur Marx (Groucho's son) and Robert Fisher (who had written for Groucho), the team responsible for the comedy hit *The Impossible Years*. Larry Grossman and Hal Hackady wrote the score, beginning their career-long series of flop musicals, Shelley Winters was hired to play Minnie, and Groucho Marx was made production consultant ("That means they give me money," said Groucho).

Minnie's Boys is a fine example of the dangers inherent in skipping a road tryout and the out-of-town reviews that go with it. The show played sixty-four previews at the Imperial, during which time the inexperienced creative team panicked, eliminating good material and substituting new songs and scenes that were often inferior to the ones they replaced. The original director, Lawrence Kornfeld, who had directed several Al Carmines musicals off-off-Broadway, was replaced by Stanley Prager (*Minnie's Boys* was Prager's third consecutive flop musical), and choreographer Pa-

○ ○ ○ ○ ○

tricia Birch was replaced by Marc Breaux. There were constant rumors about replacing Winters—with whom the show's staff was not happy—during previews, and at one point she walked out, leaving the understudy to face a sold-out theatre party with script in hand.

But Winters stuck it out, and *Minnie's Boys* opened to mixed-to-negative reviews (although Walter Kerr in the Sunday *Times* enjoyed it). It lasted a couple of months, losing $750,000 on an investment of $550,000. The show received two summer revivals, with Kaye Ballard and Charlotte Rae heading the companies, and was followed by several other stage productions (*A Day in Hollywood/A Night in the Ukraine, Groucho,* and *Groucho: A Life in Revue*) that also exploited the Marx Brothers' renown.

Minnie's Boys was problematic on several levels. First, trying to compete with the screen image of the Marx Brothers, still readily available on television and in revival houses, was, no matter how well done, probably pointless. A bigger problem, however, was the character of Minnie. *Minnie's Boys* was a lightweight version of *Gypsy*, with several parallel scenes, but its lead female character was never as fascinating or colorful as *Gypsy*'s Rose. The four boys, extremely well played in the musical, were far more entertaining and interesting than Minnie, but because a star had been hired for the part, the character had to be kept around even when she wasn't needed.

Still, *Minnie's Boys* was a moderately enjoyable show, thanks to a catchy score and the always funny Marx Brothers antics. Lewis J. Stadlen scored heavily playing what Groucho might have been like just before he became Groucho, and Stadlen went on to play Groucho again in other productions. If it never approached the quality of *Gypsy*, *Minnie's Boys* was a crowd pleaser nonetheless.

Four musicals take us from the pleasant-but-mild to the silly-and-lightweight-but-well-executed category; all four of them deserved better runs. The first of these chronologically is **Goldilocks** (Lunt-Fontanne; Oct. 11, '58; 161), a spoof of the silent-movie era written by Walter Kerr, a devotee of the genre, and his wife, Jean Kerr. The Kerrs did the lyrics with Joan Ford, and Leroy Anderson, composer of such popular orchestral pieces as "The Syncopated Clock," made his Broadway debut. David Merrick and Jo Mielziner were the original producers; when they withdrew, the job was taken up by Robert Whitehead.

Set in 1913, *Goldilocks* was about Maggie Harris, a stage actress about to leave the footlights for marriage to the wealthy George Randolph

Brown. Max Grady, a moviemaker in love with film, forces Maggie to postpone the wedding and honor a contract to make a quickie picture. Max, who dreams of making full-length movies and has secretly been using studio funds to buy elaborate scenery for an Egyptian spectacle he's planning, tricks Maggie into staying on. Max is also drawn to Maggie, although they bicker incessantly and she calls him an "on-the-make hustler." After numerous complications, George winds up with Lois, a hanger-on at the studio, and Maggie admits that she loves Max.

Dolores Gray was first announced for the female lead, but it went to Elaine Stritch, who was ideally suited to Maggie's wisecracks and brittle comedy. The part of Max changed hands twice: Ben Gazzara was originally signed, then asked to be released; he was replaced by Barry Sullivan, who had been originally sought and was now available. Sullivan opened in the show in Philadelphia but withdrew after the critics complained about his singing. Don Ameche took over at the end of the Boston stand. *Goldilocks* opened as the first musical at the newly christened Lunt-Fontanne Theatre (previously the Globe); the concern that critics would bend over backwards to praise the show because it was cowritten and directed by a colleague proved unfounded. Although Herbert Whittaker, substituting for Kerr in the *Tribune*, praised the show, the reviews were evenly divided. When the advance sale died down in December, business took a dive, and *Goldilocks* closed at a loss of almost all of its $360,000 investment. Pat Stanley and Russell Nype, who played Lois and George, won Tony Awards at season's end.

Goldilocks was far from flawless. Max and Maggie were funny but not especially likable characters, and their romance was never entirely convincing; terrific as she was, Stritch was not the kind of performer with whom audiences fell in love. The moviemaking spoofs were uproarious, but the other scenes were less interesting. Walter Kerr later said that the biggest mistake the creators made was constantly beefing up the comedy, which was already strong, at the expense of the love story: "What we should have done was forget all about working for any more comedy whatsoever, and straighten out the emotional line instead. I mean, making something real seem to happen between the principals, emotionally. And that we didn't do." The show's title, obscure in its relationship to the story, was also off-putting.

But *Goldilocks* was more than easy to sit through. The songs, particularly "Who's Been Sitting in My Chair?" and "I Never Know When to Say When" for Stritch, and "Lady in Waiting" for Stanley, sparkled. Agnes

○ ○ ○ ○ ○

Goldilocks had Elaine Stritch, a delightful score, and fine de Mille dances. It also had Barry Sullivan (in photo at top with Stritch)—but only in Philadelphia. Below: Drat! The Cat! and Foxy—two very funny flops.

de Mille's choreography was lovely, highlighted by "The Pussy Foot," a period maxixe, and by one of the last dream ballets, "Lady in Waiting," as Lois fantasized about the men of her dreams and lost one after the other. The failure of both her star vehicles, *Goldilocks* and *Sail Away*, did irreparable damage to Stritch's career. And coming as it did three years after *The Vamp*, a somewhat similar musical set in the same period, *Goldilocks* should have indicated that the silent-movie era was not fertile material for Broadway musicals. The lesson was not heeded, however, and *Mack and Mabel* turned up sixteen years later.

Foxy (Ziegfeld; Feb. 16, '64; 72) was loosely based on Ben Jonson's 1616 play *Volpone*. The musical moved the action from Venice to the Yukon Gold Rush in 1896. Foxy Jim Fox tells his three prospector friends that he's found gold in the Klondike, and they desert him to catch the first steamboat. To get revenge, Foxy and his friend, con artist Doc Mosk, set in motion a scheme whereby Foxy will pretend to be very rich and very ill, and the prospectors will cater to Foxy's every whim in hopes of sharing in his will.

Foxy was written as a vehicle for the great comedian Bert Lahr, whose last book musical had been *Dubarry Was a Lady* in 1939. Lahr was cele-brating his fiftieth year in show business with *Foxy*, which was to become his final Broadway appearance. The book was the first for Ian McLellan Hunter and Ring Lardner, Jr., and the score was by Robert Emmett Dolan and Johnny Mercer, who had collaborated on *Texas, Li'l Darlin'* in 1949.

With Robert Lewis directing, *Foxy* played perhaps the most unorthodox tryout in Broadway history. Because Canada was trying to reestablish its Yukon area for tourism, and because the show was set in that area, *Foxy* was invited to open the Dawson City Gold Rush Festival in the summer of 1962. Lahr and Lewis both disliked flying, so the show was rehearsed on trains, buses, and steamships during a month's journey to the theatre, where Beatrice Lillie showed up to introduce the show on opening night. *Foxy* ran seven weeks in the Yukon, coproduced by Robert Whitehead and the Canadian government, playing to empty houses because of the theatre's inaccessibility; weeknight audiences consisted entirely of Indians.

Back in New York, Lahr did S.J. Perelman's comedy *The Beauty Part*, then prepared to do *Foxy* again. Billy Rose took on the production, but when he and director Lewis clashed, *Foxy* became a David Merrick production. Lahr fought with the writers, who disliked his constant improvisation; with Lewis, who couldn't control him; and with his costar, Larry Blyden, who wanted changes in the show. Lahr insisted on making *Foxy* completely his, demanding that everyone on stage freeze whenever he was on. It was Lahr, however, who contributed many of the script's funniest lines. Merrick announced that he was closing the show in Detroit, where Jerome Robbins had been helping out, but Merrick changed his mind when his investors threatened to sue.

Foxy opened to love letters for Lahr, fine notices for Blyden, Julienne Marie, and Cathryn Damon, and good-to-mixed reviews for the show itself. But even before the reviews came out, Merrick, at the opening night party, decided to sell most of the show to Billy Rose, who owned the theatre where *Foxy* was playing. When Rose left town, however, Merrick found himself again responsible for a show he never really liked and—now that his recently opened production of *Hello, Dolly!* was a blockbuster—no longer cared about. Merrick did little to promote *Foxy* and even encouraged RCA Victor not to record it. It had lost $400,000 in Dawson City, and it dropped $350,000 more on Broadway.

Much of *Foxy's* book is raucously hilarious, and the show struck a nice balance between burlesquelike interludes for Lahr and musical numbers. Especially memorable was Lahr's entrance, with a bear trap on his leg, and his climbing up the side of the proscenium arch to escape a pursuer. The cast was filled with talent, the music was good, and the lyrics excellent. The score featured one semihit, "Talk to Me Baby," two good duets for Blyden and Damon, and a comic recitative showstopper for Lahr called "Bon Vivant." Above all, *Foxy* had Lahr, who was perfectly wonderful and received a Tony for the show.

Merrick is usually blamed for the quick demise of *Foxy*, but while it is true that he did not try very hard to make it a hit, he also faced insurmountable obstacles. Lahr was no longer a tremendously popular star; a new generation preferred Zero Mostel, Barbra Streisand, Carol Channing, or even Steve Lawrence, and Lahr in *Foxy* did not draw any better than Lahr in *The Beauty Part*. The reviews were not quite good enough, its theatre was off the beaten path, and business showed little sign of improvement; it's doubtful that promotion could have kept *Foxy* going after two losing months.

A throwback to the kind of shows in which Lahr had starred in the thirties, *Foxy* did what it set out to do well. Funny as it was, though, it is not especially revivable; every line in the script reeks of Lahr. If a company has at its disposal an extremely gifted clown, *Foxy* might be worth trying, but the effort might not pay off.

Far more performable is the silly but very funny **Drat! The Cat!** (Martin Beck; Oct. 10, '65; 8). A spoof of nineteenth-century melodramas and operettas, *Drat!* was about Alice Van Guilder, rebelling against her wealthy society background by becoming a jewel thief who performs thefts dressed as a cat. Policeman Bob Purefoy is assigned to track down the fiend, and Alice, with whom Bob falls in love at first sight, decides to assist him. The fairly dumb Bob unwittingly lets Alice (the Cat herself) in on police strategy and informs her of the whereabouts of valuable items, such as a Japanese idol, that are liable to be stolen by the Cat. Alice, who can never seem to remember Bob's name, frames him for the thefts, then gets him to run away with her. At Bob's trial, Alice tells the truth and is placed under Bob's permanent custody.

Drat! The Cat! was a luckless show. Ira Levin wrote the only book and lyrics of his career, and Milton Schafer, who had done *Bravo Giovanni* three years earlier, composed the music. Joey Heatherton was signed for the lead, but when she turned thumbs down on a candidate for the male lead, the producers informed her that casting was none of her business, and she departed. When the show opened in Philadelphia, Eddie Foy was playing a dual role, the fathers of Bob and Alice, but he withdrew, and the parts were given to two other performers. With fairly negative reviews, *Drat!* cut short its Philadelphia run and arrived in New York ahead of schedule.

Barbra Streisand, then married to Elliott Gould, who was playing Bob, attempted to give the show a boost by recording two of its songs, "He Touched Me" and "I Like Him," and investing in it. The show moved its opening from a Saturday to a Sunday so that Streisand could attend on her night off from *Funny Girl*. In New York, there was praise for Joe Layton's staging and for Lesley Ann Warren's Alice. Walter Kerr and Martin Gottfried were among those who filed favorable notices, but Taubman in the *Times* was negative, and with no big names and no advance sale, *Drat!* was unable to continue.

Drat! The Cat! was perhaps the most delightful show to ever run a single week. It is difficult to pull off an evening-long spoof, but *Drat!* kept tongue firmly in cheek throughout and never took itself too seriously. Layton was at his best here: as he had done in *No Strings*, he put the orchestra

○ ○ ○ ○ ○

onstage, this time on an elevated bandstand, and had them playing background roles. His Kabuki-style ballet for Alice's theft of the Japanese idol was one of those priceless bits of musical staging lost to the ages. Gould and Warren gave performances of enormous appeal, and *Drat!* boasted a score of a very high order. Schafer was a talented composer who might have gone on to a major Broadway career; discouraged by two consecutive flops, he stopped. Fortunately, a decent-sounding live tape of the score was made, which was pressed onto an LP about twenty years after *Drat!* closed.

Shakespeare's *The Comedy of Errors* had already been the basis for the Rodgers and Hart musical hit *The Boys from Syracuse* in 1938 and a Royal Shakespeare Company musicalization in London in 1976, with a score by Guy Woolfenden and Trevor Nunn. Donald Driver, who had created a smash by adapting Shakespeare's *Twelfth Night* into *Your Own Thing* in 1968, decided to reset *The Comedy of Errors* in the contemporary Middle East, and the result was **Oh, Brother!** (ANTA, Nov. 10, '81; 3). Driver wrote the book and lyrics, and directed, and Michael Valenti, who had appeared in *Your Own Thing*, composed the music. The cast of *Oh, Brother!* featured some of the better young talents in musical theatre, including Judy Kaye, David Carroll, Harry Groener, Mary Elizabeth Mastrantonio, Joe Morton, and Larry Marshall.

Oh, Brother! took place in a town on the Persian Gulf in the heart of oil territory and in the midst of revolution. Lew is searching for a pair of lost sons: his wife gave birth to identical twins in the Middle East, and the couple then adopted another set of twins born in the same hospital. One child of each pair got separated when the plane that pair was on was hijacked to Iraq; the other pair is now helping their father search for their hijacked brothers. The evening was a sitcomlike sex farce of mistaken identity involving the two pair of twins and their mates.

Word of mouth along Broadway was good on *Oh, Brother!* while it was in previews, far better than that for the musical that was previewing across the street, *Merrily We Roll Along.* But *Oh, Brother!* was just too silly to win critical approval; when it closed in two days, one cast member of the still-previewing *Merrily* expressed concern: "Everyone loved that show and it closed. Everyone hates our show—what's going to become of us?"

It is likely that a revival of *The Boys from Syracuse*, with the same leads, would have been a better bet for Broadway than *Oh, Brother!* Rodgers and Hart got there first, and their score was sublime. But *Oh, Brother!* is a good

○ ○ ○ ○ ○

bet for stock and amateur groups. It has a relatively small cast for a musical, many good leading parts, and only one set. It plays much better than it reads, so potential producers should not be put off by the printed script. Its greatest strength is Valenti's music, which elevates the farce plot from beginning to end. "I to the World," "How Do You Want Me?," and "A Man" are impressive songs; Valenti is a hard-luck talent, whose Broadway career has consisted of *Oh, Brother!*, a play with music called *Blood Red Roses* (1970, one performance), and a black concept-musical, *Honky Tonk Nights* (1986, four performances). *Oh, Brother!* acknowledges its bad puns, winks at the audience, and, like *Drat!*, never takes itself seriously.

Our last three musicals in this section were interesting, unusual, and worthy efforts, deserving of respect and reexamination. **A Time for Singing** (Broadway; May 21, '66; 41) was another unsuccessful Alexander H. Cohen production, but it was probably the best musical he ever produced. Based on Richard Llewellyn's novel *How Green Was My Valley*, already made into an Oscar-winning John Ford film in 1941, *A Time for Singing* took place in the memory of David Griffith, a Protestant minister in a Welsh mining town. It centered on the conflict within the Morgan family over the formation of a miners' union, and the romance between Angharad Morgan and David, who advises her to marry the wealthy son of the mine owner. When a strike is called, Angharad finds herself married to her family's enemy. The strikers flood the mines, two Morgan men are killed, and Angharad is finally united with David.

The music for *A Time for Singing* was by John Morris, who had composed dance music for dozens of shows, and Morris collaborated on the book with Gerald Freedman, who was the director. With English (Shani Wallis, Laurence Naismith) and Welsh (Tessie O'Shea, Ivor Emmanuel) leads, *A Time for Singing* tried out in Boston, where Gower Champion came in to restage some of Donald McKayle's numbers. During this time, Cohen's extravagant publicity machine was turned on: the first one hundred ticket buyers in line at the box office received folding chairs and a picnic lunch catered by the Brasserie restaurant. The title song was piped into the lobby, and lines at the box office were often longer than those across the street at the Winter Garden, where *Mame* would open three days after *A Time for Singing*.

The show suffered from a problem of focus; it was supposed to be about the Morgan family, but it was presented as the recollection of David Griffith, who couldn't have been privy to some of the events that occurred in the Morgan household. The original novel had been the recollection of the youngest Morgan son, Huw, which was probably a more workable concept. And there were too many principal characters in the musical, making it difficult for the audience to be sure who the show was meant to be about.

But while it was still a conventional, sixties-style book musical, *A Time for Singing* pointed the way to such later musicals as *Les Misérables* and *Grand Hotel* in its staging and use of music. Its score was richer and more serious than that of most shows of the period, and although there was dialogue, the show had far more music than was typical. There was an operatic emotionalism about the show, and much of the music was lovely. Freedman and McKayle's staging employed some of the cinematic fluidity and continuous movement of eighties shows; something of the tapestry style that became more pronounced twenty years later—weaving song, dance, and dialogue together in a nonstop staging—was attempted in *A Time for Singing*. While its authors were not quite ready to create a continuous musical, *A Time for Singing* was a significant step in that direction.

Set in Mississippi Territory in the late eighteenth century, **The Robber Bridegroom** (Biltmore; Oct. 9, '76; 145) offered characters unusual for a Broadway musical: there was dashing thief Jamie Lockhart; Clement Musgrove, a tobacco grower fooled by Jamie into believing that Jamie saved his life; Rosamund, Musgrove's beautiful daughter, who falls in love with Jamie when he's disguised as "The Bandit of the Woods" but can't stand him when he's himself; Salome, Rosamund's jealous stepmother, who attempts to do away with her; and brothers Little Harp and Big Harp, the latter a talking head without a body.

Robert Waldman and Alfred Uhry, who had collaborated on *Here's Where I Belong*, based their musical on a novella by Eudora Welty which had been inspired by a Grimm fairy tale. *The Robber Bridegroom* was first produced by Stuart Ostrow's Musical Theatre Lab at St. Clement's Church, then picked up by the Acting Company, who toured it and brought it to Broadway's Harkness Theatre for a two-week run as part of its repertory season. With future stars Kevin Kline and Patti LuPone as Jamie and Rosamund, *The Robber Bridegroom*, owing to a musician's strike, was the only musical playing on Broadway in October 1975, the Harkness

○ ○ ○ ○ ○

Above: Tessie O'Shea feeds husband Laurence Naismith in A Time for Singing. Below: Eartha Kitt and Erik Rhodes in Shinbone Alley. Both shows were interesting efforts.

operating under a different contract from other houses. LuPone received a Tony nomination the same year her brother Robert was nominated for *A Chorus Line*, and Uhry's book was also nominated.

A new production of the show began at the Mark Taper Forum in Los Angeles, and this production returned the show to Broadway, with the director (Gerald Freedman) and choreographer (Donald Saddler) of the Acting Company production, some book and score changes, and a new cast headed by Barry Bostwick as Jamie. During a dress rehearsal, Bostwick fell twelve feet to the floor when a rope on which he was swinging snapped, and Bostwick opened the show with his arm in a cast.

The reviews were rather good, and Bostwick won a Tony as Best Musical Actor, but *The Robber Bridegroom* never really caught on, probably because it was small, not what audiences expected of a Broadway show, and featured a country-flavored score unlike standard Broadway music. But it's a very witty piece, with an amusing book. The show employed a concept reminiscent of that used by Harold Prince in his production of *Zorba;* instead of that show's bouzouki circle, the story of *The Robber Bridegroom* was told by members of a country square-dance circle. The story they were telling became the show, and the members of the circle played parts and commented on the action while an onstage string band added to the air of informality. *The Robber Bridegroom* lends itself well to productions by small groups and is refreshingly different from conventional musical comedy fare.

In 1916, Don Marquis introduced a series of stories in the *New York Evening Sun* about a poetic cockroach named archy who, in a deserted newspaper office late at night, finds self-expression by telling stories of his life, in particular of his relationship with an indomitable, reckless free spirit, the alley cat mehitabel. archy (who types out his tales but, because he is not strong enough to operate the shift key, uses only lowercase letters) relates mehitabel's affairs with tomcat big bill and theatrical cat tyrone t. tattersal, who fails to make a star of mehitabel, and touchingly reveals the devotion that always causes him to come to mehitabel's aid in times of crisis.

Joe Darion and Mel Brooks wrote the book for a musical version of Marquis' stories called **Shinbone Alley** (Broadway; Apr. 13, '57; 49), and George Kleinsinger, a classical composer whose most successful pieces were children's stories for narrator and orchestra like "Tubby the Tuba," wrote the music. The musical had an unusual history. Like *Jesus Christ*

○ ○ ○ ○ ○

Superstar and *Evita* years later, *Shinbone Alley* was first an LP record, with Eddie Bracken and Carol Channing as archy and mehitabel. Then, in 1954, the forty-five-minute piece was performed in a concert version by the Little Orchestra Society at Town Hall. It was expanded into a Broadway musical, with the title changing from *archy and mehitabel* to *Shinbone Alley* and a cast headed by Bracken and Eartha Kitt. Next, the stage musical was transferred to television, with the original title and Bracken and Tammy Grimes in the leads. Finally, there was an animated film called *Shinbone Alley*, with the voices of Bracken and Channing.

A highly unconventional "back-alley opera," the musical featured a strong cast of dancers, including Jacques d'Amboise and Allegra Kent of the City Center Ballet Company, plus David Winters and several other dancers who went directly into *West Side Story* when *Shinbone Alley* closed. It was also one of the first Broadway musicals to feature a fully integrated company.

With no road tryout, *Shinbone Alley* began performances on Broadway; director Norman Lloyd, who had staged *The Golden Apple* three years earlier, removed his name after clashing with the writers and the producer. Most critics felt that Marquis' writing defied musicalization, and competition from such shows as *My Fair Lady, Bells Are Ringing, The Most Happy Fella, Damn Yankees, Li'l Abner,* and *Happy Hunting* (plus a theatre too big for it) meant an early departure for the fragile *Shinbone Alley*.

Shinbone Alley was a direct precursor of *Cats;* although it featured dialogue and a lot more characterization, *Shinbone* was, like *Cats,* a heavy dance show with lengthy ballet sequences, and its actors portrayed animals. In *Cats,* however, the actors were made up and garbed to resemble cats; in *Shinbone Alley,* the actors wore stylized human attire. While *Shinbone Alley's* plot was thin, it had abundant charm and daring, and Rod Alexander's choreography was among the best of its time. The Kleinsinger–Darion score was equally imaginative and inventive; *Shinbone Alley* is one of the few musicals of the fifties that went unrecorded but was taped through the theatre's sound system. The tapes, pressed onto acetate disks, reveal wonderful dance music and such delightful numbers as "Flotsam and Jetsam" and "A Woman Wouldn't Be a Woman." As mehitabel, Eartha Kitt (understudied by Chita Rivera) had her best Broadway role. The evening's comic high point was mehitabel's futile attempt to find happiness as a house cat; the sight of Kitt, curled up before an enormous line drawing of a fireplace and sullenly sipping milk through a straw, brought down

○ ○ ○ ○ ○

the house. *Shinbone Alley* did not play by the rules, and it lost, but it was one of the more fascinating near-misses of musical flopdom.

In the twenties and thirties, before musicals were recognized as an art form, there was room for the not bad, the in between, the almost but not quite. But the advent of the golden age of the Broadway musical—which lasted for three decades from the forties through the sixties—meant that new musicals were now judged by much higher standards. In the sixties and seventies, economics became the other enemy of the merely OK: ticket prices rose so high that many theatregoers could only go to that which was deemed the best, and higher operating costs meant that a pleasant but not great show could no longer survive by playing to medium-sized houses. While catastrophes and mistakes will never die, the "not bad" may be the most endangered of our musical flop species.

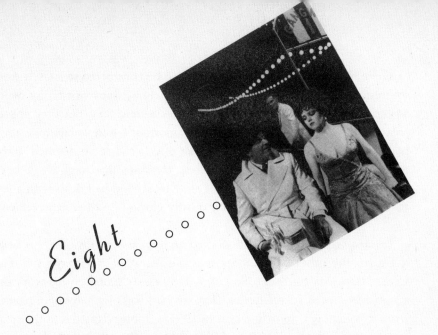

Eight

HEARTBREAKERS AND CREAM

"A really spectacular disaster . . . . Nowhere are we permitted to take a moment's shrewd delight in the sly thrust, the mockery that amuses even as it kills."—Walter Kerr, *Herald Tribune,* on *Candide* (1956)

"A largely marvelous Leonard Bernstein score that drags Alan Jay Lerner's book and lyrics behind it like an unwanted relative . . . of all the patched-up musicals that have limped into New York, this is the most pitifully pieced together one I have ever seen."—Martin Gottfried, *New York Post,* on *1600 Pennsylvania Avenue*

Robert Preston, James Mitchell and Bernadette Peters in Mack and Mabel *(above)*

There is a special brand of flop that must be considered separately from the rest. These shows may have been star flops, flops written by major writers, catastrophes, missed opportunities or mistakes. But they are set apart because they were particularly glorious—and sometimes foolhardy—in their ambition. The first half of this chapter is devoted to the real heartbreakers: the flops that dared, the flops that might have been glorious, the saddest kind of flop of all. The second half deals with a few that were, if not totally successful, mostly glorious in their achievement.

Truman Capote himself had worked on the musical version of his *House of Flowers*; the other two Capote musicals, *Breakfast at Tiffany's* and **The Grass Harp** (Martin Beck; Nov. 2, '71; 7), were based on his work but adapted by others. Like *Tiffany's*, *The Grass Harp* was originally a gorgeously written, touching Capote novella. In 1952, Capote adapted it to the stage as a nonmusical play. Starring Mildred Natwick and Ruth Nelson, and playing at the same theatre that would later house the musical version, the play lasted only thirty-six performances, indicating that the fragility of the novel made it less than ideal for adaptation. Yet Capote did a very fine job of transferring his novel to the stage: while remaining faithful to the original, he fleshed out the story with a great deal more dialogue, which took the place of the novel's amusing narration, in which cousin Collin gives the reader the lowdown on every member of the story's town.

Both the play and the later musical were centered around spinster sisters Dolly and Verena Talbo, who live with their cousin Collin and their housekeeper, Catherine. Verena's head is turned by Dr. Morris Ritz from Chicago, and together the two decide to bottle and sell Dolly's special dropsy cure. But Dolly won't give them the recipe: it's the one thing in the world she can call her own. Dolly, Catherine, and Collin leave the house to take up residence in a treehouse in the woods. In the end, Verena finds that Dr. Ritz has stolen her money and skipped town; she goes to the tree, admits her loneliness, and joins the others.

The musical had a book and lyrics by Kenward Elmslie, the author of opera libretti and protégé of John Latouche, another writer inclined toward esoteric musical subjects. The music was by Claibe Richardson. It was the first and only Broadway musical for Elmslie and Richardson, although they later collaborated on an equally rarefied off-Broadway musical called *Lola*.

The musical version of *The Grass Harp* was first produced by the Trinity Square Repertory Company in Providence, Rhode Island, in December

1966, just around the time the musical of *Tiffany's* was expiring on Broadway. The cast included Barbara Baxley, Carol Bruce, Elaine Stritch, David Doyle, and Carol Brice, under the direction of Adrian Hall. The show was then optioned for Broadway by Kermit Bloomgarden; when he asked Mary Martin to play Dolly, she uncharacteristically replied that she saw herself more as Babylove, a traveling gospel evangelist who did not enter until halfway through the evening. Bloomgarden's option lapsed, and the musical was taken up by Richard Barr, Charles Woodward, and Michael Harvey (Barr and Woodward later coproduced *Sweeney Todd*). Ellis Rabb, who was supposed to have produced and directed the musical for his own company, The A.P.A., was hired to direct his only Broadway musical.

The new production, with Barbara Cook, Ruth Ford, Brice retained from the Providence cast, and Celeste Holm as Babylove, opened the new Power Center for the Performing Arts at the University of Michigan. Holm could not handle Babylove's fifteen-minute song cycle, and she and her husband, Wesley Addy, departed; Karen Morrow, who had voice to spare, took over as Babylove. The reviews were not particularly good in either Rhode Island or Michigan, and they were no better when *The Grass Harp* arrived on Broadway. The show lasted a week, but it was recorded, and that recording assured future productions. It was performed in stock and remounted in New York by the York Theatre Company, and was seen in a half-hour television version on CBS-TV's "Camera Three."

The Grass Harp contains a ravishing score, one of the great ones as long as it is musicalizing Dolly, Catherine, and Babylove. Several of the lyrics come directly out of Capote's novel, and the others are equal to Capote's wit, while the lyrical melodies are an ideal match for Capote's style. "Chain of Love," "Marry with Me," "Dropsy Cure Weather," "If There's Love Enough," and "The Babylove Miracle Show" are the highlights of a score that, even if it fails to make Dr. Ritz and Collin sing as well as the other characters, remains a model in the area of adapting fiction into song.

But the richness of the score was partially the problem with the show: *The Grass Harp* was an overmusicalized musical. The characters are vividly realized in their songs, but because so much of the show's barely two-hour running time was devoted to songs, the action in between the songs is rushed through, and the thinness of the plot is exposed in a way it was not in the novel or play. Much of the original story is gone to make way for the songs, and the songs, wonderful as they are, are not quite enough to carry the entire evening. When one listens to the recording of *The*

○ ○ ○ ○ ○

An ad for The Grass Harp, with Celeste Holm, not yet replaced by Karen Morrow, among the stars. The glorious score was one of the show's problems.

Grass Harp, the characters and their emotions spring to life; in the theatre, the sketchiness of the story's development deprived the songs of their full impact, which may explain why the score did not for the most part receive the raves it deserved. Capote's play succeeded in making the story dramatically interesting; the musical, by thinning it out, did not.

Rabb's direction did not present the delicate conflicts and emotions of the musical as well as possible, but the leads were ideal: three of the theatre's finest voices, Cook, Brice, and Morrow, did full justice to their roles, and Ford was a touching Verena. The show would likely have fared better off-Broadway, where the audience could have been more easily drawn into its fragile web, but questions remain: could Capote's lovely story ever really have succeeded as a full-scale musical, and did musicalizing it blow it out of proportion? *The Grass Harp* receives occasional revivals, and as one watches one finds the score so wonderful and so ideally suited to the material that one continually tries to see a better musical than the one that is actually there.

It is extremely difficult to adapt truly great plays into musicals. Verdi succeeded, but with operas (*Macbeth, Otello, Falstaff*) rather than musicals with dialogue. No one has ever attempted to musicalize *A Streetcar Named Desire, Long Day's Journey into Night* or *The Iceman Cometh*, an admission, perhaps, of the high and daunting standard of the originals. But one of the twentieth century's greatest plays, Sean O'Casey's 1924 *Juno and the Paycock*, was made into a musical. The play was, for the most part, beautifully adapted, but critics refused to acknowledge the quality of the work because they did not see any necessity to touch O'Casey's original.

O'Casey had never seen a musical when the producers of **Juno** (Winter Garden; Mar. 9, '59; 16), then called *Daarlin' Man*, approached him for the rights. O'Casey granted them willingly and subsequently approved both the book by Joseph Stein and the score by Marc Blitzstein. Agnes de Mille was the choreographer, and Tony Richardson agreed to direct. The musical opened up the one-set play to include streets, a bar, and a park square, and it was Richardson who decided to put everything on a turntable. But Richardson bowed out before rehearsals began, and Vincent J. Donehue, who had never directed a Broadway musical before (he would direct *The Sound of Music* later the same year), was hired.

The story is set in Dublin during the struggle for freedom between the Irish Republican Army and the British in the early twenties. Melvyn Douglas played "Captain" Boyle, who spends his time at Foley's Bar and

An ad (with Vincent J. Donehue still billed as director) and the Playbill for Juno:
a show that demands a revival.

Two scenes from Juno. *Above: In "On a Day like This," Jack MacGowran, Melvyn Douglas, Shirley Booth, Jean Stapleton, Earl Hammond, and Monte Amundsen celebrate. Below: The troubled Johnny Boyle (Tommy Rall) dances out his anguish.*

develops pains in his legs when someone tells him of a job possibility, and Shirley Booth was his long-suffering wife, Juno, who, along with their daughter, Mary, supports the family. As *Juno* opens, Irish Republican Army soldier Robbie Tancred, in hiding from the British, is discovered and shot to death in the street. The Boyle family, which also includes brooding son Johnny, who has lost a hand in the fighting, is informed by lawyer Charlie Bentham that a relative has left them an inheritance. Boyle redecorates the house, but the inheritance proves to be apocryphal. Mary is left pregnant by Bentham, and Johnny is taken away and killed for betraying Tancred. Juno and Mary go off to start a new life as the Captain and his friend Joxer drink themselves into cheerful oblivion at Foley's as the curtain falls.

One of the main problems that *Juno* faced was simply the gloom and sadness of its source. Audiences today are more willing to accept serious musicals than they were in the fifties. *Juno*, for all its humorous byplay between Boyle and Joxer, was, particularly in its last half hour, too tragic for audiences at the time; it might have had a better chance had it been composed as an opera.

But even as it is, Blitzstein's score is the greatest ever heard in a postwar flop. "We're Alive," in which the people of Dublin affirm their belief in survival even though the streets in which they stand are "runnin' red," is one of the musical theatre's most stirring openings, and the rest of the score—including Mary's "I Wish It So" and "My True Heart," "One Kind Word" for Mary's rejected suitor, a duet for mother and daughter called "Bird upon the Tree," and "What Is the Stars?" for Boyle and Joxer—is uniformly rich and magnificent. But Blitzstein's most accessible score was still more complex than Broadway audiences were used to at the time and was not easy to fully appreciate on a first hearing. De Mille provided two fine ballets: her second act "Johnny," in which Tommy Rall danced out Johnny's emotions after being questioned by I. R. A. men, was the evening's highlight.

The dialect of O'Casey's original was watered down for the musical, as were the play's politics, but Stein's book was basically faithful to the play, and the opening-up was tastefully done. Booth and Douglas were well cast, although audiences used to Booth's earlier, endearingly comic musical roles may have been disappointed to see her in such a serious piece.

The critics, for the most part, refused to accept *Juno* from the time it began its tryout in Washington. After negative reviews there and in

○ ○ ○ ○ ○

Boston, Donehue was fired, and Jose Ferrer, never a particularly strong director of musicals, replaced him. (Donehue was later billed in the back of the Playbill as "assistant to Mr. Ferrer.") After the largely negative New York reviews, Jack MacGowran, who was playing Joxer, told the press, "O'Casey has survived stupid critics before. And he will again." But *Juno* ran only two weeks. *West Side Story*, which had moved from the Winter Garden to the Broadway to make way for *Juno*, moved back to the Winter Garden. Monte Amundsen, who had played Mary, married her stage brother, Tommy Rall, soon after.

Because of the score, beautifully preserved on the original cast album, *Juno* was mentioned for resuscitation on several occasions during the next ten years. In 1964, immediately after the opening of his *Fiddler on the Roof*, Stein announced that he was devoting himself to revising *Juno* and hoped to interest Harold Prince in producing it. *Juno* ultimately returned in a much-altered version called *Daarlin' Juno*, which was seen at the Williamstown Theatre Festival in 1974 and at the Long Wharf Theatre in 1976, with authentically Irish Milo O'Shea and Geraldine Fitzgerald in the leads, under the direction of Arvin Brown. The new version was adapted by Fitzgerald and Richard Maltby, Jr., with Maltby writing some new lyrics and Thomas Fay arranging the music for a small orchestra and writing the music for one new song. But *Daarlin' Juno* was not the answer: while more of O'Casey's original dialogue was restored, the score was vastly diminished. *Juno*, while not an opera, has a definite operatic grandeur, and scaling the score down and eliminating some of it altogether did the show no service. The lyrics, and even sections of the music, were needlessly rewritten; there was nothing the matter with the original music and lyrics, and Maltby and Fay in no way improved them with all their revisions. And the ballets, so vital a part of the original, were gone. *Daarlin' Juno* was closer to the original play but played much less like a musical, and there was really no reason why it should be one anymore.

Critics on the road and on Broadway maintained that *Juno and the Paycock* did not require a musical score and that the score added nothing to O'Casey's original. But surely the play is exactly the kind of richly emotional piece that lends itself to serious musicalization. And *Juno* was for the most part an excellent adaptation, with a score equaling the beauty of the original. The critics would not forgive Blitzstein, Stein, and company for musicalizing it, though, and audiences were not ready for a musical of such tragic solemnity. *Juno* awaits a new staging that manages

○ ○ ○ ○ ○

to scale down the original without slighting the full-bodied emotional power of Blitzstein's contribution.

Mack and Mabel (Majestic; Oct. 6, '74, 66), a less distinguished work than *Juno* but a heartbreaker nonetheless, begins with Mack Sennett (played by Robert Preston), the silent-screen director, now in his late fifties and out of place in the sound era, returning to the soundstage of his old studio. Mack, at the end of his career, resents the takeover of the industry by people who know nothing about making movies, and he begins to recall how it all began for him, flashing back to 1911 and his first studio in Brooklyn. One day, Mabel Normand arrives, delivering a sandwich from a nearby deli, and Mack immediately sees something funny in her. Mack takes Mabel and company to California, and he and Mabel become lovers, although he warns her he's no romantic and "won't send roses." Problems begin when Mabel is given a script containing a serious acting part for her; tired of Mack's not taking her seriously, she walks out, leaving Sennett to dream up the Bathing Beauties to take her place. When Mack finally asks Mabel to come back, it is too late; she is already driving away her blues with "angel dust," and what's left of her career is totally destroyed by her apparent involvement in the mysterious murder of director William Desmond Taylor. The musical ends back in 1938 on the soundstage: Mack tells us he made one final movie with Mabel, but that it was never released; Mabel has since died. When she was alive, he tells us, he was never able to tell her face-to-face what he felt for her. Mack declares, "I love you, Mabel Normand," then leaves his studio forever.

Mack and Mabel produced another of those misleading cast recordings that cause the listener to believe that the show must have been wonderful. And indeed, the idea for the show and the team assembled for it make it difficult to believe that it failed. The show began when producer Edwin Lester and writer Leonard Spigelgass approached Jerry Herman with an idea for a musical about Sennett and Normand. Herman worked with Spigelgass for a year on it, then Michael Stewart came in as librettist (Spigelgass ultimately received a "based on an idea by" credit). David Merrick became the producer, and to complete his *Hello, Dolly!* team, he hired Gower Champion to direct (Merrick, Stewart, and Champion had also done *Carnival* together).

There was a senseless to-do over the casting of Mabel. Penny Fuller was first announced, then Marcia Rodd was hired. Rodd was fired by Champion when he saw a young singer named Kelly Garrett in a show called *Words and Music*. Champion hired and then fired Garrett, announcing to the press that she couldn't act, and the role went to Bernadette Peters. With her wistful, kewpie-doll face and established talent, Peters was the obvious choice all along; why Champion went through three other women remains a mystery. *Mack and Mabel* received generally good reviews in San Diego, Los Angeles, and St. Louis, then bombed in Washington, where it played just prior to Broadway. It opened to mostly negative reviews in New York and shut down after only two months, losing all of its $800,000 investment. There were Tony nominations for the show, Stewart, Champion, designers Robin Wagner (who set the entire show in a movie studio environment) and Patricia Zipprodt, Peters, and Preston, but somehow Herman's score was overlooked, causing Stewart to pay for an ad in *Variety*, an open letter expressing his outrage at the omission.

Mack and Mabel was sent out on tour two years later, with David Cryer, Lucie Arnaz, and Tommy Tune, strangely enough, in the role that Lisa Kirk had played on Broadway. The book was revised, and the show was now directed and choreographed by Ron Field. (Merrick had attempted to replace Champion with Field in Washington, but Stewart had threatened to remove his book if Merrick did so.) This production was followed by several stock productions in America and England, and the show again received attention in 1984 when ice dancers Torvill and Dean won a gold medal in the Olympics while dancing to the *Mack and Mabel* overture. In 1988, there was a concert version in London, followed by a major revival at the Paper Mill Playhouse in New Jersey. This production used the new ending written for the tour, in which Mack made the story end the way it would have ended "if only life had been a movie," with a big Keystone Kops wedding for Mack and Mabel. This was unsatisfying and untrue to what preceded it, and far less touching than the original ending. The Paper Mill production was to have been the basis for a Broadway revival starring George Hearn and Ellen Foley and opening at the Neil Simon Theatre in the fall of 1988. But the money to produce it was not forthcoming.

It is unlikely that *Mack and Mabel*, which had failed with Merrick, Champion, Peters, and Preston, would have succeeded this time either. Herman's second consecutive flop, it remains his favorite show, but *Mack and Mabel* continues to be a heartbreaker for those who produce it and those who want to love it. It contains one of the best-liked flop scores ever, with such goodies as Mack's opening "Movies Were Movies," and

○ ○ ○ ○ ○

Most fans of musicals love the score of Mack and Mabel. *Above left photo: James Mitchell and Bernadette Peters. Photo below: Robert Preston, Christopher Murney, Peters, and Lisa Kirk.*

"Look What Happened to Mabel" and "Time Heals Everything" for Mabel. In the original, Preston and Peters were marvelous, and Champion moved his production out into the house, having Mack fly out over the audience on a giant crane during "I Want to Make the World Laugh," and girls, on the edge of the proscenium, slide down an enormous corkscrew slide from high in the flies.

But there were several problems. It's virtually impossible to do silent slapstick comedy onstage; Champion publicly expressed frustration at not being able to capture the kinetic style and elaborate mechanical gags of Sennett's films. And *Mack and Mabel* suffers from book trouble. The series of conflicts that keep separating Mack and Mabel are manufactured to keep the plot going and never ring true; they are standard, artificial musical-comedy problems, rather than those of real life. It was also hard to believe that Mabel, the Lucille Ball of her generation, was unhappy being a comic and yearned to play serious parts. For all its invention, Champion's production was not quite as imaginative as his best work, and some audience members found the second act a downer. Because the score is delightful, though, people will continue to want to try *Mack and Mabel*. But they are likely to find that for all its good qualities, it doesn't quite satisfy.

Unlike *Mack and Mabel*, our next heartbreaker may never be staged again. In the mid-seventies, Universal Pictures shelved a screenplay by Fay Kanin called *This Must Be the Place*. Ten years later, Kanin fashioned her screenplay into the book for **Grind** (Mark Hellinger; Apr. 16, '85; 79). *Grind* was set in Chicago in 1933 and took place for the most part in Harry Earle's Burlesque Theatre, where black and white acts are strictly segregated, both on and off stage. Star comic Gus, whose eyesight is going, keeps losing his stooges, so he picks up a derelict named Doyle in the alley outside the theatre and makes him his new assistant. Doyle is a former I.R.A. terrorist haunted by memories of the wife and son who died when a train on which they were traveling was blown up by a bomb he himself devised. The company's star stripper, Satin, née Letitia, who is attempting to shed her grim ghetto background the way she sheds her clothes onstage, rejects the advances of happy-go-lucky comic Leroy. Doyle helps Leroy and Satin bring Satin's little brother a bicycle for his birthday, but the sight of white Doyle mingling with blacks Leroy and Satin causes punks in the street to destroy the gift. Doyle tries to help Gus cover up his sight problem, but it's too late, and Gus takes his life.

○ ○ ○ ○ ○

Leroy shows Satin his real feelings for her, but after finding Doyle in Satin's room, he humiliates her on stage and attacks Doyle. Toughs invade the theatre and storm the stage because of the relationship between Doyle and Satin. Leroy finally realizes the need to commit himself to something, and he helps Doyle fight off the toughs, as Harry Earle's company— black and white—unites against the common enemy.

The musical's title, like those of *Follies* and *Company*, has multiple meanings: there is the grind of show after show at Harry Earle's; the bumps and grinds of Satin and the girls; Doyle's grinding of elements to make the bomb that killed his family; and the grinding down of people's spirit by the Depression. Harold Prince directed and was one of the many producers of *Grind*; like most of his musicals, *Grind* was a serious show with a social conscious. It was also his third consecutive flop.

When first announced, *Grind* was called *A Century of Progress*, and Debbie Allen and Kevin Kline were mentioned for the roles of Satin and Doyle. Larry Grossman, whose last show, *A Doll's Life*, had been directed by Prince, wrote the music for what was to be his fourth consecutive Broadway flop, while Ellen Fitzhugh made her Broadway debut with the lyrics. *Grind* tried out in Baltimore, where the reviews were negative, and arrived on Broadway at the end of one of the worst musical seasons ever. The New York reviews were no better, but the show received seven Tony Award nominations; Leilani Jones won for her Satin, and Florence Klotz took home an award for her costumes. The nominations kept the show open, but *Grind* closed shortly after the awards were distributed, losing $4.75 million.

The show's failure was later blamed by Prince and others on the compromises they made after having cast a star, Ben Vereen, as Leroy. And it is true that Vereen's role was larger than it should have been and that he was given unnecessary songs and dances (one, "New Man," staged by Bob Fosse) that took up time which could have been spent developing the other characters. But Vereen was not the main problem. *Grind* was a show so loaded with characters, ideas, themes, and plots that it tended to bewilder and turn off a first-time viewer. It tried to do too much, and there were too many diverse elements (the romantic triangle which wasn't developed until well into Act Two, the burlesque-house-as-metaphor-for-America, the I.R.A. flashbacks, the encroaching blindness of Gus, the onstage numbers, the themes of racial prejudice and violence) that did not easily fit together. Some of these elements, such as the scenes in Doyle's memory, had been more easily developed in Kanin's screenplay.

○ ○ ○ ○ ○

While the show was clearly about prejudice and violence, its statement on the subject—that we must put aside our own feelings and unite against common foes—was not made clear until the very end.

The only way this sprawling material might have been harnessed was with the kind of overriding concept Prince used in *Cabaret*. Perhaps if the whole evening had been presented as a burlesque-house show, with the plot told as acts in the show, or perhaps if the story could have been told through the framework of the Century of Progress Exposition taking place in Chicago at the time (the show's original title indicates that this was considered), Prince might have been able to pull all the strands of *Grind* together. Twice during the evening—the opening number and the finale of Act One—Prince used the "limbo" area he had used in *Cabaret*, where what the audience is watching is taking place in no real location and the stage is used for metaphorical purposes. At the end of the first act, in order to make everyone forget the ugliness of the bicycle destruction scene, Leroy turns Doyle and Satin's brother into performers in his "act," and the whole company is swept up in it, with only Satin remaining in the real world. But because the "limbo" sequences were not carried through the entire evening, their appearance was confusing; Prince never found a way to impose a unifying device on *Grind*.

But *Grind* is the show that makes us ask the question: How can such a chaotic mess be so fascinating and haunting? In spite of all its problems, *Grind* was a rich evening, one which became more and more riveting with repeated viewings. It was an uncompromising show that attempted to say something; unfortunately, because of all that was going on, sympathy for and understanding of the characters was only possible with second or third viewings. Some of Lester Wilson's musical staging, especially Satin's "A Sweet Thing Like Me," was very effective, and Clarke Dunham's three-level, three-ton revolving set was staggering, although not fully utilized in the staging. The image of Harry Earle's house divided against itself was one of the more memorable in musicals of the eighties.

Both the story and score were deliberately nerve-jangling and harsh; *Grind* was a show about violence, and it was frequently ugly and unpleasant. So *Grind* was not the kind of musical audiences took to their hearts. Many dismissed the score, which was far more interesting than it was given credit for. The most acclaimed number, the gospel song "These Eyes of Mine," performed at Gus's funeral, was actually the least interesting and relevant. The better things included Satin's aforementioned "A Sweet Thing Like Me" and "All Things to One Man," Doyle's haunting Irish

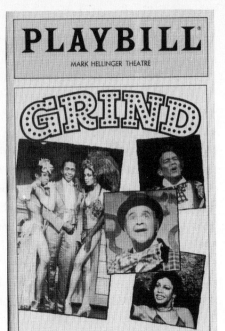

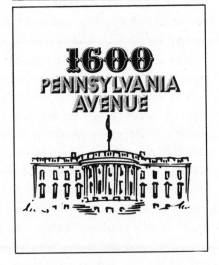

Grind *and* 1600 Pennsylvania Avenue *may never be staged again, but Rags will.*

solos, and a trio for Doyle, Satin, and Gus. Because of its size and its problems, it is unlikely that *Grind* will ever be given a second chance.

Audiences tended to dislike *Grind;* it made them nervous and was not easy to assimilate. They tended to like **Rags** (Mark Hellinger; Aug. 21, '86; 4), however, probably because for all its muddle, there was lovely music and a story that, while it may not have worked, was still dealing with issues that couldn't help but be moving.

As *Rags* begins, Rebecca Hershkowitz, a refugee from the pogroms in Russia, arrives on Ellis Island in 1910, seeking her husband, Nathan, who journeyed to America a couple of years earlier and was supposed to meet Rebecca upon her arrival in America. She and her son, David, are befriended by a fellow immigrant, Bella, and the pair are taken in by Bella's relatives. Rebecca gets a job in a sweatshop, where she clashes with Saul, a union organizer, because she won't join the union and jeopardize her job. In the next few weeks, however, Saul encourages Rebecca and David to learn English, takes them to the Yiddish theatre, and exposes them to new ideas; soon, Saul and Rebecca are drawn to each other. David tries to follow Saul's principles and stands up to a local graft collector; he is beaten. Rebecca, horrified to see the violence of Russia reappearing in America, turns on Saul, just as Nathan finally arrives. The former Nathan Hershkowitz has transformed himself into "Nat Harris," a functionary of the Tammany Hall machine looking to move uptown and become a ward leader. He is elected, but after Bella is killed in a fire at the shop where Rebecca urged her to work, Rebecca leads a rebellion at her shop and rejects Nathan and his get-ahead, assimilationist values. As the curtain falls, Rebecca and her son acknowledge that they are, for better or worse, a part of America.

Rags, with a book by Joseph Stein and music by Charles Strouse, suffered from a combination of faulty producing and unfortunate circumstances. It was first seen in workshop at Theatre 890 in 1984; directed by its lyricist, Stephen Schwartz, this version had no stars and no one central character. Two years later, it went into production as a full-scale Broadway show. Joan Micklin Silver, who had written and directed the film *Hester Street,* also about Jewish immigrants on the Lower East Side, was hired to direct but was dismissed about three weeks into rehearsal. Schwartz and Strouse took over unofficially, and *Rags* opened in Boston with no director listed in the Playbill. To add to the trouble, Teresa Stratas, the tempestuous, cancellation-prone opera diva who had been

hired to make her Broadway debut as Rebecca, missed a week of performances in Boston, including the opening, giving *Rags* the distinction of
being perhaps the only show to be reviewed on the road with a standby
(Christine Andreas) in the lead. Stratas was worth waiting for, however;
the five-foot powerhouse gave a luminous star performance and sang
incomparably in what is likely to remain her only Broadway musical.

Near the end of the tryout, Gene Saks agreed to take over the direction,
and Ron Field replaced Ken Rinker as choreographer. Saks had directed
the Robert Preston vehicle *The Prince of Grand Street*, which was set in the
same time, place, and milieu, and *Rags's* spoof of Yiddish theatre was
reminiscent of those in the earlier musical. Meanwhile, Jay Presson Allen
did uncredited book rewrites.

The New York reviews were largely negative, with scattered praise for
the score and Stratas. It was late August, and *Rags* had only a small
advance sale. After the third official performance, a Saturday matinee,
the cast marched down Broadway from the Hellinger Theatre to Duffy
Square in an attempt to halt the closing, announced for that night. But
the fourth performance was the last; the closing announcements stated
that the show would reopen in a few weeks, but this was no more than
the usual wishful thinking. *Rags* lost $5.5 million.

In a sense, *Rags* can be seen as the sequel to another Joseph Stein
musical, *Fiddler on the Roof*, showing what happened to the immigrants
when they arrived in America. But unlike *Fiddler*, *Rags* was an original,
not based on any source material, and therein lay the problem. Stein's
book was a muddle, with too many characters and subplots that couldn't
be fully developed. Bella was given the most dramatic number of the
evening, the title song, but her character was merely sketched in and not
strong enough to merit such an outburst. Rebecca was never given a
personality or much individuality; she was the symbol of all immigrant
women rather than a character. And Rebecca's husband Nathan, particularly as played by Larry Kert, was made unsympathetic and unlikable.
Nathan might have been made a sweet dupe drawn into Tammany Hall
through a desire to better his family; instead, he was a heavy, and the
audience was not happy when he turned up at the end of Act One.
Indeed, *Rags* dealt almost exclusively with the dark side of the immigrant
experience; if it was only trying to tell the truth, that truth allowed for
very few moments of joy.

There were other flaws as well. The two white-suited Americans who
sang the opening number, "Greenhorns," were set up as ironic commen-

○ ○ ○ ○ ○

tators at the beginning but didn't appear again until the finale. The final sequence, in which Rebecca leads the sweatshop rebellion, was awkwardly motivated, abrupt, and hard to believe. And Beni Montresor's spare skeletal sets were a mistake; *Rags* would have benefited from realistic scenery. The show's biggest problem may simply have been the lack of a strong directorial hand from the start. Saks clarified certain aspects of the show without really solving any of the problems; Strouse later said, "He cleaned up the loose ends of the plot, but in cutting down and explaining things, he may have taken away some of the show's charm."

Rags called into question the ability of Broadway pros like Stein, Schwartz, and Strouse to put together a successful show. Surely there was a wonderful musical in the story of immigrants taking their first steps in America, but these talents were unable to find it or bring it out clearly. It was Strouse's fifth consecutive flop, and Stein's and Schwartz's most recent musicals had also been flops. But *Rags* has had several productions since its Broadway demise, and that's because, for all its problems, it is hard to dismiss. Stein's book does at least contain some effective scenes and good moments. And *Rags* features Strouse's most ambitious score, most of which is quite wonderful. Rebecca has the gorgeous ballad "Blame It on the Summer Night" and the moving "Children of the Wind," the title song is stunning, and there is impressive use made of extended musical sequences, such as the one in which Rebecca and David learn from Saul. Revisions, some of which restore material from the tryout, have been made for the post-Broadway productions of *Rags,* and one hopes that further work will be done. Even as it is, however, *Rags* may very well satisfy audiences in stock and regional productions. It's one of the rare flops that one can find a million things wrong with, yet still enjoy.

In 1972, Alan Jay Lerner, depressed by the Nixon landslide, conceived of and began work on "a musical about the first hundred years of the White House and other attempts to take it away from us." Lerner had known Leonard Bernstein from his days at Harvard and had wanted to work with him for years, so he invited Bernstein to join him on the project. Bernstein had not had a musical on Broadway since *West Side Story,* although in the interval he had worked on a musical version of Thornton Wilder's *The Skin of Our Teeth* with Betty Comden, Adolph Green, and Jerome Robbins; a musical based on Brecht's *The Exception and the Rule* with Robbins, Stephen Sondheim, and John Guare; and a theatre

○ ○ ○ ○ ○

piece called *Mass*, which had debuted in 1971. Bernstein had only four Broadway shows to his credit, three triumphs—*West Side Story*, *On the Town* and *Wonderful Town*—and the flop *Candide*, which had turned into a hit around the time he joined Lerner's project. Bernstein hoped his new show could "rescue the word *patriotism* from the bigot," and saw it as being about "a passionate love of country."

Saint Subber was the original producer and worked on it for two years. Subber later said, "I loathed it. I tried desperately to get everyone to abandon it. After many fights, I left the production." The show, by now known as **1600 Pennsylvania Avenue** (Mark Hellinger; May 4, '76; 7), was taken up by Roger L. Stevens and Robert Whitehead. It was generally felt that major work was still required, but when the Coca-Cola Company offered to supply the entire cost of the production (which was ultimately $1.2 million), *1600* was on.

One of the main reasons why Coca-Cola footed the bill was so that the show could open in time to coincide with the nation's bicentennial. Although *1600* had not originally been conceived as a bicentennial tribute, it became one; but it was a strange bicentennial tribute, one sharply critical of many White House residents. Hired to play all the presidents from George Washington to Theodore Roosevelt was Ken Howard, who had already played Thomas Jefferson in *1776*, and Patricia Routledge was cast as all the first ladies.

1600 Pennsylvania Avenue premiered in Philadelphia to terrible reviews. Jerome Robbins and Mike Nichols came to Philadelphia and left as quickly as they arrived when the bloodbath began. Director Frank Corsaro, who later said he loved the score but always felt the book had severe problems, asked to be released, and choreographer Donald McKayle went along with him. They were replaced by the team of Gilbert Moses, who had been fired as director of *The Wiz*, and George Faison, that show's choreographer. Corsaro later said, "[Lerner and Bernstein] were terribly intimidating, and they acted accordingly. They were the power. When decisions should have been made by other people, the last word always fell to them." When Moses and Faison came in, Lerner and Bernstein found themselves locked out of rehearsals. Set and costume designer Tony Walton removed his name, and most of his work was replaced by others. The ominously titled song "They Should Have Stayed Another Week in Philadelphia," which applied a theatrical metaphor to the writing of the Constitution and contained a lyric about "fifty-six coauthors" fixing the show, was quickly cut.

○ ○ ○ ○ ○

Bernstein wanted the show closed in Philadelphia, but Lerner wouldn't allow it, and it went on to Washington, then to New York, where it was billed as "a musical about the problems of housekeeping." Coca-Cola, which had title-page program credit out of town, removed its name from the production. The New York reviews were unanimous pans, and Bernstein refused to allow the score to be recorded. The reason for this became evident when pieces of his 1600 music turned up in such subsequent works as *Songfest, A Quiet Place,* and *Slava! (A Political Overture).* One song, "Take Care of This House," snuck out and managed to get performed with some frequency.

1600 Pennsylvania Avenue had begun with the metaphor of the United States as a play always in rehearsal, and to implement the metaphor, the show, at least when it opened in Philadelphia, was a play within a play, with a company of actors playing roles and commenting on them throughout the play. In the original version, the "actor" playing the presidents and the "actor" playing Lud, the black White House servant, debated in between the scenes about the treatment of blacks through the years. Curiously, most of this was jettisoned when the two black directors succeeded the original white director; Moses and Faison set out to clarify the show and make it more entertaining. By the time it opened on Broadway, *1600 Pennsylvania Avenue* began with the cast announcing that they were about to present the story of the first hundred years of the White House; but beyond that opening and the first song, "Rehearse," little remained of the play-within-a-play concept. The audience was treated to a pageant of presidents and first ladies, set against the story of Lud and Seena, the downstairs servants. At the beginning, Abigail Adams comes upon the boy Lud, a runaway slave, and as they travel in a coach, she tells him how George Washington decided upon the site for the capital. She arrives in Washington, D.C., to become the first tenant of the White House and tells Lud to "Take Care of This House." In rapid succession, Jefferson encourages the education of the blacks below stairs, having fathered a daughter, Seena, by a black slave; the British march on Washington and burn the White House down; it is rebuilt, and Lud and Seena, now grown, are married; Eliza and James Monroe argue over the slave trading just outside their windows; the effete Buchanan dismisses threats of a civil war; and Lincoln is elected and South Carolina secedes from the Union as Act One ends. Act Two opens with the blacks reenacting the impeachment proceedings against Johnson, then celebrating the birth of Seena and Lud's baby into freedom. Garfield is assassinated; Arthur

○ ○ ○ ○ ○

tries to put a stop to the corruption around him; McKinley is shot; Theodore Roosevelt takes over; and all resolve to keep "rehearsing" until they get it right, as the curtain falls.

1600 began with a practically impossible concept. By definition episodic, the show moved swiftly from one president to the next, and there was no way of developing a story or doing more than sketching in a personality or character trait for each tenant. It was a show about a house, about democracy itself, rather than about people, and it is questionable if this idea could ever have been brought off successfully. The original play-within-a-play concept was ponderous, but when the actors-playing-roles idea and the debates about the treatment of blacks were dropped, little remained. The show that opened on Broadway was clearer, but far less rich, and played like a concert, with brief scenes in between the abundant music. The score became the whole show, and there was little surrounding the songs to support or explain them.

If it started with a difficult concept, 1600 was badly damaged in production by a lack of strong directors and producers. Stevens and White-head never exercised sufficient authority and made a serious mistake in turning the show over to relatively inexperienced hands who seem to have been selected because another, very different black musical in which they had been involved had been a hit (and was still running when 1600 opened).

It was understandable that the show was virtually turned over to the score by the time it opened, however, for 1600 contains the greatest score in post-war Broadway history that ever went unrecorded. It was Bernstein's richest and most complex work for Broadway, and it compares favorably with those he composed for *West Side Story* and *Candide*. There was enough strong material for two shows, and much that was good (e.g. Lud and Seena's searing duet "This Time" and the finale, "Make Us Proud") was left on the road. The highlights of the final version include "On Ten Square Miles by the Potomac River," Little Lud's "If I Was a Dove," "Take Care of This House," grown-up Lud's "Seena," and "The President Jefferson Sunday Luncheon Party March." There is a dazzling, scene-long duet for the Monroes in which they debate the treatment of blacks, and a lengthy series of numbers for the British when they take over the White House. Routledge, who was again marvelous in yet another flop, performed one of the most brilliant and least known showstoppers in musical-theatre history, "Duet for One (The First Lady of the Land)," a tour de force in which, during the Hayes inauguration, she alternated between

○ ○ ○ ○ ○

playing the departing Julia Grant and the arriving Lucy Hayes by a flip of her wig and a change in voice.

The critics all hated the show's concept, and the problems built into it probably doomed the show from the start. But that concept was executed with a decent amount of wit and variety. If there was too much of the bleeding-heart liberal in the writing, *1600* was not pretentious or preachy. Lerner provided numerous intricate and clever lyrics, and several of the scenes were quite affecting. The final version that played on Broadway was less effective than the original one, though, and anyone attempting *1600* again would need to examine the prerehearsal script as well as all the alterations made on the road. It is entirely possible that *1600* will never be made to work on the stage, but the over two-hour score cries out for a concert performance and recording. The Bernstein–Lerner score for *1600 Pennsylvania Avenue* should not be allowed to remain lost to future generations of musical theatre lovers.

For all their glorious qualities, none of the six shows above qualifies as a complete success. Our final group, however, approaches perfection. The first three are extremely ambitious projects which, though flawed, were vastly underrated when first presented; the other three are gems, flops only because of the length of their runs.

Can any other Broadway musical boast a star whose program bio stated that, "By the time she was eight, she was the favorite ritual singer of the sun-worshipping Andes Mountain Indians"? **Flahooley** (Broadhurst; May 14, '51; 40) starred Peruvian singer Yma Sumac in her only Broadway role, and Sumac's appearance in *Flahooley* was but one of the many bizarre things about the show.

In Capsulanti, U.S.A., "the nation's biggest toycoon," B.G. Bigelow, runs B.G. Bigelow, Inc., the greatest toy factory in the world. Sylvester, a designer of puppets at the factory, is in love with his model, Sandy, who can hear the puppets (played by the Bil Baird Marionettes) talk. Just as Sylvester is about to present his special Christmas puppet to a board meeting, the meeting is interrupted by a delegation from Arabia. It seems that they have run out of oil in Arabia, and the lamp they rub for everything is no longer working. They ask Bigelow to fix the lamp so that it can again produce a genie, and because Bigelow is attracted to one of the Arabian contingent, Princess Najala (Sumac), he accepts the challenge.

○ ○ ○ ○ ○

Sylvester then introduces his Christmas special, Flahooley, a doll that doesn't cry or wet but laughs when shaken. Bigelow is delighted and gives Sylvester the lamp for his next assignment. Sylvester works on the lamp, and when he rubs it with Flahooley's hand, a genie appears. Meanwhile, Bigelow's chief competitor has put out a doll identical to Flahooley and selling at a lower price. Sylvester, hoping to make enough money to marry Sandy, wishes every child could have a Flahooley, and the genie grants his wish. Unfortunately, the genie produces so many Flahooleys that the market is flooded: the warehouse collapses, prices lower, profits disappear, the factory shuts, and Flahooleys are given away in the street for free.

Act Two begins with a public burning of Flahooleys. The genie responsible for all the chaos refuses to stop making the dolls because he doesn't want to return to the cramped quarters of the lamp. The genie disappears, and a nationwide search is on, with Sandy ultimately tracking him down in New York. At the end, the genie helps Sylvester and Sandy get married, then decides to stay in New York to be a fifty-week-a-year Santa Claus and give things away, while Bigelow and Najala plan an Arabian honeymoon.

Flahooley was originally called *Toyland*, and Harold Arlen, then Burton Lane was announced to write the music. Ultimately, E.Y. Harburg and Fred Saidy, who had already collaborated on *Finian's Rainbow* and *Bloomer Girl* and would later write *Jamaica* together, wrote the book, directed, and coproduced with Cheryl Crawford, while Sammy Fain wrote the music and Harburg the lyrics. With typical whimsy, Harburg later said that they chose the title *Flahooley* because "it's the only name we could think of that you can't spell backwards." The numbers for La Sumac, whose voice ranged "from low contralto to A above high C," were specially composed for her by her husband, Moises Vivanco; on the road, Sumac tried to sing one song by Harburg and Fain but couldn't quite wrap her tongue around the lyrics. If Flahooley couldn't be spelled backwards, rumors persisted that Sumac was from Brooklyn and that her real name was Amy Camus, "Yma Sumac" spelled backwards. Sumac was largely peripheral to the plot, though, and the show's real leading lady was Barbara Cook in her first Broadway appearance.

In New Haven, *Flahooley* received rave reviews, although the *Variety* critic realized that there could be trouble ahead: "The show can materialize as an exceedingly novel, appealing tune-and-dance concoction, or as an exceptionally beautiful flop." The reviews in Philadelphia were good, too,

○ ○ ○ ○ ○

Blow out the trumpets for Flahooley. Above, the Playbill and the flyer for a Flahooley revision known as Jollyanna. Below, Ernest Truex (holding doll) proudly presents B. G. Bigelow, Inc.'s, newest product, flanked by Jerome Courtland and Barbara Cook.

but while there, Harburg and Saidy allowed Daniel Mann, who would direct *Paint Your Wagon* for Crawford six months later, to help with the staging. In New York, three critics approved, but five, including Atkinson in the *Times*, did not. The Korean War was on, and *Flahooley*, with its satirical jabs at capitalism and the American Way, found itself accused of being anti-American. In the *Daily Mirror*, critic Robert Coleman wrote, "The materials are there for a delightful, captivating fantasy, but, alas, they have been subordinated to lengthy passages critical of our politics, economics and ethics . . . One first-nighter was overheard to say, 'With the United States at war, this is hardly the time to condemn a production system that has given us an amazingly high standard of living and, at the same time, managed to arm us and our allies.' . . . We echo these sentiments."

Flahooley's chances of success were destroyed by such sentiments, and it closed after five weeks, although Capitol Records, with whom Sumac had a contract, recorded the score. One year later, Edwin Lester produced a revised version of the show, called *Jollyanna*, at his San Francisco and Los Angeles Civic Light Operas. New songs were added with music by William Friml (Rudolf's son) and Burton Lane, and the new version jettisoned most of the political connotations and social significance, adding a love triangle between Sylvester, Sandy (renamed Penny), and a new character, Diana, Bigelow's secretary. Bobby Clark played Bigelow, and Mitzi Gaynor was Penny. *Jollyanna* was to go on to Broadway, but it received only mixed reviews and did not.

One of the most wildly imaginative musicals Broadway has ever seen, *Flahooley*, like the Harburg–Saidy *Finian's Rainbow*, was a fantasy with underlying contemporary social satire. The targets this time were conformity and big business, and the Flahooley burnings and genie hunts were comments on the tactics of Senator McCarthy. But *Flahooley* was never solemn or preachy, and it contains a fascinating score. Fain wrote his best Broadway tunes for the show, and Harburg contributed his customary marvelous lyrics to such numbers as the brilliant opening, "You Too Can Be a Puppet," "Here's to Your Illusions," "The World Is Your Balloon," and "The Springtime Cometh." The Baird Puppets were a great plus in the Broadway production, as were Cook and Ernest Truex as Bigelow. It was all perhaps too heady a combination for Broadway audiences, who chose instead to attend such sensible fare as *The King and I, South Pacific*, and *Kiss Me, Kate*, all playing on the same block as *Flahooley*.

○ ○ ○ ○ ○

But *Flahooley* was a genuine original, and a company with a little daring and a puppeteer at its disposal should strongly consider reviving it.

The musical **Mata Hari** (Washington, D.C.; Nov. 17, '67; closed on the road) was also an original, using the real-life figure of Margaretha Gertruida Zelle, better known as Mata Hari, as the focal point of its story. During World War I, at French Military Intelligence, Captain LaFarge is disturbed that the French are losing the war and that the Germans always seem to know where and when the French will next attack. He is convinced that dancer Mata Hari is a spy for the Germans and takes charge of an investigation. Mata insists that she loves France, and LaFarge arranges to pay Mata two million francs to spy for the French, although he still believes she is an agent of the Germans. He attempts to trick her into revealing her real allegiance, but she passes his test, and they become lovers. Her first mission for the French seems to be a great success, but LaFarge, through a ruse he devised, decides that Mata is a German agent. Mata is executed by a firing squad, although her true allegiance is deliberately left ambiguous at the end.

But this plot was not really what *Mata Hari*'s authors were writing about. A preface to the script states, "Whether Mata Hari works for the Germans or not is only the superficial level of concern. It is the fact that she challenges morality which causes LaFarge to cast her in the role of enemy, and ultimately to destroy her." LaFarge's conventional, middle-class existence, with a wife and child at home, gradually crumbles as he becomes swept up in Mata's world of intrigue and mystery, and he is ultimately the one destroyed at the end.

Mata Hari was above all an antiwar musical, however, and LaFarge's gradual seduction and breakdown were interwoven with scenes involving a character identified as the Young Soldier. The show began with a prologue in which the Young Soldier lamented in song that "This Is Not a Very Nice War." Thereafter, the character turned up in between the Mata Hari–LaFarge scenes in a manner reminiscent of the M.C.'s appearances in *Cabaret*. The Young Soldier looked on as a German vendor was attacked in the street and two vaudevillians sang a recruiting song; his song "Maman," in which he described to his mother how it felt to kill for the first time, was intercut with scenes of Mata's training and the beginning of her flirtation with LaFarge; the Soldier was seen in a wheelchair on the sidelines in a scene in which LaFarge's wife discussed Mata's

○ ○ ○ ○ ○

MATA HARI

Playbill for the National Theatre in Washington D.C.—the only theatre Mata Hari ever played.

trial with her friends; and after Mata's execution, the show ended with the people of France singing "La Marseillaise," the Young Soldier, now a patriotic veteran, among them.

One of the most ambitious musicals of the sixties, *Mata Hari* was beset with production problems. Originally called *Facade*, it had a book by Jerome Coopersmith, who had written *Baker Street* and contributed material to *The Apple Tree*, music by first-time composer Edward Thomas, and lyrics by Martin Charnin. Producer David Merrick assembled a classy production team, with Jo Mielziner providing scenery and lighting, Irene Sharaff the costumes, Jack Cole the choreography, and Robert Russell Bennett the orchestrations. But Merrick miscalculated when he hired Vincente Minnelli, the celebrated film director who had not directed on Broadway since *Very Warm for May* in 1939, to stage the show. Merrick also hired two leads, the world-class beauty from Vienna, Marisa Mell, and Pernell Roberts, who did not sing well and could not begin to do justice to the score.

Mata Hari began its tryout at the National Theatre in Washington, D.C., with a benefit performance—for the Women's National Democratic Club—that became legendary. With Lynda Byrd Johnson in attendance, the show ran well past midnight, scenery collapsed, and the virtually nude Mell was accidentally spotlighted during a costume change. To cap the evening, Mell, after being executed by a firing squad, was seen scratching her nose; there was uproarious laughter and no curtain call. Merrick, who had the troubled *How Now, Dow Jones* and *The Happy Time* on the road at the same time, decided that *Mata Hari* was the least fixable of his three new musicals, and he shut it down, canceling the Philadelphia engagement and the scheduled January 13, 1968, opening at the Alvin Theatre. *Mata Hari* lost $700,000. One year later, a revised version of the show called *Ballad for a Firing Squad* opened off-Broadway at the Theatre de Lys, directed by Charnin and produced by Thomas. The score was much better sung, but reviews were mixed and the revision lasted only seven performances. A florid, operetta-like musical, *Mata Hari* demanded size and opulence; it had to be big and simply did not lend itself to a scaled-down production.

Minnelli seems to have been the main problem with the first production, and perhaps if Merrick had allowed the show to continue with another director, *Mata Hari* might have stood a chance. But even with a different director and stronger leads, it was very tricky material. Serious, enigmatic, and melodramatic, it was distinctly out of step with the musicals of its

∘ ∘ ∘ ∘ ∘

period, and unlike the similarly daring *Cabaret*, it harked back to twenties musicals in its lush music and decor. But with the exception of the heavy-handed scenes inolving LaFarge's family, *Mata Hari's* book is strong and its score striking; it ranks as the most underrated musical of the sixties.

Candide (Martin Beck; Dec. 1, '56; 73) is the only musical to flop on Broadway and later come back a hit and enter the standard repertoire. But it came back with a different book and staging and has found its steadiest success in opera houses rather than in theatres.

Musicalizing Voltaire's 1763 novel was Lillian Hellman's idea, and she wrote her only musical book for it. The original lyricist was John Latouche, who died before the show opened. Hellman, Leonard Bernstein, and Dorothy Parker contributed lyrics before Richard Wilbur took over. The music was composed by Bernstein almost simultaneously with his *West Side Story* score, and Tyrone Guthrie, who had done operas but not musicals, was hired to direct.

Billed as a "comic operetta," *Candide* received mixed reviews on its Boston tryout. Carmen Mathews, who had fifth billing in the role of the Contessa, was written out in Boston, but the show was still not destined to be a hit, perhaps because it still had floperetta queen Irra Petina playing the Old Lady, her best Broadway performance. The New York reviews were among the most varied in history, ranging from raves (including Atkinson in the *Times*) to pans (Kerr in the *Herald Tribune*). *Candide* quickly proved too special for general audiences and lasted just over two months.

But because a recording preserved what is unquestionably one of the theatre's greatest scores, *Candide* was far from dead after its Broadway production. First, there was the London production in 1959, with Michael Stewart revising Hellman's book, and Robert Lewis, who was to have done the Broadway production, directing. It too was a flop. A touring version with a new book, based on Hellman's, by Sheldon Patinkin, who also directed, went out in 1971. In 1973, Harold Prince brought *Candide* back in triumph, with a new book by Hugh Wheeler, some new lyrics by Stephen Sondheim (Wheeler and Sondheim had written Prince's *A Little Night Music* earlier the same year), and an environmental staging by Prince performed by a young cast as a madcap romp. With Voltaire himself narrating (as played by Lewis J. Stadlen, who also played Dr. Pangloss), the new *Candide* had its premiere at the Chelsea Theatre Center in Brooklyn, then moved to the Broadway Theatre for a run of 740 performances. In spite of rave reviews and a long run, however, the new

○ ○ ○ ○ ○

Candide was not a financial smash owing to the reduced seating capacity necessitated by the environmental staging and the musicians' union demand that the show employ a specific number of musicians even though they were not all needed.

Prince again directed Hugh Wheeler's book when *Candide* had its opera-house premiere in 1982 at the New York City Opera. No longer staged environmentally, the opera house version restored music that had been cut for the Brooklyn/Broadway version and reinforced the overall operatic sweep of the score, which had been severely diminished by the small orchestra and voices of the environmental production. In 1988, a better version, with Wheeler's book somewhat rewritten and direction by Jonathan Miller, was premiered by the Scottish Opera. From its Boston tryout to its most recent opera-house stagings, there have been countless changes, restorations, deletions, and additions to the *Candide* score which by now probably only John Mauceri, who assembled the opera-house versions, could unravel.

As stated, Bernstein's score is above reproach, and the lyrics, whether by Latouche, Wilbur, Sondheim, Bernstein, or anyone else, are superb. The blame for the failure of the original—which also boasted sumptuous decor—has been placed squarely on Hellman's shoulders. But, when read today, Hellman's book, with its thinly veiled allusions to contemporary issues, is a respectable job and has many funny lines, especially for the Old Lady. It follows the peregrinations of Dr. Pangloss and his students Candide and Cunegonde from their quiet Westphalian home to Lisbon, Paris, Buenos Aires, Venice, and back to Westphalia, with Candide finally rejecting Pangloss's credo that "all is for the best in this best of all possible worlds" and deciding to marry Cunegonde and "make our garden grow." The real problem with Hellman's book is that Voltaire's novel is simply unsuited to stage adaptation: it's a picaresque series of adventures with no real plot which repeats the same philosophical points again and again. There is nothing dramatic about it, and Candide, Cunegonde, and the others were not meant to be "real" people. There is no way to become involved with the plight of the characters, and musicals which prevent such audience identification rarely succeed. If Hellman's book fails to solve these built-in problems, there is really nothing else wrong with it, and it serves as a good setting for what was obviously meant to be the show's centerpiece: the score.

Hugh Wheeler's book was in no way an improvement; in fact, it's less funny, substituting camp and leers for wit. It worked well with Prince's

○ ○ ○ ○ ○

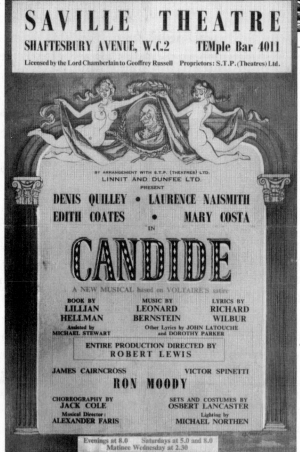

Two Broadway Candide Playbills, and the flyer for the 1959 London production.

informal, intermissionless, and giddy staging on Broadway but has become a liability in opera-house versions. It is unfortunate that Hellman's book is no longer available to potential producers of *Candide*, who must make do with Wheeler's silly, arch script or some revision thereof. The original production of *Candide*, with a glorious cast headed by Max Adrian, Barbara Cook, and Robert Rounseville, has been unjustly maligned as a misfire when it was actually superior to what passes for *Candide* in theatres and opera houses these days.

Candide was underappreciated in 1956 but never forgotten; our next show was acclaimed in 1957 but is now only dimly recalled. Langston Hughes wrote the lyrics for Kurt Weill's *Street Scene* in 1947, then the book and lyrics for *The Barrier*, an opera based on his play *Mulatto*, which ran four performances at the Broadhurst Theatre in 1950. In 1957, he adapted some stories he had written about Jess Simple, a decent black man for whom things never seem to go right but who continues to dream, into the musical **Simply Heavenly** (Playhouse; Aug. 20, '57; 62). Taking several poetic monologues for Simple directly from his stories, Hughes wrote the book and lyrics; David Martin wrote the music and orchestrations.

Simply Heavenly was set in present-day Harlem. Simple, who loves strait-laced Joyce, learns that his estranged wife in Buffalo has found a new man willing to pay for two-thirds of a divorce. But the sweet Simple is putty in the hands of "fast" neighbor Zarita; he goes for a drive with her and winds up in traction. After this experience, Simple resolves to stop using his color as an excuse for his problems and resolves to come up with his third of the divorce money. He saves his money but is laid off. To cheer him up, Zarita throws her birthday party in his room, and Joyce arrives and finds Zarita embracing Simple. A neighbor intercedes on his behalf, Joyce goes to Simple, but Simple rejects her until he can solve his own problems. On Christmas Eve, Simple presents Joyce with a ring, a divorce decree, and the deed to their own apartment.

Directed by Joshua Shelley, *Simply Heavenly* was a small, intimate musical which opened off-Broadway, at the 85th Street Playhouse, to near-raves from such critics as Kerr and Atkinson. When the theatre was condemned by the fire department, the show moved to Broadway with new producers, a new set, a few cast changes, and orchestrations instead of twin pianos. It survived two months on Broadway, then moved back off-Broadway for another two months. A West End production, directed

○ ○ ○ ○ ○

LET'S BALL AWHILE

Two obscure, wonderful pieces. Note the presence of producer Joseph Papp at the top of the Human Comedy logo.

and coproduced by Laurence Harvey, lasted two weeks the following year, and *Simply Heavenly* was seen on television in 1959 with its original leads.

While audiences flocked to see Lena Horne in the gaudy *Jamaica*, which opened on Broadway just as *Simply Heavenly* returned to off-Broadway, Hughes and Martin's musical about real black life proved hard to sell. But *Simply Heavenly* is perhaps the best black musical ever, a work of immense, unpretentious charm, extremely funny and with a great deal to say as well. The characters, especially Simple and the big-hearted domestic Miss Mamie, memorably played by Claudia McNeil in the original, are endearing, the songs are good, and the show provides the sense of an entire community and period in black history in its scenes at the local hangout, Paddy's Bar. In the wake of more spectacular and successful black musicals, *Simply Heavenly* has been forgotten, but it is a highly entertaining work that should be performed by any black theatre willing to explore its heritage.

It's 1943 in Ithaca, California, and we meet the Macauley family, consisting of a widowed mother, sister Bess, and brothers Ulysses, Homer, and Marcus, the latter away at war. Homer gets a job at Mr. Grogan's telegraph office, and he soon has to deliver a telegram to a Mexican woman informing her of the death of her son in action. Homer gradually finds that everything in his world is changing. At the telegraph office, a thief learns a lesson when he holds up Homer's coworker Spangler, who gives to the thief freely. Meanwhile, Marcus, at war, tells his best friend and fellow soldier, Tobey, an orphan, about his girl back home, and Tobey feels drawn to Marcus's family. Marcus is killed in action, and Tobey arrives at the Macauley home to become a part of the family he heard about from Marcus.

Such was the homespun, lovely tale told by William Saroyan in *The Human Comedy*. Saroyan first wrote the story as a screenplay which he was scheduled to direct; when he was fired from the picture, he turned the screenplay into a novel, which came out shortly before the movie was released in 1943. In 1983, **The Human Comedy** (Royale; Apr. 5, '84; 13) was turned into a musical-theatre piece which reunited producer Joseph Papp with composer Galt MacDermot, whose musical *Hair* had opened Papp's New York Shakespeare Festival Public Theatre in 1967 and whose *Two Gentlemen of Verona* had also been a Shakespeare Festival hit. Wilford Leach, who had directed a highly successful version of *The*

Pirates of Penzance for Papp three years earlier, directed. It was to become MacDermot's first musical to reach Broadway since *Dude* and *Via Galactica* in 1972; a magnificent work, it was to have a Broadway run no longer than those of MacDermot's twin disasters of the previous decade.

The libretto was by William Dumaresq, and a libretto it was, for MacDermot had turned Saroyan's lyrical work into an opera, all-sung, but with a sound unlike any other Broadway opera. *The Human Comedy* premiered in late 1983 at the Public's Anspacher Theatre, where *Hair*, another musical set during wartime, had opened, receiving generally strong reviews and running for two months. Papp decided to move it to Broadway, as he had such other Shakespeare Festival musicals as *Pirates* and *A Chorus Line*, and plastered his face on the ads, the poster, the Playbill cover, and the marquee; he even appeared in the TV commercial.

Frank Rich had given the show its best review downtown, but the *Times*'s policy at that time was not to rereview shows that moved from off-Broadway unless they were substantially different uptown. Those who rereviewed it on Broadway, including Clive Barnes and Douglas Watt, weren't partial to it, and *The Human Comedy* closed in ten days.

The Human Comedy was a risky prospect for Broadway. While rear projections establishing the story's various locales were added for Broadway, the show was otherwise staged starkly, in semioratorio concert style. The orchestra was onstage, at the sides, and the entire cast was upstage throughout the evening, acting as a Greek chorus, observing, and singing backup; individuals stepped forward for their scenes, then rejoined the ensemble. When the show was downtown, this staging beautifully conveyed the feeling of a whole town surrounding and embracing the audience, but much of this community feeling was lost in a large, conventional proscenium theatre. Papp would have been wiser to move *The Human Comedy* to another off-Broadway theatre, where it might have thrived, instead of to an inhospitable Broadway house.

The musical theatre of the eighties was dominated by such British pop operas as *Evita*, *The Phantom of the Opera* and *Les Misérables*; it's most unfortunate that *The Human Comedy* opened and closed on Broadway without anyone noticing that America had produced a work that could rival any of these. It is, in fact, the great American pop opera, yet it sounds no more like the British works than it does a real opera. MacDermot's music, one of the most sophisticated scores of the last decade, combined country, forties swing, and classical lyricism into a wholly unique, original mixture. Saroyan's novel was a rich subject for an American opera, and its musical version not only captured Saroyan's tone of sentimental sweetness perfectly, but actually gave the story more weight and made it more moving than it was in the novel or film. If Dumaresq's lyrics were occasionally primitive, they lay well on MacDermot's finest score. Stylistically in a class by itself, it was a beautifully executed adaptation but probably too special a show to have ever succeeded on Broadway. *The Human Comedy* is a must for community theatres, particularly since it requires almost no set and has many good roles for performers of various ages. The original cast recorded the show, but the recording has never been commercially released, thus depriving those who might find *The Human Comedy* the ideal piece for their company of familiarity with it.

Homer's *Illiad* and *Odyssey* were the basis of one of the dumbest musicals in Broadway history, *Home Sweet Homer*. But Homeric legend was also the basis for one of the most brilliant musicals, **The Golden Apple** (Alvin; Apr. 20, '54; 125). The book and lyrics for *The Golden Apple* were the work of John Latouche, whose only subsequent shows would be *The Vamp* and *Candide*; Jerome Moross, a film composer, contributed the score. Moross had already collaborated with Latouche on a difficult-to-categorize, acclaimed, and unsuccessful musical-theatre piece called *Ballet Ballads* in 1948. *The Golden Apple's* experimental nature caused several producers to shy away from it: Cheryl Crawford bowed out in 1951, Herman Levin in 1952, and Kermit Bloomgarden and Oliver Smith in 1953. It fell to the enterprising off-Broadway Phoenix Theatre to mount it in 1954. Norman Lloyd directed.

The Golden Apple resets Homer in the town of Angel's Roost in the state of Washington during the first decade of the twentieth century; Washington was chosen because it contained a Mount Olympus. Latouche, who saw the show not as an adaptation of Homer but as "a comic reflection of classical influence on the way we think nowadays," made Ulysses a veteran of the Spanish–American war, Helen a farmer's daughter, Paris a traveling salesman (and a dancing character who never speaks), and the Olympian goddesses into small-town ladies—Minerva is a schoolmarm, Mrs. Juniper (the name is a combination of Juno and Jupiter) the Mayor's wife, and Aphrodite, called Lovey Mars, the local matchmaker.

As *The Golden Apple* opens, Helen expresses her boredom with Angel's Roost, while Mother Hare, an elderly seer, has a vision of twentieth-century progress and predicts Helen will be going places soon. The Spanish–American War is over, and the heroes return, distressed to learn

○ ○ ○ ○ ○

The

PLAYBILL

for the Alvin Theatre

THE GOLDEN APPLE

The Golden Apple: *the best show ever to fail on Broadway? Above, the boys of Angel's Roost find that "Helen [Kaye Ballard] Is Always Willing." Below, Bibi Osterwald and her Sirenettes in "By Goona-Goona Lagoon."*

that Helen, their favorite, is now married to the aged sheriff Menelaus. At the country fair, Mr. Paris, from neighboring Rhododendron, arrives in a balloon. Mother Hare offers a golden apple as the prize for the best pie, and Paris is asked to judge the contest. When Lovey Mars promises Paris a beautiful woman in exchange for the apple, he awards her the prize. Lovey introduces Paris to Helen, who overpowers him, and Paris and Helen fly off in the balloon. The elders in the town shame the boys, who have just returned from war, into making war on Rhododendron, as the women despair and the curtain falls on the first act.

Early in Act Two, Ulysses beats Paris in a prizefight in Rhododendron, and Helen reluctantly goes home with Menelaus. In order to get revenge on the soldiers, Mayor Hector sets the boys on a spree that lasts ten years (and takes up most of the second act). The temptations of the big city are many: Calypso (played by the same performer who played Mrs. Juniper), a society hostess and nymph, seduces Patroclus; stockbrokers Scylla and Charybdis (the actors who played Menelaus and Hector) do a vaudeville turn, and Ajax jumps out of a window when he invests heavily in hemp and it fails; a siren (otherwise Lovey Mars) in a waterfront dive shanghais several of the soldiers; a pessimistic lady scientist (Miss Minerva) sends one of the men into outer space, but can't figure out how to bring him back; and Circe (Penelope) helps Paris, who was trying to kill Ulysses, kill Achilles. Ulysses is alone; his search for the proper set of values with which to face the new century has concluded with the realization that he must return home to Penelope to find what is most important in life.

Like *The Human Comedy*, *The Golden Apple* was through-sung and had no spoken dialogue. But it is a work utterly lacking in the ponderousness and pretentiousness of modern Broadway operas. Moross's music uses popular song and dance forms of turn-of-the-century America, with waltzes, blues, ragtime, burlesque, and vaudeville styles all making appearances. With some of the wittiest lyrics ever heard in the theatre and marvelous tunes ranging from the heartbreaking "Windflowers" to the lovely "It's the Going Home Together" to a hit blues called "Lazy Afternoon," *The Golden Apple* has one of the American theatre's finest scores.

The Golden Apple is a unique piece: it's not a pop opera, nor a musical with a certain amount of dialogue and a score of operatic length and quality like *Street Scene* or *The Most Happy Fella*. Rather, it is a lightweight, musical-comedy opera, a near-perfect piece. It was also beautifully produced, with choreographer Hanya Holm and set designers William and

Jean Eckart making invaluable contributions, and it featured irreplaceable performances by Kaye Ballard as Helen, Jack Whiting as Mayor Hector (Whiting had played another soft-shoe mayor in *Hazel Flagg* the year before), and Bibi Osterwald as Lovey Mars, who brought down the house with her siren song, "By Goona-Goona Lagoon."

The Golden Apple received numerous ecstatic reviews when it opened in March 1954 at the Phoenix Theatre: it was called "the most important musical since *Oklahoma!*" (Coleman, *Mirror*), "some sort of milestone in the American musical theatre" (McClain, *Journal-American*), and "the best thing that has happened in and to the theatre in a very long time" (Chapman, *News*). Atkinson and Kerr were less enthusiastic than their colleagues, but *The Golden Apple* won the New York Drama Critics Circle Award for Best Musical, and Alfred de Liagre, Jr., and Roger L. Stevens joined with the Phoenix to move it uptown. But like *The Human Comedy* and *Simply Heavenly*, which also began off-Broadway, *The Golden Apple* was not a hit on Broadway. It ran four months at the Alvin and lost its investment. It was revived off-Broadway at the York Playhouse in 1962 and has had several off-off-Broadway productions ever since.

If *The Golden Apple* was so brilliant, why didn't it run longer on Broadway? There were those who maintained that it was somewhat lacking in emotional involvement, but emotion is there in the music for Penelope and Ulysses, and the sheer theatrical imagination of the piece provides sufficient excitement to make up for any lack of feeling. No, *The Golden Apple*, perhaps the most neglected masterwork of the American musical theatre, was simply caviar to audiences more attuned to *The Pajama Game*, *Kismet* and *Can-Can*, all playing nearby. Most of the shows in this book failed their audiences; it was the audience that failed *The Golden Apple*.

○ ○ ○ ○ ○

EPILOGUE

CARRIE: HOW DID
IT HAPPEN?

○ ○

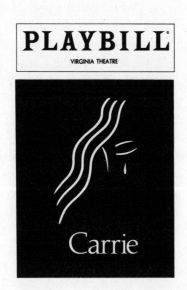

PLAYBILL®

VIRGINIA THEATRE

Carrie

Stephen King's 1974 novel *Carrie* is a tour de force of science-fiction writing which manages to make an impossible story plausible and even touching, combining horror with a study of awakening sexuality and the torments of adolescence. In 1976, King's novel was made into a film, directed by Brian DePalma, with a screenplay by Lawrence D. Cohen. It was an effective, often humorous adaptation, wisely sticking to strictly realistic, small-town locations and making the progress of Carrie's telekinetic powers clear and central throughout.

Betty Buckley, who played the sympathetic gym teacher in the film, would play Carrie's horrific mother in a musical version of King's novel twelve years later, a musical that from its initial conception took seven years to arrive on Broadway. Michael Gore and Cohen, author of the film script, attended a performance of Alban Berg's opera *Lulu* at the Metropolitan Opera House and decided that if Berg were alive and writing operas today, he would choose *Carrie* as the basis for one of them. Gore, who wrote the music for *Carrie*, had done the score for another high school saga, the movie *Fame*. Dean Pitchford, who had collaborated with Gore on *Fame* and written *Footloose*, another youth-oriented film, joined Gore as lyricist, and Cohen again adapted King for the musical's book.

There was a workshop production of the first act of the musical at 890 Broadway in August 1984, with Annie Golden in the title role, Maureen McGovern as Mrs. White, Laurie Beechman as Miss Gardner, Laura Dean as Sue, Liz Callaway as Chris, Todd Graff as Tommy, and Peter Neptune as Billy. At this point, the show seemed to be on the right track: there were still realistic scenes in Carrie's school, including one in the principal's office and one in English class, a substantial amount of dialogue, most of which Cohen took from his screenplay, and Carrie's powers were pointed up clearly and imaginatively. The fist act ended with Carrie demonstrating those powers to her terrified mother by shutting down every window in the house during a storm without lifting a finger. The White home had a sewing machine (on Broadway, there would not be a clue as to how Mrs. White supported her daughter), religious objects, and a radio playing a gospel broadcast which cued Mrs. White's first song, "Open Your Heart." The script for Act Two at the time of the workshop indicated that the musical would end realistically, too, with a scene back at the White home rather than the "stairway to heaven" *Carrie* ended with on Broadway.

After the workshop, *Carrie* was announced for a Broadway production in the fall of 1986, to be produced by Barry and Fran Weissler and Fred

○ ○ ○ ○ ○

Zollo. But the money could not be raised, and the show lingered in the pages of *Theatrical Index*, a publication which lists forthcoming New York shows, for years. The musical was finally taken up by West German producer Friedrich Kurz, who had produced *Cats* and would later present *Starlight Express* in West Berlin. Kurz arranged a coproduction with the Royal Shakespeare Company, which had done well with their 1985 co-production (with Cameron Mackintosh) of the musical *Les Misérables*. At this point, Terry Hands, then artistic director of the Royal Shakespeare Company, joined the musical as director. Although he would later use inexperience with musicals as his excuse for the show's Broadway debacle, Hands had in fact already directed a complex musical called *Poppy*, by Peter Nichols, for the Royal Shakespeare Company; it had won the Society of West End Theatres' Best Musical award in 1982. Also coming on board at this time was Debbie Allen, a Broadway dancer—actress who had appeared in and choreographed *Fame* on screen and on television and would choreograph *Carrie* in exactly the same frenetic style.

By special arrangement with British and American Equity, *Carrie*'s cast was half American and half English, and its creative team was also split fairly evenly, with an American choreographer and writers and an English director and designer. A special coup was obtaining the services of Barbara Cook for the role of Mrs. White; Cook had not appeared in a musical since *The Grass Harp* seventeen years earlier. *Carrie* was booked to play a three-week engagement in February 1988 at the Royal Shakespeare Company's mainstage theatre at Stratford upon Avon; Kurz supplied most of the money, and the Royal Shakespeare Company profited from the brief but sold-out Stratford run.

The Stratford booking raised an outcry of controversy. Newspaper articles appeared justifiably accusing the R.S.C. of using subsidized funds to mount a Broadway tryout. The Stratford reviews were terrible, and Cook, after nearly being decapitated on opening night by the set, decided to part company with the production immediately. She later said, "When someone first mentioned to me that they were doing a musical of *Carrie*, my first thought was, 'You've got to be kidding.' Then I heard the music, and thought some of it was quite good. I was still wary of it because of the subject matter. But Terry's vision of the material intrigued me. There were many, many things about the production that were ineptly done. A lot of it came from lack of experience. For some unknown reason, they were not willing to get people in who had experience with musicals and listen to them. I'm not at all sorry that I did it, but I did absolutely the

○ ○ ○ ○ ○

Betty Buckley and Linzi Hateley square off near the end of "And Eve Was Weak" in Carrie.

right thing in leaving it. I thought, 'There isn't a chance in hell that they'll be able to pull this off.' They really didn't have any ideas about how to fix it, things were really set in concrete, and they did nothing but polish the same killing dance numbers. Going in, I thought, 'This man is the head of the Royal Shakespeare Company; if a scene isn't working, he's going to see it's not working.' Well, he didn't."

Cook played out the remainder of the Stratford run while the producers began the search for a replacement, and Harold Wheeler, who had reorchestrated *Dreamgirls* on the road, was brought in to reorchestrate much of the score, as if the orchestrations were the show's biggest problem. *Carrie* was never planned for London, only Stratford, so Broadway was to be the next stop. Rumors began to circulate that the show would not continue, and indeed it almost shut down when CBS pulled out its investment. By the time New York previews began, *Carrie* found itself the first show of the 1988–89 season and no longer eligible for 1988 Tony Awards. By now, it was clear that Kurz's producing left much to be desired: the show arrived in New York with little advance sale (contrary to published reports) and most of its money depleted. It was thus totally dependent on reviews, which no one involved had any right to expect would be raves. Throughout Broadway previews, *Carrie* was greeted with one of the most varied reactions ever, with derisive laughter and some boos mixing with cheers and wild applause.

As was to be expected, *Carrie* opened on Thursday, May 12, 1988, to horrendous pans, even worse than the Stratford notices, with the exception of Clive Barnes's in the *Post*. There was no reserve fund to run the show for a few weeks with the hope that it might be able to find a youthful MTV-oriented audience. The creators were told on Saturday morning that the show would stay open, but a few hours later they and the cast were informed that *Carrie* would close with the Sunday matinee. It was the most expensive flop in Broadway history, losing the $8 million which had been contributed by British and West German investors.*

Clearly, a musicalization of King's *Carrie* was a questionable project to begin with, one that might never have worked completely. Daring and ambitious, it was also rather foolhardy, but the workshop production

*The New York production of Andrew Lloyd Webber's *Aspects of Love* lost the same amount three years later. But *Aspects* was a long-run hit in London, so the profits from the West End version and the cast recording offset, to a degree, the New York loss.

○ ○ ○ ○ ○

demonstrated that there was indeed potential. The only way King's story can possibly work when dramatized, however, is if Carrie's supernatural powers are set against a realistic, average, typically middle-American town and school (the novel was set in a small town in Maine). Instead, Hands opted for a nonrealistic, abstract production inspired by Greek tragedy and morality plays. Hands, who said he was creating "the first serious music drama since *West Side Story*," set the show in a white box and had his small-town girls wearing togas and red and pink body stockings, and his boys studded leather. Along with any vestige of realism went most of the dialogue; the Hands–Kurz–R.S.C. *Carrie* was almost through-sung. Hands' staging of *Carrie* ranks as one of the most misconceived in theatre history, often wildly off in tone and unintentionally comic. The destruction scene at the prom poses perhaps insoluble staging problems, but Hands' solution was halfhearted and laughable. Yet it must be said that his staging of the scenes between Carrie and her mother was, albeit excessively abstract, frequently exquisite. And Buckley, who replaced Cook, gave a heroic performance in a role ideally suited to her steely voice and chilling intensity. If the contrast of voices in the mother–daughter scenes that was there with Cook, who sang in an ethereal soprano, was gone when the same scenes were performed by twin belters Buckley and Hateley, Buckley, unlike Cook, hurled herself into the role of Margaret White and gave an unforgettable performance.

As for the material itself, *Carrie*'s stunning mother–daughter scenes constitute the most genuinely operatic material to be found in any pop opera and feature often gorgeous music. There were a couple of decent pop tunes plus a number of perfectly awful songs, but the Gore–Pitchford score is salvageable. There was little book left on Broadway, and neither the book nor Hands' staging ever established Carrie's powers very clearly in the Broadway version; they were barely mentioned until the end of Act One, and only those familiar with the novel or film could have fully understood what was going on.

What makes *Carrie* so unique in flop musical history is its combination of soaring, often breathtaking sequences and some of the most appalling and ridiculous scenes ever seen in a musical. It alternately scaled the heights and hit rock-bottom. *Carrie* also had nonstop energy and, unlike so many flops, was not dull for a second. But there was something ominous about it all, a feeling that it was playing to the lowest common denominator, to people who had never been to the theatre and would respond only to jolts of pop music.

○ ○ ○ ○ ○

Carrie's act endings. Above, the floor has opened, Betty Buckley is pinned to her chair (the only furniture in the White home), and Linzi Hateley's hands are aflame, as the curtain falls on Act One. Below, Buckley lies dead as Hateley descends the enormous staircase and the second act ends.

While the response of those who saw *Carrie* varied wildly, the response of those who missed it was uniform. Never have so many people who missed a flop musical wished so fervently that they had seen it. Many of those who did see it found themselves unable to stop talking about it, and live tapes of the score were widely circulated and treasured. When flop musicals opened during the season that began with *Carrie*, critics and audiences had to admit that the new flops did not begin to live up to the standard set by *Carrie*. *Carrie* was fascinating, thrilling, horrible, and un-believable. The ads said, "There's never been a musical like her"—and there never would be again.

Like *Kelly*, *Carrie* was a catastrophe. Like *Rockabye Hamlet*, *Carrie* was often campy. Like *Pousse-Café*, *Carrie* had made a better movie than a musical. Like *Prettybelle*, *Carrie* made the mistake of attempting to musicalize that which could not be musicalized. Like *Candide*, *Carrie* had wild ad-herents and others who strenuously objected. And like *Grind*, *Carrie's* strengths made it a heartbreaker. *Carrie* was to a degree a star flop—had it succeeded, Buckley would have entered the top stratum of musical-theatre stars, and Hateley would have been made. It was also at least partly a missed opportunity; while Carrie and her mother had been strongly musicalized, the other characters were wildly misconceived. *Car-rie* was, in fact, every kind of a musical flop; it seemed as if every flop there ever was was piled high, and *Carrie* was playing on top of them all. *Carrie* was the apotheosis of flop.

Carrie once again brought up the same questions raised by most of the musicals discussed in this book: How do these things happen? Why didn't anyone stop it? Didn't they know it wouldn't succeed? How did they ever think they could get away with it? *Carrie* provided no answers, but then those earlier flops didn't either. If not always as bizarre and fascinating as *Carrie*, these things do keep happening.

One might hope that readers of this book who are also involved in creating musicals, after attending the tales of woe of so many musicals, would be discouraged from repeating the same mistakes. But this hope would be entirely in vain; flops are here to stay, and each successive Broadway season will always bring more flop musicals than successes.

True, there are flops and there are flops. There are those that are the work of hopeless amateurs or people with little experience in the difficult art of creating a musical. It can almost always be safely predicted that

○ ○ ○ ○ ○

shows involving such practitioners will fail. But then there are the flops that involve the most celebrated names in musical theatre. The flops that result from the collaboration of proven talents are the most difficult to explain. Why, if these people have done such good work in the past, did they not realize this time out that the show was unworkable? First, when one is so close to a project over a long period of time, it becomes very difficult to stand back from it and assess its strengths and weaknesses. Very often, those involved in a flop will never really know why it failed. And just as often, if one asks the librettist, star, director, composer, or producer of a flop why it failed, each will blame one of the others involved, and each will provide an entirely different diagnosis for the outcome.

Then too, a flop is often the result of the fact that each of the talents involved, while working on the same project, may in effect have been working on a different show from all the others. If all contributors do not share the same vision of the evening, the end product will not evince the harmony of diverse elements—the seeming inevitability of book, score, and staging—of a good musical. While this has always been the case, the problem of faulty collaboration has become greatly exacerbated in the last two decades because of the decline in producing know-how. In the fifties and sixties, there were producers like David Merrick, Kermit Bloomgarden, and Feuer and Martin; while they all had flops, they all knew how to put a musical together, how to assemble just the right people for the project, and how to orchestrate the creation and fruition of that project. There seem to be very few people working in today's musical theatre with the ability to find the right properties and develop them with the care and strength required.

Of course, producing skill is not entirely dead; certainly Cameron Mackintosh is as powerful and successful a producer of musicals as the theatre has ever known. But Mackintosh and Andrew Lloyd Webber's Really Useful Company tend to produce huge musicals, and there can only be so many such shows mounted each decade. And if there are fewer producers around with the know-how, some who might have the ability required simply can't raise the money. The theatrical economics of the fifties and sixties allowed the production of a vast number of shows each season. Almost anyone could produce a musical, and the abundance of product meant that there would be many musicals each season, a number of them flops, some in between, and several outright hits. The changing economics of Broadway in the last twenty years means that those days are over; it is now not only fiercely difficult to finance a musical, but

○ ○ ○ ○ ○

virtually impossible to make money on a musical that is not an immediate smash hit. It has become hazardous to even run a musical that does not receive rave reviews or open with a huge advance sale. So musicals that are dismissed by critics, some of which may have merit, have little chance of survival. The stakes have risen tremendously; the nineties will see fewer musicals produced and even fewer that last.

The serious decline in musical-theatre talent also means that flops will persist. The decades studied herein saw the death or slowing down of such major musical-theatre contributors as Richard Rodgers, Alan Jay Lerner, Frank Loesser, Leonard Bernstein, Harold Rome, and Jule Styne. Talents commensurate with these have simply not emerged, and still-active veterans like Stephen Sondheim, Cy Coleman, Charles Strouse, John Kander, and Fred Ebb cannot be counted on for very much of the twenty-first century. Then there was the retirement of Jerome Robbins from Broadway and the deaths of Gower Champion, Michael Bennett, and Bob Fosse: with the notable exception of Tommy Tune, there is at the moment an appalling dearth of musical-theatre directors with the imagination, skill, and power to get the job done right.

If it seems inevitable that flops will remain an integral part of Broadway-musical history, flops may actually have one or two salutary effects. Flops help us to appreciate the better shows that do turn up from time to time; indeed, the shows that receive the greatest acclaim nowadays are often shows that are merely better than most of the other junk. Above all, though, flops give the flop connoisseur something to treasure, dissect, laugh at, and collect. Fans of the genre will not simply be content to recall *Breakfast at Tiffany's, 1600 Pennsylvania Avenue,* or *Prettybelle.* They rely on the fact that every Broadway season will make its own contribution, and they live for the arrival of each new debacle. "How was it?," they are asked, after witnessing a tryout or preview performance of an especially unbelievable musical evening. "Not since *Carrie,*" their reply will begin.

INDEX

○ ○ ○ ○ ○ ○ ○ ○ ○ ○ ○ ○ ○ ○ ○ ○ ○ ○ ○ ○

○ ○ ○ ○ ○

NAMES INDEX

○ ○ ○ ○ ○

○ ○ ○ ○ ○

o o o o o

○ ○ ○ ○ ○

○ ○ ○ ○ ○

○ ○ ○ ○ ○

○ ○ ○ ○ ○

○ ○ ○ ○ ○

○ ○ ○ ○ ○

○ ○ ○ ○ ○

○ ○ ○ ○ ○